Remembering and Imagining the Holocaust

This is a meditation on memory and on the ways in which memory has operated in the work of writers for whom the Holocaust was a defining event. It is also an exploration of the ways in which fiction and drama have attempted to approach a subject so resistant to the imagination. Beginning with W. G. Sebald, for whom memory and the Holocaust were the roots of a special fascination, Bigsby moves on to consider those writers Sebald himself valued, including Arthur Miller, Rolf Hochhuth, Peter Weiss and Jean Améry, and those whose lives crossed in the bleak world of the camps, in fact or fiction. The book offers a chain of memories. It sets witness against fiction, truth against wilful deceit. It asks the question who owns the Holocaust – those who died, those who survived to bear witness, those who responded to it as metaphor, those who appropriated its victims to shape their own necessities?

CHRISTOPHER BIGSBY is Professor of American Studies at the University of East Anglia and has published more than thirty books covering American theatre, popular culture and British drama, including *Modern American Drama* (Cambridge, 1992), *Contemporary American Playwrights* (Cambridge, 2000) and *Arthur Miller: A Critical Study* (Cambridge, 2005). He is co-editor, with Don Wilmeth, of *The Cambridge History of American Theatre* (1998), which received the Barnard Hewitt Award for Outstanding Research from the American Society for Theatre Research. He is also an award-winning novelist, has written plays for radio and television, and is a regular radio and television broadcaster.

Remembering and Imagining the Holocaust

The Chain of Memory

Christopher Bigsby

CAMBRIDGE
UNIVERSITY PRESS

CAMBRIDGE UNIVERSITY PRESS

Cambridge, New York, Melbourne, Madrid, Cape Town, Singapore, São Paulo

CAMBRIDGE UNIVERSITY PRESS

The Edinburgh Building, Cambridge CB2 2RU, UK

Published in the United States of America by Cambridge University Press, New York

www.cambridge.org

Information on this title: www.cambridge.org/9780521869348

First published 2006

Printed in the United Kingdom at the University Press, Cambridge

A catalogue record for this publication is available from the British Library

ISBN-13 978-0-521-86934-8 hardback
ISBN-10 0-521-86934-x hardback

To the memory of Max Sebald

Contents

1 The past remembered *1*

2 W. G. Sebald: an act of restitution *25*

3 Rolf Hochhuth: breaking the silence *115*

4 Peter Weiss: the investigation *149*

5 Arthur Miller: the rememberer *176*

6 Anne Frank: everybody's heroine *219*

7 Jean Améry: home and language *258*

8 Primo Levi: from the darkness to the light *285*

9 Elie Wiesel: to forget is to deny *318*

10 Tadeusz Borowski: the world of stone *341*

11 Memory theft *357*

Coda *377*

Notes *384*

Index *395*

1 The past remembered

> The pages before you are segments of contemplation and
> memory. Memory is elusive and selective: it holds onto what it
> chooses to hold on to ... Very like a dream, memory takes
> specific details out of the viscous flow of events – sometimes
> tiny, seemingly insignificant details – stores them deeply away,
> and at certain times brings them to the surface. Like a dream,
> memory also tries to imbue events with some meaning ...
> Memory and imagination sometimes dwell together ...
> memory and oblivion, the sense of chaos and impotence on one
> side and the desire for a meaningful life on the other.[1]
>
> Aharon Appelfeld, *The Story of a Life*

The Russian writer Andrei Vosnesensky spoke of what he called a
nostalgia for the present. For a man who had escaped repression, there
was nothing to yearn for, no past to be burnished by memory. Instead,
he projected himself forward, already imagining looking back on
himself reborn. The idea of Eden offers a powerful metaphor of
innocent beginnings, recapitulating, as it does, the processes of
human development from child to adult, knowledge and sin becoming
coterminous. Yet there are those born with the taste of the apple
already in their infant mouths or at least those whose memories will
not permit the notion of a paradise lost.

This book began with a desire to celebrate the work of
W. G. Sebald, a friend and colleague. Max, as he was known to his
friends, began writing late. As an academic he became discontented
with the self-denying ordinances of his profession, the restrictions of

an approach that seemed to militate against the imagination. He began, instead, to create works that defy precise definition. He was inclined to call them fictions but in truth they were a blend of autobiography, biography, literary criticism, intellectual history and much more. Fact and invention jostled one another. Borders of all kinds were dissolved. They were lyrical, playful, touched with melancholy. He had something of the romantic's interest in decay and dissolution, in ephemerality. His were books in part concerned with memory, its necessity, its unreliability, its generative power. In his work, memory has a moral force even as it is a mechanism for exploration, the source of reproach, a means of resurrecting the dead. It is also the cause of a certain vertigo as individual and nation stare down the vortex of time.

Like Vladimir Nabokov, of whom he was an admirer, he was aware that memory changes with place and language, drawing attention to the autobiography of a writer whose national identity was itself instructively ambiguous. An early paragraph from that work by Nabokov, significantly entitled *Speak, Memory: An Autobiography Revisited*, expresses precisely the awareness of death that would lace its way through Sebald's writing, as it does of the ironies which that writing would delineate with a quiet humour.

> The cradle rocks above an abyss, and common sense tells us that our existence is but a brief crack of light between two eternities of darkness. Although the two are identical twins, man, as a rule, views that prenatal abyss with more calm than the one he is heading for (at some forty-five hundred heartbeats an hour). I know, however, of a young chronophobiac who experienced something like panic when looking for the first time at homemade movies that had been taken a few weeks before his birth. He saw a world that was practically unchanged – the same house, the same people – and then realized that he did not exist there at all and that nobody mourned his absence. He caught a glimpse of his mother waving from an upstairs window, and that unfamiliar gesture disturbed him, as if it were some mysterious farewell. But what particularly frightened him was the sight of a brand-new baby carriage standing

there on the porch, with the smug, encroaching air of a coffin; even that was empty, as if, in the reverse course of events, his very bones had disintegrated.[2]

Part of *Speak, Memory* was first written in French. It was then translated into Russian, 'the amnesiac defects of the original, [the] domains of dimness' (9) being rectified and flooded with new light, before being translated back into English. 'Copious' additions and changes were introduced at this stage. Nabokov lived, it seemed, a different life in different languages. In seeking to describe this process he turned, unsurprisingly, to the figure of the butterfly. 'This re-Englishing of a Russian re-version of what had been an English re-telling of Russian memories in the first place, proved to be a diabolical task, but some consolation was given me by the thought that such multiple metamorphosis, familiar to butterflies, had not been tried by any human before' (10).

He was dealing, he explained, with 'the anomalies of memory', of which he was both 'possessor and victim', but it was clear that he was dealing with a good deal more than that. He was seeking to engage a self translated from language to language with, seemingly, different memories inhabiting those different languages, moments located in contrasting cultures with contrasting, if overlapping, histories. Even time was unstable since east and west located themselves according to different calendars. 'By the old style I was born on 10 April, at daybreak in the last year of the last century, and that was (if I could have been whisked across the border at once) 22 April in, say, Germany.' He travelled, though, with a passport which registered his birth on neither date. He had, he explained, 'journeyed back in thought – with thought hopelessly tapering off as I went – to remote regions where I groped for some secret outlet only to discover that the prison of time is spherical and without exits.' Initially, he explains, he 'was unaware that time, so boundless at first blush, was a prison' (18), and that, perhaps, is the starting point and destination of the autobiography as a form. It is a journey in search of a purpose.

He is not concerned to locate a primal trauma, rejecting, as he does, the 'medieval world of Freud' with its 'bitter little embryos spying ... upon the love life of their parents'. Instead, he looks down from his 'present ridge of remote, isolated, almost uninhabited time', at moments when he revelled in sharing existence, in time, with others, conscious that 'the first creatures on earth to become aware of time were also the first creatures to smile' (19).

In telling his story, however, there were not only omissions, conscious and otherwise, translations, between languages, cultures and histories, between remembered older selves and present consciousness, but erasures. To protect others, names were changed. His autobiography is crafted, as few lives are. Serendipity assumes the shape of purpose; the arbitrary becomes part of a design. Memory is selective and selected, honed over time, modified to serve the purpose of plot, the plot of a life which can only be retrospective.

Max Sebald also moved between countries and languages. At a crucial stage in *Vertigo* he (or his narrator) even loses his passport and with it a clear sense of national identity. He, too, seems to float in time, the past as real and compelling as the present which, indeed, is oddly attenuated. He was an immigrant and not an exile and yet there were aspects of his own original society that disturbed him and prevented his permanent return. He lived in England for more than thirty years but wrote in German. There were, indeed, different memories back in a country whose own memories seemed to him occluded. There were absences that eventually he felt obliged to fill, silences he felt impelled to break. And though his work was by no means all focussed on such concerns, it is nonetheless true that he was increasingly pulled, in memory and present concern, towards the question of the Jews, a principal absence in his life and the centre of troubling personal and national concerns. Born in the final year of the Second World War, he became increasingly aware of discontinuities, of the damage done even to language in the Germany of his birth, though there were others more uncompromising than he.

George Steiner spoke of the deforming influence of Nazism on language, a deformation, he suggests, which hardly ended with the war. Indeed, it seemed to him that the language was already corrupted by ponderousness and an academicism that made it vulnerable to such a crude assault. The German language, he suggested, was no longer lived, merely spoken. It cannot, he insisted, 'be a mere accident that the essentially philological structure of German education yielded such loyal servants to Prussia and the Nazi Reich'.[3] There was, he acknowledged, a counter-current in the work of George Grosz, Bertolt Brecht and Thomas Mann, who shocked the language into different shapes. Rilke, Kafka, Musil all reached out along the shimmering international path of modernism. But to Steiner this offered little respite. What had followed was more than a linguistic reversion for, and here Steiner is absolute, 'the German language was not innocent of the horrors of Nazism. It is not merely that a Hitler, a Goebbels, and a Himmler happened to speak German. Nazism found in the language precisely what it needed to give voice to its savagery.' Hitler, Steiner suggests, 'heard inside his native tongue the latent hysteria, the confusion, the quality of hypnotic trance' (210). He sensed in German another music than that of Goethe, Heine and Mann; 'a rasping cadence, half nebulous jargon, half obscenity. And instead of turning away in nauseated disbelief, the German people gave massive echo to the man's bellowing. It bellowed back out of a million throats and smashed-down boots' (211). He quotes Klaus Mann as asking, 'can it be that Hitler has polluted the language of Nietzsche and Hölderlin?' (212). Unsurprisingly, his answer is 'It can.'

Conceding that Hitler would have found reservoirs of venom and moral illiteracy in any language, in Germany, he insists, 'they were near the surface of common speech'. After all, a 'language in which one can write the "Horst Wessel Lied" is ready to give hell a native tongue' (211). What happened under the Third Reich, he suggests, was not silence but wholly serviceable and practical words with which the Nazis were entirely content to address their chosen victims and to record the details of their genocide. The Jews were 'vermin' whose eradication was thus sanctioned at the level of language. There was a coded word for the transports which took them to their deaths as there was for the liquidations themselves, but for the most part they were willing for their words to be more transparent. The poet Paul Celan, who had escaped shooting by the SS in Romania but suffered two years forced labour, wrote in a German which he confessed had had to 'pass through the thousand darknesses of death-bringing speech',[4] Steiner suggesting that he spoke German as if it were a foreign language.

Nor was culture a defence, and here was the source of a deep anxiety. For Matthew Arnold it was a protection against anarchy. For the Nazis it was enrolled in the cause of anarchy. In *Auschwitz*, Peter Barnes's 1978 play, a character recalls that 'Reichsführer Heinrich Himmler himself decreed that our first complex should be built in the forest outside Weimar, the very seat of German classical tradition. Didn't he leave Goethe's famous oak tree standing there in the middle of the compound and construct the ramps, and block houses around it? You see, even in times like these, in places like that, for people like them, German culture is made available to all. We think transcendentally. We raise our eyes to the hills; the soul, the soul, the German soul!'[5]

The Jews were not permitted to have a history. Their religion existed only to be mocked, its self-evident failure to protect them a further mark of their absurdity. Meanwhile, the language which specified the instruments of torture, the logistical complexities, swirled around the vortex of an inhumanity so profound as to defy articulation. There was a bureaucratic language drained of pain, abstracted from the living flesh, but this was designed precisely to bear no organic load, no history outside of its own reflexive exigencies. It carried no memories but, filed away, would provide the skeletal meaning of actions otherwise denied by those few called to account for their actions despite their apparent success in burrowing down into a postwar Germany concerned only to reconstruct.

What to do, however, when language is compromised? 'Should a German writer', asked Thomas Mann, 'made responsible through his habitual use of language, remain silent, quite silent, in the face of all the irreparable evil which has been committed daily, and is being committed in my country, against body, soul and spirit, against justice and truth, against men and man?' (214). The answer was clearly, no. Yet he could ask and answer that question because he, in common with so many other German writers, was in exile, though the very fact of exile threatened both memory and language, now detached from the reality it had once expressed. Others, such as Walter Benjamin and Stefan Zweig, chose a radical silence, committing suicide. Sebald was

6

aware of those others who had been drawn to suicide, including Jean Améry, whom he admired and about whom he wrote.

Aharon Appelfeld speaks of another kind of silence:

> we didn't speak during the war. It was as though every disaster defied utterance: there was nothing to say ... In the ghetto and in the camp, only people who had lost their minds talked, explained, or tried to persuade. Those who were sane didn't speak ... I've carried with me my mistrust of words from those years. A fluent stream of words awakens suspicion within me. I prefer stuttering, for in stuttering I hear the friction and the disquiet, the effort to purge impurities from the words, the desire to offer something from inside you. Smooth, fluent sentences leave me with a feeling of uncleanness, of order that hides emptiness. (102–3)

There is a chain of memory (Freud's phrase) in Sebald's work, his own, along with that of others, real and fictional, and he travels along that chain, reaching back into the past through photographs, his own recovered youth, and through writers, writers in particular, though by no means exclusively, drawn to the plight of the Jews. I have followed him, writing, as he did, about Rolf Hochhuth and Peter Weiss (and Arthur Miller who attended the same Auschwitz trials as Weiss and who Sebald came briefly to know at the end of his life), as about Améry. But Améry, in turn, led to Primo Levi, while Levi led to another survivor of Auschwitz, Elie Wiesel. These had shared a plight, as they had with a young woman who had thought herself secure only to find herself in that anus mundi, the name given to Auschwitz by a contemptuous German officer. Her name was Anne Frank.

And so the chain of memory extends. Nor does it end there. For others also sought to use their memories or, indeed, their very identities, to reach back to an event whose significance, so long denied, now seemed a key to understanding history and human possibilities. This book, then, is a meditation on memory, on the ways in which memory has operated in the work of writers for whom the Holocaust was a defining event. But it is also an exploration of the ways in which fiction and drama have attempted to approach a subject so resistant to the imagination.

For Elie Wiesel, a novel about Auschwitz was either not a novel or not about Auschwitz. Irving Howe insisted that the Holocaust was not, essentially, a dramatic subject: 'Of those conflicts between wills, those inner clashes of belief and wrenchings of desire, those enactments of passion, all of which make up our sense of the dramatic, there can be little in the course of a fiction focused mainly on the mass exterminations.'[6] As Aharon Appelfeld observed of the 1950s when he began to write, 'What had been written about World War II had been mainly testimonies and accounts that had been deemed authentic expressions; literature was considered a fabrication' (105). Others felt no such inhibition. Indeed, there were even those who would seek to appropriate the lives and experiences of those who had known the reality of the camps, even if the truths they offered were defined by the particularities of their experience, survivors of places from which no one had been supposed to escape alive.

There was, of course, drama, and other entertainments, within the ghettos and, indeed, the camps themselves, often, though not invariably, at the behest of those in command. Those who worked away to forge British banknotes as part of a plan to destabilise the economy took time out for a regular cabaret which they confessed to enjoying as much as the guards. In Sweden, in 1943, Nelly Sachs, who escaped from Berlin in 1940, set herself to write *Eli: A Mystery Play of the Sufferings of Israel*, in which a voice is given to the chimneys through which the smoke of the dead passed. To write so soon was unusual. It was 1967 before Liliane Atlan, whose brother was sent to Auschwitz and who herself survived the war years in hiding, wrote *Mister Fugue or Earth Sick*, later creating *Un Opéra pour Terezin*. It was plainly possible to address the subject of the Holocaust. The question was to what effect?

A nine-year-old girl in the concentration camp at Majdanek secreted a piece of paper, on which she had written a verse, under the sole of her shoe, along with instructions as to the tune to which it was to be sung. In Eva Hoffman's translation it reads:

There was once a little Elżunia,
She's dying all alone now.

For her daddy's in Majdanek,
Her mummy in Auschwitz-Birkenau.[7]

The tense of the first line suggests that she was already projecting a future in which she herself would no longer exist, a future to which she wished to bequeath her truth. She was a witness to something more than her own desolation.

Zalmen Gradowski, a member of the Auschwitz *Sonderkommando*, buried his diary near the crematoria at Birkenau shortly before his death. He, too, could imagine the future he would not live to see and understood the need to bear witness. That imagination was his only victory. At a time when all the evidence was of the total victory of those who had set themselves to liquidate an entire race, he and others like him sustained the idea of another world in which there would be those anxious for the truth, ready to initiate justice. Others secreted messages for the future they would never see in sealed bottles and jars which they placed amidst the pits of human ashes in the belief, or perhaps simply the desperate wager, that they would one day be disinterred. Their memories were preserved against a tomorrow in which they should have ceased to believe. Gradowski's diary was later discovered. The justice was long delayed and deeply imperfect.

When Claude Lanzmann set out to capture the past in his film *Shoah*, he did so less through memory than by taking those who had experienced it and placing them in the world they thought to have escaped. He distrusted memory. He was concerned to stage a drama. As he explained, 'The film is not made with memories; I knew that immediately. Memory horrifies me. Memory is weak. The film is the abolition of all distance between the past and the present; I relived this history in the present.'[8] What he shows is real enough, even as it is contrived and, whatever he says, it is suffused with memories, but memory alone is insufficient for him. It lacks the immediacy of the present suffering which he sets himself to orchestrate, taking survivors back to the place where they suffered. Yet any mediation in such a context breeds suspicion, still more any attempt to imaginatively recreate that past, the imagination being both inadequate and suspect. As Dominick LaCapra observes, 'For both survivors and those born later, the imagination may prove super-fluous, exhausted, or out of place with respect to limit-events; even their allegorical treatment, transformation, or reduction in scale poses difficult, perhaps intractable, problems of tact and judgement' (181). Somehow, the unadorned fact seems to carry authenticity, moral authority, but are memories ever truly unadorned more especially when they are retrieved and articulated to serve a purpose?

Then again, since these are memories of trauma, there is another degree of problem. Dominick LaCapra has spoken of 'the difficulties of memory with respect to traumatic events that are invested with devastating phantasms' and which 'generate anxiety-ridden uncertainties, create disorienting holes in experience' (183), while insisting that much can still be reconstructed subsequently. Aharon Appelfeld, author of *The Story of a Life*, in which he describes his experience as a child in the Ukraine, his parents murdered by the Nazis, observes that 'Profound experience, I've already learned, is easily distorted.' He still, he confesses, had not 'found the words to give voice to those intense scars on my memory' (50).

There is an etiquette for approaching the past. A certain respect, if not a protocol, is required along with an acknowledgement that its shape shifts under the pressure of attention. A rear-view mirror, as drivers are warned, can make the calculation of distance hard to achieve. There is risk of spatial and temporal distortion. There is a tide running. A memory frequently invoked wears smooth like a pebble on the foreshore tumbled by each incurving wave until it seems a work of art, inviolable, complete. Remembering remembering risks an hermetic reflexiveness. As Michael Frayn has suggested, memories 'are like legends. They take particular form when they are told – and when they are told again they are made incarnate in a different body.'⁹ Memories are stories and stories have their own history. As Primo Levi said of his own story of Auschwitz-Monowitz, *If This is a Man*, 'I've constructed a sort of legend around that book, that I wrote it on impulse, that I wrote it without reflecting at all ... Now that I think about it, I can see that this book is full of literature, literature absorbed through the skin, even while I was rejecting it.'¹⁰ As he confessed of his second book, *The Truce*, which details his return after his time in Auschwitz, 'It tells the truth, but a filtered truth ... I had recounted each adventure many times ... and had retouched it *en route* so as to arouse [the] most favourable reaction' (18).

There is no such thing as that to which witnesses are required to swear an oath, committing themselves to telling the truth, the whole truth and nothing but the truth. As Levi remarked, 'while I thought I was writing the authentic story of the concentration camp experience, I was telling the story of my camp, just one ... all stories of people who survived concentration camps have no general application. Every survivor is an exception' (5–6). Yet what else is there if forensics are incomplete and the accused deny their crimes? In World War II people did die, cities were bombed, casual cruelties and calculated murders were as much facts as the periodic tables and all the misprisions and misremembered moments cannot diminish that unleavened fact.

There is a difference between the misremembered and a lie, a flat denial of fact and agency alike and in the courtroom at Frankfurt, when those who had served as guards at Auschwitz were belatedly put on trial two decades after their crimes, memory was countered with calculated amnesia or the claim of necessary acquiescence. These were trials which profoundly influenced Max Sebald but also Peter Weiss, Jean Améry and Arthur Miller. George Steiner, meanwhile, has spoken of what he calls 'the acrobatics of oblivion'.[11] Those who worked in the camps claimed not to have known, not to have seen and if, on occasion, they might have glimpsed something disturbing they were themselves no more than passing observers of a mystery from which their own minds, they assured their inquisitors, had shied away. Meanwhile, those who confronted them had misidentified, misconstrued, misunderstood if not the fact itself then the role they personally might have played. And besides, of necessity they had lacked the perspective, the wider knowledge that might have made them hesitant to level accusations at those who were no more than agents and never principals.

And what happens when the writer, product of another context, one transformed by a shifting politics, by changed assumptions, as Peter Weiss was, seeks to take this material and reshape it as an entertainment for which people will pay money, buy programmes, and during which they will pass the candy, check their watches with public transportation or baby sitters' wages in mind? Is the product uncontaminated history, that pure revelation of fact which places the past, cold in its purity, uncompromising and uncompromised in its precision, in the hands of those who can be invited to weigh it for its truth value and arrive at unchallengeable verdicts? And if not, what is the motive and what are the ethics no less than the aesthetics of this gesture?

Beyond that, however, is an issue addressed by W. G. Sebald and, at greater length and more detail, by Lawrence L. Langer, who reviewed the testimonies of many survivors. Even retrieved memories have to be shaped into a form in which those survivors believe they can be understood by their listeners. As one such, known as Chaim E., explained to an interviewer, 'I try in my best words to bring the picture out of it. But you see, when I ... I see the picture in *front* of me; you have to *imagine* something. So it has a different picture for me than for the one that imagines it.'[12] An inevitable act of translation occurs in moving from experience to language, by way of memory, and in moving from actual to imagined experience. As the same man explained, on hearing his story retold by the interviewer he already ceased to recognise it as his: 'sometimes I hear telling back a story that doesn't sound at all the same what I was telling'. In part that is a product of the intransitive nature of extreme experiences but in part it is a consequence of the survivor existing in a wholly different world: 'It was horrified and horrible, and when you live once with this tension and horrification – if that is the right word – then you live differently' (62–3). The difficulty is to speak out of this different world.

Another survivor explained the problem of describing that world when the available language was so manifestly inadequate. Even simple words like 'hunger', 'thirst', 'dirt', 'cold', 'illness', have a meaning which is literally incommunicable to those for whom they are mild irritants or at worst descriptions of temporary conditions to be ameliorated. How to communicate the sheer contingency of life, the knowledge that at any moment, on a whim, life could be ended to those who know it as an ultimate truth but seldom as a moment-by-moment fact? To say 'My family were killed' could never suffice, nor could 'My mother and brother and two sisters were gassed' (61). The failure of language breeds a mixture of despair, irony and even doubt as a present self is confronted with a past self which may seem no more than a stranger. The move from event to narration of event is a measure simultaneously of the imprecisions of language and of the gulf between raw experience and its communication. To suffer a blow is not to be able to express the truth of that blow, merely the fact that it occurred.

In one sense the camps were a black hole from which no light could emerge. Attempts to shine the bright light of attention and concern into that darkness potentially constitute a denial of the reality so sought. Even those deliberate attempts made by some to lay down the material of memory against some future and necessary retrieval were confronted by the temporal distortions of the camps in which there was no imagined tomorrow: 'In normal life, you think about tomorrow and after tomorrow and about a year, and next year a vacation then, and things like that. Here you think on the moment. What happen *now* on the moment. *Now* is it horrible. You don't think "later"' (63). As Lawrence Langer points out, some of the survivors even spoke of the impossibility of accessing the self which inhabited the camps as if it were wholly separate from the self which now attempts the near impossible act of remembering. Thus, Charlotte Dembo writes of living ' "beside" Auschwitz' which remains 'wrapped in the impervious skin of memory that segregates itself from the present "me"' (5). Aharon Appelfeld has similarly remarked that 'sometimes I felt it wasn't I who was in the war, but someone else, someone very close to me, and that he was going to tell me exactly what occurred, for I don't remember what happened and how it happened' (89).

Dembo confessed that 'Today, I am no longer sure that what I have written is true, but I am sure that it happened' (42). Dembo makes a crucial distinction between what she calls a deep and an external memory and the gulf which lies between experience and its expression:

> When I talk to you about Auschwitz, it is not from deep
> memory my words issue. They come from external memory ...
> from intellectual memory, the memory connected with

13

thinking processes. Deep memory preserves sensations, physical imprints. It is the memory of the senses. For it isn't words that are swollen with emotional charge. Otherwise, someone who has been tortured by thirst for weeks on end could never say 'I'm thirsty. How about a cup of tea.' This word has split in two. *Thirst* has turned back into a word for commonplace use. But if I dream of the thirst I suffered in Birkenau, I once again see the person I was, haggard, halfway crazed, near to collapse; I physically feel the real thirst and it is an atrocious nightmare. If however you ask me to talk about it ... That is why I say today that while knowing perfectly well that it corresponds to the facts, I no longer know if it is real.[13]

Appelfeld confirms this conviction: 'The strongest imprints those years have left on me are intense physical ones. The hunger for bread. To this day I wake up in the middle of the night ravenously hungry ... I eat as only people who have known hunger eat ... Everything that happened is imprinted within my body and not within my memory.' While insisting that he remembers little, 'sometimes just the aroma of a certain dish or the dampness of shoes or a sudden noise is enough to take me back into the middle of the war, and then it seems to me that it never really ended' (89–90).

The camps were so profoundly outside the parameters of normal thought and experience that some spoke of inhabiting another planet so that to understand life there it became necessary to reconstruct an entire ecology, an alien social system, a morality largely contained and defined by the exosphere of this place where people died by ice and fire, where the rise of the sun meant neither warmth nor hope.

And when those same memories make their way into written accounts another level of difficulty occurs in that there are conventions to the written word. Writing has its own history. We enter the world of aesthetics. And so the survivors reach for metaphor seeking for some analogy that will aid the reader, thereby retreating from the thing itself. Langer quotes from a survivor who, in the middle of an interview, asks to be permitted to read from her written account. Immediately, she steps into the conventions of writing, speaking of people being 'vomited into an impenetrable black night' as they leave the cattle trucks. Screams 'knife the air', torches 'lick' the sky. There is a step here away from the event and into the imagined event. The vivid writing risks dimming the immediacy of feeling, though that immediacy of feeling is itself difficult to preserve through the years.

To be sure, there comes a moment in many interviews in which survivors are brought to a halt by their own accounts. They are unable to continue even as they feel the obligation to do so, offering apologies to the invisible interviewer and, beyond him or her, to those who watch. For a second they are, it seems, back there in the place on which they had desperately tried to slam a door. But whether they are feeling now exactly what they felt then it is impossible to tell. Then, everything was a shock. It was not just the loss of their immediate family but the moment-by-moment process, beginning with ignorance and hope of a kind, only later ending with a knowledge which even then required the imagination to complete, where imagination was the enemy, for who would wish to witness even thus what they had been 'spared' as they were directed one way and their family another? What is it that stops their speech but loss, or the memory of loss, images of those who they loved and who they are now obliged to offer up again as the price of fulfilling their obligation?

W. G. Sebald recalled Kafka's remark that 'we cannot do without pictures, but they torment us too', himself adding that we 'are so moved by photographic images because of the curious aura of another world that emanates from them'.[14] The 'other world' in the context of the Holocaust is not the camps but that curiously innocent place that preceded knowledge of what was to come. Steiner has said that, 'It is not the literal past that rules us, save, possibly, in a biological sense. It is images of the past.'[15] He did not, perhaps, mean it in terms of physical images but it explains something of the urgency of the project. As Steiner continues, 'the echoes by which a society seeks to determine the reach, the logic and authority of its own voice, come from the rear' (3). A society, he insists, needs its antecedents. How much more so when systematic attempts had been made to eradicate that past, when that past was turned to ash. Yet that past exists in images invalidated by what followed as innocent childhood, family excursions, ended at the doors of the gas chambers.

It was not, of course, that there had been an absence of information. The Germans may have attempted to destroy the evidence of their crimes but they had a counter instinct, which was to record and catalogue. Holocaust survivors have told bewildering stories of the extremes to which German officialdom would go to see that every regulation had been obeyed, every detail filed away. Nor were the smudged photographs smuggled out by inmates the only images to hand. In Warsaw, the underground established a secret cell in Foto-Rys, a photographic shop where German soldiers obligingly took their snapshots of atrocities for developing and printing. Copies were smuggled to the Polish government in exile. Andrzej Honowski was executed for his part in the operation. One German officer even gathered together his pictures of the Krakow ghetto, its empty streets filled with the abandoned suitcases of those taken away to die, and had them mounted and leather-bound to take home. W. G. Sebald's father, whose activities in Poland were never to be spoken aloud, nonetheless himself presented a similar album to his wife. These were mementoes, memories being laid down against an unimagined future but with no apparent sense of shame even if those memories could never be spoken, quite as if, like Arthur Miller's Eddie Carbone, in *A View from the Bridge*, they thought that what was not spoken did not in truth exist.

Yet, the question of remembering was by no means clear. What, after all, was to be remembered, and why? Was the past to be a burden carried into the future and, if so, for how long was it to be borne? George Steiner quotes Albrecht Goes's *The Burnt Offering* in which he asks himself the legitimacy of stirring the ashes of the past: 'One has forgotten. And there must be forgetting for how could a man live who had not forgotten?' Steiner's reply is 'Better, perhaps.'[16] Nietzsche however rehearsed the necessity for forgetting, the Nietzsche whose complete works, printed on Bible paper, were presented by Adolf Hitler to Mussolini on his sixtieth birthday.

Yet the impulse to forget, to suppress, is entirely understandable. Lawrence Langer has described the case of a woman whose baby was snatched away from her as she left the Kovno ghetto. She later married a former inmate but could not even tell him what she had experienced, a man, after all, who it might be thought would understand if anyone could. 'I think all my life I have been alone', she explained, 'Even when I met Jack ... I didn't tell Jack my past. Jack just found out recently [1979]. To me, I was dead. I died, and I didn't want to hear nothing and I didn't want to know nothing ... I didn't want to talk about it, and I didn't want to admit to myself that this happened to me ... I wasn't even alive ... I don't know if it was by my doing, or it was done, or how, but I wasn't there. But yet I survived.'[17] How far survival depended on the denial of memory is not clear. Eventually, her husband discovered the truth and she offered herself for archive interview but that new openness clearly did battle with the conviction that her former self had died, along with her child. It is not entirely clear that the request that she should revisit this time was consonant with her psychological well-being. On one level she acknowledged the necessity to break her silence. On another, to force her back into the past was to insist that she re-experience not only the death of her child but also her own death as a fully functioning individual.

Another survivor spoke of knowing a truth concealed from others which made it impossible to have trust in anything or anybody, aware, as she was, of the ease with which civilities, humanities, could be stripped away. She had lived on into a world of illusion in which people behaved as if such revelations had never come, unless they had been processed into reassuring narratives in which past errors had been transcended, in which human imperfections were in process of being eliminated. But remembering did not occur in the past. It was a present activity and the consequences of remembering were carried not by that distant self but by a new self, forged out of a forgetfulness which was perhaps a necessary precondition for survival.

Even the notion that testimony is justified as a Catonian warning, that future cataclysms can thereby be avoided, depends on a certain view of history and the human sensibility which may have been precisely what died in the camps, as people were stripped to bare necessities. King Lear was equally stripped of the habiliments of civilisation in order to learn a truth about human demands, his role in a tragedy, however, giving him an exemplary force and an abiding dignity at odds with his situation. In the camps there was room neither for tragedy nor for dignity. Edgar is blinded the better to see. Those who were maimed in the camps were the victims of arbitrary diktat. They died fighting for breath, climbing over one another to reach what they thought might be the salvation of fresh air. This was the birthplace of the absurd and not tragedy and the recuperation of that fact was not a self-evident necessity unless we presume to deny the lesson most clearly presented there. This was the world of Camus's *Caligula*, of Beckett's *Act Without Words*, *1* and *2*, not of *Oedipus* or *Lear*.

In his book *The Ethics of Memory*, Avishai Margalit reconstructs a debate between his parents.

MOTHER: The Jews were irretrievably destroyed. What is left is just a pitiful remnant of the great Jewish people [which for her meant European Jewry]. The only honorable role for the Jews that remain is to form communities of memory – to serve as 'soul candles' like the candles that are kindled in the memory of the dead.

FATHER: We, the remaining Jews, are people, not candles. It is a horrible prospect for anyone to live just for the sake of retaining the memory of the dead. That is what the Armenians opted to do. And they made a terrible mistake. We should avoid it at all costs. Better to create a community that thinks predominantly about the future and reacts to the present, not a community that is governed from mass graves.[18]

Are we, is anyone, obliged to remember, more especially if there is no redemption in memory, only the blunt fact of suffering and the accusation, no matter how pitiless, of passivity? Is it a legitimate function to sustain the memory of injustice? Holocaust survivors, Aharon Appelfeld has said, 'had faced excruciating choices, the main one being whether to continue living with the memory of the Holocaust or to start a new life'. Many 'had chosen the new life. The choice was not lightly undertaken. They had wanted to spare their children the memory of suffering and the shame; they wanted to raise them to become free men and women, without that dismal legacy' (170). Those emigrating to Israel were treated with suspicion and urged to set aside their memories and with them the taint of a supposed passivity. In a new state the past was suspect and ambiguous. The future was to be unambiguously good.

On the other hand, memory is a defence against oblivion. Those who would deny the past are confronted by those who recall it because they were there. Oscar Gröning was an SS guard at Auschwitz in September 1942. Though he felt uncomfortable about his presence there, and even requested a transfer, he believed that it was legitimate to rid Germany of alien cultures. Life was not too bad. There was a good social life, with parties and dances. The murders were 'something that happened in war'. Two years later he was transferred to the front, the Ardennes, and surrendered to the British in 1945. In the postwar world he prospered. When his parents-in-law criticised him for his war service he was angry. He eventually became an honorary judge of industrial tribunal cases. Finally, and in the face of those who denied the truth of the camps, he confronted the past: 'I would like you to believe me ... I saw the gas chambers. I saw the crematorium. I saw the open fires. I was on the ramp when the selections took place. I would like you to believe that these atrocities took place, because I was there.'[19]

As confessions go, it falls somewhat short of deserving absolution. In truth, it seems more as if he were tidying his desk, sorting things out before the end, this man who had been a bank clerk at seventeen and whose job in the camp was to count the money stolen from those who were to die. He always knew which group were dying by the currency he received. But the last words, 'I was there', are offered as an assurance of truth (though witnesses are notoriously unreliable: 'This book is drenched in memory', warned Primo Levi, a man for whom memory seemed finally to get too much for him).

Barbara Stimler now lives in London. She suffered in Auschwitz-Birkenau. She arrived in Britain in 1946. She had a nervous breakdown ten years later and on the advice of her psychiatrist had her camp tattoo removed. She chose not to speak of her experience, even to her husband who had fought in the Polish army. Then, she was persuaded to record her experiences for an archive, subsequently visiting schools. 'When I speak to the children,' she has explained, 'I ask myself, "Do they believe me?" Because sometimes I don't believe myself' (5).

Mayer Hersh, a Polish Jew, also ended up in Auschwitz, although as the war wound down he endured the forced march to Buchenwald. He came to Britain and only in the 1970s began to speak of his experiences. 'To me', he explained, 'this is a fulfilment. But why is it a fulfilment? Because I am talking about my family, whose lives were extinguished and whose voices were obliterated. The perpetrators also wanted the memory of these people to be obliterated, and that's something I don't want to happen. I want their memory to be preserved for an eternity' (11).

Yet the need to remember and, having remembered, to bear witness may be in the service of other necessities. Memory is sometimes shaped into a public form. In 2005, the new Yad Vashem Museum opened in Israel. It cost $56 million and was larger than the first which had opened in 1957. In the intervening years, especially in the 1980s and 1990s, other memorials had sprung up around the world (in the United States there are more than a hundred) and there was a risk that Jerusalem would lose its primacy. That earlier one had stressed Jewish resistance and the flight to Israel. The new one told a different story, tracing the path from persecution through to deportation and murder. It was to be entered via a downward sloping tunnel whose walls slowly narrow, a recreation of the experience of those whose possibilities had themselves slowly narrowed to a nullity.

There was, though, suggested Tom Segev, author of *The Seventh Million*, a politics to the museum. As he told the *Guardian* correspondent Chris McGreal,

> The new museum's a statement of two things. It tells you that
> nowhere in the world should there be a more magnificent
> Holocaust museum than in Jerusalem, not in Washington, not
> in Berlin. This is the reason why it was built in such a way.
> There's an element of competition here. The other thing is that in
> the past decade, the Holocaust has become a universal code of
> the ultimate evil. By building this kind of museum, Israel is

trying to gain back the monopoly on the Holocaust; the Holocaust is ours and ours alone, and no humanistic or universal values should overtake what we feel about the Holocaust.[20]

Who owns the Holocaust – those who suffered there, their descendants, those who see in it an image, a metaphor, an expression of inhumanity? Yad Vashem is a house of memories. The question is, whose are they and what is the reason for preserving them? For the Museum's curator, Avner Shalev, the Holocaust was 'the formative experience on which the modern world was established'. Yet its specificity to the Jews meant that it also served a more immediate purpose. For Israel, it was part of the cement of the state. Even those young Jews who had no familial connection with those events in Europe, indeed with Europe itself, thought of themselves as Holocaust survivors because it had become the master story of their country, its justification, a collective memory to which they could lay retrospective and vicarious claim. It was not their memory but they claimed presumptive rights to it via their religious and national identity. Memory had become a statement, a present and political fact.

The Museum deliberately lays stress on the individual lives at risk of being lost a second time in the statistics with which subsequent generations were terrified. Those terminated lives took with them their own memories. What they left, occasionally, was a photograph – and they are collected and named at Yad Vashem – a document, a trace. In place of anonymous victims it lays stress on documented lives. In the Hall of Names portraits of the dead are displayed around the dome. Those whose ashes once swirled up through the chimney now rise up to the apex of that dome, their faces preserved, their lives memorialised.

Ralph Waldo Emerson, in 'Nature', regretted that 'Our age is retrospective. It builds the sepulchres of the fathers. It writes biographies, histories, and criticism. The foregoing generations beheld God and nature face to face; we, through their eyes. Why should not we also enjoy an original relation to the universe?'[21] He spoke, it turned out, not just for a confrontation with the natural world but for a culture which felt the wind of the future in its face and would become synonymous with the modern. It had escaped aristocracy and autocracy, sailed away from the dead hand of tradition. Here, self-invention was the mode. A man could be remade out of his encounter with the new. Yesterday was prelude to the present which was itself a temporary condition. The past was discarded because it was the site of trauma or guilt. An 1890s guide for immigrant Jews travelling to America advised them to forget their customs and ideals and hold fast to the new country. This was to be what Gore Vidal called the United States of Amnesia.

In Europe, the past is never dead. Borders between countries follow defensive topographies or simply mark the line where the fighting last stopped. They are signs of victory, defeat or pressured negotiations. They are marked in blood and are temporary. National identity and language are subject to political will and liable, under pressure, to be exchanged for others. Yesterday survives into today through individual and collective memories but these are themselves subject to other necessities than mere recall. In such circumstances, nostalgia is seldom uninfected with irony. Memory, anyway, is subject to biological process and social necessities.

Freud once remarked that 'Childhood memories are only consolidated at a later period, usually at the age of puberty ... and involve a complicated process of remodelling, analogous in every way to the process by which a nation constructs legends about its early history.'[22] Memory, in other words, is constituted of something more than retrieved images of a former self in a former life. It serves present needs even as it offers to fuse together disparate experiences into a master story.

At Salisbury Cathedral, a gardener died of tetanus when he pricked his finger on a rose in the graveyard and succumbed to the infection drawn up from the dead buried beneath. Death born out of beauty born out of death. The connection between now and then is organic. The past is the source of meaning, a place it is necessary to visit if the present is to make sense. And the path to that past, the wormhole through which we travel, is memory. As individuals, as communities, as nations we are about the business of remembering and forgetting and our identities are intimately involved in this process.

Anna Akhmatova once wrote that 'In the terrible year of the Yezhov terror, I spent seventeen months waiting in line outside the prison in Leningrad. One day someone in the crowd identified me. Standing behind me was a woman with lips blue from the cold, who had of course never heard me called by name before. Now she started out of the torpor common to us all and asked me in a whisper (everyone whispered there) "Can you describe this?" and I said "I can." Then something like a smile passed fleeting over what had once been her face.'[23] That smile was a justification for Akhmatova, but witness depends on memory and memory and imagination are kissing cousins. Where does the chain of memory take us as it goes from testimony to play to novel?

Lawrence Langer asks to whom the story of the Holocaust will be bequeathed: 'To the historian? The critic? The poet, novelist or dramatist? To the surviving victim? ... In some ways ... with the exception of the surviving victims, all are witnesses to memory, rather than rememberers themselves.'[24] As Stephen Smith observes,

> If we consider the witness of the witness as the first link in the chain of witness, each 'generation' becomes less authoritative with each link in this chain. The survivor bears witness to the death of the true witness of the 'Final Solution', as an eye-witness of inevitable and ultimate death. The story is in turn witnessed by a third party observer. This personal testimony is then re-told or re-presented in alternative forms, such as film or literature, to be in turn re-witnessed by an audience for which personal contact with a survivor may not be possible. This chain of witnesses results in subjecting the eye-witness of the individual who was there to the opinion or re-representation of those who were not. (439)

What, then, lies at the end of this chain of memory and witness, enlightenment or obfuscation? Does the truth lie only at the beginning, in that compacted atom from which this dark universe was born, or are there other truths generated as the story echoes down the corridor of time, a story changing with the telling? The British playwright David Hare, speaking in 2005, insisted that 'the crimes committed in the concentration camps are not available to be used in the common currency of figurative speech. They stand alone. They are different.'[25] Yet, for all its harsh particularities there were those for whom the essence of the Holocaust lay in its power as a warning, a template and, indeed, a metaphor while memory itself was a more subtle mechanism than a simple recorder.

At times, even addressing such issues is to hear the ice begin to crack beneath one's feet. For some two decades it was if not a secret then a story few were willing to tell and to which few were willing to listen. Now it is told in survivors' tales, recounted in schools, dramatised, filmed until there is a risk that its images will become too familiar to carry the sense of trauma it induced in those who suffered but also in those who contemplated the implications of what occurred in the middle of Europe, in the middle of a century that had seemed to carry the promise of a new Enlightenment but which devolved into the deepest of horrors.

2   W. G. Sebald: an act of restitution

The moral backbone of literature is about the whole question of memory ... Memory, even if you repress it, will come back at you and shape your life. Without memories there wouldn't be any writing.

W. G. Sebald, 'The Last Word'[1]

Time past
Grows no more real
Through sufferings endured.

W. G. Sebald, *After Nature*[2]

Our world is a cracked bell that no longer sounds.

Goethe, quoted in *The Emigrants*

... if I see before me
the nervature of past life
in one image, I always think
that this has something to do
with truth. Our brains, after all,
are always at work on some quivers
of self-organization.

After Nature[3]

W. G. Sebald disliked his first name, Winfried, both because it would have had to be on the approved list published by an edict of the Third Reich and because, in England, it was close to a girl's name, Winifred; he disliked his second because it had been his father's and he had a problematic relation to him. He was born in Wertach im Allgäu, a village three thousand feet up in the Bavarian Alps in 1944, the only son of Rosa, the daughter of a country policeman. His father, Georg, came from a family of glass makers and was himself a locksmith. There were three daughters.

The village, which had some one thousand inhabitants, was isolated. There was snow for five months of the year. There were no cars or machinery and hence, no noise, except, perhaps, for that emanating from the zither which he struggled for three years to master and played to the dying grandfather he loved before abandoning it. He was four before the first tractor arrived. To the end of his life he was sensitive to noise and refused to work with a computer, computers, he insisted, being given to muttering under their breath. He read almost nothing in his early years. Even the two-page newspaper appeared only once a fortnight. There was no library and little music, though at five he recalled playing a card game which featured pictures of German cities as they had been before the war rendered them to ruins. His time was spent looking after cows, tobogganing or, as he explained, fiddling around with odds and ends, a habit which he later suggested determined his working methods: 'I always begin by scratching around for bits and pieces and then seeing what I can do with them.'⁴ Time moved at a different rate in Wertach im Allgäu.

His father, like Sebald's mother of working-class background, was unemployed for several years in the 1920s and then, in 1929, joined the 100,000-strong German army permitted under the Versailles Treaty. When the National Socialists came to power he stayed and flourished. The family began its climb into the middle class. They were Catholics and anti-Communist. In 1939 he was among the troops that invaded Poland and that Christmas gave his wife a celebratory album. It included photographs of the Polish campaign and, oddly, a picture of gypsies behind barbed wire somewhere in Slovakia, a puppet state, interned in an open-air camp. Later, Sebald realised its significance. It was 'an indication that these things were accepted as part of the operation right from the beginning'. As a young teenager, however, when he first saw the picture, he had failed to understand its significance. 'I looked through this album as a thirteen-year-old', he explained, 'blindly, as one does at that age, without noticing it; only much later did it strike me that there was a whole tale in that image',[5] and, indeed, it found its way into his book *Vertigo*.

Later, in Manchester, he came across a postcard from Stuttgart, dating from 1939, on which a young English girl had recorded her attendance at a Hitler Youth rally. The picture reminded him not only of what that city had looked like before Allied bombers had reduced it to rubble but that his father, at that moment, would have been part of a convoy of trucks driving east to initiate the catastrophe his country had brought down upon others and itself. Memory of this card and of the memories which it, in turn, stirred in him formed part of an address he made in the final year of his life at the opening of the House of Literature in Stuttgart. His presence in Stuttgart led him to think, by way of Hölderlin, of the French town of Tulle (Hölderlin having travelled from one city to the other) where, exactly three weeks after Sebald's birth, ninety-nine men had been hanged by the SS and the remainder of the male population worked to death. So what, he asked his Stuttgart audience, 'is literature good for?' The title of his address, however, was 'An Attempt at Restitution', and he ended by insisting that 'only in literature can there be an attempt at restitution over and above the mere recital of facts and over and above scholarship'.[6] Those remarks explain why Sebald himself moved beyond the scholarship to which he had devoted the first part of his life. His career as a writer was in effect an act of restitution.

Though this was not a story that Sebald invoked, it was through the bomb-wrecked streets of Stuttgart that Simon Wiesenthal made his way in 1945 in search of the mother of an SS officer. While still a prisoner of war Wiesenthal had been summoned by that man who lay dying of his wounds. The officer had sent a nurse to find a Jew, any Jew, to whom he could confess his crimes. He looked for forgiveness and was forced, therefore, to turn witness against himself, to lay his memories before a man who must stand in place of those who could not offer forgiveness because they were dead at his hands.

The story he told was a brutal one and he made no attempt to evade his own involvement. He and others had rounded up Jews and forced them to carry cans of petrol into a house. They had then thrown hand grenades in and shot anyone who tried to escape. The rest were burned to death. Now, on the edge of death, the SS officer looked for the grace of forgiveness from a Jew who must stand for those other Jews. A lapsed Catholic, he stared into a darkness that terrified.

Wiesenthal listened in silence. Several times he tried to leave, only to be called back. The man had not finished his story. And as he sat beside him so a certain human sympathy seemed to evidence itself, not in anything he said but in his actions. He held the man's hand and brushed a fly away from his face. These were no more than instinctive gestures. It was as if his body retained a memory of certain civilities. But for the man confessing to his culpability such gestures were not enough. He wanted this Jew, whose name he seems never to have asked, to grant him absolution.

When he died shortly afterwards his possessions were offered to Wiesenthal. Had the man so misunderstood his gestures as to believe he had offered what in fact had been withheld, for Wiesenthal had left the room without speaking the words the man needed? Could the holding of a hand, the brushing away of a fly have assumed an unlooked-for significance? He refused the possessions, which were therefore sent to the man's mother.

When the war was finally over, Wiesenthal made his way to Stuttgart. He had recalled the address of the SS officer's mother on the package that had been offered to him. Why did he recall the address and why go to see her? In part, perhaps, because he was uncertain about the legitimacy of his actions, felt a degree of guilt that he could not earth in anything so definite as a moral cause. He found her among the ruins. Her life had fallen apart. Her husband had been killed in the bombing, her son in circumstances that were unclear to her. She had had her differences with him. He had joined the Hitler Youth against his parents' wishes. He had then volunteered for the SS. They could not understand him. However, with her husband gone, it was the memory of that son that sustained her. Should Wiesenthal tell her the truth of that son's depravities? Once again he left without speaking. Two varieties of silence. The one silence was a refusal to offer forgiveness. The other was a gesture of compassion. In the ruins of Stuttgart he reached into himself and discovered if not sympathy then an inability to injure, to exact a price for his own suffering or for that of the anonymous Jews killed by a young man who had regretted his actions only when confronted with his own imminent death and the return of religious convictions conveniently laid aside while he committed murder.

Yet this was the same Simon Wiesenthal who would devote his life to tracking down those Nazis whose hands were stained with blood, the same man who would rely on the memories of survivors such as himself to see justice done decades after the perpetrators had slid effortlessly back into civilian life, beneficiaries of the wilful forgetfulness against which Sebald would rail and which would characterise more than one society in the decades after the war. Sebald stood in Stuttgart and recited the crimes of the SS, as he envisaged the possibility of restitution if only within the constructed parameters of literature. Yet, even there, restitution depended upon memory and for Sebald memory, literal, fictive, was anyway a central concern.

His father was taken prisoner in France not long after Sebald's birth and did not return until the summer of 1947 by which time he had the rank of major (on another occasion he remembered him as a captain) and even then worked in a nearby town, only returning at weekends for the next three years. Significantly, Sebald insists, 'We should recall ... that the horrendous occurrences and atrocities that are now recorded happened not only in the latter part of the war, they happened as soon as the Germans marched into Poland in 1939.'[7] Precisely what involvement his father may have had was never clear. 'You didn't know what your parents had done but, perhaps more decisively, you didn't even know what they had seen or not seen. And the question, to my mind now, is: What did they witness? What did they see? The first line of defence was always, "I can't remember exactly what happened"' (143). As he explained,

> In most German families this kind of topic was taboo ... of course, you tried to talk to your parents about it. But these attempts invariably ended in family drama and arguments, so you left it after a while. I think there was certainly what has

often been described as a conspiracy of silence. I don't even
think that couples talked to each other much about that sort of
thing. One had tacitly to agree to leave this behind and
developed an attitude that was entirely forward-looking,
which was bent on *not* remembering ... We never had that
conversation ... The first line of defence was always, 'I can't
remember exactly what happened.' If you pressed harder then the
atmosphere would become increasingly uncomfortable. (142–3)

The past, then, was problematic and memory denied. He
derived from his failed efforts to penetrate what seemed to be family
secrets linked to a larger silence an unfocussed feeling of responsibility and a sense of the indeterminate nature of the past. In some way
he was aware that private biography and national history were
intertwined but what the nature of that connection might be was
unclear, as was the precise shape of the past itself. As he remarked,

it is extremely difficult to determine what the past contained in
terms of the personal experience of others. The accepted version
of the past is largely of a fictional nature, or large tracts of it are.
As regards the lives of your immediate relations – your parents,
for instance – there are stock memories which are constantly or
repeatedly reeled out when people start talking about the
past. Between these 'stories' there are enormous lacunae of
non-memory, of a past that somehow seems to have no
existence at all. (143–4)

After a time working as a locksmith, his father joined the new
German army, the Bundeswehr, in the mid 1950s, Germany already
turning its back on the past and emerging as a new force in Europe, its
economy renewed with the help of the Marshall Plan.

As he grew up, Sebald learned nothing about the Holocaust, or,
indeed, the catastrophic effects of the air war on Germany's cities,
except that suddenly, one day, his class was shown a film about the
concentration camps. There was no discussion and afterwards he and
his fellow pupils went out to play. It remained as a curious incident,
not explored at the time, but recovered in memory as a first

intimation of something that lacked either a private or a public context. 'It was a long drawn-out process to find out, which I've done persistently since.'[8]

It is an experience I shared. In the 1950s, when television was still a rarity, programmes were only broadcast in the evenings. During the day, however, a test card, along with occasional random films, was transmitted to assist engineers installing sets and aerials. One day, I turned the set on only to see a film of a concentration camp. It showed piles of skeletal bodies being thrown into a pit and what seemed to be living corpses walking round. It showed what were called gas chambers and crematoria. After what I suppose was half an hour the screen reverted to a test card. There was no indication as to why it had been shown. There was no context. But it left its mark.

For the most part, Sebald's was a protected upbringing, though the later death of his father left him feeling exposed. For all his problematic relation to him, years later he still missed this man with whom politically he had felt at odds. There was, he confessed, a hole in his universe.

Sebald's education took him from the Bavarian Alps to the University of Freiburg, where he enrolled in 1963, and where he had a special interest in the German Romantics. It was now a time when the Holocaust first began to impinge on public consciousness. Indeed, 1963 had marked the first performance of *The Deputy* (which concerned Pope Pius XII's attitude towards the Jews during World War II), by Rolf Hochhuth, whose work Sebald admired and whose documentary approach stirred his interest, more especially when he went on to write *Soldiers*, which dealt with the air war against Germany. Drama (and Sebald's *The Emigrants* would itself be dramatised in 2005), it seemed, might make up for what he later described as 'the moral and artistic deficit which [Germany] had incurred since the desertification of the minds had been systematised in 1933',[9] the year of Hitler's accession to power. What he called 'the German desire to silence and end the witness',[10] was showing signs of coming to an end. This documentary theatre refused to close its eyes to a conspiracy against humanity. This does not, though, mean that Sebald was content with the idea of what in Balzac had seemed to him a mania for reality, which he thought an act of authorial prostitution as if mere submission to fact generated its own self-justification. What he looked for was an aesthetic with moral sense.

His ambiguous feelings about Alfred Döblin, the subject of his doctoral thesis, did not stop him respecting the lure of documentation charged by the imagination or recognising the world that in documenting Döblin wished to preserve, the Jewish society of the late 1920s on the brink of catastrophe. He wished, Sebald observes, to wrest individual lives from 'the river of oblivion'. The tenor of the work, he said, 'corresponds to the attitude of the messenger in Greek tragedy who as a survivor announces in a voice of shaken indifference a disaster that has already taken place. The report is directed didactically at posterity so that by studying the example it may avoid the same fate.'[11]

Yet the risk of the documentary style was a 'rather questionable predilection for gloomy fortune-telling from the tea-leaves of history' (226). In the end, it seemed to Sebald, Döblin's novels, in spite of themselves, were 'testimonies of a period when the resistance of the artist is broken and art is made to serve the purposes of terror' (232). Not for nothing did the Nazis omit his *Wallenstein*, a novel about the Thirty Years War, from the list of books for burning, since in its pages, 'Jews are burned and we are told how the executioners tear off the skin of their victims in strips, so that the fat begins to boil', scenes which, it seemed to Sebald, Döblin described with altogether too much relish and which recalled the obvious truth that 'the aesthetic reproduction of pain does nothing to alleviate it. Art simply transposes it on another plane' (264). In his own work Sebald would display a certain reticence even as he acknowledged the reality and force of pain. Complicity with those who inflicted pain was to be avoided even as it was necessary to bear witness to it. Yet it is worth recalling that Döblin would refuse to be interned in Germany and was buried by his son, Wolfgang, who committed suicide rather than be captured by the Germans.

Sebald found his university experience unsatisfactory. The system itself remained unreconstructed and authoritarian while classes could range up to a thousand students simply listening to professors who, it later occurred to him, had begun their careers under National Socialism and whom he describes, with uncharacteristic casualness, as 'dissembling old Fascists'.[12] Only Theodor Adorno seemed to offer anything worth reading, though even he would later begin producing what seemed to Sebald to be turgid, programmatic, works. The libraries, meanwhile, were chaotic and the education on offer suspect.

As a result, at the age of twenty-one, he transferred to the French-speaking part of Switzerland, thereby moving outside his home language, though later he would write his books in German and rely on others to translate them, despite his fluency in English, despite, indeed, the carefulness with which he checked those translations. This, he explained, was because, though by then he had lived in England for more than two decades, as a Professor of German he worked in that language even as his daily speech was English. English was simply a language in which he did not feel at home as a writer. But he did not feel entirely at home in the German language either, though for rather different reasons, and increasingly felt suspended between two language, seeing each from the outside. So, he would explain of writing *Austerlitz*, 'I reached a point where I thought I can't string together another German sentence at all and I wondered whether I was now faced with this notorious problem of having to change my coat, my linguistic coat, as happened to some other writers.'[13] He was aware that even Nabokov, often invoked in his work, a figure with a butterfly net glimpsed on a mountainside both as a young child and an adult, had struggled to locate a secure linguistic ground on which to stand. Now Sebald himself felt that sense of insecurity.

Before he moved to Switzerland, an event occurred that would prove of central significance to him. The Eichmann trial seems to have passed him by but the Frankfurt trial of a number of guards from Auschwitz-Birkenau, in 1963–5, did not. For Sebald the significance of the trial was that this 'was the first *public* acknowledgement that there was such a thing as an unresolved German past'. He read the daily reports in the *Frankfurter Allgemeine Zeitung* 'and they suddenly shifted my vision. I realized that there were subjects of much greater urgency than the writings of the German Romantics. I understood that I had to find my own way through that maze of the German past and not be guided by those in teaching positions at the time' (147). It gave him, he explained, 'an understanding of the real dimensions for the first time: the defendants were the kind of people I'd known as neighbours – postmasters or railway workers – whereas the witnesses were people I'd never come across – Jewish people from Brooklyn or Sydney. They were a myth of the past. You found out they too had lived in Nuremberg and Stuttgart. So it gradually pieced itself together, along with the horrific details.'[14] He realised that he was living among at least tacit accomplices and that he was himself thereby an accomplice. It was difficult, he explained, 'to say you haven't anything to do with it', and as a result he felt he 'had to know what happened in detail, and to try to understand why it should have been so'. To his dismay he realised that few if any German writers had sought to address these concerns and when they had done so, it was with a lack of 'tact or true compassion'.[15]

His next step seemed a strange one. Fluent in German and French, and with a background in Greek and Latin, in 1966 he decided to go to England, a country of which he knew nothing and whose language was as yet a mystery. He also exchanged the beauty of German and Swiss towns for Manchester (where he was to be a language assistant at the University), and, unsurprisingly, was thrown into a temporary depression. But England seemed attractive none-theless. It offered an efficient library system and a heated office, both novel to him. The pound was strong and as an assistant lecturer he was earning real money. He also valued the lack of an authoritarian system. For someone like himself, he insisted, with 'something of an anarchist streak', it offered a new sense of freedom. Many years later, when his reputation was established, he was tempted back to Germany but found he could no longer face it. There was still a hierarchy in place that he felt repellent and the job market a matter of influence and intrigue.

In moving from Germany to Britain, however, he was exchanging a country in which the war was not to be mentioned for one in which it was a matter of obsessive concern. He became aware that in his own country there was not even an account of the destruction of German cities written by German historians, hence his own later work in that area. But there was another absence, both in German historiography and in his own life: the Jew. One of the consequences of the Final Solution, he explained, was that in growing up in Germany after 1945 it was entirely possible never to encounter a Jew, though there had been Jews in villages and the small town in which he had gone to school, one of whom he would memorialise in *The Emigrants*.

In Manchester, he met one, his landlord, whose parents had been deported to Riga where they were killed. The encounter proved crucial. 'To my mind', he insisted, 'there is an acute difference between history as historiography and history as experienced history.' Here was a man who embodied the past, whose memories constituted a counter history to that on which he himself had been raised, though this ex-patriated survivor, no less than Sebald's own father, was hesitant to re-animate ghosts, if for wholly different reasons.

However, the fact that this awareness came to him in Britain, and that he was later inclined to find this a more accommodating country, more liberal, less willing to deny its own history, should not be taken as evidence for its genuine engagement with those aspects of the past which the British themselves chose to mythify. There is a sense in which he grants England more than its due when it comes to remembering the war. It was a particular version of it that was celebrated. It was a victory for the human spirit, a triumph for an island kingdom that had stood alone. There was, though, a silence which was not so different from that which pertained in his native Germany. The Jewish experience did not burn itself into the national consciousness. Its record of accepting Jewish refugees before the war was as patchy as others, though the *Kindertransports* were welcomed with seeming generosity. When the camps were overrun, reporters did their best to convey something of what they had found, recognising the importance of bearing witness to what they instinctively felt might not be fully believed. In his book on the Holocaust and the liberal imagination, Tony Kushner quotes the BBC's Richard Dimbleby remarking to a colleague: 'I must tell the exact truth, every detail of it, even if people don't believe me, even if they feel these things should not be told.'[16] At first the BBC refused to broadcast until it had further confirmation. Ed Murrow, broadcasting to America, said, 'I pray you believe what I have said about Buchenwald. I have reported what I saw and heard, but only part of it, for most of it I have no words' (214). The particularity of Jewish suffering, though, was lost in the general shock.

After the war generosity to those who had suffered was hard to find. Major exhibitions of photographs from the camps were held, one, indeed, in the very heart of London, at Trafalgar Square. A department store gave over its whole window to a display of gaunt figures in striped clothes, to pictures of the skeletal dead, where once mannequins had displayed fashionable clothes, but these tended not to stress the specifically Jewish nature of the cataclysm. A government delegation to Buchenwald included only one Jew, and that a person standing in for another who had fallen ill. The impact on those who went was considerable, one member of the delegation committing suicide, but the emphasis was placed on what it said about man's inhumanity to man rather than on what it said about Hitler's genocidal policies which had sparked so little response from the Allies during the conflict. Here, as in Germany, it was not that the Holocaust was denied but that it could not be sorted out from other aspects of the war.

Writers were no faster in Britain than in Germany or the United States to grapple with the idea of the Holocaust. Indeed, they were somewhat slower. And though the bombing campaign was the subject of investigations, the sheer ferocity of it was put out of mind. 'Bomber' Harris was the only wartime military leader not publicly recognised for his work, as if this were a secret best kept, a policy that could not bear much scrutiny. Dresden was a word whispered but it was two decades and more before it entered the public consciousness. Sebald, though, carried to Britain a burden different from that of a country which had been attacked and which had gathered its citizens within the castle walls.

In 1968, he completed his master's degree in German literature and briefly returned to Switzerland as a schoolteacher before going back to Manchester a year later and then on to the University of East Anglia, in Norwich, a medieval city in rural Norfolk. He returned to Germany briefly, in 1975–6, working at the Goethe Institute in Munich, but neither then nor on later visits did he feel at home. Nor did he feel affinity with a neighbouring German-speaking country: when he published a book, largely concerned with Austrian writers, he called it *Unheimliche Heimat, Alien Homeland*. He preferred England, with its liberal university system and its respect for privacy, though in the 1980s and 1990s he felt increasingly uncomfortable with the political mood and with what seemed to him to be the abandonment of certain civilities, along with respect for the past. When he was interviewed for Channel 4 television, on the occasion of the publication of *The Rings of Saturn*, it was this dimension that he wished to stress to a background of scenes of mostly elderly people wandering around seemingly with neither purpose nor direction in a decaying environment.

Sebald makes indirection a moral as well as an aesthetic choice. It is not that he does not wish to confront the thing itself but that a slowly focussing awareness reflects that process which allows the unthinkable to make its way into thought and then experience. There is a sense of a man circling around a centre, spiralling in towards a meaning which becomes slowly clearer. He comes at this truth in retrospect, gradually working his way back to it. As he grew up the truth of the past had been a matter of peripheral vision, as it was for a country which both consciously and unconsciously put it out of mind. And because he travelled back to it, remembering and forgetting became something more than matters of detached concern. It became the essence of his writing and his moral commitment.

In some ways a quotation from Michel Foucault's *Madness and Civilization*, which appears as an epigraph to Sebald's essay on Peter Handke's play *Kaspar*, explains both his method and the necessity which drove him:

> We must therefore listen attentively to every whisper of the
> world, trying to detect the images that have never made their
> way into poetry, the phantasms that have never reached a

waking state. No doubt this is an impossible task in two senses: first because it would force us to reconstitute the dust of those actual sufferings and foolish words that nothing preserves in time; second, and above all, because those sufferings and words exist only in the act of separation.[17]

Kaspar, a boy who suddenly emerges, with no language, is, in a phrase from Nietzsche quoted by Sebald, 'totally unhistorical' (57). Like Faulkner's Benjy, in *The Sound and the Fury*, he has no sense of time past and hence sidesteps the moral world. The past, by implication, is an ineluctable aspect of our humanity, the burden and also the redemption of self and society alike. For Nietzsche, paraphrased by Sebald, 'there was nothing more sinister in the prehistory of mankind than the combination of pain and recollection to construct a memory' (62), but that, Sebald insists, is part of the process of emerging as a moral being, and is captured in language, though that language equally possesses the potential for a coercive functionalism, a destructive cruelty. Hence, Sebald's desire to re-establish a connection with the past, to listen to the whisper of the world and reconstitute the dust of sufferings.

He was not unaware, however, that, as Handke remarked, 'the utmost need to communicate comes together with the ultimate speechlessness' (67). Where images escape such a paralysis, Sebald observes, they do so through fact and fiction 'inseparably linked together', as they would in his own work. The risk is that language captures not the 'individual fullness of existence, but only a dead abbreviation of it' (67). In such circumstances literature has a special obligation to transcend this dilemma, by using a subversive language and 'opaque images', those opaque images inviting concentration, exploration.

In exploring the difficulty of inhabiting the German past in particular, with its burden of guilt not only for actions taken but for having survived those in whose annihilation they collaborated, or those fellow citizens whose deaths had left them unquestioning survivors, Sebald remarks, 'Reflections on the guilt of survival were probably presented most cogently by Elias Canetti, Peter Weiss and

Wolfgang Hildesheimer, which suggests that not much might have come of the process known in Germany as "coming to terms with the past" but for the contribution made by writers of Jewish origin' (79). But, then, he was prepared to consider, with Walter Benjamin, that the Jewish tradition had always constituted 'a leaven of the German mind' and had continued to do so 'at a time when the academic establishment was busy transforming German literature into a pure product of Aryan creativity'.[18]

Significantly, his first published monograph, in 1969, was on Carl Sternheim, German and Jewish. His Ph.D. thesis at the University of East Anglia was on Alfred Döblin, also Jewish and an exile (driven, Sebald suggests, 'into a state of linguistic homelessness' (118)), though he would convert to Catholicism. A debt was being acknowledged. Indeed, he was inclined to see in Döblin's work a reverse memory, that is a shadow cast forward. Commenting, in 1973, on a chapter from *Berlin Alexanderplatz*, which relates to the process of organised death in an abattoir, he remarks, 'Far more horrifying than the chaotic destruction of the Apocalypse is the well-ordered mass destruction contrived by man himself. Today as we read how the unwitting beasts are transported by rail from the provinces of the Reich, how they are driven long distances, packed into goods trucks and jolted along before being sorted out in the pens to meet their fate – as we read this today, after all that has happened in the meantime, we cannot ignore the prophetic implications of the chapter Döblin wrote in 1928.' This was a world, after all, where 'the very hecatombs are administered with painstaking meticulousness by an utterly dispassionate bureaucracy' (68).

There is a passion in the analysis which belies its status as a formal academic thesis. Indeed, he goes on to describe Döblin walking through the Warsaw *Judenstadt* and acknowledging the 'atavistic despair' (72) of those he sees, aware of their hopeless position. During his Polish journey, Sebald suggests, Döblin 'speculated whether in the end these intolerable social tensions would not be dissipated by some terrible catastrophe'. His, Sebald reminds us, was 'one of the last accounts of the world of the Ashkenazim before their dreadful extermination' (129), almost as if he were trying to fix in the memory something about to disappear. Even this early, Sebald was reading Gershom Scholem on spiritual developments within Jewish theology, recalling the trauma of 1492 when the Sephardic Jews of Spain were banished, an event which, Sebald insisted, gave birth to a conviction that salvation could only follow apocalypse. It was this apocalyptic strain in Jewish thought that Steiner hinted might make Jews seem complicit in their later fate as if catastrophe and hope were perversely allied.

Sebald also worked on Gottfried Keller and Robert Walser, but became increasingly irritated both by the self-imposed restrictions of scholarship and by the reductive attitude towards research, a certain Stakhanovite attitude which marginalised the eccentric vision, eccentric in terms of the character of teachers but also in the sense of existing at a tangent to some supposed centre. As he explained, 'I always felt somewhat hemmed in by the discipline of academic writing. I was always intent on developing hypothetical notions to suggest that there is circumstantial evidence for a certain case' (151). He began to 'work with very fragmentary pieces of evidence to fill in the gaps and blank spaces and create out of this a meaning which is greater than that which you can prove' (152). He wrote articles in which the strict division between fact and fiction was no longer respected. 'I moved from the straight monograph to essayistic exploration, dealing with my subjects in an elliptical sort of way. But even so I constantly came up against a borderline where I felt, well, if I could go a little bit further it might get very interesting, that is, if I were allowed to make things up' (152). The result was work that he defined by what it was not. It was not, he explained, history, literary criticism or sociology but all 'of these things together'. That, he explained, was how the writing of his literary texts began.

Sebald was an admirer of Hans Erich Nossack, whose account of the bombing of Hamburg gained its force from the fact that he combined an almost documentary directness, which he claimed derived in part from Stendhal, a figure who recurs in Sebald's work, with a view from the periphery, not observing the thing itself but the human tremors it prompted. Memory, meanwhile, Sebald observes, 'and the passing on of the objective information it retains must be delegated to those who are ready to live with the risk of remembering'.[19] That risk, as Sebald was to discover, could be acute. It is a risk, he says, because 'those in whom memory lives on bring down upon themselves the wrath of others who can continue to live only by forgetting' (87). But that would prove to be not the only risk in that sometimes memory can prove a burden too heavy to bear.

Nossack's work proved to Sebald that 'an attempt to write a literary account of catastrophes inevitably, if it is to claim validity, breaks out of the novel form' (88). He also found evidence of this in the work of Alexander Kluge whose *New Stories. Nos 1–18*, published in 1977, 'resists the temptation to integrate that is perpetuated in traditional literary forms by presenting the preliminary collection and organization of textual and pictorial material, both historical and fictional, straight from the author's notebooks' (89). He generated 'complex linguistic montages … maintaining a critical dialectic between past and present', imposing neither a pattern of retrospective historiography nor a determined fictional story but a reflection on those means of understanding the world (99). Kluge, too, worked 'by events peripheral to his own existence past and present' (90). His work, Sebald explains, in what could surely be taken as a form of self-description, 'consists in using *details* to illustrate the main current of the dismal course so far taken by history'. What immediately follows is a reference to fallen trees and silk-moth caterpillars, both of which would feature in Sebald's *The Rings of Saturn*.

Kluge's power lay in his ability to bring the past into the present. An author 'on the perimeter of a civilization to all appearances intent on its own end is working to revive the collective memory of his contemporaries' (100). It is tempting, then, to see the origins of Sebald's style as deriving in part from these authors, from his admiration for the documentary theatre which flourished in Germany in the 1960s, and from his fascination with Stendhal and Borges.

Max Sebald became centrally concerned with the nature of memory, private and public. He wrote what his publisher chose to call prose fiction (though occasionally that publisher would offer a portmanteau description, 'Fiction/Travel/History') for want of a better description since the books include acknowledged fiction along with history, autobiography and biography. He was an admirer of the British travel writer Bruce Chatwin precisely because he mixed genres with a seeming promiscuity. It is also tempting to think that he owed something to the man about whom he wrote so movingly: Jean Améry. He, after all, once described his own work as 'a kind of autobiographical essayistic novel'.[20] 'I always proceed', he explained, 'from the concrete event, but never become lost in it; rather I always take it as an occasion for reflections that extend beyond reasoning ... to areas of thought that lie in an uncertain twilight' (xi). Where to place Sebald's work along the spectrum from fact to fiction? The very question ceases to make sense in books designed in part to demonstrate the degree to which each is infiltrated with the other. This is not to say that he grants no authority to the real, seeks to suggest that we inhabit a kaleidoscope of fictions with varying density. There is a moral core to his work. It is a moral core laid down as he grew up in a small village with no electricity, no reading matter, no distracting noise, no sense that history was gathering to a point.

Yet how was that history to be located and expressed? For a writer so concerned with the past, he was acutely aware of the difficulty of constituting it and the near impossibility of generating a language capable of capturing its totality. In *Austerlitz* the central figure, trying to reconstruct his own past and therefore the past of which he was a product, begins to assemble details, statistics, facts, only to discover how far short this falls of what he is looking for. As Sebald has said, 'fact and fiction are, as it were, both hybrids. They are not alternatives. They are both hybrids with the constituent parts in different measure'[21] (153).

How, anyway, is it possible to capture the truth of the past? In contemplating the battle of Austerlitz, a teacher in *Austerlitz* provides a detailed and apparently authoritative account which lasts for hours and could, he explains, have lasted longer. Indeed, that is precisely the point: 'it would take an endless length of time to describe the events of such a day properly, in some inconceivably complex form recording who had perished, who survived, and exactly where and or how, or simply saying what the battlefield was like at nightfall, with the screams and groans of the wounded and dying. In the end all anyone could ever do was sum up the unknown factors in the ridiculous phrase, ''The fortunes of battle swayed this way and that''' (101).

As Austerlitz observes, 'It does not seem to me ... that we understand the laws governing the return of the past, but I feel more and more as if time did not exist at all, only various spaces interlocking ... between which the living and the dead can move back and forth as they like' (261). This is more acute for him because his past has been falsified and so much of it has been wiped away, but there is a deeper truth here and a justification for Sebald's own approach which allows the living and the dead, the past and the present, implicitly to converse. Certainly, there is no doubt that he feels an obligation that draws him back. As Austerlitz again remarks, 'might it not be ... that we ... have appointments to keep in the past ... and must go there in search of places and people who have some connection with us on the far side of time' (360).

It was not, however, a case of an untainted world that would become the location of pure values. It was instead a matter of an irony that he would find ever less sustainable. Six boys had left a farm in the village in which Sebald had been born to lend their efforts to the army of the Third Reich. All perished on the Russian front. Nothing much else, however, marred the quiet pleasures of village life and it was precisely what did not happen that would later seem to him unbearable. There were a series of absences, for long not perceived as such, that would eventually demand his attention, lead him on a series of journeys, physical, emotional, moral. 'Now', he explained, looking back over many decades, 'I have a sense that while I grew up in what was, after all, quite an idyllic environment, at the same time the most horrendous things had happened in other parts of Europe. While I was sitting in my pushchair and being wheeled through the flowering meadows by my mother, the Jews of Corfu were being deported on a four-week trek to Poland. It is the simultaneity of a blissful childhood and those horrific events that now strikes me as incomprehensible. I know now that these things cast a very long shadow over my life' (*Writers in Conversation*, II:144). One of those deported in the same month he was born, May 1944, was Kafka's sister who began her journey towards Auschwitz quite as if she were realising the force of her brother's prophecies.

For his part, Sebald felt, he explained, no guilt, no sense of responsibility but he did feel an irremediable 'sense of shame' (144). Interestingly, it was a distinction that would be made by someone a good deal closer to the centre of Nazi power who nevertheless, by virtue of her age, also felt free of guilt but not obligation. Hilde Schramm is the daughter of Albert Speer. She was nine years old at the end of the war. Asked, in 2005, what her feelings were she remarked, 'Instead of using guilt, there is a better word to describe my feelings, and that word is shame. I feel ashamed of what happened in the past, and of course I feel ashamed that it happened so close to me, in my own family. For that I still feel shame.'[22] More strangely, Major Karl Plagge, a German officer credited with saving three hundred Jews from the Vilnius ghetto, did use the word guilt and later wrote: 'I was not able to recognise the boundaries where the limit of guilt began or ended and in a broad sense, as a German, I myself bear this guilt. From this plague there is no refuge.'[23]

Even Primo Levi, who had suffered in Auschwitz, confessed to feelings of shame not only because he was a member of the human race that could perpetrate such atrocities but because he had been allowed to survive when his skills as an industrial chemist became known to those with the power to stay his execution in the name of vital work for the Reich. In his case, though, he did also use the word guilt, knowing it to be unjustified but knowing, too, that he could never purge it from his mind so long as his memories continued to haunt him, shaping themselves into an accusation. And when a German with the initials W. G. (also Sebald's, an echo he himself would have noticed) wrote to Levi it was to confess that though himself a child at the end of the war and hence one who could not take on himself any share of the guilt for the crimes committed, 'yet I am ashamed of them'.[24]

Born when the war was all but over Sebald, of course, had no involvement in it and no memory of anything but the quiet solitude of his early years. It was the fact that he had, as he pointed out, remained untouched by the catastrophe unfolding in the German Reich that gave him his subject, though his work shows that despite his protestation he was anything but untouched by it. The cold wind of those times came to him later but it was no less cutting for that. To be sure, he was never a victim in an obvious way any more than he was a perpetrator, but there was an obligation, it seemed, born out of what seemed his immunity. Why, though, feel shame, as he confessed he did? Because, he explained, 'although I was born "late" and consequently was spared direct responsibility, I naturally feel at the same time that this is where my origins lie'. They lay, he explained, a long way back.[25]

How far was apparent in a prose poem first published in German in 1988 and not translated into English until after his death: *After Nature*. The first section explores the life of the artist Matthias Grünewald of Aschaffenburg (1475–1528), an account, however, that takes the poet back to Frankfurt in 1240 when some 173 Jews were slaughtered or died, as he says, ironically, 'of their own free will', in a fire, then on to a massacre in 1349 in another fire that cleared the view from the Cathedral Hill to Sachsenhausen, a name that echoes forward through time. For Jews, it appeared, it was never a question of the fire next time. Then, in the mid fifteenth century a clothing statute was issued requiring all Jews to wear yellow rings on their tunics. And so this pre-history gathers pace, as a ghetto is established from which one girl escapes by converting to Catholicism and marrying the artist whose work would be celebrated in a book, in fifteenth-century Schwabach type, to mark Hitler's birthday in 1938, part of a reinvented past, folkish, Aryan, evidence of a national spirit centuries before the nation was born. The book was about Grünewald. And no mention of the Jewess Enchin who wed herself to a man who would be retrospectively claimed as the carrier of a culture. The arrow which left the bow in 1240 finally reaches its target. When, then, is the beginning and when the end? From fire to fire, yellow armband to yellow star.

In the final section of the poem the narrator, whose biography shadows that of the author, asks himself 'How far, in any case, must one go back / to find the beginning?',[26] and settles on his grandparents, who gave birth to a child who on 27 August 1943 would travel to Dresden, soon to be a destroyed place, of whose beauty his memory 'retains no trace' (82). On 28 August 582 aircraft flew to attack Nuremberg, as his mother watched, though later she could not recall 'what the burning town looked like / or what her feelings were / at this sight' (84), the beginnings of a forgetfulness that her son would one day seek to address. That son, 'W. G. Sebald', later travelled to England, where he met a Jewish man, Mr Deutsch, born in Kufstein, who, we learn in the final section of the poem, had arrived in England in 1938, and of whom he says, 'There were many things he could not / remember; some others he could not erase / from his mind' (100). There is a connection, then, between Frankfurt in 1240 and this Jewish exile in Manchester, as there is between that past and the poet who lays before himself the evidence for that connection. The poem tracks back and forth through time, pulling together private and public histories, the poet hearing assonances and dissonances, observing what is remembered and what forgotten and how together those absences and presences create what passes for reality, albeit a reality whose present force seems always to be fading to transparency.

It was that conviction that would send Max Sebald back and forth in time, crossing boundaries of different kinds until the crossing of boundaries becomes both a method and a subject. This man, who met his first Jew in England, unaware until then of their absence from his life, ended up writing the story of the *Kindertransport* which ferried Jewish children across the boundaries of Europe even as he himself had slept soundly in a world in which no sound intruded. He could not, though, bring himself to visit an actual concentration camp, the ultimate destination for six million, the destination, too, of the history he had traced, the source of the unmeaning that had to be granted meaning without denying its decreative essence. This was a pilgrimage which he believed was 'not the answer' (146), not least because they have become tourist museums through which people walk, discarding their rubbish as they go, as if this were just another sight to add to an itinerary.

He was, though, a traveller, and travel was to be important for his work, but the most important journeys were journeys of the imagination. Nor was he interested in describing violence in a realistic fashion, which he called 'the trap of action writing'. 'The only way to write about persecution and its consequences', he insisted, 'is to approach the subject obliquely ... it is always there. Even if you concentrate very hard on what is good and promising in life somehow this is always there at the edges' (146). This was to be his aesthetic.

In another sense, his aesthetic reflected that of an artist whom he admired and knew and with whom he planned a cooperative venture: Jan Peter Tripp. It seemed to him that Tripp was concerned in part with the 'depiction of a species becoming more and more monstrous in the course of a civilization's progress'.[27] His seemingly realistic portraits were of the individual as 'an abnormal creature forcibly removed from all connection with nature and society'. His still lifes 'bear witness to the former presence of a peculiarly rational species' (79). Since the objects pictured often outlive those who use them they become 'the book of our history' (79), images of the past, of what is most enigmatic about human life ... the estate we leave behind' (80).

What he admires in the painter is that he relinquishes 'our too facile knowingness'. Beyond the apparent realism of Tripp's work, which seems to inspire what Sebald calls, 'the tiresome question of realism' (80), he sees an ironic commentary on the impossibility of recuperating the real by way of a perfected surface precision, even as we are tempted to believe that its reproduction of a familiar world is so exact as to invite us to feel it no more than an extension of our own world such that we could step within the frame of his art and feel no dislocation. His occasional resort to a *trompe-l'oeil* effect provokes observers to believe that he is interested in a kind of trickery, merely the effect of the real. For Sebald, though, what is at stake is divergence and difference. What art requires, he insists – and in this he is describing his own style, as in many ways he was in identifying those other aspects of Tripp's work that appealed to him – was 'ambiguity, polyvalence, the resonance of a darkening and illumination, in short, the transcendence of that which in an incontrovertible sentence is the case' (84).

Photography, by contrast, is a kind of 'undertaker's business', an 'agent of death', since it captures 'something like the residue of a life perpetually perishing'. For the artist, 'life's closeness to death is its theme, not its addiction'. Tripp, in particular, deals with additions and subtractions; something 'is shifted to another place, emphasized, foreshortened or minimally dislocated. Shades of colour are changed, and at times those happy errors occur from which unexpectedly the system of representation opposed to reality can result. Without such adjustments, divergences and differences there would be no line of feeling or thought in the most accomplished of depictions' (84–5).

Here is what was to be Sebald's approach. It seems to be rooted in the familiar, even the personal and the realistic. Yet that real swiftly dissolves. There is no facile knowingness. He is precisely concerned with ambiguity, additions, subtractions, divergences, with shifts to another place, transcendence. What there is is precisely a line of feeling. Like Tripp, he is interested in 'the metaphysical lining of reality'. Painting, Sebald suggests, is 'a kind of dissection procedure in the face of black death and white eternity', and in the case of Tripp reflects a concern with 'passing, past and lost time', like Proust focussing on ephemeral moments 'and configurations taken out of their sequence' (89). There is an aura of remembrance 'in which melancholy crystallizes itself'. He is about the business of salvaging the past, and here, too, is Sebald describing his own approach in describing that of another. He, too, after all, takes experiences out of sequence and is fascinated by passing, past and lost time in the name of a resistance to death. Acknowledging a mood of melancholy in his work, he insisted that it was entirely respectable, not least because it is a product of that isolation required to work. Writing difficult, complex sentences, he suggested, 'takes the sort of attention which makes you appear to the outside world like someone who keeps staring into the same hole'. Even comedians, he observed, tend to be 'of that dark bent'.[28]

Tripp, then, it seems to him, is about the business of remembrance and remembrance 'in essence is nothing other than a quotation', while quotation, incorporated in either text or painting, takes us 'into time recounted and into the time of culture' (90–1). Referencing a specific painting, *La Déclaration de guerre*, one featuring abandoned shoes, Sebald comments on the 'connections' and 'interweaving' in the image. Not merely does he himself deal in precisely such connections and interweaving but the questions that the abandoned shoes provoke in him were to be the questions provoked by his own later use of shoes. What was the prehistory that explained the abandoned shoes? 'To what woman did these shoes belong? What became of her?' There was, it seemed to him, a privacy here. This provoked a desire to know without the objects in themselves rendering the information necessary to an understanding. This was to be Sebald's approach, a withholding that nonetheless provoked a need for knowledge. What is not there is to be inferred from what is. Sebald points out that in a later reworking of Tripp's painting, in which it is seen hanging from a gallery wall and watched by a woman wearing similar shoes, there is a quotation from a fifteenth-century painting by Jan van Eyck. A clog from that painting lies in the foreground of Tripp's work, seemingly brought there by a dog with the power to move through time, creating a new meaning by that fusion of moments.

There is another such dog in *Austerlitz*. Looking at plasterwork relief on a building, the protagonist sees a small blue dog carrying a branch in its mouth 'which I could tell,' he explains, 'it had brought back out of my past' (213). Walter Benjamin had called the dog the emblematic beast of melancholy while for Kafka it was a symbol of the darker aspects of melancholy and its tenacity, thus its ability to resist the passage of time. Elias Canetti, too, seized on the dog as a symbol of melancholy, what Sebald had earlier called a 'cipher of ceaseless activity'.[29] In a way, Sebald is those dogs, free to roam through time and space and bring back to our attention what he has found there. Yet at the same time, not mentioned in his analysis of the painting, the subject of abandoned shoes can never be as innocent as this meta-artistic gesture presupposes to a generation haunted by the displays in concentration camps of entire rooms of shoes, abandoned by those on the way to their deaths, believing themselves to be proceeding to cleansing showers. It is the unspoken subject which perhaps unites the image with the painting's otherwise gnomic title.

After Nature was followed, in 1990, by *Vertigo*, whose title has a double meaning in German, both the fear of falling and a fraud, a trick. It can stand as an introduction to his method and an indication of his apparent feelings about the past and memory, in a book which includes, as he himself acknowledged, crime fiction, autobiography and travelogue. There is a playfulness to Sebald as he establishes a figure called, at least by implication, 'Max Sebald' who nonetheless is constantly evading definition, his stories morphing into those of others, his journeys taking the reader through time and space, following an associational logic. Like Jean Améry, who was surely an influence, and about whom he would write admiringly, he scattered his work with invocations of other writers. Yet at the same time there is a moral imperative at work, those he encounters assuming an exemplary status, being part of a larger story to do with need and pain transmuted into experience. The prose, meanwhile, he insisted, had to be weighed as carefully as a poem.

Vertigo, which he said was about the 'problem of love', though 'not in a standard way',[30] consists of four sections, the first of which is called 'Beyle, or Love is a Madness Most Discrete'. At the beginning of this he reproduces a sketch map drawn by seventeen-year-old Marie Henri Beyle, who accompanied Napoleon over the Great St Bernard Pass in 1800. The map apparently marks his position as he comes under fire. He drew it because it 'seemed to him that his impressions had been erased by the very violence of their impact'.[31] Trauma, in other words, wipes away a detailed memory of its cause. But the sketch itself, we are told, is unreliable, depending, as it does, on a perspective that would have been denied to him by virtue of where he had been standing: 'he will not have been viewing the scene in this precise way', observes the narrator, for 'in reality, as we know, everything is always quite different' (7).

The formulation is deliberately odd. It is not simply that Beyle was part of what he observed, and hence unable to see it in a detached way, that he imagined himself located somewhere other than he had been, but that his impressions had been erased and, in that striking and un-delimited phrase, 'as we know, everything is always quite different'. From what? Reality? The way things actually were? Hardly.

What is proposed is a kind of flux, a viscosity to experience. And this is the story through which we enter *Vertigo*. What, though, of those impressions which have not been eroded but are preserved in memory? 'Beyle ... writes that even when the images supplied by memory are true to life one can place little confidence in them' (7). His conviction that he could remember every detail of his journey – with the town of Ivrea off to the right, where the valley opened out onto the plain, and, to the left, the mountains, 'the Resegone di Leco ... and at the furthest remove, the Monte Rosa' – is exposed as false when he realises that what he remembered was not the actual scene that had confronted him but an engraving entitled *Prospetto d'Ivrea*. His memories were stolen, derivative, aesthetically shaped, part of that library of images to which we are exposed. How do we see except in those ways in which we have been trained to see, or seduced into seeing? Memory and desire are intimately connected and both have the ability to create form out of need.

In a similar way, and perhaps with more than a passing relevance to those fraudulent accounts presented by Jerzy Kosinski and Binjamin Wilkomirski (to be considered later), when he attends a performance of Cimarosa's *Il matrimonio segreto*, he finds himself 'actually' within the opera, not simply moved to tears by what he observes but drawn into the drama, convinced both that he is a participant and that the principal actress is attracted to him. Ostensibly a mere observer, he is pulled into it by his own gravitational need for centrality. He wishes to eschew his marginality, become the protagonist of something more than his own life. He is constantly having to negotiate between his need and his experience. When he has an actual sexual encounter, however, the 'overpowering sensation ... blotted out the memory entirely' (11), its facticity being affirmed not by his ability to recall but by the venereal disease which becomes its best evidence. In other words, the fact of that event is indirectly confirmed, not in and through itself but by its consequences. And this would become a marker of Sebald's approach, intense events being registered by the invisible ripples sent out across time.

Memory alone is insufficient. Indeed, since memory is present tense it is liable to be shaped by immediate necessities. The past, Sebald remarked, 'is always being re-edited in the interests of what one attempts to do at a certain point of time. People make up myths about themselves and they stick very closely to those stories that they have once "written" about themselves in their own minds. I believe that any form of historiography, whether it is personal or professional, is largely based on figments, on stories, that we make up about the past.'[32] Kosinski and Wilkomirski wrote themselves into existence as victims, taking fragments from their own lives and locating them in a story to which they were then obliged to remain loyal.

The young sub-lieutenant in *Vertigo* is offered a series of lessons. When he visits the site of the Battle of Marengo he is thrown into 'a vertiginous sense of confusion' (17) by the contrast between the event as he has imagined it and as popular myth and, indeed, history has recorded it, and the bones of 16,000 men and 4,000 horses that he now sees scattered over a bleak countryside. Yet this is not to say that the meaning of that battle is circumscribed by those bones, merely that meaning depends upon something more than assembled evidence.

Beyle later becomes a writer, in *De l'Amour* describing a journey with a Mme Gherardi whom he later claimed never to have existed 'despite all the documentary evidence' (22). The narrator, indeed, casts doubt on whether the journey itself had ever taken place. The past seems increasingly problematic. Later in *Vertigo* the narrator of 'Il Ritorno in Patria' remarks that the 'more images I gathered from the past ... the more unlikely it seemed to me that the past had actually happened in this way or that, for nothing about it could be called normal: most of it was absurd, and if not absurd, appalling' (212).

Nor are the various illustrations and photographs which appear in Sebald's text themselves an unassailable source of authentication. Sketches are fragmentary to the point of meaninglessness, pictures ironic and partial. At one stage we are told that Beyle inscribes initial letters in the dust, only to have those initials reproduced as if they were a record of the occasion. He takes to making calculations in cryptographic form, one such 'impenetrable note' being helpfully reproduced. But there is another level if not of mystification then of legerdemain here, for Beyle is in fact a portrait of a real writer, Stendhal (whose name was Marie Henri Beyle), and much of the material in *Vertigo* comes from his autobiography (a book which also includes drawings), a work, though, which, instructively, Sebald insists, 'is full of false memories. Almost nothing', he points out, 'could have been as he describes it. Obviously there are terrible flaws in all these constructions and you very easily fall through trapdoors, several storeys down' (*Writers in Conversation*, II:157).

Those flaws are not, though, only a product of literature, though that plainly deals in falsifications. As he confesses, the 'text is a sort of confidence trick by the writer who is able to pull the wool over the reader's eyes and who is ... engaged in a morally dubious exercise, particularly when that exercise is executed with a great deal of virtuosity' (157). They have to do with the nature of perception and memory itself, both of which are subject to need and desire, both of which are in the service of an imperial self which pulls all experience towards a suspect centre.

This story unfolds through the first thirty pages of the book. In the second section we follow a narrator who travels from England to Vienna in 1980. In a confessedly strange frame of mind, he wanders, seemingly aimlessly, though always, he gradually realises, within certain parameters. He telephones acquaintances but there is no reply. He begins to imagine that he sees friends on the street whom he has not known for years. He even imagines he sees the poet Dante. He begins to deteriorate physically and mentally until he comes upon a Jewish community centre in a building which also houses a synagogue. He looks down at his shoes, which are in a state of dilapidation, and sees 'heaps of shoes' (37). No explanation is offered. The image is born out of his desperation and despair. The journey which was to have been to Vienna was, it seems, in fact a journey to this pile of shoes. As he later says in describing his writing, 'my papers and notes spread out around me, drawing connections between events that lay far apart but which seemed to me of the same order' (94). Piles of shoes, after all, have assumed a particular significance in a post-Holocaust world standing as emblems of absence, of the many who had no more need of shoes having no more hold on life.

What the narrator remembers most acutely from what he calls 'the village of W', where, like Sebald, he grew up, is a ceremony of remembrance as the villagers attended family graves. A memory of rememberers. 'What relationship was there', he asks himself, 'between the so-called monuments of the past and the vague longing, propagated through our bodies, to people the dust-blown expanse and tidal plains of the future?' (106). How, in other words, could past and future not merely be reconciled but be seen to stand justified in relation to each other? And what is the present except the place from which past and future can be viewed?

The third section of the book, 'Dr. K Takes the Waters at Riva', draws on Kafka's diaries and letters. It chronicles the Jewish writer's trip to a sanatorium. He is already dying of tuberculosis, though it is not his death but that of another (a suicide) which gives the story something of its tone. Kafka was curiously uninformative about his journey and Sebald offers to fill some of the vacancies in the account he left, focussing in particular on a platonic but emotionally laden relationship with a young girl, whose recommendation is precisely that it carries no commitment, that it takes place out of time. When he returns to Prague, he follows an unattractive Jewish man (who appears to sell pornographic materials) with aspirations to be thought German, another doomed relationship and one which unavoidably prompts thoughts of what lies ahead when homosexuality – if that is what is hinted at – and pretensions to German nationality would prove no defence for the Jew.

The final section sees the narrator return to his native village, 'W', a journey which necessarily stirs memories. He sees the world refracted partly through such memories and partly through art. What overwhelms him, though, is a sense of loss. His home is no longer home, though broken images come back to him. In a cemetery are buried boys who died, purposelessly, in the last year of the war. He recalls gypsies and the family album that had pictured them, a seemingly innocent memory now stained with a knowledge that came with the years, though Sebald makes no comment, relying on a quiet confederacy with the reader. The order of the world he discovers, once so reassuring, is itself now alien. And so, fragmentary memories, fictions, sherds of the past begin to form themselves into a meta-story having to do with violence, death, loss.

It is with *The Emigrants*, though, that Sebald moves the Jewish experience to the centre of his attention. We enter the first section of the book by way of an epigraph: 'And the last remnants memory destroys.' It is an enigmatic and troubling observation, as if memory itself were a destroyer, transforming, denaturing the thing recalled. Is it that memory delivers the quietus and if so what exactly are the last remnants that memory destroys? Or could it be that memory destroys what has been denied? It is an ambiguity sustained in a book in which memory invokes a past of pain, a past occluded but never finally erased, being the burden to be carried until the weight can no longer be sustained.

It is also a book with a central irony. Only the narrator and one of the central figures is a true emigrant. The others whose stories are told are all exiles, literal or symbolic, the difference, of course, being one of choice. Those he explores have all lost agency. They have been dispossessed of their lives and end up literally or effectively committing suicide.

The book is in four sections, each named for an individual. It opens with the narrator describing the arrival, in Norwich, of himself and his wife and their renting a flat in the nearby town of Hingham. There they meet Dr Henry Selwyn, who, at the age of seven, had left Grodno in Lithuania with his family. Despite his name, that family was Jewish. They were inadvertent immigrants to England having set out for the United States only to arrive in London, which they believed at first to be New York.

He mastered English, we learn, quickly, changing his name from Hersch Seweryn and becoming a doctor. He married, at first concealing his origins. Gradually the marriage had failed and eventually he retired to Hingham and his garden. He describes his life openly to the narrator except that 'The years of the second war, and the decades after, were a blinding bad time for me, about which I could not say a thing even if I wanted to.'[33] The overwhelming mood is one of loss. Selwyn's life has narrowed down until it seems circumscribed by a decaying garden in a remote part of the country. Obscurity is a last protection, but he cannot escape his own notice. A few weeks after this encounter, he shot himself. And there the story almost ends except that a memory of Henry Selwyn returns to the narrator as he travels in Switzerland.

The most intense friendship of Selwyn's life had been with an alpine guide who had disappeared decades earlier. Now the narrator reads an article in a Swiss newspaper which reports the discovery of the man's body, finally surrendered by the glacier into which he had fallen seventy-two years earlier. 'And so', the narrator observes, 'they are returning to us, the dead' (23). Here is that layered time which is equally central to Sebald's method as a writer; here is memory made immediate in the present.

Did Selwyn, born Seweryn, kill himself because he had survived the man who meant most to him, as he and his family had survived those who never left Grodno? What was the nature of this bad time during the war and afterwards that could never make its way into language and whose logic had finally worked itself out in this solitary death? Did the Jew never escape the identity he had relinquished as if a change of name could deny the past? And why is the narrator drawn to the story of a man he knew for the briefest of times, to the extent that the I of the narrator seems to blend with the I of the person he is describing, with no grammatical markers to indicate the transition, the memories of the one seeming to migrate into the other as if burdens cannot be borne alone?

The second section also concerns a suicide – that of the schoolteacher Paul Bereyter, a last name which also features in Stendhal's *Life of Henry Brulard*. The names of writers and characters surface repeatedly in Sebald's work, along with literary quotations and allusion, fact and fiction being given if not quite equal weight then at least equal substance, blurring, merging and overlapping being a clue to his sense of how we constitute our sense of the real. It was belated news of this event, indeed, which prompted the book, not the only time lag between suffering and consequence noted by Sebald in his work. The narrator, whose biography seems to overlap with that of W. G. Sebald, had left the small town of S in 1952, a town in which the buildings were punctuated by patches of wasteland, fire-scorched walls, broken buildings. Unbeknown to him, these were markers of the war but the war had never really entered his consciousness. To him, towns simply had fire-scorched walls.

Paul had been an inspiring teacher, intimidated neither by the syllabus, which he was happy to ignore, nor by the Catholic church, which constituted the ruling orthodoxy of the region. Later news of his death stands as a mystery which sends the narrator on a journey to Germany but also into the past. He tries to reconstruct his teacher's life from a series of photographs which give him the feeling that 'the dead were coming back, or as if we were on the point of joining them' (46).

Slowly, the trauma that would lead to depression and death becomes apparent, for it was while Paul Bereyter taught in S that he had been served with a notice that he would not be able to remain a teacher 'because of the new laws', plainly the Nuremberg laws. The young woman to whom he had been drawn, meanwhile, had seemingly been deported, 'On one of those special trains that left Vienna, probably at dawn, probably to Theresienstadt in the first instance' (50). Paul himself, it turned out, was only three-quarters Aryan. His father, a store owner, had been harassed and forced to pass the family business to a non-Jew. Paul became a private tutor in France but in 1939 returned to Germany, Berlin, indeed, the very centre of the madness, a city previously unknown to him, and it was there that, despite his status, he was called up by the military, serving in Poland, France, the Balkans and Russia. As a result, we are told, 'with every beat of the pulse, one lost more and more of one's qualities, became less comprehensible to oneself' (56).

Thereafter, he returned to teach in the very place from which he had been ejected. It was as though he were erasing everything that had happened, though in fact he became increasingly obsessed with the past and the violence that had infected the region even before Kristallnacht. On retirement, like Selwyn, he retreats to another city and to his garden, though making occasional, and unaccountable trips back to S. Despite fading eyesight, he devoured books, mostly by those who had committed suicide. Finally, he killed himself on a railway line, perhaps, the narrator suggests, because 'he felt they were headed for death' (61).

The story of the schoolteacher is, Sebald has affirmed, entirely authentic, including the manner of his death. The photographs in *The Emigrants* come from the man's own album. However, Sebald briefly intrudes a parallel with Wittgenstein's time as a teacher in Austria, drawing that material from Wittgenstein's biography. It was Wittgenstein and not Paul Bereyter who boiled a dead fox to prepare its skeleton for his pupils. So, not entirely authentic and that level of uncertainty is significant for a writer who despite his desire to authenticate a forgotten and suppressed past is also conscious that the real is unknowable in its totality or even in its most intimate intensities. Paul's death is both explicable and a mystery, as his inner life must be closed even to those most committed to acknowledging its integrity.

The third section, 'Ambros Adelwarth', begins with an epigraph, 'My field of corn is but a crop of tears', which, Mark R. McCullah has pointed out, comes from Chidiock Tichborne, words written shortly before he died in the Tower of London. The narrator had been seven when he last saw his Great Uncle Adelwarth on the occasion of the latter's brief return from America. His aunt, who accompanied him on the visit, had left Germany in 1927, before Hitler came to power, but there is a photograph of her, and the narrator's mother, on a school trip and we are told that the teacher 'was one of the very first National Socialists' (75).

Great Uncle Adelwarth himself had emigrated before the First World War while one of the narrator's uncles, Kasimir, had left after renewing the roof of the Augsburg synagogue, the Jews having donated the copper from the original for the war effort, a gesture of inclusion that they can never have expected to turn to dust. Sebald, though, makes no comment, any more than he does on the hint that Adelwarth was homosexual which would, of course, have rendered him vulnerable had he chosen to stay. He is, we learn, of 'the other persuasion', a phrase used for Jews and gays alike. People 'like us simply had no chance in Germany' (80), his uncle Kasimir remarks. The homeland for which the aunt cries is the homeland that would liquidate both Jews and homosexuals with perfect equity, though there is nothing in this story that suggests as much.

Kasimir tells of his own journey to America and his arrival in the Lower East Side in Manhattan and his literal elevation to working on skyscrapers. The story of Adelwarth emerges only gradually. He had worked for a rich Jewish family whose members slid, one by one, towards deep seclusion, and only later did he begin to tell of his time in America. As the narrator observes, 'I gradually became convinced that Uncle Adelwarth had an infallible memory, but that, at the same time, he scarcely allowed himself accesss to it' (100). Shortly thereafter, though, he commits himself to a sanatorium, speaking obscurely of the butterfly man (a reference to Nabokov), and slipping into a deep melancholy before submitting to electro-convulsive treatment which slowly dissolves his sense of self.

Adelwarth suffers from what is called Korsakov's syndrome, an illness which supposedly causes memories to be replaced with fantastic inventions. He is not, it seems, alone in that. In a diary entry he also observes that 'Memory often strikes me as a kind of dumbness. It makes one's head heavy and giddy, as if one were not looking back down the receding perspective of time but rather down on earth from a great height, from one of those towers whose tops are lost to view in the clouds' (145). It is tempting to see this as a description of Sebald's style, not because he is omniscient – he rejects those works in which the narrator knows everything – but because with the vertigo that comes from such a perspective there also comes an awareness of connections.

'Ambros Adelwarth', part story within story, part dream, builds a portrait out of partial memories, hearsay, rumour, fragmentary diary entries. The pseudonymous protagonist moves in a Jewish world, which cuts across national boundaries, but that Jewishness is no more than a context. What Sebald offers is a picture of a man who never quite comes into focus, who is seen for the most part in terms of others not so much living a life as turning personal reticence into a way of being, disappearing into his own unarticulated dreams.

The fourth section, which concerns a man called Max Ferber (based in part on Sebald's Manchester landlord and the painter Frank Auerbach), begins with an epigraph that anticipates something of what is to follow: 'They come when night falls to search for life.' The narrator seems once again to be 'Sebald'. Certainly it mirrors his life, as he arrives in Manchester, an immigrant city, in 1966, as a student planning research. He discovers what had once been the Jewish section, now represented by a single row of buildings, the inhabitants having moved out to the suburbs. It is here in the inner city, however, that he discovers Ferber, an artist working in a dingy space he calls his studio. He had arrived in Manchester in 1943 and lodged for a time in the same house once occupied by Wittgenstein, but the narrator learns of his past only two decades later, in 1989, and then by chance, through an article in a Sunday colour supplement, Ferber having by then been recognised and having works in the Tate Gallery. He had, the narrator learns, left Munich, where his father was an art dealer, in 1939, at the age of fifteen. His parents had contrived to get him out of the country but delayed their own departure too long. In 1941 they had been deported to Riga where they were killed. Only now does the narrator realise that he had failed to enquire into that past, never asked the questions which surely the artist might have expected him to ask. Accordingly, he returns to Manchester to seek him out, much as Sebald had begun to ask himself questions about the past.

Despite his success, Ferber continues to work in the same studio, making his drawings in charcoal which he repeatedly rubs out, a process which concludes seemingly only by virtue of exhaustion, the end product showing shadows of those earlier portraits, 'a long lineage of grey, ancestral faces, rendered unto ash but still there, as ghostly presences, on the harried paper' (162). Just as his art contains its own past, haunted, it seems, by what went before, never entirely erased, past and present co-existent, so, too, he, solitary now, retains his own litany of memories, partly obscured, memories of those similarly rendered into ash, surviving only as traces in the mind.

Ferber's method is equally Sebald's with respect to his writing. As the latter explained, two months before his death, 'My texts are like palimpsests ... They are written over and over again, until I feel that a kind of metaphysical meaning can be read through the writing.'[34] What follows, in *The Emigrants*, is the conversation that should have taken place earlier, as for three days, and far into the night, the two men discuss their separate pasts which intersect in a common German identity and present displacement. For both of them that national origin is flooded with ambiguity but for the narrator unease is in part second hand.

For Ferber, four and a half decades after his flight to England, time has no immediate meaning. It is no more than 'a disquiet of the soul'. There is, he insists, 'neither a past nor a future' (*The Emigrants*, 181), at least not for him. His present is invaded by broken images from the past which have become obsessive. He has never returned to Germany for fear that the disturbances in his mind might still have their objective correlative in the Germany of today, because for him 'Germany is a country frozen in the past, destroyed, a curiously extraterritorial place' (181). When he thinks of it he sees people still dressed as they were in the 1930s. His memories seem to stop in 1933, except for random images of marches and parades, uniforms, sharp but disconnected. He recalls marchers carrying a banner through the Munich streets emblazoned with the word *Blutfahne*, the banner of blood. It was, he now says, 'as if a new species of humanity ... was evolving before our eyes' (182). But what he recalls most clearly is a sense of exclusion which has left him with a tracery of guilt.

At home, he recalls – and as he speaks so more memories begin to come, detailed memories from the time of which he said he recalled almost nothing – no one spoke of these developments, even after his father had to surrender control of his gallery, even after his grandmother had, seemingly unaccountably, committed suicide and his uncle was dismissed from his job as schoolmaster, though he now, and for the first time, remembers a photograph which that uncle had shown them of a book-burning on the Residenzplatz in Würzburg in 1933. This was a photograph which that uncle had insisted was faked because the poor light had made photographs impossible. It was not that the event had not happened but that the photographic record was unreliable and for his uncle this had been proof of the falsity of everything.

Prompted by this memory, others now come, as sight of the reproduction of a painting a few months earlier had stirred yet another. He recalls a visit, with his uncle in 1936, to see Tiepolo's ceiling fresco in the Residenz and his return to the family home afterwards where the silence was deepening, even as the Nazis confiscated family possessions on the grounds that they had no right to the German heritage. Then had come Kristallnacht, and a six-week internment in

Dachau for his father. Finally, his parents had acted and secured a visa for their son. Fifty years later he recalls the details of the journey to the airport but not his final moments with them. 'He no longer knew what the last thing his mother or father had said to him was, or he to them, or whether he and his parents had embraced or not' (187). Everything else stood out in perfect clarity, down to the minutest detail, but not this moment which in retrospect became the most important.

A final letter from them arrived at his English school in 1941. When no more followed he was, he now confesses, at first relieved that he would no longer have to send replies. When their deaths were confirmed, he suppressed thoughts of their suffering and never revisited Germany or spoke the language again. But 'that tragedy in my youth struck such deep roots within me that it later shot up again, put forth evil flowers, and spread the poisonous canopy over me which has kept me in the shade and dark in recent years' (191). So it is that year on year he works away in a semi-abandoned building, in the gloom, drawing and erasing, in an echo of his frame of mind as memories ebb and flow. He had decided to settle in Manchester, he explains, believing that it would help to banish painful memories, only to discover that as an immigrant city it had attracted Germans and Jews for a hundred and fifty years, and that his fate was 'to serve under the chimney', a phrase meant to reflect the fact of industrialisation but whose other meaning floats, ungrounded either by Ferber or by the narrator.

As that narrator prepares to leave he is handed a manuscript which turns out to be a memoir written by Ferber's mother between 1939 and 1941. It contains nothing more than 'the odd oblique glance' at the situation in which she found herself. Instead, she wrote of her childhood. Memory, it seemed, had been a recourse, a protection, except that in reading it later Ferber himself could only see those earlier years as an ironic prelude to what would follow. So, a double memory is in play, as are overlapping time periods, that of her early life, the painful period in which the document was written, and the later period in which it was read. Now, another emigrant reads it, the narrator of *The Emigrants*, with his own necessities, his own sense of the past.

Her family, she had recorded, had lived in the village of Steinach since the seventeenth century. There are, though, the narrator notes, no Jews there now, and few who remember, or care to remember, their fate. What follows is an account, dense with life, of the daily doings of her family, though in passing she notes a young Russian boy with a butterfly net, an echo of an instance earlier in *The Emigrants* of an encounter with an adult Russian also hunting for butterflies and plainly a reference to Nabokov. The memoirs continue for twenty-five pages, reconstituting a life now lost and a way of life efficiently eliminated, rendered ironic, irrelevant.

The reading of them leads the narrator to visit the two places where the family had lived, first Steinach and then Kissingen, both places of absences. In the latter, there is no longer a synagogue, destroyed at Kristallnacht, while the Jewish cemetery is in a state of abandonment and neglect. There, however, he discovers the grave of Lily and Lazarus Lanzberg and of Fritz and Luisa Ferber. The inscription notes that Lazarus had died in Theresienstadt in 1942 while the Ferbers had been deported in 1941. Only Lily, who had committed suicide, lies in the grave. Otherwise the graves are empty.

What strikes the narrator is a more profound absence, an absence of memory: 'I felt increasingly that the mental impoverishment and lack of memory that marked the Germans, and the efficiency with which they had cleaned everything up, were beginning to affect my head and my nerves' (225). He begins to have doubts about the enterprise on which he has launched himself, the telling of the story of Max Ferber and still more the greater story which his family embodied. His scruples concern not only the subject of his narrative, to which he doubts he can do justice, but 'the whole business of writing' (230). He finds himself crossing out, discarding and obliterating his text, in a gesture which effectively mirrors Ferber's own artistic process. What has survived, it seems to him, is no more than fragments.

Later, as Ferber lies ill in hospital, the narrator recalls one of a batch of photographs he had seen in Frankfurt of the Litzmannstadt ghetto established in 1940 in Łódź, a place known as the Polish Manchester, the two places suddenly fused together, both with their

Jews, one group doomed to die and the others doomed to be haunted by the memory of their death. Another photograph had featured the city's Mayor and a table laden with food. It is not the contrast, though, that disturbs him. It is another picture of three women sitting at a loom. It is disturbing because they seem to look directly at him with a gaze he cannot meet for long, as if they were appealing across the decades, unaware of their ultimate fate and yet looking to him to deny the ostensible truth of the photograph as they work, seemingly normally, displaying their industry, their essential role in the wartime economy in what was a deliberately staged piece of propaganda. This is the lie he is obliged to refute. For the truth is that they exist only in a photograph which denies rather than reveals the truth of their lives, lost now, as they are, to all but the artist with his charcoal, rubbing out and redrawing, or the writer, overwhelmingly conscious of his inadequacy, writing, erasing, re-inscribing, going about the impossible task of breathing life into the dead and doing so in the very language which Max Ferber refused as if a language could itself be a facilitator and carrier of infection. This, after all, is the language which once described Jews as shit, lice, vermin, fit only for death with an insecticide as if the use of that chemical were a proof of what the Nazis asserted, as if language could validate inhumanity. And if that was so, could language, the same language, be deployed to reinstate that humanity? That was the scale of the task that W. G. Sebald saw as confronting him.

Asked why he was drawn to the Jewish experience, he explained that it was because 'the persecution and the attempted eradication of the Jewish people by my compatriots loomed largest among the historical experiences of my life. When you first learn about these things, at the age of seventeen or eighteen, you stare at them with incomprehension. So you carry on as if nothing had happened. And then there is a gradual process of becoming aware of it, which in my case went into a quite different mode as soon as I arrived in Manchester.'[35]

His compatriots had been nothing if not thorough, their thoroughness being one of the particular gifts they had brought to genocide. Suddenly, however, it was not a question of anonymous victims but real people. There was, perhaps, no artist, struggling towards a meaningless fame, working in his darkened studio, but there was his landlord whose parents had been deported to near Riga. There were Jews in nearby old people's homes whose books would turn up in the local bookstores on their death (and which Sebald would buy), often books of nineteenth-century German literature, the culture they had been told they contaminated, the tradition to which they had been told they had no claim.

Those who in Germany, in the 1950s and 1960s, had tried to write literary texts about the Fascist period seemed to Sebald to have failed. Their work he regarded as tactless and reflecting a dubious moral position with respect to representing Jewish lives. So, he explained, 'I felt that it was necessary to at least attempt to write about these lives in a different sort of way' (161).

In *The Rings of Saturn* (Saturn, the planet of melancholy) the Holocaust is hardly mentioned. Yet the book is haunted with death and dissolution, and the briefest of mentions of Bergen-Belsen, a matter of no more than half a dozen words, prompts a two-page photograph of bodies scattered among the trees of that camp in April 1945. Neither here nor elsewhere in his books, however, are his photographs captioned. An account of the assassin Gavrilo Princip, killer of the Archduke Franz Ferdinand, recalls his being imprisoned in the Theresienstadt casements, a reference which neither needs nor receives comment in a book which works in part through echoes, repetitions, coincidences, overlapping histories, assonances, imminent connections. In *Austerlitz* references to 'Theresienstadt Wasser' and 'Auschwitz Springs' play a similar role. These are apparently no more than healing waters, the latter incongruously curing obesity. The ironies are left hanging as later events reach back to corrode an earlier innocence. It is not only the future that was to be forced to bear the burden of genocide, but the past. Language itself must bear a taint which spreads out in all directions. The Holocaust, it seems, has the power to deform time.

The seventy-fifth anniversary of Princip's death, the narrator notes, is celebrated in 1993, on the verge of an ethnic slaughter which is also not mentioned, though its invocation recalls another act of ethnic cleansing fifty years earlier in which the Germans and Croats had collaborated to slaughter the Serbs, the deportation order for whom was signed by an Austrian officer called Kurt Waldheim (though Sebald withholds his name) who far from being punished for the crime was rewarded by being made Secretary General to the United Nations, in which capacity he recorded a message to be taken into outer space by Voyager II. What message about mankind, coming from such a person, we are implicitly asked, could be carried to alien beings other than of man's inhumanity to man?

A country house in Suffolk, meanwhile, prompts memories of the aircraft which at twilight once took off from the nearby airfield on their way to Hamburg, Munich and Schweinfurt. A gardener remembers not only the planes but his own thoughts of the destruction the bombs would have caused. He had even learned the names of those German cities as, after the war, he had learned German as part of the occupation forces in the hope that he could read accounts of what he had imagined, only to discover that there were no such accounts and that his memory of imagined events perhaps offers a truth not available from other sources. Sebald himself would be moved to write his own response to the air war precisely in response to this silence which stood as a mystery and a reproach.

At the end of the book an account of silk making gains a new significance when we learn that the Nazis had a plant to produce it not far, as it happens, from Bergen-Belsen where the naked figures of the dead and dying had been captured in the earlier photograph, a thread connecting experiences otherwise separated by time and space quite as if history were all of a piece.

And so the text moves back and forth like the shuttle in a loom, a pattern slowly emerging from what seems no more than a scatter of stories. As space travellers will supposedly be able to move from one space time to another by way of wormholes, so Sebald moves back and forth registering the temporal and spatial anomalies generated by this signal event so that incidents in different times and places seem to co-exist, creating interference patterns.

Though the spine of the book is constituted by the author's walk through the Suffolk countryside, this serves as a springboard for historical, philosophical, biographical disquisitions. That it begins with reflections on Sir Thomas Browne, author of *Urn Burial*, itself in part a contemplation of death, sets the tone for what follows, a text threaded through with massacres, suicides, ruins, fallen dynasties, graves, decay, disease, destructive gales. Friends die mysteriously. The author himself falls ill, is injured. Here, as elsewhere in his work, his sentences flow, sometimes at considerable length, as did those of Sir Thomas Browne whose steady progress he describes as resembling 'processions or a funeral cortège in their sheer ceremonial lavishness' (19).

This is the Sir Thomas Browne who may have attended an autopsy pictured by Rembrandt, a painting whose partial fraudulence (both hands are right hands, and plainly copied from a medical textbook) is underlined by Sebald in what amounts to a warning about the status of his own documentary gestures. In the following section, the narrator, in a dream-like state, believes himself in a balloon rising above mountains. As Mark McCullah points out, part of this description is taken directly from a story by Adalbert Stifter – a fiction within a dream within a narrative. The world, for all the urgencies of its demands, does not offer up its meanings directly, at least not in Sebald's work. Meaning comes in images, memories, memories of memories, negotiations between fact and fiction.

At the heart of *The Rings of Saturn*, as of his other books, is a sense of loss. 'That is what life is about to a very large extent', Sebald has insisted,

> when you grow up promises are held up in front of you ... but the more you are lured along this road, the more is taken away from you, the less the scope becomes. Day by day you leave things behind, ultimately your health, and so loss is perhaps the most common experience that we have. I think somehow this has to be accounted for and as there are few other places where it is accounted for it has to be done by writing ... it is just a matter of fact that somehow this whole process is one in which you get done out of what you thought was your entitlement. (163)

For some, that entitlement is life itself.

The book is in part a contemplation of history but the history that it contemplates is at times suspect, a product in part of a need for coherence, for completed stories. The narrator visits the Waterloo Panorama, a mural a hundred and ten yards by twelve painted in 1912 on the inner wall of a circus-like structure. This was history as seen by Louis Dumontin, the artist, history as pictorial representation. Neat phalanxes of armies charge gallantly forwards amidst the smoke of battle. What the narrator says of this, however, could be said equally of the problems confronting not only the historian but also anyone trying to understand the past and in this case, though largely unmentioned, the Holocaust. 'It requires', he confesses, 'a falsification of perspective. We, the survivors, see everything from above, see everything at once, and still we do not know what it was.' Now there is silence where once there was the sound of pain. 'Are we', he asks, 'standing on a mountain of death? Is that our ultimate vantage point?' (125). Only in his imagination, he confesses, can he see the scene and even then he places at its centre not an actual soldier but Fabrizio, Stendhal's hero. The imagination has already been colonised.

Among those he encounters on his journey through rural East Anglia is the translator Michael Hamburger. His family had fled the Nazis, abandoning to her fate the grandmother who had refused to leave. He had been nine when he left and the few memories he has are 'barely enough for an obituary of a lost boyhood' (177), memories seeming, as they do at times, more like dreams and hallucinations. Berlin is merely a 'grey smudge ... a slate pencil drawing', like the painting of Max Ferber or the writings of Max Sebald, 'blurred and half wiped away' (177–8). 'Sebald' and Hamburger meet in a gothic landscape in which the birds have ceased to sing and everything 'is on the point of decline. Only the weeds flourish' (181). Even the sheets of paper on which he endeavours 'to put together a few words and sentences seem covered with mildew' (181). Writing, indeed, begins to seem divorced from the real as the mind constructs its own coherences out of a need to resist the very unspooling of order that had prompted the author to put pen to paper.

Austerlitz, the book Sebald published three months before his death, and which the following year, somewhat paradoxically, went on to win the *Independent*'s Foreign Fiction Prize, was described by him as a sequel to *The Emigrants*. It was inspired by his watching a Channel 4 documentary, *Into the Arms of Strangers: Stories of the Kindertransport* (2000), which featured Susie Bechhofer, who in middle age remembered having been brought to Wales on the *Kindertransport*. *Kindertransport* was the name given to trainloads of Jewish children shipped originally from Austria and Germany and subsequently from Czechoslovakia to Britain, with the agreement of the British and German governments. In the end, 10,000 were saved. Sebald, not untypically, was struck by the fact that she shared a birthday with him. Such echoes had always mattered to him, as if there were invisible lines of force, something more than the merely fortuitous in such connections reinforcing, as they did, both his convictions about connectedness and his methods as a writer. He was, however, hesitant to model his central character too closely on Bechhofer, and the abuse she had suffered in Wales, because he did not think he had the right to intrude. He approached her, therefore, at an angle, not merely transposing her experiences.

He felt the same way with respect to the Holocaust, his explanation of his strategy for approaching it further elucidating his characteristic style. 'I don't think you can focus on the horror of the Holocaust. It's like the head of the Medusa: you carry it with you in a sack, but if you looked at it you'd be petrified. I was trying to write the lives of some people who'd survived – the lucky ones. If they were so fraught, you can extrapolate. But I didn't see it; I only know things indirectly.'[36] That indirection was not merely a matter of discretion. It was necessitated by the nature of the experience: 'you could not write directly about the horror of persecution in its ultimate forms, because no one could bear to look at these things without losing their sanity. So you would have to approach it from an angle and by intimating to the reader that these subjects are constant company; their presence shades every inflection of every sentence one writes. If one can make that credible, then one can begin to defend writing about these subjects at all.'[37]

His doubts were reflected in a later documentary which celebrated Nicholas Winton, the British man who organised the trains that set off from Prague station at midnight and deposited over five thousand children at Liverpool Street Station, the London terminus, too, as it happens, of those travelling from Sebald's home city of Norwich. 'How can you find a way of approaching something that repels', the survivor asked, 'articulate something that resists articulation?' And that was the central problem for Sebald, as for so many others.

The book is concerned with Jacques Austerlitz, who, in 1939, had been sent from Prague to Britain, where he was taken in by a dour Welsh couple, fundamentalist Calvinists, for reasons the young boy could never understand. His own mother, of whom he knew nothing, was already on her path to extinction as the Germans moved in and the Jewish laws slowly tightened around her. His father, again unknown to him, had travelled to Paris and an undocumented oblivion. The story, Sebald has said, was based on 'two and a half real-life stories', and involved 'a process of collation'.[38] One of those stories was that of an architectural historian whose photograph appears on the front cover.

The adoptive father, in *Austerlitz*, ended up in a mental asylum while the mother died early. They hugged the secret of the past to them perhaps, as they thought, for the young boy's own good, perhaps because they saw themselves as rescuing him for their own unforgiving religion, this boy whose Jewish faith would have made him doubly alien.

For the first two hundred pages there are few markers of the underlying story Sebald is so determined to tell, not least because the young boy has no idea of his own past. What he was concerned to do, as he explained to the *Guardian*'s Maya Jaggi, was to explore the 'effects political persecution produces in people 50 years down the line, and the complicated workings of remembering and forgetting that go with that'.[39] What interested him, he explained, 'was the fact of this young boy's hidden identity'. He was raised, as was Sebald in his own remote village, in a world of silence, literal, in so far as his foster parents disliked noise, but also with respect to his past, which appears to him as no more than a dream. 'There you have a situation', Sebald further explained, 'of someone who has been deprived, by active intervention or default, of any knowledge of his own origins and who later resolves not to investigate his own case.'[40] He had even been raised under another name than his own: Dafydd Elias. Only late in life does he feel able to revisit that lost past.

In that sense, it is a book of silences. His real parents have faded into the silence of the grave. His adoptive parents, who live an inward life, have decided that they will remain silent with respect to his past while he himself has, until the end, decided against hearing the voices which in some moods he is desperate to recover. Beyond these silences, however, is that greater one, of those who suffered and cannot speak, of those who watched their suffering and said and did nothing, of history which, through the years of his adolescence, had little or nothing to say to him or the world.

We first meet Jacques Austerlitz, however, not as a young boy living in a loveless house, but as an adult who nonetheless at first keeps the details of his life to himself. He is interested, it seems, in architecture, and therefore in the past, and accordingly he and the narrator, who has a similar interest, fall into a series of conversations which gradually reveal a personal dimension to that interest. The book opens with the narrator's visit to Belgium during which he encounters the adult Austerlitz (whose name, not inappropriately, occurs as a minor character in Kafka's diaries). It is the first of a series of seemingly coincidental encounters. So unlikely are the places they meet that there appears to be some hidden principle at work, though what it might be is by no means clear.

Though the conversations, initially conducted in French, seem innocent enough, there are already hints of something more ominous. In relation to a visit to Breendonk, a fort completed before the outbreak of the First World War, we are told that in 1940 the Germans had made it into a reception and penal camp presided over by SS guards. An ominous pit, with an iron hook hanging from a cord in the ceiling, reminds the narrator of a butcher's shop in his home town and of the terror he used to feel, a terror, however, which he is incapable of communicating. 'No one can explain exactly what happens within us when the doors behind which our childhood terrors lurk are flung open', the narrator observes. And not only childhood terrors, it seems, for he now recalls Jean Améry's description of the torture to which he was subjected in that place, precisely the same torture which Gaston Novelli suffered and which was described by Claude Simon, descending, we are told, 'once more into the storehouse of his memories',[41] though in the case of Novelli it is not his own memory we are offered. Novelli was subsequently taken to Dachau. The details of the torture are supplied. Words, however, necessarily fall short of the experience, which we approach by indirection. Novelli, surviving, had fled his own country and lived in the jungle with a native tribe whose language he learned. When he returned, he painted pictures, but these consisted of no more than endless repetitions of the letter A, looking at times like a cipher or 'rising and falling in waves like a long-drawn-out scream' (36).

The passage, not yet rooted in the personal history of the stranger the narrator had encountered, foreshadows the story that is to follow but also stands as a warning of the near-impossibility of recovering certain truths and as a justification for the oblique nature of the narrative whose serpentine shape nonetheless twists around a central concern. The ominous Breendonk, meanwhile, whose bleakness and surviving paraphernalia of torture brings back a distant past, underscores another aspect of Sebald's approach in so far as he has explained that 'Places seem to have some kind of memory, in that they activate memory in those who look at them.'[42] Memory, then, may be contained within the self but it is also in a curious way invested in places. Plainly those who returned to Auschwitz in 2005, for a commemoration of the liberation of the camp sixty years earlier, scarcely needed the literal architecture of mass slaughter to remind them, but to Sebald all places have the power to prompt recollections, gather to themselves the ghosts of a past seemingly lost or set aside; and, as he remarked, ghosts and writers meet in their concern for the past.[43]

Austerlitz's identity seems insecure in more ways than one. He is one person until the age of fifteen, when his original name is revealed to him by a schoolteacher, and another after that. He seems to change when he moves from French to English (as Nabokov suspected he did) while another language (Czech) and self are compacted within, waiting only for some sudden prompt to bring them back. He had, we later learn, been sent on the *Kindertransport* at the age of four and a half and virtually everything before this moment had slipped away from him. What had survived was a fascination with trains and a sense that they were associated with happiness and misfortune. In a television documentary one of the survivors of the *Kindertransport*, who obsessively drew trains, remarked that they were symbolic for her because any picture of a concentration camp will feature a single track line leading to death, just as it was a railway which led her to life. In *The Drowned and the Saved* Primo Levi observes that, 'at the beginning of the memory sequence, stands the train ... There is not a diary or story, among our many such accounts, in which the train does not appear.'[44] In his autobiography, *All Rivers Run to the Sea*, Elie Wiesel remarks that 'Ever since my book *Night* I have pursued those nocturnal trains that crossed the devastated continent. Their shadow haunts my writing. They symbolize solitude, distress, and the relentless march of Jewish multitudes toward agony and death. I freeze every time I hear a train whistle.'[45]

Austerlitz prefers not to send letters to Germany. When he discovers his real name he is inhibited from beginning the journey on which he will later set out. All that remains are fragments of memory. Yet there are constant reminders of concealed truths. For if he resists travelling to that moment in his own past which may have a clue to the mystery of his being, his restless intellectual fascinations offer him exemplary truths. Thus, he discovers that Broad Street station, in London (situated alongside Liverpool Street Station), built in 1865, when excavated in 1984 had revealed four hundred skeletons underneath a taxi rank. Partly because of his interest in archaeology, he explains, and partly 'for other reasons which I could not explain even to myself' (*Austerlitz*, 184), he takes a series of photographs of the remains of the dead. It feels to him, he confesses, as if the dead are returning from exile.

This is in part how the book works. Austerlitz may have consciously set his face against disinterring his own past but the need to do so emerges with every move he makes. The past draws him, he believes, because it is a matter of intellectual concern while it becomes ever more apparent that there is a current running in his life, drawing him back, dissolving the boundary between then and now, the dead and the living. In an essay on Nabokov he toyed with the idea that there might be a position from which the landscape of time could be seen in a synoptic view, what had slipped away from view now being observable alongside the present. But the past is never to be retrieved in generalities. It is always details that open the time portal.

Finding himself in an abandoned waiting room at Liverpool Street Station (stations again) Austerlitz remembers fog spilling into a Norfolk church, slowly rising up his body as though it would cover him. This, he confesses, is something to which he has accustomed himself, 'memories behind and within which many things further back in the past seemed to lie', annihilating time and bringing back 'all the suppressed and extinguished fears and wishes I had ever entertained' (192–3). At the same time he resists these memories. As far as he is concerned, the world ended in the nineteenth century. He avoided knowledge of the German conquest of Europe, did not read newspapers or listen to the radio. His life has been a triumph of denial, though the cost of that denial becomes ever greater prompting a literal illness, this being the price to be paid for denial. Then, appropriately enough in an antiquarian booksellers, he inadvertently hears a radio programme about the *Kindertransport* in which one of the women taking part recalls having travelled first by rail and then a ship called the *Prague*. The name of this ship, in the context of the programme, unlocks a memory and he realises, for the first time, that this had been his own experience, that his interest in the distant past had been serving only to distract him from a more recent past.

It is page 200 of a 415-page book. The circumlocutions and evasions of the central character have been replicated in the reader, who, like that character, has previously been offered only oblique clues, hints, brief memory flashes. Now Austerlitz decides to retrace what he suspects had been his own steps, those years before, to Prague. The space which he had thought he was content to fill with a restless scholarship, seemingly random journeys, must now be filled; the silence in which he had conspired has finally to be broken.

Speaking not of the children of the *Kindertransport* but of those other children who were given into hiding by their parents to wait out the war in families that embraced another religion and who were no more than strangers, Elie Wiesel asks,

> What took place in their still fragile but already wounded subconscious? A rejection? A betrayal, perhaps? How long did it take before they grasped the full meaning of what their parents had to do on their behalf? How long has it taken to overcome the anger some of them might have felt toward their parents as they held them responsible for their separation? When exactly did they understand the fathomless strength their parents needed to give up their children to a stranger in order to spare them their own fatal destiny? On the brink of death, their parents pulled themselves away from their children so as to shield them from death.[46]

The young Austerlitz was not concealed in the presence of danger but he was concealed nonetheless, from himself as much as others. He did find himself in an alien world, though without understanding just how alien it was until he discovered his identity at which point the feelings described by Wiesel flooded in.

Accordingly, he sets off for Prague and, after a visit to the archive, discovers not only his parents' former address but their next-door neighbour, Vera, who decades before had once acted as his nursery maid. There is something about him which leads her to identify him immediately and in the days that follow he learns more of his past and retrieves not only his previously suppressed memories (which, Vera suggests, are like looking through a glass mountain) but also a language of which he had imagined himself ignorant.

His mother, he learns, had been an opera singer, his father a union organiser. They had not been married. He had left for Paris while she had stayed on too late, slowly being dragged down by restrictions which at first limited her movements and then saw her lose everything she owned including, finally, her life. As he rediscovers himself, so he loses his parents a second time as if he himself had set a machine in progress.

Each place he visits liberates more memories seemingly locked up in those places for him to release, like souls in torment awaiting the benediction of attention. And, indeed, for Austerlitz those brought back into existence by memory stare out at the world which for them lacks substance 'so that it seems to me that we who are still alive are unreal in the eyes of the dead' (261). Austerlitz himself feels unreal, unclear as to who he is. 'At some time in the past', he confesses, 'I must have made a mistake, and now I am living the wrong life' (298), the mistake being that which led to the death of his parents and the suspension of his own life. He has one foot in a world in which he has unknowingly played a role, the other in a world only just beginning to come into focus.

His search now takes him, in his mother's footsteps, to Terezín (Theresienstadt), a limbo en route to annihilation where people had been held, living out a parody of normal life. It is here that he visits a ghetto museum, only to discover that for all the information gathered there he is no closer to the knowledge he seeks: 'I understood it all now, yet I did not understand it, for every detail that was revealed to me ... far exceeded my comprehension' (279). It is not merely that, as we learn later of the Theresienstadt ghetto, the Nazis fabricated a version of that experience for the sake of a visiting Red Cross team, and recorded that fabrication on film, in a corrupt documentary, but that even true documents remain remote from experience. Memory itself begins to seem suspect. As Vera asks, 'how do we remember, and what is it we find in the end?' (287), the last a question posed by the book itself.

By degrees, the burden of what he learns works to edge Austerlitz towards breakdown. He suffers a three-week 'mental absence' (323). The identity for which he had been searching, tied up as it was with the fate of parents who he has no sooner rediscovered than he has to relinquish them to time, comes under stress again. The past is not available for exorcism. It is immanent.

In Paris, where his father's trail had gone cold, he contemplates the wasteland between the new Bibliothèque Nationale, with its accumulation of history and stories, including Balzac's account of a man who, in the course of a battle at Eylau, had been thrown into a mass grave, and the Gare d'Austerlitz. This, decades earlier, had been the site of a huge warehouse complex in which had been gathered the goods stolen from Jews who had been killed in the gas chamber. Like the trains that had taken those Jews on their last journey, some of which will have left from the marshalling yards alongside the warehouse, this had been a triumph of fastidious logistical organisation, requiring the skills and contributions of tens of thousands. And where had all those possessions gone, possessions picked over by privileged members of the SS and the Wehrmacht?

About that there is silence, as there is about the contribution made to the Holocaust by so many, as there is in the library and as there is, by chance, on the railways because a strike has brought to a halt all rolling stock. Had they been brought to a halt during the Holocaust, perhaps his parents would have survived. But it was the railway that had gifted him life, as his parents would lose theirs. And here he stands, a man called Austerlitz at a place called Austerlitz, a confluence of stories and fates. He recalls having visited the station as a student, being fascinated by it, but also curiously threatened. He remembers 'scaffolding reminiscent of a gallows with all kinds of rusty iron hooks'. These had been no more than mechanisms for storing bicycles but he had felt himself on 'the scene of some un-expiated crime' (407), and now such vague feelings have seemingly been earthed in a literal history.

Elie Wiesel's *Night* has a foreword by François Mauriac. He recalls a visit by a young Israeli (Wiesel) which led him to remember a particular event in the Occupation. 'I confided to my young visitor that nothing I had seen during those sombre years had left so deep a mark upon me as those trainloads of Jewish children standing at Austerlitz station ... I believe that on that day I touched for the first time upon the mystery of iniquity whose revelation was to mark the end of one era and the beginning of another.'[47] It was the end, he believed, of Enlightenment values. He was wrong in thinking that Wiesel had been on one of those trains. He travelled from another country to his appointment with potential oblivion. But Austerlitz had such a resonance for Mauriac that it came to stand for those others, as it did for Sebald.

Sebald's book ends as the protagonist contemplates a work by the South African writer Dan Jacobson in which he recalled a field of oats in Lithuania under which were buried 30,000 people, brought there by train and killed by the Germans over the course of three years. He, too, it seemed, saw the evidence of inhumanity buried beneath history.

Walter Benjamin's angel of history, invoked by Sebald in another book, has his face turned to the past, a past which is not a narrative but an instantaneous accumulation of debris. Even as he is drawn towards the future by the storm of progress, to which he resolutely turns his back, he sees that debris building ever higher. It is that angel which presides over Sebald's work. Compacted within a present already leaning into the future, and heavily compromised, is an un-inspected past whose truth he watches with a steady gaze. Yet there is a sense in which perhaps he doubts the integrity of his own method.

In his book *On the Natural History of Destruction* he upbraids an author for his aesthetic interventions in an account of the destruction by bombing of a German city, while praising another, Hubert Fichte, whose novel, *Detlev's Imitations*, incorporates within it a genuine account of the raid on Hamburg that dispassionately describes the resultant horrors. This documentary account, it seems to him, carries real authority, the elaboration of brute facts 'before which all fiction pales'.[48] The strength of Fichte's novel, set in 1968 on the anniversary of the bombing, seems to him to offer, through its 'discontinuous notes[,] ... a very plausible literary approach, probably because they are not abstract and imaginary in character, but concrete and documentary' (59). In this he seems to suggest that certain material is incommensurate with traditional aesthetics.

It is tempting to feel that Sebald's praise derives in part from the fact that he recognises a kindred spirit. The medical report which it incorporates opens up 'a view into the abyss'. In like manner he responds positively to Alexander Kluge's account of a raid on Halberstadt, written twenty years after the event, and which, like Sebald's work, incorporates photographs. It is, he says, an archaeological excavation 'of the slag heaps of our collective existence' (61). Sebald's appreciation for and justification of Kluge's account takes a revealing if convoluted form: 'the retrospective learning process ... is the only way of deflecting human wishful thinking towards the anticipation of a future that would not already be pre-empted by the anxieties arising from the suppression of experience' (64). Implied here is a question about the legitimacy and possibility of hope but here, too, is a statement of aesthetic values. In certain respects Sebald's description of Kluge could apply to himself. Both have a respect for history, for facts seen in the context of a contemplation of human possibility. For both, photographs simultaneously offer information and disinformation – pictures of a ruined city providing evidence of ruin, of one kind of absence, while lacking a human component, sound, smell, context.

For postwar Germans, Sebald implies, such a picture would be embraced only as a 'before' for which the 'after' was the economic miracle that would justify wiping out the past with its burden of memory, suffering and guilt, whereas for him the past is a critical component of personal and public reality if also something more than a justification for the extinction of hope.

What he accused his fellow countrymen of was a failure to apply 'a steadfast gaze' (51). The 'construction of aesthetic or pseudo-aesthetic effects from the ruins of an annihilated world', he suggests, 'is a process depriving literature of its right to exist' (53). What, then, to make of his own books which undoubtedly operate according to their own aesthetic rules? In part, his remarks come in the context of two writers whose aesthetic values seem to him to be suspect – hence his reference to 'pseudo-aesthetic effects' – but his critique goes further. It would seem to imply a humility in the face of fact, a primacy to raw evidence. But he, himself, is plainly not content with pure fact, despite the emphasis he gives to buried histories. How, then, to defend himself against his own accusations? In part it is because he sets himself to disinter a disregarded past, to fill in lacunae, yet he readily accepts that

> anything one does in the form of writing, and especially prose
> fiction, is not an innocent enterprise. It is a morally question-
> able enterprise because one is, of course, in the business –
> however honest one's attempts to be a writer – of arranging
> things in such a way that the role of the narrator is not an
> entirely despicable one. There is no way around this ... Writing
> is by definition a morally dubious occupation, I think, because
> one appropriates and manipulates the lives of others for certain
> ends. When it is a question of the lives of those who have
> survived persecution the process of appropriation can be very
> invasive ... A writer's attitude is utilitarian. I think Graham
> Greene said somewhere that most writers have a splinter of ice
> in their heart. This seems to me a very perceptive remark
> because writers have to look at things in a certain way. There is
> a horrible moment when you discover, almost with a sense of
> glee, something that, although itself horrid, will fit in exactly
> with your scheme of things. (153)

The truth is that he accuses himself. He is, indeed, committed
to a suspect enterprise but it is the nature of the enterprise that it
should be suspect. There is, he insists, an integrity to the text. This,
though, does not neutralise the accusation of bad faith. Such an
accusation is the price to be paid for the imaginative appropriation of
experience. What is required is a certain level of moral discretion.

Despite what he says, there are descriptions of violence in his
work, even if these are distanced through character and narrative voice.
To stare into the experience of the Jews and not acknowledge this, after
all, would be a gross act of distortion. What he works to avoid is a
pornography of violence. He operates by simple description, by
indirection, implication, inference. He listens for the echoes of the
blow, observes those whose sensibility and language carry the markers
of distress. As the origin of a radio signal can be located by triangulation,
so he carries us back to a particular time and place through intersecting
memories, histories which meet at a particular site, figures whose
seemingly random journeys bring them to moments of consonance.

There is, of course, a documentary element in his books – the photographs which appear in all of them, as if these were family albums in which the past could be identified. As he has explained, as a child he used to spend much of his time in the darkroom and had always collected photographs, not least because 'there's a great deal of memory in them'.[49] That memory, however, is itself complex. To a visiting reporter in 2001, he pointed out an old family photograph of a young boy on his office wall and explained that he had returned from the First World War mentally disturbed after electric shock therapy. The photograph, however, had been taken before he had gone to that war. What Sebald found disturbing was the impossibility of knowing what lies ahead. The memory induced by this photograph was prompted not simply by what was there but by what was not. The boy's future became the unavoidable lens through which it became necessary to read it. To another eye, however, it would be no more than a picture of youth, an innocence preserved against assault.

Photographs have, he explained, 'an uncanny ability' to suggest that 'there is another world where the departed are'. They are documents of absence and in some way 'curiously metaphysical ... They represent a sense of otherness.' The figures in photographs 'stare out at you as if they were asking for a chance to say something',[50] so that he becomes a kind of ghost writer. The pictures are, he has said, part of the way in which he declared his position. They are simultaneously in time and out of it, offering reproach and consolation.

His photographs are ambiguous and as complicit in the author's aesthetic as the words which appear between them. As he has said,

> I think they have several functions. The main device is certainly one in which, I think, every writer of fiction has to have an interest: the narrator wants to tell the reader that he has been there and that he has seen all this with his own eyes and what better proof than a photograph ... As it happens, the vast majority of pictures in my books are in fact authentic, that is, they come out of the albums or boxes of people like the ones whom I am trying to describe, whose life I am trying to relate.

Sometimes these pictures contain very dense information
which it would take a long time to get across in writing ...[51]

He recalled in particular the photograph in *The Emigrants* of a
large Jewish family, resident in Munich, dressed in traditional
Bavarian costumes, with lederhosen and Tyrolean hats. It seemed to
him that this conveyed, in an almost farcical way, the extent of that
family's assimilation and acculturation. Beyond that, of course, was
the knowledge that this acculturation will have served as no
protection and hence was never what they believed it to be. Language
could never have expressed this cascade of meanings, a past frozen at a
moment of pleasure that was now flooded with irony and pain. If a
photograph is a memory it is subject to transformation by a shifting
context. A photograph, he explained,

> can be something like a very condensed account or a shorthand
> cipher. It can also put a different angle on things and it can have
> [an] ironic quality ... A very small proportion of the pictures are
> retouched. I change things in them, brush things in or cut things
> out or make them more gloomy or lighter, depending on what I
> need to do. I write up to these pictures and I write out of them
> also, so they are really a part of the text and not illustrations ...
> They must not stand out; they must be of the same leaden grain
> as the rest. (154)

In seeking to explain something of his style, and, interestingly,
identifying himself as a novelist in doing so, he acknowledged the
importance of the vogue for documentary writing in Germany in
the 1970s, which perhaps explains something of his fascination with
the theatrical work of Peter Weiss. It was a movement which he
confesses 'opened my eyes'. It was, he thought, an 'important literary
invention'. Yet it seemed to him no more than a starting point
because it was 'artless'. For himself, he was 'trying to write something
saturated with material but carefully wrought, where the art
manifests itself in a discreet, not too pompous fashion'. The major
events, he explained, were true while the details were liable to be

invented. 'Every novelist', he insisted, 'combines fact and fiction ... In my case there's more reality. But I don't think it's radically different; you work with the same tools.'[52]

Sometimes, he confessed, 'I make up one out of two or three stories but, in essence, what I write is how it happened ... the most shocking, the most hair-raising, the most coincidentally absurd moments are precisely how things did happen. The fictional changes are on the margin.'[53] Seen from the outside, it seemed to him, 'some stories have more truth than others, but the truth value of the story does not depend on its actual truth content. The truth value depends on how it is framed and phrased. If a story is aesthetically right, then it is probably also morally right. You cannot translate one to one from reality. If you try to do that, in order to get at a truth value through writing, you have to falsify and lie. And that is one of the moral quandaries of the whole business.'[54]

Of course, it is not true that documentary theatre is 'artless'. Its claim to authenticity is necessarily limited by its shaping of information, its selection of material. A documentary play is a construction. There is, almost invariably, a polemical intent. The necessary self-denying ordinance has to do with the exclusion of the manifestly fictive. For Sebald, what matters is that what he writes should 'in essence' be true but that truth is itself a product of indirection, implication, peripheral vision. Uncertainty about the nature of the real felt by the people in his books is designedly replicated in readers, never entirely certain about the parameters of the terrain they enter. At the heart of the Holocaust experience was a radical disbelief. Could these things be happening, could these words be being spoken? In later years that disbelief remained. Could these things have occurred in this way? How was it possible that this could have happened? Sebald saw himself as a messenger whose job it was to bring the news, news which on occasion seems literally unbelievable. The very calmness of the prose, its sometimes lyrical arabesques, meanwhile, belie the nature of what is described or intuited, but that tension is a part of his strategy.

In his own life, he confessed, it was what had seemed the secret of the past which drew him, the vacancy which demanded peopling.

The beauties of nature which had indeed surrounded him appeared no more than a lie concealing the greater truth of a destruction whose clues were there had he, even as a young boy, chosen to see them. People had, after all, been torn from their families across Europe, even as German accounts of those years concentrated on family celebrations.

A picture on his parents' bedroom wall had, he discovered, been purchased in 1936 when his father had been in a cavalry regiment in which earlier Count von Stauffenberg, Hitler's would-be assassin, had served. Such, he insisted, was the 'dark backward and abysm of time' in which everything 'lies all jumbled up'.[55] Here is the basis of his books. Separate events appeared to have hidden connections, a thought which he confessed instilled a sense of vertigo. Thus he notes, for example, that among those who died in a bombing raid on his own town of Sonthofen (the S of his books) was a nun by the name of Sebalda. In like manner, in writing of the crash of a Dornier aircraft not far from what would be his own home near Norwich, he notes that one of those who died – Lieutenant Bollert (and it is significant that he offers his name) – shared his birthday and was the same age as his father. His work is full of such coincidences, connective tissue linking people, places and times as if all were part of some meta-narrative whose theme, ultimately, is one of loss. His is a literature of ghosts. Looking at the abandoned airfields of East Anglia, he senses 'the dead souls of the men who never came back from their missions' (77) and beyond them of those who died in the fires they flew so far to start. In his work, indeed, no man is an island entire of itself and time is no barrier to membership of that main.

Sebald wrote his 'novels' out of a desire to 'cast some light on the way in which memory (individual, collective and cultural) deals with experiences exceeding what is tolerable' (79). But what of those whose memories are presumably central to that enterprise? What of those whose authority lies precisely in the fact that they were present at the moment of apocalypse? They, at least, surely, had not turned their eyes away, could not be accused of denial. Sebald did not doubt their utility but he was struck by what seemed the stereotypical way in which many recalled or expressed their recollections. He was, moreover, aware of an 'inherent inadequacy, notorious unreliability and curious vacuity' (80), a tendency to restate familiar material in familiar ways. Their accounts, he suggested, were subject to the psychological effects of the very traumas they endeavour to recall. As a result, he distrusts the form of such recollections, including the literary form, and distrusts in particular a connection between these private recollections and public consciousness whose focus is on reconstruction and not destruction, a reconstruction which extends to the sensibility. In part the suppressions on which he comments are connected with the nature of the Third Reich but in part he traces them to the German sensibility, to what he calls the regulation of intimate feelings within the family, a kind of bourgeois fastidious-ness. He comes close to suggesting, indeed, that the war itself, with its deformations of the human soul, had its psycho-social origin in the German mind.

Yet, he has to concede the right to silence of those whose experience is, indeed, too traumatic to bear. It is, he confesses, 'as inviolable as that of the survivors of Hiroshima, of whom Kenzaburo Oe says, in his notes on that city written in 1965, 'even twenty years after the bomb fell many of them could still not speak of what happened that day'. This silence was earned. The price had been paid. What surprised and dismayed him with respect to Germany was that silence should have become a socially sanctioned strategy, the wiping out of the past seen as a necessary path to the future. This, however, seemed to him to place an even greater burden on the writer since the writer's task is 'to keep the nation's collective memory alive' (98). It is certainly the task that in his novels and unforgiving essays he accepts for himself.

Yet he is aware that art 'is a way of laundering money'. The Nazis deployed architecture, where the stones to create their monumental buildings were quarried by prisoners whose lives were in the hands of the SS. Music, art, literature were all enrolled in the Nazi cause. It is that fact, however, that creates its own necessities. 'It would be presumptuous', he accepts, 'to say writing a book would be a sufficient gesture ... But if people were more pre-occupied with the past, maybe the events that overwhelm us would be fewer.'[56] Yet there is something safe even about the worst memories. As he confesses, they represent a 'haven of safety' because 'it's already happened – the pain is already past'.[57] The problem, therefore, is to disturb that sense of safety, to allow the pain to seep into the present riding on something as insubstantial as words. What he sets out to do is 'reinvent a life almost lost or something that perhaps nobody thought might be recovered'.[58]

Memory is a contended site. Collective memory is what the present chooses to make of the past. Julius Novick has pointed out that one of the first people to use the term, the French sociologist Maurice Halbwachs, was interested less in 'the past working its will on the present' than in the ways in which 'present concerns determine what of the past we remember and how we remember it' (Halbwachs was to end his days in Buchenwald). Perhaps that was never clearer than when, as Novick recalls, Chancellor Helmut Kohl responded to proposals to make denial of the Holocaust a crime by suggesting a corresponding law making it illegal to deny the suffering of Germans expelled from the East in 1945. It was a breathtaking suggestion, an offer to trade one trauma for another as if there might be an official rate of exchange for suffering, a retrospective equivalence between forced exile and mass slaughter. Memories were simply to be balanced, with the help of a thumb on the scales of history, negotiated in a kind of treaty in which concessions would be required before truths could be conceded. Until then, denial, by implication, was to be the default setting. Indeed, a sixtieth anniversary commemoration of the victims of the Dresden bombing, in 2005, attracted 5,000 members of the neo-Nazi National Party of Germany, which the previous year had won 9.2 per cent of the votes in elections in Saxony. They carried banners declaring, 'Never forgive, never forget', as a band played Wagner. One of its supporters, Annie Lutzner, was quoted as saying, 'We believe that the German state favours foreigners and the Jews.'[59] Chancellor Gerhard Schröder insisted that he would resist such attempts 'to reinterpret history'.

What was it that drew Max Sebald to a past towards which it might be felt he had no obligation? The answer perhaps lies in a question posed by Jean Améry. What obligation did the Holocaust place on those others who 'didn't know, or were too young, or not even born yet?' Améry's answer explains something of Sebald's work: 'You should have seen, and your youth gives you no special privilege, and break with your father.'[60] In effect, that is what Sebald did with respect to the father whose secrets he could never penetrate, the father whose death nonetheless left him distraught. For the past is not sealed off from the present. It lays obligations on it, and those obligations were accepted by a man who, like Améry, was born in one country and moved to another. The one spoke out of immediate experience, the other out of a debt he felt the necessity to discharge.

Sebald's work was not, of course, limited to a concern with the Jews and with the Holocaust. His shuttling back and forth through time, his blurring of the boundaries of fact and fiction, his transgression of genre boundaries, his crossing of frontiers, literal and figurative, his elision of the 'I' of the narrator and the 'I' of the figures who drift like so many ghosts through his books, was an assertion about how we construct the world which we inhabit, about what is shared rather than what divides. The echoes, coincidences, analogies, rhymes which engage him hint at a hidden structure to experience, an uncanny coherence in what otherwise he celebrates as sheer and compelling variety.

He shows a Whitmanesque respect for detail and simultaneously for the meaning immanent in such detail which grants access to the metaphysical. His melancholy does concede a force to what is lost and what is fast fading. Death, disease, decay lace through his prose, but they are a provocation to consider life and its beauties, the integrity of individual lives, not least when those lives seem most threatened. The photographs, often faded, partial, distant, are the shadow of a past brought into the present. They are not the evidence against which to test the text. They are of a piece with words which seek to approach truth by indirection and even untruth. And if that seems a paradox it is the paradox of art, a dubious enterprise but necessary for what it tells us about the story that is history and the story that is a life.

For Sebald, 'Melancholy embodies the peculiar ambivalence of human life'; she is 'not only an illness; she is also the patroness of creativity'. For him, 'the resistance offered by melancholy becomes the last bastion of a humanist world-view in the great novels of this century'. In his 1973 doctoral thesis he offered an image for a melancholy which manages simultaneously to express despair and its transcendence:

> There is a Dürer engraving which shows a dark Angel surrounded by allegorical instruments – a pair of scales, an hour-glass, a death knell and a plane, a knife and a goat; but there is something else in the picture, a piece of rock with crystalline surfaces. Thus although the inorganic goal is represented in the picture, regression is itself transcended by the unflinching calm with which the Angel stares death in the face. In this way both the Angel itself and the tools of destruction appear to have their activity suspended: under the protection of melancholy the prospective victim savours a final interlude of living peace.[61]

There may be a sadness to personal memories, as past and present are set side by side providing evidence of decline, the eclipse of hopes, the erosion of youthful grace, but for Sebald the past is not projected as a paradise lost. Indeed, there is evidence enough in his work of a shadow cast both forwards and back. At times there is a pervasive sense of melancholy, that black bile that was once thought to be one of the governing principles of the human organism. He recalls, indeed, in an essay on Günter Grass, that in the sixteenth century black bile had been a synonym for a writer's ink. He insists, however, that melancholy, about which Robert Burton had written and which, he noted, is the subject of an engraving by Dürer, is 'a very respectable mood to be in, whether you are a philosopher or a writer or indeed a physicist', though in his essay on Grass he comments that 'a writer who uses black bile as a medium for creative work risks taking on the misunderstood depression of those for whom he writes' (*Campo Santo*, 120). Sebald's stance is of one who is outside the world, observing, looking for patterns. One aspect of that dark bent in his own case, meanwhile, was a product of his own particular past which had exerted a pull upon him, not least because there was a vacuum at its heart.

That fascination with melancholy was apparent as early as 1973 and his thesis on Döblin. His experience of the horrors of the

First World War had generated precisely this mood which Sebald saw as paralleling that outlined by Burton, who had identified the various sicknesses of the world but insisted that for a country suffering thus, melancholy must be a stimulus for reform, for restitution. That would become a central concern of Sebald's.

There is, though, perhaps another source for his interest in melancholy. In her book on the Holocaust, *After Such Knowledge: A Meditation on the Aftermath of the Holocaust*, Eva Hoffman recalls Freud's essay on 'Mourning and Melancholy', in which he suggests that in order to mourn it is necessary to understand what has been lost. Failure to reconstruct that lost individual or world is productive of melancholy. The issue, in other words, is absence. For Hoffman, this is acutely felt by the children of survivors. A chain of memory has been broken. The past has been winnowed. People, proof of their existence, photographs of those rendered into ash, are missing. The key word is 'loss', directly connected, for Hoffman, to the uncanny, another Freudian concept, one with which Sebald was surely familiar. 'Transferred loss', Hoffman suggests, 'more than transferred memory, is what children of survivors inherit; and how do you get over loss that has no concrete shape or face? That way, placeless loss itself, a dimensionless melancholia, may become the medium in which we live.'[62] What is the solution? 'Just as for some survivors only fully remembering could bring about some catharsis, so for the second generation, only a full imaginative confrontation with the past – however uncanny, however unknown – can bring the haunting to an end' (73). That past contains pain and may contain shame; it is part real and part fictional, part tangible and part imagined. But the past cannot be left to look after itself. It has already been carried into the present, like a child carried within a child. The ghost is within and hence the key to confronting it lies, as it would for Sebald, in part through autobiography, in part through fiction, in part through documented truth, in part through a re-animated history contained within a narrative of the present.

Sebald, of course, was not the child of a survivor, beyond the fact that he, too, could look back to an absence, an unspoken, unacknowledged truth and his father, whose loss he felt, was doubly lost to him because he suspected a shame he was long hesitant to confront. But he behaved in some senses like the child of a survivor, not in any presumptuous sense, not because he was guilty of what Hoffman calls 'significance envy', wishing to attach himself to the historically significant, but because he was aware that history, and hence memory, has become unstitched. He had felt drawn to re-establishing that missing connection and hence was increasingly attracted, though by no means exclusively, to those to whom he felt a responsibility merited only by his awareness that he came from a people who had conspired against memory, who had sought to precipitate a radical discontinuity. So as he seemingly meandered back and forth through history and fiction, taking private journeys which mysteriously turned out to be metaphysical journeys, so he was drawn more and more to those who themselves either sought to insulate themselves from a past they still forbore to confront or to travel along the chain of memory in search of themselves as much as of the history of a people and hence of all.

In the late 1990s, Sebald published *On the Natural History of Destruction*, which in its English edition contained essays about three writers. What tied them together was their concern to recapitulate the past, particularly the past of the Third Reich and the concentration camp. What separated them was their handling of that past, the uses to which they had put memory and, beyond that, their right to enter this territory.

The first of these essays dealt with the work of a respected German author, respected by many, Alfred Andersch, the latter two with Jean Améry and Peter Weiss, for whom the Holocaust was a central fact. Though perhaps these essays set out to be dispassionate accounts, they are anything but that. Aesthetic discriminations are offered but these are intimately invested in moral discriminations which in turn reach out beyond private proprieties. The fact is that these are deeply felt pieces in which critical analysis is no more than a dissecting tool. The stakes are higher than a mere academic polemic. For Sebald, a silence about events half a century before had been broken. The question was with what authority, with what degree of integrity. For the fact is that he was not neutral. He was removed in time and space from the events which generated these fictions, and despite his own German passport might be thought to have a certain detachment. But he never accepted the immunity from his country's past that might have been a gift of his own emigration to Britain in 1968 and his date of birth, 1944. What he says about these writers is implicitly a statement of his own stance as a writer, a writer whose accomplishments, in a brief passage of years, established him as a leading voice of his generation.

In one of his essays he recalls Nietzsche's remark, in *Genealogy of Morality*, that forgetting is the doorkeeper of peace and order (187), not least because memories carry forward what continues to give pain. Forgetting is an analgesia, yet it is clearly not without a moral dimension. This is not a casual inattention, but a wilful refusal to allow the past to be explored for its human content, not least because of the power of that past to disturb the present. Doors are closed in the name of equanimity. A continuous present or anticipated future evacuate precisely that responsibility for past actions which is the basis for a moral system. Forgetting swims in the same dark pool as denial and refusal. The torturer may choose to forget; his victim can only try. The absolute nature of pain may cause a lesion in the memory but the lesion itself is evidence for the pain.

Memory is not nostalgia, which is what the present invents for consolation, a past turned on the lathe and shaped to serve new requirements. It is a ghost which haunts the present and which is released by places, echoes, coincidences, Proustian moments of recall triggered seemingly arbitrarily. For Sebald, it is not that the past contains a secret to be disinterred. He knows well enough its capacity to change shape. He himself would not so much uncover it, strike it to see if it rang true, as honour its power to enter into a dialogue with the present. His books contain conversations but in many respects are themselves conversations between different times, places, experiences as if there were a connective tissue. Except in his essays he is not concerned with accusations, though certain facts, documents and lives might form themselves into such. What he is concerned to do is follow the paths worn down by memory, trace patterns detected by mind and imagination, the human necessities compacted in the past and at times the betrayal of those necessities.

The first literary essay in *On the Natural History of Destruction* focusses on a man who did not write overmuch about the camps, though he had spent three months in Dachau and another period imprisoned in the Munich police headquarters, but whose books seemed to be generated out of a need to rewrite his life, to deny the betrayals, subtle and overt, for which he had been responsible. And what emerges most clearly from the forty-page essay is Sebald's contempt. Indeed he struggles to grant either integrity or literary accomplishment to a man who had a considerable literary reputation.

Alfred Andersch, who emigrated to Switzerland in 1958, was respected in the Federal Republic. As a journalist, and then a novelist, he seemed willing to explore something of the war years. His were novels in which Jewish characters would make an appearance. He had been married to a partly Jewish woman, a marriage he claimed to have contracted in order to protect her from the Nuremberg laws. For Sebald, though, he was a man who deployed memory highly selectively, omitting decisive tracts of experience entirely. He was, in short, a construction, desperate for success and respect, whose honesty in approaching the past was almost wholly factitious. It was merely a novel means of forgetting.

He had, indeed, married a Jewish woman, but in 1943 he divorced her, knowing in what jeopardy it would place her, her mother having been sent to Theresienstadt the previous year. For several years he could have left for Switzerland, which he would do after the war, but chose what was called internal exile instead, a process which inevitably meant compromise. This man, with his acknowledgement of the plight of the Jews, had worked for an enthusiastically anti-Semitic publishing house, responsible for some of the more scabrous output of the Nazis. He served in the military, from which he eventually deserted, and after the war claimed to speak on behalf of those loyal members of the Wehrmacht whom he absolved of any responsibility for genocide. He had ended up in a prisoner of war camp in Louisiana in which he suddenly remembered the utility of his one-time wife who he described, in a curiously revealing deposition, as 'a mongrel of jewish [sic] descent' (122).

Sebald's point, though, is not simply that he was a morally suspect individual whose books simultaneously drew on and distorted his biography (in one, his central character rescues a Jewish woman where Andersch had abandoned his own Jewish wife). Not merely, Sebald insists, does Andersch use 'literature as a means of straightening out one's own past life' (142) but in doing so he contaminates his fiction, whose aesthetics become meretricious, as cheap and formulaic as his simulated ethical stance. As Sebald insisted, 'when a morally compromised author claims the field of aesthetics as a value-free area it should make his readers stop and think' (133). Think what, one is inclined to ask? Did Céline's or Pirandello's politics poison their art? Literary talent and liberal politics, or even human decency, do not always come into neat alignment. There is, at times, perhaps a sentimentality to Sebald who wishes to see the world at moral attention and literature as an agent if not of redemption then of a clarifying integrity. Céline and Pirandello, however, did not use Auschwitz as a scene-setter and Sebald reserves a special contempt for those who claim suffering as a *mise en scène*.

Sebald accumulates biographical and critical evidence for Andersch's bad faith and poor literature but the real interest lies in the fact that he feels obliged to write this essay at all, to correct what he presents as a false reputation. Who, after all, cares? Sebald does and he does so because if he was bewildered by an initial unwillingness by German writers to explore the darkness of the war years, so threatening to a Republic busy presenting itself as the bastion of democracy and the foundation of international fiscal integrity, he is particularly concerned with the honesty or otherwise of those who offer to break that silence. If Andersch is, finally, as insignificant a literary figure as he suggests, it would hardly be worth crushing him. The fact is that he sees him as a threat to the past and to literature itself.

George Steiner wrote of those German writers who chose to stay behind, rejecting the terrible solution of suicide or the option of exile, as being always touched with ambiguity. The inevitable compromises, it seemed to him, and not only him, opened a gulf of understanding that was all but unbridgeable. He quotes one such as complaining 'You did not pay with the price of your own dignity. How, then, can you communicate with those who did?' Steiner forbears even to offer his name. 'What, then', he asks, 'of those writers who did stay behind? Some', he explains, 'became lackeys of the official whorehouse of "Aryan culture", the *Reichsschriftumskammer*. Others equivocated till they had lost the faculty of saying anything clear or meaningful even to themselves.'[63]

He quotes Klaus Mann's parody of one such, Gerhart Hauptmann. It is a cruel piece. Others he identifies as taking what Gottfried Benn called 'the aristocratic form of emigration' (216), joining the Army, believing it to be immune to the pollution of Nazism. Ernst Jünger, he notes, wrote an elegant book called *Gärten und Strassen*, about the French campaign, which managed to avoid all unpleasantness, subsequently withdrawing, Steiner remarks, into 'obscurity of style, then into silence' (216).

There were, he conceded, those who stayed to conduct resistance. One such was Ernst Wiechert, who spent time in Buchenwald in 1938 and then buried his description of that time in his garden, digging it up and publishing it after the war. Andersch's aristocratic emigration, his decision to join the Army, proved short-lived, though he seems to have had fond thoughts of it subsequently, while his time in Dachau was not recorded and buried against a future when it could be disinterred and presented as witness and accusation. He chose another path. Steiner's barely suppressed contempt for those who stayed is explicable, given his Jewish identity, given, indeed, his seemingly acute sense of guilt at avoiding the fate of those who died while he flourished. Sebald's anger, and that is clearly what it is, is of a different kind. It is born out of a sense of complicity at several removes.

Andersch's compromised position is highlighted by the fact that Sebald places this essay next to another, one celebrating both the life and the writings of Jean Améry. He, too, had been silent for twenty years but when he broke that silence he did so as someone who had himself suffered, and he did so not in novels but essays. A new generation of writers 'were anxious to compensate for the huge moral deficit which, until about 1960, had been a feature of the literature of the post-war period' (149). But it seemed to Sebald that 'the alacrity with which literature was now reclaiming "Auschwitz" as its own territory was no less repellent than its previous refusal to broach that monstrous subject at all' (149–50). He commented on the 'astounding efficacy with which moral capital was now being made from denunciation of the collective amnesia encouraged by the literary world itself', a process which could easily marginalise those who had actual and immediate knowledge and who wrestled with the simultaneous need to remember and forget.

Améry had been tortured by the Gestapo in Fort Breendonk, which Sebald had visited and which features in *Austerlitz*, and had spent time in Auschwitz. He was, in a sense, at risk of being defined by his victimhood, doomed to be the literal dangling man (he was suspended from his dislocated arms), never able to forget, never able to speak. For Sebald, what impressed was 'the way in which he tried to break through the silence imposed on him by the terrorism, in the face of a situation where those who came after the Fascist regime, and were at most only indirectly affected themselves, were usurping the victim's cause' (*On the Natural History of Destruction*, 152).

Memory plainly lies at the core. The mental state of victims of persecution is determined in part by the fact that 'a memory can hardly be endured – memory not only of moments of terror but also of a more or less untroubled time before then' (153). That earlier normality becomes impossible to reach in its truth. It is blocked off by what followed, as Sebald's own protected childhood was mocked by the disasters then unknown to him but to which he felt himself umbilically connected. It was not only Améry's arms that were dislocated. Something happened to time: 'the thread of chronological time is broken', Sebald insists, 'The experience of terror also dislocates time, that most abstract of humanity's homes' (154). That, of course, had been a central truth of the camps. Those who entered had their past smeared away. What did it matter who they had been, what they had accomplished? The families who contained that history were destroyed immediately with a mere wave of Dr Mengele's imperious hand, the gesture of what Primo Levi called a conductor's baton, as if he were directing some orchestra of suffering, sensitive to the crescendos and diminuendos of pain. The future, meanwhile, did not exist, could not be imagined when moment-to-moment survival was the sole priority.

In Auschwitz there was an area of the camp known as 'Canada' (described by Fania Fénelon, an inmate of Auschwitz-Birkenau who played in the women's orchestra, in her book *Playing for Time*, adapted for the screen and stage by Arthur Miller). It was so called because Canada itself seemed a place out of time, secure, magical. 'Canada' was a place where prisoners' clothes and belongings were sorted through in search of loot for the Reich (and, not incidentally, for the SS, who were corrupted in this as in so much else). It was a place where survival was a possibility, not least because among the gold and jewellery was secreted food. 'Canada' was a perverse Shangri-La, existing in a timeless void, a parody of a world beyond that could never be anything else but a fantasy. But the camp itself existed outside of time. Nothing mattered but the moment.

Améry worked as a journalist after the war and for twenty years said nothing about his past. It was not that he had forgotten or repressed it but that he could not find a language in which to express it. When he did begin to write, his chosen mode was understatement, allied as it is to irony, a Hemingwayesque tactic. There is even an irony in the seeming precisions of language. When recalling the moment he was suspended from his twisted and dislocated arms at Fort Breendonk, Améry remembers that the word 'torture' derives from the Latin *torquere*, to twist. The torture itself is intransitive. It is itself. It leads nowhere. It is defining of nothing but the unimagined limits of pain. But Améry contemplates torture where Andersch and others used it. He could not believe in a history which simply swerved around such events, like a car avoiding a rabbit, as if it were no more than an inconvenience. He does not, however, write to exorcise or offer a benediction so that business may be resumed. What lies in the road is a rock. Nor can writing contain or transcend it, the mind and imagination having, willingly or otherwise, always bent the knee to power. Yet what is to be done with that knowledge except embrace the Sisyphean truth and yet protest again the irreversible?

What appeals to Sebald about Améry's work is its refusal to compromise, to believe that the waters can remain untroubled. The death sentence on Améry pronounced by the Nuremberg laws had effectively never been revoked. What he resents is resignation and indifference and his essays are a testament to this. He writes not to lay the past to rest but to insist on its substantiality and continued relevance. The past world of the Austrian province from which he came, once seemingly secure, had been exposed by events as no more than a temporary parole for the offence of being Jewish. There is thus no past to which he can return where justice and security had prevailed. The past was deeply compromised and history no more than evidence for an insecurity which deepens from a social into a metaphysical condition. Everything was always a temporary reprieve and living a result of wilful forgetfulness and denial. He was dispossessed of himself as of his home and country. That Sebald, a non-Jew, should respond to this is in a sense surprising, though its logic would slowly emerge. In retrospect his own securities, he came to feel, had been built on similar suppressed truths slowly exposed, and he felt a similar need to break the silence, though he had never been the victim and hence simple testimony could offer no adequate or even legitimate route to the past.

It is tempting to feel that Sebald's description of Améry's condition, as he crossed into Belgium, and into another language, bore on his own situation in leaving Germany for Britain, though without any presumptuous desire to elide his own unthreatened existence with that of his subject. Améry did not know how hard it would be, Sebald observes, 'to endure the tension between his native land as it became ever more foreign and the land of his foreign exile as it becomes ever more familiar' (165).

In his Ph.D. thesis Sebald had noted how German writers in exile during the Nazi period tended to turn to the past, producing voluminous historical novels as if to be severed from the home country required a retreat to the apparent security of the past even as language came under pressure. With respect to Nazi genocide Sebald had insisted that 'only a few authors, for instance Peter Weiss, managed to find the linguistic gravity of language for the subject and make the literary treatment of genocide something more than a dutiful exercise marked by involuntary infelicities' (150). Beyond that, however, was the special fate of those looking for a legitimate language while themselves abandoning the language of their birth. At the same time, language represented its own country, a seeming security. Sebald remarks that 'for those whose business is language, it is only in language that the unhappiness of the exile can be overcome' (166).

Nor was it simply a question of the transition from German to French. Améry had to make his way back to a language in which he could place his trust because it had been so severely and profoundly compromised. He deserted his mother tongue as Sebald did not and clearly they were in different positions. For all that they shared certain dilemmas the gulf between them was extreme, a fact underlined when this man, whose companion in Auschwitz was Primo Levi, took his life, like so many who survived the camps eventually feeling that survival was not enough, indeed was the root of a more profound sense of guilt and anxiety, though such neat explanations can only distort the complexities of even such a seemingly implacable gesture. Sebald does not so much offer an explanation for Améry's death as a certain logic, quoting E. M. Cioran as observing that continued life was only possible, 'par les déficiences de notre imagination et de notre mémoire' (by deficiencies of our imagination and our memory) (169).

Sebald's *On the Natural History of Destruction*, based on his Zurich lectures about the air war on Germany, is both angry in itself and anger-inducing in readers. If he and others had been struck by the silence provoked by the Holocaust, why, he enquired, were the Germans silent about the violence they had experienced in an aerial bombardment which had proved annihilating? The Jews burned, and so did the Germans, 600,000 dying in air raids, a tenth the number of Jews who died but a startling number nonetheless. Much had been written about the deferred attention accorded to German genocide, virtually nothing, he suggested, had been written about another silence, that of the Germans themselves not simply about the sufferings they inflicted but the sufferings they experienced. There was a curious absence of any real consideration, by historians or literary writers, of the cataclysmic air war launched on German cities (though in 1977 Götz Bergander had published *Dresden im Luftkrieg* (Dresden in the Air War)).

Both silences seemed to him to be related and though in a series of lectures he would focus on the latter, the explanation, at least in part, lay in the former while both perhaps had a common root. The essays were called 'Air War and Literature' but when he came to publish them as a book he chose another title. A founding professor of the University of East Anglia, who had been a scientific adviser to the government, had planned to write a study of the bombing campaign under the title *On the Natural History of Destruction*. His name was Solly Zuckerman. He never wrote the article, though he did later have conversations with Sebald, who chose to appropriate his title if not his approach for the lectures that he delivered in Zurich in 1997.

Sebald points out that it is almost a commonplace to remark on the absence of a great German epic of the wartime or of the postwar periods but to him that is evidence of a larger failure to address the humiliation felt by Germans in the last years of the war and thereafter. It seemed to him that today's Germans are blind to history and lacking in tradition, an odd fate for a nation which during the Third Reich was assured of the existence of a glorious, albeit mythical, heritage. The central problem was, in his own words, that his was a morally discredited society. Those authors who had stayed on during the war seemed to him later to be more concerned with re-making themselves than addressing the nature of their society. The process of re-making involved deletions, adjustments, silences and the central silences were to do with the violence inflicted and suffered.

Beyond the 600,000 dead in bombing raids, three and a half million Germans lost their homes in the air war. Forty per cent of male children born in 1920 died in the war, half in its final year, though the figure included military deaths. What surprised Sebald was that it 'left scarcely a trace of pain behind in the collective consciousness' (4). Perhaps, he suggested, the commitment to the reconstruction effort and the insistence on the future inhibited a concern with a suspect past. There certainly seemed to him to be a tacit agreement that the real state of 'material and moral ruin in which the country found itself' (10) would be ignored. It was taboo territory. Only Heinrich Böll's *Der Engel schwieg* (*The Angel Was Silent*) seemed to capture the mood but its publication was deferred for fifty years, finally appearing in 1992. What Sebald looked for was some evidence of moral trauma, some overt expression of the catastrophe that the country had experienced as well as the damage it had done.

It is hardly surprising that his Zurich lectures provoked a hostile response. He quotes Hans Magnus Enzensberger as suggesting that it is impossible to understand German energy if we fail to understand that Germans make a virtue of their deficiencies. In particular, insensibility was the condition of their success (12). The familiar German work ethic, meanwhile, had been learned under totalitarianism where Germany had also picked up its skills in dealing with foreign labour. Sebald spoke of 'the corruption of the Germans' and of the 'fault line' that ran through the German mind during the first half of the twentieth century. And when he later received angry letters in response to those lectures, he published a further piece which was even more direct in its accusations. He recalled that the dead of Dresden had been buried by a detachment of the SS that had honed its skills in Treblinka. He was unequivocal in acknowledging 'the immeasurable sufferings that we Germans inflicted on the world' and the fact that 'we provoked the annihilation of the cities in which we once lived' (104), recalling the pleasure with which Hitler had anticipated the possibility of London being reduced to ash by incendiary bombs of the kind that would only later fall on Germany.

This was brutal stuff, more especially when he suggested that Bomber Command had assisted modernisation by eliminating the medieval buildings that had once contained German industry. German energy, he suggested, derived from 'the well-kept secret of the corpses built into the foundations of our state, a secret that bound all Germans together in the postwar years, and indeed still binds them, more closely than any positive goal such as the realization of democracy ever could' (13). The influence of the Deutschmark, meanwhile, extended precisely to the limits once occupied by the Wehrmacht in 1941.

Perhaps it was as well these lectures were delivered in Switzerland, more especially when he suggests that the parasites which crawled over the dead bodies rotting in the streets of Germany's bombed cities could not be acknowledged by a country that had set out to sanitise Europe, regarding others as vermin, not least because they suspected that they might themselves be that vermin.

But note that this expatriate, a mere twelve months old at the end of the war, does not distance himself from those he denounces. The pronoun he uses is 'we', as well as 'they'. If it had been otherwise he would hardly have been moved to speak and write as he did. The Zurich lectures simply make clear the nature of the silence that he had felt obliged to break, a silence with respect to the Jews but also with respect to his own people whose denials seemed rooted in the very history they were so committed to denying.

The British and American bombing campaign, which began in 1942 and which prompted considerable contemporary moral debate in Britain, to his surprise prompted no such debate in postwar Germany. In part, he suggests, this may have been because of awareness that millions of people had been killed or worked to death and that there was thus no moral high ground on which to stand. He hints at this when he recalls that the impact of the bombs which destroyed Dresden was heard seventy kilometres away by a prisoner at Theresienstadt, as those that landed on Munich were heard at Dachau.

Immediately after the raid, he concedes, people were too shocked to remember, observing that in such circumstances 'lives do generally have something discontinuous about them, a curiously erratic quality, one so much at variance with authentic recollection that it easily suggests rumour-mongering and invention' (25). Confronted with this, writers resorted to cliché and convention, thus distorting the thing they tried to capture. In surveying the literature that came out of this time, Sebald looks for but does not find evidence of a distortion of language under the impact of such extreme experiences.

The response to the Zurich lectures surprised him. He had thought he might be refuted, offered evidence that writers had indeed addressed the nature and extent of the catastrophe suffered by Germany. Instead, he received confirmation. Indeed, the silence, it seemed to him, had extended outwards to all areas of private and public life. Historians had simply turned the page without pausing but the family accounts sent to him seemed less concerned with trauma than celebrating a triumphant continuance, focussed, as they were, not on ruined cities but on the natural world. He might have found an answer in Primo Levi's observation that 'many survivors of wars or other complex and traumatic experiences tend unconsciously to filter their memory: summoning them up among themselves, or telling them to third persons, they prefer to dwell on moments of respite, on grotesque, strange or relaxed intermezzos, and to skim over the most painful episodes which are not called up willingly from the reservoir of memory'.[64]

Some of the letters he received were simply abusive, some anti-Semitic. More sought to assure him that the traumas suffered by Germany had not failed to find their way into writing. He had half suspected he might have been ignorant of some texts which contra-dicted his thesis, but what was on offer was less academic correction than family reminiscences from the war years, dutifully sent to him by way of gentle reproach. These were accounts of family life, of resilient normality, picnics in the countryside, celebratory enco-miums. There was at their heart precisely that void that had led him to write the lectures in the first place. There seemed no sense that the moral world had been in free fall, that there was either fault or catastrophe. What was reflected there was a national desire to ignore what seemed unavoidable, to speak of continuity, the German homeland, even a triumphant justification. These were the written memories now invoked as evidence. He understood such preserved relics not least because he was aware in his own family of the absoluteness with which events had been suppressed and domestic tranquillity substituted. It was this, indeed, which had set him writing, a man drawn to telling a story of the Jews and the Holocaust, though himself a non-Jew, a German writer with no immediate contact either with the Holocaust or, indeed, for the first two decades of his life, with Jews.

Thus, he praises Günter Grass's *From the Diary of a Snail* saying that without the passage 'describing the fate of the persecuted minority [it] would surely have remained a work written on a single level. For only the dimension of concrete remembrance lends substance to the central story ... and on another level substance to the reflections on melancholy' (*Campo Santo*, 112). But since at the time the German literati still knew little in detail about the fate of the persecuted Jews this could not have been written by Grass himself and indeed was derived from material developed by a Jewish historian living in Tel Aviv. That, in turn, it seemed to Sebald, 'shows that literature today, left solely to its own devices, is no longer able to discover the truth' (114).

In his work as a critic Sebald was drawn to Jewish writers, even chastising German critics for failing to emphasise this dimension of Kafka's life, permitting himself a fantasy based on the fact that his friend Peter Tripp had painted a portrait of Kafka as he might have looked had he lived for a further eleven or twelve years. This would have brought him to 1935 when Leni Riefenstahl was filming a Nazi rally and Kafka would have been on his way to the gas chamber, thus fulfilling his implicit prophecies. This was the Kafka who obsessed the Wiesel who lost his mother and sister to the gas chamber.

Sebald's bitterness at the German response to the Jews, not merely during the war but afterwards, explains a great deal about his later commitments. He recalls, for instance, a visit in 1976 to see a production of Lessing's *Nathan the Wise*, a play he disliked in a production which he thought unspeakable. What stayed with him, however, was the comment of a German woman as she came out of the theatre, who whispered in her friend's ear. 'Well, he certainly played Nathan well. You might have thought he was a real Jew' (170). So impossible did he find it to unpack the meaning of this remark that it left him, he said – and the word is significant in the context of Sebald's work – with a sense of vertigo. Even his comments on a non-Jewish writer, the exiled Vladimir Nabokov, are earthed in the fact that his brother died in a concentration camp.

For his last thirty years W. G. Sebald lived in what to many must seem the quiet irrelevance of the small East Anglian city of

Norwich, one hundred and ten miles north-east of London and sixty miles from Cambridge as its citizens are used to intoning, as if the best way to locate it were in terms of somewhere it is not. This must have seemed as distant from the horrors of the camps as it was possible to be. Yet, in truth, there is tarnished thread connecting this place with those others, though it lies far back in history. But all things have their beginnings, a truth which explains something of Sebald's methods in books which shuttle to and fro between past and present, gathering up stories and myths along with dates and places, in the process constructing a melancholic account of foundered hopes, desires too often betrayed in their own imagining.

For all its remoteness – today it is at the end of a railway line, a destination and not a place for passing through – Norwich was for long a centre of power, the second city of England until 1740. That power came from money and the money came from the wool trade. Not far away was the small village of Worsted, whose cloth would be known around the world. There were links to Amsterdam, and many of Norwich's buildings still sport Dutch gables. Indeed, even today Amsterdam remains a focal point since planes from the local airport fly to Schiphol, from which it is possible to journey anywhere. It enables its citizens to travel without a detour through London and the plane from Norwich to Amsterdam was often taken by Sebald when he returned to Germany or travelled to France, Belgium or Switzerland, for Sebald was a traveller, in more than one sense. He died on a journey, though one of no significance beyond the fact of his death, travelling on a small country road only miles from his home.

Travel, as the eponymous Austerlitz observes, can seem illusionistic and illusory to the traveller, with space and time expanding and contracting. And certainly Sebald is always recounting dreams (in which, he once observed, the dead, the living and the still unborn come together) which seem to braid effortlessly into his observations about the places he visits quite as if they were spectral extensions, as if the thoughts and images they inspired were part of their reality as their reality is subverted and metamorphosed by those who see and describe them. Those places also exist in the paintings and photographs which equally make their way into his texts and which have the power to usurp their subjects, to blend with them, to flow. This flow is reflected in Sebald's prose style. There are few paragraphs in his books; in *Austerlitz* there are none: it is a feat comparable to Alexander Sokurov's *Russian Ark*, a ninety-minute film made in the Hermitage in St Petersburg in one continuous shot. Eight hundred and sixty-seven actors, portraying real and imaginary characters, play out scenes in the glittering rooms quite as if they were ghosts oblivious of the camera as it passes by, apparently with no more substance than a random thought. For them, after all, it is our present that is unthinkable, even though this is the direction in which they are, without knowing, moving. Sebald moves towards the point at which he wholly abandons paragraphs because, as he explained, the whole concept of his work 'is based on patterns of association, and so one moves fairly easily from one thing to another'.[65] But, then, his ideal reader, he explained, was one who did not read the text but sees it, as one sees a picture, one who 'lifts it out of the perennial wasting which occurs in time' (156).

But the crucial link between Norwich and the Jews, curiously never explored by Sebald, who was otherwise so fascinated with identifying invisible connections, lay further back than 1740. In 1144 a young apprentice called William was found murdered on Mousehold Heath, a gorse-flamed heath that looks down on what was then the newly completed Norwich Cathedral. He had been tied up in what appeared to be a ritual way. Though today we would suspect child molestation (and in a play written by a man with Norfolk connections, Arnold Wesker (*Blood Libel*), that was how it would be presented), then there was a different way of seeing. The rumour swiftly spread that he had been killed by the Jews as part of a ritual requiring Christian blood. It was this blood libel which spread not only through the city but through the country. In 1190 Jews were attacked in the streets of Norwich and many other cities and a century later expelled from the country. The blood libel crossed into mainland Europe, starting in Blois and seeping north where it would flourish for centuries, sinking down into the soil of Russia and Poland and what would become Germany. What happened in Norwich in 1144 sent ripples through time and made Majdanek and Auschwitz-Birkenau seem sanctioned by something more than the corrupt dreams of a man who sought to re-invent history to make himself its apotheosis.

Norwich, then, was not such an unlikely place for a man to sit in the quiet of a once medieval city and explore history for signs of a virus as for evidence of those who had sought to shape the world by their actions, the images they generated, the dreams they dreamed, the words they wrote.

There is, however, another link between the place in which Sebald decided to settle in 1970 and the concerns that would lead him to write something other than the articles and books required by his academic calling. For the flat land which stretches out from Norwich, to the North and East in the direction of the sea, to the West towards Ely, where Cromwell had his home, was a natural site, for half a dozen crucial years, for airfields, over seventy of them. It was from these that bombers set off, a thousand at a time on occasions, towards Germany. First, the pathfinders would seek out the heart of the medieval cities, tinder dry, and drop their multi-coloured flares. Then the other bombers would follow, the British by night, the Americans by day, and create an inferno, with howling winds and fire so intense that it fed on the oxygen it sucked from the lungs of those who huddled together in cellars that became their tombs. It was this experience that Sebald was shocked to find absent from postwar German literature. For twenty years the culture seemed in denial, though the occupying powers themselves had a vested interest in assisting what seemed a collective amnesia.

In the mid 1990s, W. G. Sebald travelled to Corsica, subsequently writing a book, *Campo Santo*, which includes an account of his visit. He went alone because this was not to be a family holiday. As he explained, he could not expect others to be interested in 'the abandoned places' that attracted him. He needed solitude to follow the unexpected paths that opened up and whose arabesques carried him towards a constructed meaning, albeit one rooted in the ostensibly real. In Ajaccio, he wandered down the streets, venturing into the tunnel-like entrances of buildings, 'trying to imagine what it would be like to live in one of these stone citadels, occupied to my life's end solely with the study of time past and passing',[66] though this was precisely one of Sebald's own preoccupations.

He usually had no time for tourist venues, but now he did venture into the Musée Fesch, in whose basement he discovered Napoleonic mementoes (from the Latin imperative, 'demanding memory'), the existence of which stirred other memories, in particular of Franz Kafka's attendance, in 1911, at a conference on the legend of Napoleon. From the museum he progressed to Napoleon's house, recalling as he did so Flaubert's visit to Corsica and his description of this same place, never quite the same place, of course, as that described by others. In one of the rooms he noted steel engravings of Napoleonic battles, including Austerlitz, a name that would stay with him and reappear several years later as if the past could not only be summoned into the present but projected into the future. In this museum, history appeared to shape itself into coherent form, as if there were an irresistible logic to it, but what, he asks,

> can we know in advance of the course of history, which unfolds according to some logically indecipherable law, impelled forward, often changing direction at the crucial moment, by tiny, imponderable events, by a barely perceptible current of air, a leaf falling to the ground, a glance exchanged across a great crowd of people? Even in retrospect we cannot see what things were really like before that moment, and how this or that world-shaking event came about.

The most precise study of the past, he insists, 'scarcely comes any closer to the unimaginable truth' (14) than the most far-fetched theory. In such a place, time seems to travel in both directions and the assurance of museum directors and custodians of the past that it is fixed, that there is a true taxonomy to events, seems dubious. As a writer, Sebald would be drawn to the past, literal and fictive, searching out those imponderable events, without any assurance that they were the motor force of history but also granting them their own integrity, creating thereby his own plausible fictions, while time seemed to him anything but fixed and implacable. Often what lay in that past was death and suffering, whose wounds in some way or another we still bear, but you could say of his work what he says of a painting by Pietro Paolini of a woman with melancholy eyes, that it is 'an annulment of all the unfathomable misfortune of life' (5). For Sebald, there is a music to time, a music with its own restorative powers.

Remembering, imaginative recall, the linking of past and present, are essential to Sebald's literary method as to his philosophy and moral sensibility. His remembering, though, is not a matter of simple recall (if the process of recall could ever be said to be simple), the disinterring of disregarded fact; it is not a question of breathing on a tarnished mirror to see what might once have been written there, though all these are present in the verbal and emotional mosaics he would create. He also remembers other people's remembering, a cascade of stories and images which flow with the freedom of the imagination and the control of thought. The memories are not, then, all his, except in so far as he commands them and thereby makes them his own. They are, in part, constructed, as he brings together seemingly discrete events, images (photographs, works of art), histories, biographies, in striking them against one another releasing a spark of meaning. He is in the business of forging metaphors out of such collisions. For him, the past and the present are co-existent, the one inhering in the other.

No wonder that Arthur Miller and his wife, the Magnum photographer Ingeborg Morath, were so delighted to meet him in Norwich, a year before his death, since they dealt in the same currency. When they returned he sent them each a copy of one of his books, an English edition for Miller, a German edition for Morath, itself something more than an exercise in tact. Morath had by then been nearly forty years outside of her native Austria (as Sebald was over thirty years out of Germany) and was fluent in half a dozen languages but just as he still felt marginally more secure in what remained his home language so, he assumed, did she, a woman whose father had joined the Nazi party (though only because it was thought wiser to do so than not) and had urged her to do likewise. She refused. On the verge of marrying Miller she had taken her Jewish husband-to-be to Mauthausen concentration camp, not far from her Salzburg home, because she, too, had ghosts to confront and a debt, not truly her own, to acknowledge. They recognised something in each other that it was perhaps difficult to express in the language of the culture that had once nurtured and betrayed them.

In Piana, Sebald was drawn to the local cemetery, whose fretful reductiveness seemed to him to stand in contrast to the 'diverse beauty of life' (19). It is a typical remark and that co-presence of death and beauty in his work – not simply a romantic gesture – stakes out the boundaries of human existence even as it describes the essence of his own work, drawn as it is to an awareness of mortality even as it exemplifies the shaping power of the imagination. On the same occasion he had swum out to sea, feeling himself drifting into the night, only to 'obey the strange instinct that binds us to life' (19). This tension typifies his work. His books are full of the dead and dying, from the cemeteries of Corsica, to Sir Thomas Browne's *Urn Burial* and those finally so overwhelmed by their memories that they take their own lives. Yet he observes with an eye to sudden beauty, a resistant spirit, detecting a coherence which may be the product of imagination wedded to mind but which is no less valid for that.

In that Corsican graveyard, he saw the faded photographs which tell so little about those who lie there, as, ironically, he noted the inscription, '*Regrets éternels*', the promise contradicted by the brevity of its expression. There is an echo here, perhaps, of Jean Améry's observation of the mausoleums in the Parisian cemetery Père-Lachaise where the words written on them in faded gold are *Concession à perpétuité*, as if, Améry remarks, 'a bourgeois fortune could at least acquire a pseudo eternity in space'.[67]

Sebald stands in the present looking at these images from the past which look forward to an indefinite future, time flowing in all directions. Grief, he acknowledges, exists both in its emotional immediacy and in the cultivated aesthetics of mourning, learned and carefully modulated. On the death of their husbands, Corsican women were required to go into mourning for the rest of their lives, as if life carried death at its very heart. They exude, he says, an 'aura of melancholy' (*Campo Santo*, 28), these representatives of our 'severely disturbed species' (27). Yet he remembers, as a child, seeing his dead grandfather in an open coffin and being struck by the 'shameful injustice that none of us could make good'. But 'the more one has to bear, for whatever reason, of the burden of grief which is probably not imposed on the human species for nothing, the more often do we meet ghosts' (33). His work is full of such ghosts, a work which itself constitutes a response to that shameful injustice.

Yet the passage to that past seems ever more difficult to locate. There is a bias against memory. As he says, in the urban societies of the late twentieth century, 'where everyone is instantly replaceable and is really superfluous from birth, we have to keep throwing ballast overboard, forgetting everything that we might otherwise remember: youth, childhood, our origins, our forebears, our ancestors'. It is this shallow current that he resists. His distaste for so many aspects of modernity lay in the evidence they offered of a degradation of the spirit, in the casual dismissal of the past as no more than a pre-history. He feared that 'the whole past will flow into a formless, indistinct, silent mass'. The consequence of this, he insisted, could only be disastrous and here is the fear that drove him to write as he did, to recuperate the past not as artefact, nor simply as an explanation of who we are, but as evidence of our imperilled sense of existence. Leaving 'a present without memory', he asserted, 'in the face of a future that no individual mind can now envisage, in the end we shall relinquish life without feeling any need to linger at least for a while, nor shall we be impelled to pay return visits from time to time' (35).

Travel, for him, was never something he conducted only in space. There was always a vertical dimension to it. To look at woodland in Corsica was to recall how earlier travellers and writers had described it, how artists had rendered it. The wood contained its own past not simply in the rings laid down by time's passing but in its refraction through human thought, the shifting aesthetics that accompanied historical process. It is also the associative power of place that drives him. He remembers, as a child, seeing a dozen dead deer tipped in front of a butcher's shop. From this comes a reflection on the decorative display of that meat in the shop, as if to conceal its true nature, and from that the thought of the absolution this gesture seemed to reflect, if also the cheapness with which that absolution was sought. So, memory leads to social comment and on to metaphysics.

From this springs another thought as he recalls discovering an old volume of the *Bibliothèque de la Pléiade* in the bedside table in his Corsican hotel room. In this he had read Flaubert's version of the legend of St Julian (a legend also invoked by Bruce Chatwin, about whom he wrote an admiring essay), a man who had learned to kill animals until he was surfeited to the point of self-disgust before redemption came. And what this recalls is 'the despicable nature of human violence', a thought implicit in his memory of the butcher's shop which now stands more clearly as a displacement of a more disturbing historical alarm.

Yet his contemplation of death, the melancholy which characterises much of his work, is not a reflexive gesture, an obsessive regard for mortality. As he himself remarked in 1985, 'Melancholia, the contemplation of unhappiness as it is occurring, has nothing in common with the desire to die ... and at the level of art in particular its function is anything but reactive or reactionary ... The description of unhappiness carries with it the possibility of overcoming that unhappiness.'[68]

The essence of Sebald's work, surely, lies precisely in his desire not to deny or even transcend the darkness that has flooded much of human history but to recall it, and the art and literature which has explored the world, and in so doing generate a moving and compelling justification for human survival. Memory is in the end not, as Nietzsche thought, the enemy of peace but ultimately its repository. In one sense we are all exiles, speaking a language inadequate to express our needs and fears, yet exile offers its gifts, a perspective, a different sense of time and place which has its own acuities. In an essay on the Austrian Adalbert Stifter, he spoke of a consciousness concerned with the continuance of life which he found inherent in art and literature, as opposed to photographs which he saw as mementoes of a world in league with dying. That was Sebald's commitment, to the continuance of life however bruised by the blows mankind has directed at itself.

In the final year of his life, speaking in Stuttgart, he explained both what he had committed himself to doing as a writer and how he had set about accomplishing it. 'I have kept asking myself', he explained, 'what the invisible connections that determine our lives are, and how the threads run.' What, for example, was the connection between his own presence in Stuttgart and the fact that in 1946, not yet a year after the end of the war, a police raid on a camp of displaced people, in search of black marketeers, had resulted in the death of a man who had only just been reunited with his wife and children? (In fact eight US military police accompanied a raid by German police on a camp in the Reinsburg Strasse. They found only a few eggs. The American Military Government immediately barred German police from entering Jewish camps.) Why, he asked himself, could he not get such episodes out of his mind? The answer in part lay in the fact of columns of refugees who continued to trail along dusty roads the world around. His lament, in other words, had not only been for the human dereliction at the heart of German history but for something still more disturbing, something that justified his own restless literary wandering, for 'how far is it', he asked himself, 'from the point where we find ourselves today back to the late eighteenth century, when the hope that mankind could improve and learn was inscribed in handsomely formed letters in our philosophical firmament?' (*Campo Santo*, 211).

It was a question which haunted him in his contemplation of the past and which forced itself on his attention precisely because of those whose lives had been forfeit even as notions of perfectability and progress were paraded by those whose hands were stained with blood. Speaking in relation to Hölderlin, but surely with relevance to himself, he wrote, in the final year of his life, that the 'synoptic view across the barrier of death ... is both overshadowed and illuminated ... by the memory of those to whom the greatest injustice is done' (*Campo Santo*, 215).

When Max Sebald was made a member of the German Academy he accepted the honour but in the briefest of speeches recalled the absences which had marked his education. The German present had found no room for the violence of the immediate past. There had been what he called a premeditated blindness. It was only his distance from Germany, his emigration, that had enabled him to see what should have been clear to him. Now, to look at the country of his birth was 'like a never-ending déjà vu'. Even in England, he confessed, he felt suspended somewhere between familiarity and dislocation, as if, finally, he belonged nowhere.

Perhaps that was what gave Sebald his particular perspective. He had found somewhere to stand that enabled him to look back over what he called 'the unlimited chasms of the past', in order to rectify 'the short memory of mankind'. Given the place of his birth and the language in which he wrote, however, the memory that cut deepest was that which led him, by way of shame, to the displaced, the bereft, the victims of a history he felt obliged to acknowledge as his own even as he shaped his work into an accusation.

To the guests assembled to see him accepted into the Collegium of the German Academy he confessed the contents of a dream he had had in Paris. He had dreamed, he said, that he had been unmasked as a traitor. Perhaps, he said, his admission to the Academy was an un-hoped-for form of justification. The question was, for whom? How tempted he must have been to quote the words which Rolf Hochhuth gives to SS Obersturmführer Kurt Gerstein, who had worked, unsuccessfully, to persuade the Vatican to intervene on behalf of the Jews:

> The traitors, they alone, today
> Are saving Germany's honor.[69]

Sebald died not long after publication of his last major book, *Austerlitz*, killed on the Bungay to Poringland road only a few miles from his home and from his place of work. Driving with his daughter, he allowed his car to edge to the wrong side of the road where he crashed into a truck. His daughter survived. He did not. It seems his heart may have failed before the impact. At the very moment his reputation had become established on both sides of the Atlantic he died, that rarity in Britain, a truly European writer.

George Szirtes, another displaced writer, who had left Hungary for Britain in 1956, exchanging one language for another, was a friend. In a poem in which he named him for his character, Austerlitz, and with which he marked his death, he observed that

> I could not believe that Austerlitz was dead.
> Though others had died that year his death was strange.
> His voice had internalised itself in my head

and I kept listening to see how it would arrange
the furniture it found there.
... He would unwind
the world of memory and wind it up again
a little off-centre as though it were a blind
or hedge against bad luck. *You can't explain
history to itself,* he said. *It has
neither ear nor eyes. Humankind must train
itself to refocus or play mirror.*[70]

Max Sebald was about precisely that process.

3   Rolf Hochhuth: breaking the silence

The world is silent. The world knows what is going on
here – it cannot help but know, and in the Vatican, the deputy
of God is silent, too.

> From an underground Polish pamphlet, August 1943

This statement, from another time, shaped into an accusation, opens
the printed version of the third act of a play written by a thirty-
two-year-old German author who as a child had been a member of the
Deutsches Jungvolk, a Hitler youth group, the young members of
which, in 1943, were set to collect leaflets dropped from Allied planes
telling the Germans of the extermination of the Jews.

Rolf Hochhuth was born in 1931 in Eschwege, in Northern
Hesse, the son of a man who worked in a shoe factory founded by his
great-grandfather. That father had served in the First World War and
went on, briefly, to serve in the second. Rolf met his wife-to-be while
still at school. Her mother, a Social Democrat councillor, was
removed by the Nazis, imprisoned and decapitated. Her father died
while serving in the Wehrmacht.

Rolf's parents were anti-Nazi but had to keep their views to
themselves. Their son, by contrast, looked for the German victory
that they feared. Where W. G. Sebald protested that postwar Germans
were silent about the catastrophe they had suffered, Hochhuth would
be one of those who broke that silence, in 1964 observing that
'because of the bombing of the Allies, we hated the Allies ... the
English destroyed Kassel. We saw the town burning ... and my
14-year-old brother had to go there at night to help. The English didn't

care where they bombed, but', he added, 'now I understand the English point of view.'[1] The understanding came as a result of his learning the extent of Nazi crimes, though there had been clues enough had he not been too young to understand the implications of what he saw.

The Jews of his home town had been driven out to Kassel and from thence to Riga where they were worked to death or killed. He recalled the fate of the Jewish wife of a cousin, a doctor from Wiesbaden:

> A Jew married to a non-Jew was considered half-Jewish so they were not deported in 1941, but they had to wear the yellow star. My parents invited her here in 1943 and we boys were ashamed and wondered what people would think. She was very sweet to us and grateful. She stayed for a few weeks although people wondered and talked in a small town. When she returned to Wiesbaden, she had an 'invitation' to go to the Gestapo and she poisoned herself. Her husband was asked to help revive her, but he would not because he had promised to respect her wishes about her own fate.
>
> (*The Storm Over the Deputy*, 46–7)

As a child, Hochhuth had been taught in school that Jews were *Untermenschen*. Only when the war was over did he see photographs of the concentration camps and begin to make sense of his relative's fate. His first reaction was shame but then, like others, he turned to other things, to his books, mirroring his society which had no desire to revisit a traumatic past, though the reading of Thomas Mann would bring him back again to what he had escaped. As he acknowledged, 'The people who were adults at that time and who silently feel guilty do not want to go near these problems.' They had losses of their own. They quickly grew tired of stories of torture. 'They want to be left in peace from politics', he explained. As for the young, like Sebald, 'They don't know Jews' (48).

First at the university of Heidelberg and then at Munich, he studied history and philosophy before becoming an editor for a book club in which capacity he worked on a collected edition of the work of the caricaturist Wilhelm Busch, being sure to omit pictures of the Jews for fear they would reinforce old prejudices. During this time he wrote, but did not publish, a novel called *Occupation*, about the fall of the Nazis and the beginning of the occupation. However, it was while reading about the Nuremberg trials that he came across a man who would become a key figure in *The Deputy* (or *The Representative*), the play that Sebald would admire as marking the beginning of a literary acknowledgement of the German role in the war.

First produced in 1963, *The Deputy* is not so much a play of witness, authenticated by memory, nor yet entirely a documentary drama, though the apparatus of such is elaborately gathered in an appendix. It is based on a number of verifiable facts, as pins set into a skull facilitate the reconstruction of the face of a long-dead person, but these are no more than the starting point. Much of the play, indeed, is built around encounters that did not happen between people who did not exist, at least not in the precise form that Hochhuth chooses to give them. They say things, some of which were said and some of which perhaps they, or others like them, should have said but did not. In a sense this is to say no more than that this is a play, with its own necessities, except that in the furore which accompanied productions much was made, both by those who attacked and those who defended it, of its accuracy, its symbolic if not actual truth. Here, after all, was a play that was as likely to be discussed in the news sections of newspapers and magazines as in the review section. And there was something else about this play. In its original form it would have run some eight or nine hours. As a result no one saw it in that form. Each production edited still further a work which was itself the distillation of research refracted through the sensibility of the author and with each editing a new balance was achieved or, perhaps more likely, a new imbalance. *The Deputy* played its role in helping to generate a renewed interest in documentary theatre but in doing so it also raised issues that were inseparable from the form.

The plot is, in a sense, about a plot, or several of them, conspiracies whose form was prompted by events in the real world but which are registered here in the constructed form of a drama shaped by polemical and aesthetic needs. The play is about silence, but of necessity fills the air with speech, speech, indeed, which has been crafted into verse whose very announced artifice might seem at odds with a claim to veracity, if not naturalism. Those who played a role in a national drama become characters playing a role in a drama in which conflicting ideas must be embodied in conflicting individuals. What is true and what is dramatically plausible do not necessarily come into alignment and if it is the truth value of the work that is at stake how are the falsifications, the lies of art, to be accommodated and justified?

This is not a question raised solely by *The Deputy*. Anne Frank's diary was undoubtedly true, if we mean by that that she wrote it in the secret room which cut her off from so much of life, even as her own life and the lives of her family were threatened. In the stage version, however, those diaries became something else and there were those, especially Jews, who were unhappy with the end result both because of what they took to be an obscuring sentimentality and because she was celebrated not as a Jew, conscious of the traditions, the values, the faith of a Jew, but as a victim, an everyman whose fate we know but neither learn nor see in the play. *The Deputy*, however, raised further issues.

There is no, or little, question of sentimentality, unless it might be thought that the sight of individuals – men, women, children, marched to their death – could be accused of provoking such, but there is the unavoidable question of melodrama, unavoidable since the collision of innocence and evil can hardly be recast to avoid accusations of bad faith. Are we, then, being invited to respond to a play or a polemic? And can a play sold by the yard possibly invite the kind of textual attention it seems to demand? In certain productions key figures were reduced in significance, whole speeches, indeed several hours of material were stripped out. What is the principle behind such excisions, beyond the pragmatism of those concerned to attract and retain audiences while allowing them to return home before the last bus? Was it the central argument that had to be protected, the most vital and commanding performances, or those moments when language seemed at its most resonant?

In some ways, such problems might seem irrelevant. Was O'Neill's *Strange Interlude* not so long as to require a dinner break? *Strange Interlude*, however, was not offered for filleting nor was it attempting to rectify history, to expose a moral and historical flaw in the representative of one of the world's great religions at the very moment that the fires of Auschwitz were being stoked by the antichrist. Hochhuth was deliberately playing for high stakes. He had news to rush out and the theatre, the most social of all the arts, was his chosen vehicle.

The theatre is a present-tense art. From the Greeks onwards, it has been where a society debates with itself. It offers immediacy. During the civil war in Russia the *Zhivaya Gazeta* staged contemporary events, reading out newspapers and other accounts, along with a commentary. This led to the 'Blue Blouses', founded not by playwrights but by the Institute of Journalists. In the United States, the Federal Theatre staged 'Living Newspapers', which also used journalists, along with actors who performed plays about contemporary events based directly on public documents. The same year as *The Deputy* saw the production, in the United States, of *In White America* by Martin Duberman, a play drawing on documents of African American history. Duberman did not invent characters but interwove dialogue, narration, song. He staged it in the conviction that the past had something to say to the present. Later, Eric Bentley, in *Are You Now or Have You Ever Been*, explored the investigation of show business by the House Un-American Activities Committee in a similar documentary way.

Even when the theatre reaches back to the past it does so, Hochhuth has insisted, by bringing the past before us. As he has a character say in *Soldiers*, the play in which he engages with that other question which had so engaged Sebald, the wartime bombing of Germany:

The theatre isn't a museum.
History only ceases to be academic
When it can illustrate for *us* and *now*
Man's inhumanity to man

It was not that history had a fascination in its own right, inviting nothing more than a detached interest in a past exhausted in its own presentation. What mattered was the pressure the past exerted on the present because

> ...what we and the Germans did twenty years ago,
> has become the A.B.C. of the airmen of *today*.
> Korea, Vietnam, the murdered civilians there –
> That is *our* teaching, the Anglo-Saxon precedent![2]

The risk, of course, was that this instrumental use of the past would devolve into little more than a finger-wagging warning to his contemporaries, bereft of dramatic conviction, beginning with its conclusion, an indictment against which there was to be no appeal since he would choose to articulate the case for the defence when the reason for the play's existence was that there could be no legitimate defence.

Beyond that there lay another risk. The very insistence on contemporary relevance risked denying the unique nature of what he chose to engage, implying that some equivalency existed between willed, systematic genocide and wars which he might choose to identify as unjust. He was inviting judgement. The stage was to be a court, though there was no question, surely, that the verdict could be anything other than guilty, even as he was prepared to make space for pleas in mitigation. He would explain that in *The Deputy* he allowed the accused – Pope Pius XII – to offer an articulate defence on the public platform that he had never offered even in the privacy of the Vatican. But this was not to be a work in which the scales hovered uncertainly between innocence and guilt. A crime had been committed, a crime past understanding. Now a man stood before us whose sin was not to have committed that crime but to have done nothing to prevent it and thus to have been an accomplice before and after the fact.

He becomes a representative, and not simply to the extent that he was God's representative on earth. He was to be representative of all those who, from Hochhuth's point of view at least, failed to meet the challenge. George Steiner observed that

> Below his breath, the Jew asks of his gentile neighbour: 'If you
> had known, would you have cried in the face of God and man
> that this hideousness must stop? Would you have made some
> attempt to get my children out? ...' The Jew is a living
> reproach. *Men are accomplices to that which leaves them
> indifferent* ... The house of civilization proved no shelter.[3]

Indifference on the part of one who seemingly had the power to
rescue the children was a greater crime.

At the heart of the play, besides the forbidding figure of Pope
Pius, are two men prepared to sacrifice themselves for others. Though
one, Father Riccardo, strictly speaking did not exist, being a
composite of others, one certainly did, a man who wore the uniform
of the most dreaded of organisations, that of the SS. As a young man,
Kurt Gerstein, a Protestant, had been a member of a German Lutheran
and Evangelical movement which, from 1934, drew up plans to resist
Hitler's attempts to infiltrate Nazis into church positions. He wrote
articles and distributed anti-Nazi literature, an offence for which he
was imprisoned in a concentration camp. On his release, he was
shocked by the death of a mentally ill relative, murdered by gas as part
of the Nazi programme to destroy the unfit. Anxious to uncover what
was going on he took the extraordinary step of enlisting in the SS,
slowly rising to the rank of lieutenant in which position he found
himself involved in the extermination programme, becoming responsible for the delivery of Zyklon B. In August 1942 he visited Belzec
and the site of what would be Treblinka.

He now set himself to spread knowledge of what was going on,
confronting religious leaders, trying, in particular, to meet with the
Apostolic Nuncio in Berlin. He took amazing risks. In September,
1944, he, and a group of other men, met with Cathedral Capitulary
Buchholz (who ministered to those condemned to death at Plötzen-
see), in his own apartment in order to hear details of the killings. In
his turn, Gerstein offered details of the death camps, the numbers of
those dying and the manner of their deaths. He also passed reports to
Bishop Otto Dibelius, who in turn passed the information on to the

Bishop of Uppsala, though in truth the news had already been passed to the Church.

Having escaped from Birkenau (one of only five Jews to do so), Walter Rosenberg (number 44070), along with his companion Alfred Wetzler, compiled a detailed report of the gassings. He had worked in 'Canada', meeting the reportees and sorting their belongings. He escaped, he later explained, not so much to report a crime as to prevent one, warning of preparation for the arrival and liquidation of Hungarian Jews. He even brought with him a label from a Zyklon B tin. The Vatican's chargé d'affaires in Bratislava smuggled the report to Rome, though it took five months to get there. Meanwhile, it was passed to the Czech Government in Exile in London, the World Jewish Congress and the International Red Cross in Geneva. On 14 June 1944 the Czech and Slovak Service of the BBC broadcast news of the gassings.[4] They were no longer a secret.

Rosenberg escaped as Rudolf Vrba, a name that he kept until his death in 2006, celebrating as his birthdate 7 April, the day of his escape. Once Vrba's reports reached the outside world protests forced Admiral Miklos Horthy, regent of Hungary, to suspend deportations. Some 200,000 Jews in Budapest were saved as a result, though 50,000 of those would die at the hands of Hungarian Fascists. Vrba's memoirs, published in 1963, were called *I Cannot Forgive*. None of this diminishes Gerstein's bravery. All this time he was a trusted SS officer supposedly committed to the destruction of those he risked his life to defend. He was a double agent, a mirror image in some ways of the young Nazis that Heydrich had proposed infiltrating into Catholic seminaries in an attempt to subvert religion from the inside.

Gerstein's was a necessarily equivocal position. He had to simulate loyalty to his leaders while desperately working against them. In the words of Pastor Martin Niemöller, who wrote to the state prosecutor after the war, he 'was prepared to give up honor, family, and life for his cause, and did give them up'.[5] He seems to have succeeded in maintaining his disguise so successfully that after the war he was in all probability killed by the French, having been held in a Paris prison, though his posthumous testimony was presented to a number of trials. In May 1945 he wrote a report, detailing the location of the camps and their methods. It was accurate in almost every detail except the estimated number of victims. When he surrendered to Allied troops he gave them a series of bills for the purchase of Zyklon B written in his own name. The Americans opted not to use this material in the subsequent trials while the French chose to distrust them.

In an essay that accompanies the published version of the play, Hochhuth sets out the evidence on which he had drawn. It includes a letter sent by Gerstein to his father in March 1944, at a time when the war had more than a year to run, and the killings in the camps were accelerating. 'At some juncture', he wrote, 'you will have to stand up with the rest of your times, for what has happened in them. You and I would no longer understand each other and would no longer have anything meaningful to say to one another if I could not say this to you: Do not underestimate this responsibility and this obligation of an accounting. It may come sooner than people think. I am aware of this obligation, granted; I am gnawed by it' (294).

Gerstein was to prove a key figure in Hochhuth's play, and he had begun thinking in terms of drama though he had never written a play before. But on his own Gerstein was no more than a rebel whose actions lacked resonance. Then, another event occurred which would create something of that tension necessary for drama. In 1958, Pope Pius XII died, a figure whose three closest advisers had been German and who was himself much loved in Germany. He was celebrated as a potential saint. Gerstein had never met him, though he worked desperately to provide the information that would lead the church to act. What if the two had confronted one another, the SS lieutenant and God's representative on earth? In the person of Gerstein there was a man who knew at first hand because he was to be implicated in the deaths he struggled so hard to prevent. The Pope had, of course, been in possession of this information, but what if he had been forced to defend himself to the very man charged with bringing about the deaths against which he had so signally refused to protest?

What puzzled Hochhuth was that while 2,500 Catholic priests had died in concentration camps the Pope had never rescinded the concordat between Nazi Germany and the Vatican (though his predecessor had publicly warned against giving racist values priority), never taken overt actions, or made unequivocal statements about the fate of the Jews, even when they were dragged away from under the very walls of the Vatican and within sight of St Peter's. Though Camus had asked, as early as 1944, why Pius had remained silent, Hochhuth himself had not known of it and now set himself to undertake research, though when he did so he found, among much else, Hitler's statement to the Reich Cabinet in July 1933: 'This Concordat, whose contents do not interest me at all, nevertheless creates an area of confidence which will be very useful in our uncompromising struggle against international Judaism' (298). As a result of its utility, however, the Vatican, and the Papal Legations, it seems, were the only authorities Hitler respected after the entry of the United States into the war in 1941. Indeed protests led to a cessation of the euthanasia programme. Why, then, not protest against the genocide? There was certainly no lack of information about the situation of the Jews. People risked their lives to get it out. Public protests were made in Britain and the United States. The Vatican itself had what was effectively an intelligence network, with priests scattered throughout Europe. Yet it offered nothing but the most general of protests, never uttering the word 'Jew', and only once using the word 'race', which it evidently believed would be sufficient.

Gerstein, a Protestant, had risked his life. The Pope, it seemed, had risked nothing, being obsessed with the threat supposedly constituted by a godless Soviet Union against which Germany, whatever its faults, was a bulwark. In the name of realpolitik, it seemed to Hochhuth, he had been prepared to sacrifice millions of Jews and even Catholic clergy, some of whom showed far greater courage than did the Pontiff, guided as they were less by pragmatic politics than by human sympathy. Beyond that lay the still less penetrable mystery of a God who could watch without intervening, a God, indeed, for whom the Pope was a Deputy. In the face of Pius's inaction, the Nazis had seemingly believed there would be no sanction in this life or the next, like Camus's Caligula testing the proposition of actions without consequence: a world ruled not by God but by absurdity.

The second of the play's rebels, Father Riccardo, was invented, though even he was in part modelled on a real figure, Provost Bernhard Lichtenberg of Berlin, who publicly prayed for the Jews and died in Dachau. Lichtenberg is one of two people to whom the play is dedicated. The other is Father Maximilian Kolbe, who died in a starvation cell at Auschwitz, taking the place of another prisoner. Gerstein could not plausibly be permitted access to the Pope; Father Riccardo could, and challenges the Pope because he and his father are presented by Hochhuth as being in the Pope's favour. For W. G. Sebald, Riccardo would be a somewhat suspect figure, like Hermann Ott in Günter Grass's *From the Diary of a Snail*. Of the latter Sebald said he was 'a retrospective figure created by the author's wishful thinking; structurally no different, if of far less fateful import, than the angelic young Father Riccardo Fontano ... who provides evidence that goodwill still exists even in the face of mass annihilation' (*Campo Santo*, 115).[6]

Despite Sebald's enthusiasm for the 'documentary theatre' of the 1960s, this is not a neutral description, not least because he regarded Ott as modelled on what seemed to him to be the suspect notion of the 'good German' much evident in postwar German literature, though in truth Riccardo, unlike such characters, could not be said to have been one of those who 'failed to understand the grave and lasting deformities in the emotional lives of those who let themselves be integrated into the system without questioning it' (116). He did challenge it, and, indeed, sacrifice himself. He was, though, a retrospective figure, and does function in the way Sebald suggests, but there were antecedents.

The play opens in 1942 with Gerstein forcing his way into the presence of the Papal Legation in Berlin. The nuncio, we are told in a note, was described by Baron Ernst von Weizsäcker, State Secretary to the Foreign Office and later Hitler's Ambassador to the Holy See, as preferring to avoid 'elevating the irreconcilable differences between the Curia and the Third Reich into matters of principle' (*The Deputy*, 13). This is the man Gerstein tries to persuade of the urgent need to take a stand against the horrors he has seen. Riccardo had already been urging such action. Both men succeed in doing no more than prompting a justification for inaction.

In the second scene, Gerstein is seen in quite different company, that of Eichmann, a bureaucrat of death so anonymous, Hochhuth notes, that when the war was over nobody bothered to search for him until the Israelis tracked him down in 1960, and Dr Mengele, never named, being merely identified as the Doctor, the 'handsome devil' who made a point of giving sweets to the children on whom he would experiment, and who would console those he parted even as he sent them to the gas chambers. These were, Hochhuth, observed in a note, 'surrealistic scenes'. The scene in his play is no less so as the two men are seen in the company of a German academic, a collector of human skulls. They are relaxing, with drink and a game of bowls.

Hochhuth makes no move to flesh out the figure of Mengele, his refusal to name him being confirmation of the fact that since 'this uncanny visitant from another world was obviously only playing the part of a human being, I have refrained from any further effort to plumb its human features – for these could contribute nothing to our understanding of so incomprehensible a being or its deeds' (32). The use of the third person singular suggests the extent to which he thinks of Mengele as an abstract force. On the face of it, this is an odd decision in the context of a play but, for Hochhuth, Mengele is to perform a part in what is essentially a morality play. He is no more than he seems, an embodiment of evil, towards the end of the play perhaps too completely so, but here is the essence of Hochhuth's problem in trying to shape such experiences into aesthetic form.

Here, too, is another difficulty in that he is anxious to stress the ease with which the business of liquidating millions was accommodated to the quotidian. The instinct is to suggest that those who perpetrated such acts must lie outside the parameters of the human, while he was concerned to demonstrate the more disturbing truth that they were all too human. How, then, to place so close to the centre of his work a man about whom he can say that he 'stands in such contrast not only to his fellows of the SS, but to all human beings, and so far as I know, to anything that has been learned about human beings' (32)? The only defence seems to be that he is in some sense a marker, signifying the extreme outer edge of human possibility, the anti-matter of humankind.

The Deputy may have its roots in historic fact; it may have been seen as an example of documentary theatre. In fact, it leaves documentary behind in a number of ways, nor was this unintentional. Hochhuth did not set out to create a simulated trial, an oral history. Characters grouped together in the *dramatis personae* were to be played by the same actor. Thus the Pope and Baron Rutta of the Reichs Armaments Cartel were to be played by the same person, just as an equivocating priest in the Vatican was to be played by the same actor who assumed the role of an SS sergeant. A cardinal was to be played by the same actor as the collector of skulls. They were so grouped, he claimed, because 'recent history has taught us that ... it is not necessarily to anyone's credit or blame, or even a question of character, which uniform one wears or whether one stands on the side of the victims or the executioners' (12), except, of course, that it manifestly is. We are invited to draw our own conclusions even as those conclusions are shaped for us by his casting strategy.

Beyond that, this is a play in verse: a device, he explained, to enable him to concentrate language. This was a practice also followed by Arthur Miller, who often wrote his plays in verse before moving them into prose. But there is also a sense in which it creates a degree of linguistic distance, even as the language carries with it something of the formality with which, in the play, moral failings are concealed rather than exposed by language. The blunt facts deployed by Gerstein break not so much on the indifference of the Pope as on what are presented as higher principles identifiable as such in part because of the elevated language in which they are expressed. A central strategy deployed by this temporising Pope is precisely to retreat into words, without Hamlet's self-accusing sensibility.

In the second scene of the first act, the Nazis, and those who hope to make or sustain their fortunes by consorting with them, are seen at play. A young woman, seduced by Mengele, is engaged to a lieutenant at Auschwitz and herself hopes to be sent there to be close to him. For her, it is no more than a posting, a place where she might be able to be reunited with the man she believes herself to love, a desire which, for the audience, stands in contrast to those separated in that place. Yet, in the midst of this social occasion there is a brief conversation about the Church's attitude to the deportations. Eichmann is disturbed when he is told that a papal nuncio has been making complaints about them. Bishops, he explains, are insignificant and, indeed, members of the Catholic People's Party had assisted in rounding up the Jews. A nuncio, however, is a representative of the Pope and this can only mean trouble, an indication that the Vatican is to be feared, that it has precisely the power that the Pope disavows and fails to deploy.

For Hochhuth, the point of this early scene is in part to expose the degree to which the death camps did not lie outside daily life. They were discussed at parties as much as at formal meetings by people who, among other things, took pleasure in the arts. We learn that Eichmann played the harmonica, Mengele sang, Heydrich, who is described as having 'a 'Jew's nose for artistic quality', played the cello and read Kleist, activities plainly not incompatible with what happens in the camps but continuous with it, not least because men and women were snatched from death to play in camp orchestras, partly for the entertainment of camp personnel and partly to beat out the rhythm to which the prisoners would march. Art is thus exposed as collaborative. Perhaps, indeed, it is that fact which seems to give a primacy to the documentary as if this alone were purged of a suspect aestheticism. The scene, however, is also plainly designed to establish the vulnerability of the Nazis to church intervention, the possibility that history could have been deflected.

Both issues are picked up in the following scene, in which Gerstein, who has been keeping a Jew hidden in his apartment, meets with Riccardo. Gerstein speaks with 'intense disgust' of the Auschwitz orchestra and challenges Riccardo to commit himself both publicly and personally, the former by confronting the Pope, the latter by giving his passport to the Jew to enable him to escape, receiving in return that Jew's yellow star. Gerstein has committed treason. He is now testing the metal of a man who can gain the access he is himself denied.

The guilt, though, does not, he confesses, lie in Rome alone. 'We Germans are no worse', he insists, than 'the other Europeans.' There are, he accepts, 'scoundrels everywhere' (80). There were, after all, those who helped to hide Jews while the French, Hungarians, Poles and Ukrainians were enthusiastic collaborators. There is, however, something a little less than convincing in this speech, as though it served less the character of Gerstein who, after all knows the truth about the camps, than of Hochhuth, who saw the play as something other than an indictment either of the Germans or, indeed, of Pius XII. What was at stake was a principle. What concerned him was a refusal to accept responsibility for one's actions, a turning aside from human solidarity out of disregard, political or strategic calculation, a denial of that connection between the individual and that wider society of which he was a part. Gerstein accepts that the 'Germans bear the greatest guilt' (81), and there is nothing in the play that would suggest otherwise, but Hochhuth's focus, nonetheless, was designedly broader.

The fact is that for all the particularities of *The Deputy* Hochhuth's target was not, finally, Pope Pius XII. As he confessed, 'To me ... Pius is a symbol, not only for all leaders, but for all men – Christians, Atheists, Jews. For all men who are passive when their brother is deported to death. Pius was at the top of the hierarchy and, therefore, he had the greatest duty to speak. But every man – the Protestants, the Jews, Churchill, Eden, Cordell Hull [Secretary of State of the United States] – all had the duty to speak.' He was not, he insisted, as he was accused of doing, attempting to absolve the Germans by directing attention elsewhere. As he remarked, 'The arsonist does not become less guilty because a fireman resigns in front of a great fire.'[7] Nonetheless, the play is entitled *The Deputy*, and his attention is not primarily on those who lit the fire but those, like Pope Pius, who watched it burn, intent primarily, as it seemed to him, on seeing that it did not extend onto their own territory. The Pope is not accused of cowardice. Who could know how they would fare if confronted with the need to take actions that could endanger them or those for whom they care? He is charged with calculation, with a hierarchy of values that places the saving of Jews below the safeguarding of an institution, that hesitates to condemn one criminal on the grounds that he might safeguard against a greater.

For many, there were a number of problems with Hochhuth's defence. Firstly, what were the Jews doing in his list? Secondly, in so far as he was concerned with a generalised passivity he was deflecting attention not simply from the Germans but from the Holocaust, whose specificity was, to some, central, unique, isolated in both its enormity and its procedures. Indeed, he specifically insists that 'the terror against the Jews in our time is only one example of the terror which reigns on earth at all times, in all epochs, in all centuries' (43). He even invokes the Christians in Rome, the Inquisition and, in what struck some as an ultimate reductiveness, McCarthy's persecution of the Communists, who, to be sure, lost their livelihoods and the freedoms they thought granted by the American Constitution, but not their families, their humanity or, for the most part, their lives. Arthur Miller, in *The Crucible*, wrote an allegory prompted by that same McCarthyite assault on individual integrity, and confessed to seeing a shadow reach out from the Holocaust, but no more than that. When, in *After the Fall*, Miller asserted a connection between private acts of betrayal in the family and the camps, he was challenged not merely for his presumption but for failing to understand that questions of scale may become questions of kind. When he wrote *Incident at Vichy*, a play that concerns the rounding up of Jews in Vichy France preparatory to sending them to a fate not known in its details to the characters but known to us, who watch, he sought to relate this to the situation in Harlem. Both writers trod a dangerous edge and were upbraided accordingly. The wider the circles spread, in time and space, the more the immediate and irremediable pain seems generalised away. And besides, Pius was at the top of one hierarchy, but only one. What gave him primacy?

Hochhuth's point about the Jews was contentious but not without some justification. Many American Jews had been nervous, before the country's direct involvement in the war, that too active a pressure would make them appear anxious to edge America into the conflict. Zionists, in particular, felt that their priority lay in the establishment of a Jewish state, doubting that anything much could be done for those beyond their reach. For Hochhuth, then, Pope Pius was to stand for all those who looked away, refused to act, found personal, social, political, justifications for a failure of moral purpose.

The second act takes the action to Rome, where Riccardo confronts a cardinal. In the third act, a German staff sergeant of the Waffen-SS and two Italians of the Fascist Militia seize a Jewish family in that same city even as they plan escape. Some, we learn, have escaped, being hidden by a religious order, representative of the Church's effort to protect a few in the city's monasteries, though often on the assumption that they are baptised and therefore legitimately part of the Church's concern. In the office of one such order, Gerstein, desperate to urge action, some acknowledgement of the nature and extent of the problem and the obligation, comes face to face with a cardinal. The cardinal takes pride in what he takes to be a humanitarian gesture, especially if 'a good many of the Jews / will be converted to the faith', a statement which undermines his apparent generosity of spirit (143). A confrontation with Gerstein and Riccardo, however, disturbs his complacency: 'why won't you stop / that business with the Jews!' he asks, insisting that their intervention might force the Pope to act, as if that were not the point of the argument. 'Are you so limited', he asks, 'as not to see / that any anathema against Hitler by the Curia / will become a fanfare of victory / for the Bolsheviks?' (147).

Gerstein pleads for even a secret threat to break the Concordat. The cardinal appears to bow to the argument, only to repeat his point, suggesting to Gerstein that 'the smoke of the crematoria / has blinded you to the fact that there must be / an alternative to conquest of the territories by the Red Army' (149). With the future of Europe in the balance, he suggests, Gerstein is advancing the cause of the few against the many, the relief of immediate suffering against the movement of history. Nonetheless, even the cardinal feels that deportations at the heart of Rome have raised the stakes and may precipitate action. For Riccardo, if no action is taken silence will incur a guilt on the part of the Church for which there could be no atonement.

For his part, Gerstein goes to the Gestapo headquarters in an effort to deflect the fate of those arrested, though a note warns that the Nazi officer to whom he speaks was later sentenced to life imprisonment for his murder of thirty-five hostages, one more than required by his orders. Gerstein hints that the higher command may already be in negotiations and that should the war end anyone thought to be involved in deportation and murder might find themselves exposed. His suggestion that the Pope might himself be about to intervene disturbs the equanimity even of such a man as this. Hochhuth is plainly suggesting that even hints at papal displeasure might have been sufficient to have some effect, as they do in this scene. A reported letter from the bishop is dismissed as being of no account. 'If only this damn Pope / would tell us bluntly where he stands!' laments the SS officer. 'If he gives us a free hand the way he's done, / and thinks this letter from the bishop is enough / to square things with his dear old Christian conscience – then I've got to start deporting tonight' (189).

It is only in the fourth act that we enter the Vatican itself. The Pope's first words in the play are expressions of concern for Italy's factories, power plants, railroad terminals and dams, all of which, he insists, are in need of protection. He has issued a plea to be followed by a protest, and fully expects a positive response. The Germans, on this and other matters, have, he confesses, shown 'more friendliness' than the Allies who have destroyed Church property. At this moment he receives two cheques from the Jesuits, removing his glasses to see the figures more clearly. After three acts which have focussed on the plight of the Jews the irony is too pointed. He regards the deportations as no more than 'tactless', 'extremely bad behaviour' (198). What he will not do is protest.

The Pope portrayed by Hochhuth swings from wilful denial to naivety. 'Hitler', he declares, 'is no longer dangerous' (200). He looks to a negotiated peace that will leave Europe secure from the atheistic Communists. For a Machiavelli, he seems remarkably uncertain in his grasp of geopolitics, tactics or strategy. 'Hitler alone', he declares, 'is now defending Europe' (206). It is August 1942. The Europe Hitler is supposedly defending is largely under his heel.

Hochhuth has provided sources for much of his material. He has also, however, given himself licence. The confrontation between the Pope and Riccardo did not occur, nor that with Gerstein. It follows that the debate itself did not take place, nor did the Pope mimic

Pilate's gesture: 'We are – God knows it – blameless of the blood / now being spilled. As the flowers / in the countryside wait beneath winter's mantle of snow / for the warm breezes of spring / so the *Jews* must wait, praying and trusting / that the hour of heavenly comfort will come' (220–1). The comfort they can expect is made manifest in the final act, which takes the action to Auschwitz.

Here he confronts a familiar problem with the Holocaust – how imaginatively to enter the camps, this man who never himself went there. As he explains in a note to the text – a confession, incidentally, invisible in the stage production – 'We lack the imaginative faculties to be able to envisage Auschwitz, or the destruction of Dresden and Hiroshima.' Oddly, though, he adds to the list 'exploratory flights into space, or even more mundane matters such as industrial capacity and speed records', and, still more oddly, the observation that 'Man can no longer grasp his accomplishments.' What is the connection between Auschwitz and human accomplishments? The challenge to the imagination, it seems, is presented by a whole range of events and discoveries.

The representation of Auschwitz itself led Hochhuth away from any attempt at documentary realism. There should, he insisted, be no attempt 'to strive for an imitation of reality – nor should the stage set strive for it' (223). He was equally wary, however, of metaphor which seemed to him more likely to conceal rather than expose the cynicism of a site of mass murder. The problem, clearly, was that 'a reality so enormous and grotesque' left the writer disabled, not least because the unreality of such a place seemed to lead in the direction of apocalyptic fable. Nor was he drawn to Brechtian alienation techniques in that the detachment they were designed to promote could only struggle against the gravitational pull of events which precisely conspired against rationality. He acknowledges the difficulty even in visiting Auschwitz, where the immediate surroundings are designed to prompt an imaginative possession of the place and its meaning. It is precisely the systematic processes that led to this place, the murders conducted by people who came from their ordinary occupations and were to return to them that defies the mind. Only 700 of the 8,000 who served at Auschwitz were ever tried for their crimes, many of whom, indeed, continued to deny either that they were involved or that they were crimes, since only a handful of the SS were actually involved in the gas chambers or the crematoria. Faced with these problems, Hochhuth places weight on the fact that the Doctor remains anonymous, not specified by name precisely because he is the embodiment of a particular evil (though it is hard to see how this militates against apocalyptic fable), and on a number of features, including monologues, designed precisely to disturb what he plainly fears will be the reassurance of familiar forms.

Thus it is that we enter the final act in near darkness and with a series of monologues 'spoken and thought' inside a freight car en route from Italy. There is a radical break between the preceding acts and this place, isolated, seemingly, in its own particularity. This is the place about which the arguments between the Pope and those urgent to engage him had waged. In the background we hear the pounding of the train's wheels.

The first monologue is that of an Old Man, no more identified by Hochhuth than he would be by the Nazis, a man in contention not with a Pope but with God himself. It is this argument which surely lies behind Hochhuth's with his Deputy if this play is to grapple with anything more than the pragmatics of government, a failure rooted in concerns of state. Whatever the controversy that would rage over Hochhuth's portrait of the Pope, his concentration on Catholic responsibility when the perpetrators came from a partly Protestant Germany and those with real power commanded regiments on earth, what stunned a generation into silence was a far more profound abandonment, a version of mankind not as cynically manipulative but capable of the unimaginable, and God as denying his grace to those in extremis.

The old man's words are shaped into a poem which is less a lament than an accusation:

> Whatever You may be, You terrible God
> Your heaven is above us, and the hangmen
> Are men like us, authorized by You.
> Are You watching now?

It is not that he has lost his faith. He does not doubt God's existence, merely his nature, asking a question that fuses depraved man with the God who created him.

> Untrammelled God – is man most like You
> At his most untrammelled? Is he
> Such a pit of depravity, because You
> Have created him in Your own image? (224)

The irony is that beside this desperation, what has preceded it in the play seems both prosaic and beside the point. Of course, if the Pope had been persuaded to intervene and if his intervention had indeed been able to overturn such a fundamental commitment of the Nazi state, this man would not have been on this train. But before the death camps became policy, they were imagined. They existed in the human mind. If the police in the conquered countries had not collaborated, even enthusiastically, if the railway lines had been bombed, if declarations had been made more loudly, more unequivocally, there might have been some ameliorisation. Some, at least, could thereby have been saved. But the thing itself, planned in great detail, a triumph of logistics, of genuine rigour, came unbidden into an individual mind and from thence into the minds of others because, it turned out, there were no limits, no constraints. The difficulty of *The Deputy* is that until this moment, and for all the recitation of horrors, and the identification of failures to protest, this truth has been held at arm's length.

In the elaborate notes which Hochhuth assembles to support the published version of the play, he gathers together examples of bishops or priests who protested with some effect, almost as if he were desperate not merely to indict the Pope for his failures but to sustain a version of man and even God that merited something more than despair. The play, indeed, risks sliding into melodrama in its final section as German depravity comes up against the flawed goodness of the martyr, as if Hochhuth wished to withdraw from too absolute a contemplation of the void. There is something more than a tonal change when the action moves through the limbo of the freight train to the hell of the camp by way of the Old Man who clings to his fate even as he recognises the corruption of his God. His prayers now smack of a tainted bargain. All he asks in return for belief is not to die in front of his grandchildren, even as a young woman beside him feels the threat to the child in her womb which, if it is born at all, will indeed, as Beckett said, be born astride the grave. A young girl, herself next to the pregnant woman as she approaches the fires, is struck by the certainty that 'God is cold' (226). Even the lyrical prose of her lament creates an ironic tension as she pitches her memories against a frightening reality, regretting that she had not surrendered to her lover as if this were a metaphysical poem about a coy mistress and not one last desperate cry of pain.

At this point a different sound cuts across this bruised language. Even as she addresses her absent lover, saying, 'Take, take once more / The sand of Ostia into your hands / And throw a handful to the waves, / As though it were my ashes, / And call my name, / As you did that time, in Ostia' (226–7), so the noise of shunting and sliding doors, the brutal orders of the Kapos, rings out. Dogs bark, whistles are blown, steam escapes from the engine and a woman shouts out 'Rachele', the name of the Biblical figure whose children were scattered. They have arrived.

This is only the first of a series of disjunctions. In four pages of notes, Hochhuth describes not only the set as he imagines it, but the world which he cannot imagine. The set is 'dreamlike' and 'ghostly', even as the underworld of the crematorium 'exceeds imagination', there being 'no way of conveying it' (228). As the men and women move across the back of the stage, behind an unnaturally orderly guardroom, towards their death, so Helga, the attractive switchboard operator, is woken by an alarm clock for the beginning of a day which to her is part of the normality of life at Auschwitz, a normality described by the Commandant of the camp in the memoir he wrote as he awaited his execution. It is precisely this normality, this accommodation of mass slaughter not only to the routines of military life but the daily business of social life, that is the root of a particular horror. It was, as Hochhuth reminds us, a place of work, where the Germans conducted love affairs, partied, played games.

The killing of huge numbers of people was normalised, broken down into discrete tasks, many of which involved no contact with those who would be killed and incinerated, though the pall of smoke which lingered over the camp and the omnipresent smell must have caused at least some inconvenience when it came to picnics or party clothes. Meanwhile, those prisoners not immediately murdered were sent to work at the I. G. Farben factory, processed by those who Hochhuth assures us will move with ease into the world of postwar Germany ostensibly with scarcely a glance back to the days when their skills were deployed to eliminate an entire race.

The remainder of the play essentially concentrates on the fate of Riccardo and Gerstein, the former having joined the deportees from Rome, partly to comfort them, partly as a gesture of martyrdom, the latter attempting to rescue him. They are confronted by the Doctor, a man whose dialogue is at times naturalistic, at times not. He declares, 'I cremate life, / I create life – / and always I create suffering' (237). He is, it seems, the Devil incarnate, sleeping with a Jewish woman whose children he has had killed for the sheer pleasure of seeing her reaction when she learns the truth. He is a scientist in more than his profession. He is curious to dissect more than the bodies of the children to whom he distributes sweets before having them killed. He is drawn to those who resist for the pleasure of breaking their resistance.

Riccardo, he decides, is not to be permitted the role of martyr, implausible anyway in a place where people die anonymously, 'like a snail crushed under an auto tire' (245). The Doctor insists, indeed, that he has been conducting an experiment with God, killing with impunity. 'I took the vow to challenge the Old Gent, / to provoke him so limitlessly / that he would have to give an answer. / Even if only the negative answer / which can be His sole excuse, as Stendhal put it: that He doesn't exist' (247). Auschwitz has destroyed the concept of God, unless it be a God who takes pleasure in 'turning the human race / on the spit of history' (248), unless it be this man with the power of life and death. And along with God, the very idea of tragedy collapses, based, as it is, on the individual's struggle with determinism, snatching a subjective victory from an external defeat. Here death is designed to be meaningless.

Auschwitz, the Doctor insists, serves to refute not so much God as the idea of a meaningful existence, just as the Church, he is inclined to say, has done in slaughtering the innocent through the ages to serve its own idea of power, its definition of what was of value and what was dross. Life as an idea, he observes, 'is dead' (248). Auschwitz is no more than the logical extension of a resisted truth. 'Your church', he tells the young priest, 'was the first to show / that you can burn men like coke' (249). Riccardo is to be kept alive as the Devil's chaplain. His function is to dispute with him and, indeed, they continue with a Shavian dialogue as Riccardo suggests that since he is standing next to the Devil that in itself is the evidence for the existence of God. Even as they speak, however, in the background figures move towards their death, a fire glows red and we hear a crescendo of sound.

At this point Gerstein arrives, determined to rescue Riccardo, now forced by Mengele to work at the crematorium extracting teeth from the dead. He claims that he is under instruction from Eichmann himself to secure his release. Riccardo refuses, insisting that another man should be smuggled out in his place, the very man to whom he had given his passport earlier in the play and who is living under his name, a rather too neat coincidence which gives him the chance to rescue the same man twice. However, the Devil is everywhere and the Doctor discovers their plans. The play ends in a curiously maladroit way. A woman who has witnessed the plot collapses in madness. The Doctor shoots her in the head. Riccardo is then shot by an SS man. Gerstein is led out as the taped voice of an actor reads a statement released by the Pope on 25 October 1943, in which he extended his paternal solicitude to all men without distinction of nationality and race. This was the closest he came to speaking out for the Jews.

For Erwin Piscator, director of the Freie Volksbühne in Berlin, who first staged the play in 1963, a year after the execution of Eichmann, it was a historical drama in Schiller's sense, depicting man as a free agent, acting in knowledge of 'categorical ethical, essentially human behavior' (11). There is something decidedly odd about such a comment, as there is in his assertion that this freedom was possessed by all under the Nazis. Without accepting the fact of such freedom, he insists, we disclaim the guilt which sprang from our inaction, and

138

block true access to the past. The comments are clearly directed at those who chose to conspire or resist. What they do not do is address the supposed freedom of the victims. His comments address the moral, social and political within the play but not the metaphysical. The play ends with martyrs, who die knowing why they meet their deaths, but in the final act we also encounter those who drift across the back of the action, driven into the gas chambers and thence the ovens. What freedom did they have? There was no time even to shape their deaths into some meaning. The real terror of the camps, after all, was that they meant nothing. They served no purpose beyond themselves. This was a reflexive, self-referring world.

The argument with the Pope is with a man, who did indeed have a choice, even if the debate as presented in the play never in fact took place. The argument with God is a monologue. As Mengele is made to say, his silence offers a sanction to one whose choice is annihilation. The Pope is silent for reasons of state. God is silent for reasons which are as impenetrable as they are implacable. There are, in other words, two plays in *The Deputy*. The Pope, by his office, is a deputy, an agent. He refuses to intervene because to do so, he fears, would be to threaten the Church and risk the souls of those who might fall under the heel of Communism. The Nazis are not good Catholics or Protestants, but they do at least simulate belief. The principal does not intervene because once freedom is granted it becomes necessary to accept the consequences even if at the extreme that freedom is rendered null.

Hochhuth travelled into the past to indict. Initially that indictment is directed at a man, and through him at other men. There is, however, another indictment lodged which depends less on a particular time and place, less on a specific ideology. The play was indignantly rejected by many, especially those in the Church who sought to defend the reputation of a dead prelate. They appear not to have noticed, perhaps because Hochhuth drew no attention to it, that beyond the attack on the Pope lay a far more profound assault. Those who killed so mercilessly killed because they could, because they were sanctioned, because they had the capacity. They had it in them to do this and if they, then us. Piscator responded to the play precisely because, as he explained, he wished to 'check [a] general forgetfulness, this general desire to forget in matters of our most recent history' (12). Piscator's experiences of the First World War had taught him which realities he had to deal with. They had to do with the political, with economic and social oppression, with 'political, economic, social struggle' (14). Theatre was a place where such concerns could be staged. It was designed not as a contemplation of the past but as an agent of change through understanding. It was to break a silence in order to make it possible to speak again of what had been suppressed, to accept what had been denied. In short, the play he welcomed was the play he wished to see staged.

Nor was he wrong in thinking that Hochhuth shared such a vision. It is just that there is a counter current in *The Deputy* which dares to question the logic of its own polemical stance. Hochhuth suggested that 'history is man's great fatality' (*The Deputy*, 56), a phrase inspired by his reading of the German historian Mommsen and Theodor Lessing's *History as Rationale of the Irrational*, whose thesis seemed to have found its apotheosis and vindication when the latter himself was shot dead by the Nazis as he sat in his study. While insisting on the human capacity to act, Hochhuth was equally struck by the near impossibility of doing so. At one moment he is suggesting that in life as in drama the existence of choice is fundamental; at the next he is recalling a sentence from Mommsen concerning the invasion of Sicily – 'The men were killed; their women and children distributed among the soldiery' (56) – a sentence which strikes him as containing the whole of history and which anticipated the apparently intransitive nature of mass killing in the Third Reich.

The contradiction between history as fate and the necessity of choice was, he explained, the essence of the fatality to which he referred. Man should be master of his fate, yet he is always being defeated. For some, of course, that is the substance of tragedy and there seem moments when Hochhuth appears to be shaping himself to create such. But again there is a counter current since tragedy – and he uses the word several times – is precisely what was destroyed in the camps, which were less the continuation of history than its end, less evidence of the need for individual action than proof of its impossibility. The Pope might have been persuaded to speak out – his predecessor might have done so – but this in itself seems evidence for a more profound irony. Hochhuth reports a visit by a Jesuit priest who protested against what seemed to him the humanism of the play, saying that 'man is not really the measure of all things. Antiquity is wrong when it asserts that man is the measure of all things ... Man is excrement, at least in the aspect of eternity' (60). Hochhuth offered the story as a justification for his own humanism but the problem he confronts, and which he is honest enough to allow to bleed into his play, is that history seems not to dissent from this proposition.

This is not to suggest that he has created a play in which Beckett nestles inside Brecht but that he glimpses issues which transcend the question of whether the Pope wilfully betrayed the Jews, or was simply guilty of the sin of omission. Bring the background figures, the shadows at the rear of the stage, into the light, and move the melodrama of good confronting evil closer to the cyclorama and the emphasis changes. Yes, there were questions to be answered about strategy, tactics, policy, polity. The questions which stunned a generation, however, were not these, which were easily if not always convincingly answered: American Jews remained silent because they had no wish to have people believe that this war was of their making or for their advantage; the railway lines were not bombed because precision bombing in World War II was seldom precise and anyway such lines could be repaired within hours; the camps were not bombed because there were other priorities and perfectly sane and reasonable men believed that more would be saved by bringing about an early end to the war; the Pope did not speak out because he feared that the Soviet Union was more of a threat, Jesuitical reasoning perhaps but in the end not wholly wrong given Stalin's destruction of millions simply because they were an obstruction. (For his part, Primo Levi did ask why the Allies had not acted but at the same time insisted that 'one cannot speak of a true complicity, and the moral and judicial difference between those who do and those who allow it to be done remains immeasurable'.[8])

The real question, which seemed to block off avenues to thought itself, was how such a thing could have happened, how we should look on our shared humanity now that we knew of what we were all capable, what we truly share. This did not lend itself to polemics. This was not the play that the self-confessedly optimistic Piscator wished to stage or even recognised behind the immediacy of disputation, heroics, private decisions raised to the level of general principle. The Catholic clergy who sprang to Pius's defence sought to defend the head of the Church; they did not challenge the silence of God that gave birth to other silences which lasted decades. *The Deputy* is, indeed, a subversive play, but its subversiveness cuts a deal deeper than its first director and perhaps its author fully understood.

Hochhuth's 'lecture for the future', itself something of a reductive description, is presumably based on the faith that in future authority should speak out, that moral paralysis should be recognised for what it is. The odd thing, though, is that this is a secular lesson. God was dead and it was that which made everything possible and therefore some things necessary. There were others who drew a far more radical lesson from the past which they then passed onto the future. Arthur Miller put it well when he indicated that with God dead it was necessary to re-invent him as men sought sanction outside themselves for the necessity that they felt within. God was the projection of their own best possibilities. The dialogue which mattered was thus with their own capacities, which extend across the whole spectrum from the Devil Doctor to the man who offers his own life for that of another, as he does here and as he would in Miller's *Incident at Vichy*, a play which also had its roots in fact but for which fact was not the true source of legitimacy. Art, after all, has its own structures and language. It creates the metaphor within which it chooses to operate. It works on the mind, however, not by insisting on the precision with which it refracts history or even re-invents it to give it a keener edge, as in *The Deputy*, but by creating tensions born out of its own propositions.

The Deputy is not a documentary drama, though Hochhuth assembles sixty-five pages of notes and at least one production used elements of this. The notes are offered as a claim of authenticity. In a play about good and bad faith this was clearly perceived as vital. Yet the mere act of shaping such material into art only begins the process of refashioning that past to serve a dramatic purpose and here the transformations the writer effects are considerable, beyond the moulding of prose into verse. Much of the action, in strict terms, never happened. The confrontations which focus the debate are Hochhuth's invention. The play is threaded through with material for which he can offer a source but most of it is reconceived by the imagination, albeit working under the pressure of a moral imperative.

Two years later, Robert Lowell would plunder less history than history as refracted through literature in *The Old Glory*, a response, in part, to the first stirrings of the Vietnam war but, beyond that, an exploration of American racism and violence. Hochhuth turns to historical records and such documents as he can assemble, shaping the past. If memory plays its role it is at more than one remove. The story that memory and history tell, however, was entirely his choice.

Perhaps the most forensic critic of the play was Karl Jaspers, German, anti-Nazi, who admired it for the attention it attracted to the plight of the Jews but suspected a fundamental evasion. It was not, after all, entitled 'The Murder of the Jews', he pointed out. It was an attack on the Pope, and that, he suspected, was what had given it much of its appeal. The guilt of the German was present but not the point of the play. It was the Pope who was the focus of opprobrium. To be sure, beyond him were others who failed to act, but they are listed in the notes, called, perhaps oddly, 'Sidelights on History', as if these were less significant failures. What Jaspers wanted was a different history, one that would track back through a history of anti-Semitism. For Hochhuth, a non-Catholic, to suggest that the Pope must bear the burden struck Jaspers as unacceptable, the more especially since the Catholics, whose sacrifices had led him to dedicate the play to them, had never expressed doubts about the Pontiff while Riccardo seems curiously void of a faith to be tested. He is prepared to challenge the Pope because he is not presented as someone who has any respect for the Papacy beyond its potential as a sounding board for essentially humanistic concerns. Finally, Jaspers notes that the dialogue with an absent God is not simply logically intransitive, it is simply not examined for its implications in terms of the rest of the play.

What, he seems to ask, is this play, an indictment of a flawed Pope, of the Western powers, of the Germans, or of God? To that last concern he discerns not only no answer but a hesitation to venture into the void which Hochhuth had apparently so carefully opened up. Indeed, in a sense this theological, anti-theological argument is beside the point. For the fact is that it amounts to an argument about the meaning of genocide, as if it were a proposition that could be usefully debated. The true terror is that it existed entirely to one side of logical discourse and ontological inquiry. There was no meaning. Even Hitler's tendentious justifications were rooted in mythologies with no substance. Beyond the Jews were homosexuals, Communists, the Poles, Russians. Hell was not a concept; it was an ever-expanding proposition based on the conviction that human life was a currency with no worth. Nor was the slaughter carried out by those who had any need of a theology, an ideology, or anything beyond obedience to command and a relish for the rigour and inventiveness with which they went about what they had been told was their difficult business.

Hochhuth had, Jaspers concedes, forced his audiences to think. The fate of the Jews lies at the very centre, even if they (somewhat curiously) do not, existing to the side of the arguments which swirl around them, seemingly accepting their lack of agency. Hochhuth had broken a silence, and that was what had attracted Sebald. What he had not done, as it seems to Jaspers, was to follow the logic of his own play, distracted by his ostensible subject, a man who was God's deputy, but also a man.

What he had also not done, unfair though the criticism might seem, was to see the Jews outside the role in which they were cast by the Nazis but also – and in a wholly different way – by the playwright himself. The paradigm of those who act is Riccardo, a Catholic. We are told of two other Catholic martyrs, as we are of Jews sheltered in monasteries. A German shelters a Jew who not once but twice puts others at risk in order to escape himself. The other Jews we see fail to act in time and are swept off to the camps, are driven mad by the world in which they find themselves, or trudge, so many shadows, towards what they seemingly accept as their fate. It is not that he should have written against the grain of history and shown them as rebels, resisters (though there were such, and not a few), but that the very emphasis on those non-Jewish individuals who act seems to suggest a world in which free action was a sustainable proposition for some but not for others.

As a play, *The Deputy* is an unwieldy piece. Even Piscator, having said that people should be prepared to sit still for as long as it took to play, cut the text, as did virtually everyone who produced it. How are we to feel if we are bored by a play seemingly about the destruction of the Jews? The result was that there was not one play but many. Nor did the verse function as it did in *The Old Glory*, a play, admittedly, by a poet. There is little evidence that it did encourage brevity and concision and, except in a few speeches, little evidence that it served to raise polemic in the direction of tragedy. The play also had a curious impact. In Paris, some audience members shouted out insults against the Jews, while in America not only Catholic but Jewish organisations opposed its production. The Jewish Anti-Defamation League went so far as to defend Pope Pius's silence, one of its members writing a pamphlet for the National Catholic Welfare Conference insisting that for the Pope to have spoken out would have inhibited the Catholic Church from working for the Jews in other ways. Meanwhile, neo-Nazis picketed the play when it was produced.

The Deputy is not a product of testimony. It is history shaped into an accusation. It is, though, as if one indicted the witness of the crime for failing to do his duty and thereby compounding the crime, while at the same time recoiling from the crime as if it is past examining. There is guilt enough to share around, and none too distant in time or place not to deserve a share. Hochhuth had every right to indict those he chose and suggest that one man's failure can stand for the failure of all. Yet somehow he permits himself to go to the very heart of a mystery only to turn away as if the answer is not to be sought in such a place. If the Pope had spoken unequivocally, perhaps some mitigation might have come about, not only in the immediate horrors but in those which had been gathering force through the centuries and which had erupted in the past and would do again, though that past, and the questions it raised, is not interrogated. But there is a prior question, altogether more terrifying than one's man's failure of nerve, one man's calculation, a question which would still lie on the table when Pol Pot slaughtered his millions, and the Pope could have done nothing, or when, in Rwanda, tribe slaughtered tribe and the cries once again were heard by no one, or if heard were ignored almost as if such events were like a tide that must ebb and flow.

As a play *The Deputy* has its weaknesses. Its tumble of characters often seem to exist as exemplary figures. The moving verse of the monologues highlights the arbitrariness and perhaps necessary flatness of many of the other speeches, where the verse form seems without purpose. The Pope is presented as autocratic yet is oddly prepared to listen to harangues from a young man with no real standing. Within the larger play are a number of others not so much implausible as clichéd – a realist sketch about Jews who fail to escape being rounded up by the Fascists, another about a Jew who attempts escape dressed as a cleric. The final section, in Auschwitz, of necessity represents a shift in style, but the Doctor becomes such a conscious diabolist that there seems no attempt to do anything with him but make him a figure in a morality tale, which in itself is to risk giving meaning to the ultimately meaningless. Alfred Kazin, a subtle critic, thought this pretentious and false. Certainly it seems to belong in another play. This is not a figure who would have cared what the Pope thought or said. It is also a protection against the wider significance of the play, a significance brought out by Peter Brook in his Paris production in which all the actors wore the same plain clothes, merely putting on identifying elements as they played their roles, thus undermining any suggestion of a distinction between those who, offered the opportunity, killed, and those who thought it politic to look away.

The Church in Germany capitulated early, not least because Nazi anti-Semitism built on the foundations of centuries of such. Ideas of racial purity found fertile soil. As Guenther Lewy pointed out, Cardinal Faulhaber even denounced the Jews as wanderers to whom he owed no duty. Bishop Hilfrich of Limburg insisted in 1939 that the Jews were guilty of the murder of God while a handbook edited by Archbishop Gröber referred to 'the Jew Karl Marx' and spoke of bolshevism as in the service of 'a group of terrorists led by Jews' (199). The Pope spoke for a Church whose history was intimately involved with anti-Jewish sentiment. To expect it to risk itself in the name of those it had historically rejected was perhaps too much to hope for and certainly not an idea explored by Hochhuth whose interest in history stops short at the Nazis.

Nearly forty years later the controversy still raged on the pages of the Catholic *Commentary* magazine. Kevin Madigan noted the success of Hochhuth's play, translated into more than twenty languages, but dismissed it for the crudeness of its portrait of the Pope, a crudeness 'that marks every line of his drama'.[9] He then observed that the Jewish-owned *New York Times* had praised the Pope as 'a lonely voice crying out of the silence of a continent', and that the Reich's principal security office, at least, had seen the Pope's intervention as 'one long attack on everything we stand for', and him as 'the mouthpiece of the Jewish war criminals' (50). Golda Meir, then foreign minister of Israel, had praised Pius XII on his death in 1958, while a committee set up by Pope Paul VI to investigate the justice of the accusations vindicated him. However, Madigan also noted that by October 1943, at the absolute latest (*The Deputy* opens in August, 1943), the Vatican had detailed knowledge of the camps. The Pope had not, he acknowledged, been silent, but he had not been anywhere near as robust as he was on other matters. He permitted members of the Church to assist Jews without himself taking the kind of stance that might have made a difference.

The article, scarcely unbalanced, inspired a ferocious response. Critics pointed out that the British historian Owen Chadwick had praised the Pope for putting himself at risk by relaying a secret offer of surrender by the German general staff in 1940, the courier who had brought the offer to him being captured and tortured by the Gestapo. They stressed that by his actions he had saved many more Jews than Oskar Schindler or Raoul Wallenberg, the Swedish diplomat. Correspondents itemised the consistent failure of America's Jewish leaders to speak out, from 1933, when the American Jewish Committee with B'nai B'rith opposed demonstrations for fear of inflaming matters, to the American Jewish Congress opposition, in 1935, to laws which would have eased Jewish immigration to America, to the inaction of Jewish organisations immediately after Kristallnacht. Even following

Hochhuth's play, it was pointed out, the Anti-Defamation League concluded that a public protest by the Pope would have provoked a brutal retaliation while inhibiting Catholic efforts on behalf of the Jews. After all, when the Dutch Catholic bishops protested in 1942, the Nazis deported Jews who had converted to Catholicism.

Where does this leave Hochhuth and his play? It was never offered as a balanced account. It was a response to what he perceived to be a betrayal. There is no doubt that his thumb was securely on the scales. On the other hand, it is a rare dramatist that can provoke a papal enquiry and the release of some, if not all, relevant Vatican documents. As a drama it was in many respects crude. Its approach to character was far from subtle, its language, for all its presentation as verse, frequently flat. The idea that a play could simply extend towards eight hours and that directors should be invited to cut to size hardly suggests a form whose integrity was to be respected, even by its author. He revisited the past not through memories – he had access to none – but through those public documents which are the stuff of national memory, though when he wrote by no means all of these were available to him. But, as Primo Levi remarked, documentary evidence is itself inadequate. It 'almost never has the power to give us the depths of a human being; for this purpose the dramatist or poet are more appropriate than the historian or psychologist', though whether such depths are plumbed by Hochhuth is doubtful.[10] Meanwhile, the failure of others than the Pope did not form part of his concern, and as a result he tended to place a significance on his actions that is difficult to justify, alongside the responsibility of national leaders and the silence of so many Jewish organisations.

Should this be the concern of a writer? What, indeed, were Hochhuth's priorities? If it was to poke a stick in the wasp's nest, it had its desired effect. If it was to create a powerful play which staged a genuine dialectic through believable characters speaking a believable language, it is hard to believe he succeeded.

This, however, was not the end of *The Deputy*. Almost forty years after its premiere, in 2002 Costa-Gavras released a film version with the somewhat ambiguous title *Amen*.

4 Peter Weiss: the investigation

W. G. Sebald was not simply drawn to the past, to history, biography, buildings and places that retained an aura of people and events long disappeared. He travelled, in fact and imagination, in memory, his own and that of others, to remote times and places to which he felt a thread of connection, obscure sometimes, a product, perhaps, of echoes and seeming chance. The dead exerted a particular pull, as if they were the conservators of knowledge, holding the answer to mysteries which defied easy understanding. At times they seemed to speak to him.

He was attracted to the work of Peter Weiss for a number of reasons but perhaps this was one cause of his feelings of affinity. After all, Weiss himself remarked that 'we live with our dead. Each of us has memories of persons no longer present. As long as we exist they also endure. We often get into conversations with them. Our very existence is a consequence of theirs ... I live with many dead.'[1] As Sebald would move, in his career, towards a fascination with the dead of the camps, and the anguished survivors, so, too, did Weiss. Friends had died in the camps. He tried to secure the release of one of them, Lucie Weisberger, from Theresienstadt. Perhaps that was why, many years later, when he wrote a play about the camps, *The Investigation*, it was the fate of one young woman that clearly fascinated him. In a play in which the victims have no names, only one is singled out as if he could at least rescue this one person in memory if not in fact.

Sebald had chosen to approach the camps obliquely, indeed scarcely to enter them at all, in fact or imagination. Weiss would choose a seemingly more direct method, seemingly, but not actually, as he staged a documentary drama in which concealed truths would tumble out and judgements be invited. Yet in the end he, too, had his indirections. The fact that the text is constituted from an actual trial does not, in the end, deny the imagination its role or mean that the shape is determined solely by transcriptions of evidence offered under oath. Weiss was a playwright, with a politics and an aesthetics of his own, and memories deployed in the service of justice proved memories deployable for other purposes, too.

He began his play convinced of two things. The first was that a way had to be found to tell the truth of the mass exterminations. The second was the near impossibility of doing so, and for Weiss Rolf Hochhuth's play had seemed to clinch the case. In art – for Weiss was an artist as well as a writer – he had perhaps hinted at some elements of a conspiracy against the self, of a society sliding towards dehumanisation. Words, however, seemed to stop short as if inadequate to the task. Yet there had been visions of hell before and as he contemplated the problem confronting him so he was increasingly drawn to Dante, as in art he had been drawn to Brueghel and Giotto, while not wishing to suggest that art or literature offered a sufficient correlative, not least because hell was reserved for sinners and these victims were guilty of nothing but existence. Robert Cohen notes the moment when Weiss jotted in his notebook: 'Dante and Giotto stroll through the concentration camps' (78).

In March 1964, even as his immensely successful play *Marat/Sade* was in rehearsal, he attended the Frankfurt trials. Eight months later he went to Auschwitz, returning to the trials the following year. The play he produced was originally called *Anus Mundi*, a term whose resonances were too severe to be allowed to stand. He renamed it *The Investigation*, a phrase intended to imply a certain neutrality as well as a process. As a reminder of Dante, its sub-title was *Oratorio in 11 Cantos*.

The play was to be set not in the past but in the present, its presentness being part of its justification. To be sure, it was a play of contending memories, with the audience in the position of jury, but the audience was not to feel that these events, or the implications of these events, were safely sealed in the past, awaiting only the solemnities of justice. The play ends with an implicit ellipsis, with the jury never required to deliver a definitive judgement not least because they are presumed by these revelations to be complicit with the accused, if not before then after the fact.

Oren Baruch Stier opens his book *Committed to Memory* by quoting from the American professor of folklore Henry Glassie. Writing about Ulster, but plainly with wider relevance, Glassie observes that 'History is not the past, but a map of the past drawn from a particular point of view to be useful to the modern traveller ... Reality is not the present but between the past and the future.'[2] The writer plainly stands somewhere yet where he stands is defined in part by the past interpreted to serve present needs, and already that past is being reshaped in preparation for an imagined future. Concern with the past is not merely a disinterested inquiry into ascertainable past events, but an effort to understand and expand our notion of the present. This is not a mere instrumental use of the past, though there are instrumentalities enough on the part of those who wish to displace present issues into a reconstructed past. It is an acknowledgement that there are crucial absences which make the present an insecure environment. The other side of the coin from laying claim to a 'relevant' past lies less in willed forgetfulness than in a casual disregard as if the authority of the present were enough and all that precedes it mere prelude, used up in the realisation of what followed. Yet what are the terms on which that past may be reclaimed? Is fiction a mechanism, a film such as *Schindler's List* a television docudrama? It is such thoughts, of course, which give primacy to witness though it is not only lawyers who are aware of witness's potential unreliability if necessity.

In his account of what he calls the 'missing camps of *Aktion Reinhard*', the German name for the process which encompassed the murder of all Jews in occupied central and south-western Poland, together with Galicia in the east, Donald Bloxham notes a con- temporary tendency to edit out the centrality of Jews and the distrust of eye-witness accounts as opposed to a reliance on German documents. As he points out, most memoirs encouraged by the Allies in 1945–6 were written by political prisoners. Only three of the forty-two released in the British and American zones, he indicates, concerned Auschwitz, none mentioning the extermination centres and only one written by a Jew. None had been held at Auschwitz-Birkenau, instead being imprisoned at the main camp. The crimes were seen as being against humanity rather than the Jews and to have been committed by the Germans, in some large degree against the Germans. What was being shaped, he suggests, was a sense of collective guilt subsequently to be purged by a radical reshaping of German society along lines already being formulated by the Allied powers.

Bloxham quotes a report produced by the joint military command SHAEF on the making of a documentary on the camps aimed, as he says, ' "to promote German acceptance of the justice of the Allied occupiers by reminding Germans of their past acquiescence" and, therefore, their "responsibility". However, it also aimed to show specific crimes committed in the German name to rouse the populace against the Nazis.'³ At the same time, a 1945 edition of *Welt im Film* emphasised the story of German resistance in the camps while ignoring Jews.

In fact few Jews survived the camps. As he points out, only one inmate survived Belzec, thirty Jews survived Sobibor and sixty-seven Treblinka. Even so, at the Nuremberg trials survivor testimony took second place to survivor documents, the former distrusted as partial, both in the sense of prejudiced and in the sense of having a limited perspective. Ironically, those who had administered the camps, and the records they kept, were seen as the true source of authenticity. Thus Kurt Gerstein's report was ignored (the Kurt Gerstein who would feature in Rolf Hochhuth's play), along, largely, with the testimony offered by Konrad Morgen, an SS investigator, and Christian Wirth, an inspector of the camps.

It was against this background, and the twenty years of near total silence which followed, that Peter Weiss chose to give prominence not to documents but to the testimony of those who had been in the camps, as guards and prisoners. If the past is preserved in documents, albeit documents provided by those who might be thought to have motives for distorting them, then it is preserved in another sense by the memories of those who were present. And if those memories were themselves subject to deletions, distortions, reconstructions, then the context of a courtroom would provide an opportunity for them to be tested against one another in the hope that truth would become apparent or that within the competing and overlapping versions some approximation to the reality of the past would emerge.

Even so, the journey into the past, like the carrying of that past into the present, can never be without its ambiguities. Nobody walks naked in either direction. Nor did Peter Weiss make his way to Frankfurt for the Auschwitz trials on a whim. It was a decision that grew out of his own ambivalent identity as also out of his concerns as a writer and artist. That the trial took place at this particular moment was itself no arbitrary decision. It was part of a reawakening. Nor, at a time when Germany was divided, was it without relevance to debates about what German identity might imply. Klaus L. Berghahn quotes a rallying cry by the playwright Martin Walser in 1965: 'Today a German author has to present exclusively characters who either conceal or express the years from 1933 to 1945 ... Every sentence by a German author which says nothing about this historical reality conceals something.'[4] It was plainly a piece of rhetoric, too severe in its demands, yet it was an appeal to which Weiss implicitly responded in that same year.

Weiss, who died in 1982, was born in Nowawes, near Potsdam, in 1916, before moving with his family to Bremen in 1919 and then, in 1929, to Berlin. His father was a Slovak Jew, his mother a Swiss actress. Bullied at school, Peter later suffered from Jew-baiting. In 1934 his sister was killed in a traffic accident, and the family emigrated to Britain where, at the age of twenty, he staged an exhibition of his paintings, albeit in a small storage room rather than a gallery. For two years, from 1936 to 1938, he studied at the Art Academy in Prague, one reason, perhaps, why Kafka would prove an important figure for him. He spent the war years in neutral Sweden, working as a farmhand and lumberjack, but secure where others were not. It was not until 1947 that he returned to Germany as a journalist, writing about the devastation he found there. He began to publish prose poems and plays, now as a Swedish citizen.

His early work bore little relation to the apparently documentary drama he would later write, though as a founder member of an avant-garde film group he made a documentary about a prison. As Michael Hamburger (the same Michael Hamburger to whose house W. G. Sebald had made his way in *The Rings of Saturn*) observed, he was drawn to surrealism, both in his art and in his literature. Thereafter, as he himself explained in an essay published in 1967, he had passed through periods of scepticism and belief in the most absurd concepts, to radical commitment, the latter involving an embrace of Marxism. The year 1967 was not perhaps the best of moments to arrive at Marxism, not least because Soviet troops marched into Prague, his home for two years in the thirties, the following year. His international reputation, however, had come in 1964 with the Artaud-influenced *Marat/Sade*.

In his essay on Peter Weiss, W. G. Sebald begins not with his play about Auschwitz but with a painting, *Der Hausierer* (The Pedlar), which dates to 1940. It shows, he points out, a dark industrial landscape in the middle ground and in the front a small circus. In the foreground is a young man, a pedlar it seems, about to descend a path towards the circus. The white of the tent, lit, he suggests, by a setting sun, contrasts with the darkness inside it towards which the man is making his way. To Sebald, it is an allegory as what he takes to be a homeless man makes his way through life towards this darkness. In truth, it could equally well be a commentary on the destructive power of industry, the dark plume of smoke from a chimney and the blackness of a gasometer being reflected in the oily blackness of a contaminated nature which exists now almost as a memory, a group of dancing people being shown as seemingly oblivious of their fate. Beyond that, though, to Sebald, it is a self-portrait which 'expresses the artist's need to enter the dwellings of those who no longer live in the light of day and shows him intent upon his own end, for even later, with persistence bordering on monomania, Weiss remained faithful to the programme it presents. All his work is designed as a visit to the dead.'[5]

And he had dead of his own: his sister, his friend Uli (whose body, Sebald notes, was washed up on the shore of Denmark in that same year, 1940), his parents and 'all the other victims of history who are now dust and ashes'. Quoting directly from Weiss, Sebald notes that writing itself is a struggle against 'the art of forgetting', an attempt 'to preserve our equilibrium among the living with all our dead within us'. In this context memory becomes crucial since, he insists, 'it alone justifies survival in the shadow of a mountain of guilt' (176).

Nor is the point a generalised memory, still less simple pity. What Sebald chooses to see in Weiss is a sympathy that finds expression in a precise retrieval of the past, particularly a past which proves resistant to exploration and retrieval. Not the least fascinating aspect of Sebald's account of Weiss, in an essay called 'On Memory and Cruelty in the Work of Peter Weiss', is the fact that he sees this concern as pre-dating the Holocaust. He notes, in particular, a painting called *Alexanderschlacht* (Battle of Alexander) which portrays a chaotic scene of sinking ships and raging fires. What he sees in this and other paintings is a sense of catastrophe, of individuals isolated from history, staring blindly ahead, though scarcely into a redemptive future. *Das grosse Welttheater*, which dates from 1937, features a similarly apocalyptic landscape, nature turned against itself.

If he is a memorialiser here, the memorials he constructs are ominous. Sebald was drawn to Weiss not least because he recognised in him a fellow melancholic whose melancholia is a function of his willingness to stare into the face of darkness in an attempt to make out the features of those in need of rescue from time. Reality, he seems to suggest, needs breaking open, like the human body lying on a dissecting table presented in a 1944 picture and echoed in another, *Anatomie*, two years later. The end of the war brought *Der Reiche und der Arme*, 1946, in which a naked man, streaked with blood, carries an overweight man who digs spurs into his flesh. *Der Krieg*, in that same year, features men thrusting knives and spears into one another, as in *Kindesmord (Skizze)*, again in 1946, a man tears a baby from a woman's arms. It is hard not to see in such pictures a sense of crisis, of trauma.

Weiss, himself, underwent Freudian analysis, itself a process that involves a breaking down, a recapitulation of memories linked to traumas now manifesting themselves as neuroses, not unconnected with the process of writing. And Freud would for some be a crucial figure in suggesting an instrumental use of the past just as in the theatre Stanislavsky would direct the actor backwards in order to draw on emotions stored away against the future. In America, Arthur Miller, a writer who always insisted on the central significance of the past, underwent analysis and duly noted down memories and dreams as if they were, indeed, keys to understanding, necessary to present identity. But the memories thus invoked almost invariably involve pain, and so they seem to do for Weiss, as they did for Nietzsche. That pain would be explored in *Marat/Sade*, his play set during the French Revolution and in a mental hospital, an example of Antonin Artaud's theatre of cruelty and performed as such in London, with Peter Brook directing, as part of a series of productions called the 'Theatre of Cruelty' season. But as a part Jew there was another subject waiting for him as though the logic of his own interests would inevitably lead him in this direction, he the young man, this the darkness glimpsed through the doorway of the tent in *Der Hausierer* otherwise shining white in the sun.

It was the logic of his development as a writer that would lead him from the private to the public, from personal anguish to a perception of the social and political forces which turned individual loss into historical fact. It was a logic that would take him to the Auschwitz trials in part, Sebald speculated, as if, at least within his own psyche, his presence could be a compensatory fact as he suffered vicariously the accusations directed at those with whom he shared if not the same guilt then guilt of a kind even as, a part Jew, he was one of the accusers. Yet, of course, as Sebald acknowledges, the very form of the trial made the idea of compensation for cruelty impossible. Instead, those who witnessed were required to slide down the razorblade of memory and those who were accused could experience again the power they had once possessed even as they refused the consequences of that power.

Yet, to Sebald, what he took to be Weiss's ambivalent position, his awareness that 'exploiters and exploited are in fact the same species', and his willingness to acknowledge that he was at least an accomplice to the crime, was that which gave his work its power and integrity. His 'willingness to take this heaviest of moral obligations on himself' in his view 'raises his work far beyond all other literary attempts to "come to terms with the past"' (190). He noted that in his novel *Nacht mit Gästen* (Night with Guests) Kaspar Rosenrot is a mixture of German and Jew and that the names of the Nazi criminals he wrote in his notebook as he was working on *The Investigation* derive from a history of assimilation. He notes, too, that one of the orderlies who had held victims down as they were injected with phenol in Auschwitz bears Weiss's own name. Sebald speaks of 'the long paroxysm' of Weiss's memory, acknowledging in that the price to be paid for sifting through the detritus of the past in search of the complicit self no less than the victims and the guilty perpetrators.

Sebald was drawn to Peter Weiss for a number of reasons. In Weiss he found someone who saw autobiography as one weapon of the writer, albeit within the context of works which he believed should challenge conventional forms. In his three-volume novel *The Aesthetics of Resistance*, published between 1975 and 1981, Weiss mixes literature and philosophy within a story about those who fought against the Nazi regime from within. The characters are based on actual people but he invokes literary figures, including two significant to Sebald, Dante and Kafka, as he explores paintings and photographs. Sebald must have been struck, too, by the fact that, like himself, the narrator of *Fluchtpunkt* (*Vanishing Point*) first learned of the Holocaust by watching a documentary:

> Then in the Spring of 1945 I saw the end of the development in which I had grown up ... [and when the pictures were shown on the cinema screen] they were from now on part of our existence, they could no longer be dismissed from our thoughts, and often they had made every spoken word, every written note, into a lie and a mockery.

In this context, and in the demand for truth, 'only the most intimate personal statements were valid. Diaries, case histories, reports from prisons deprived novels of their force.'[6]

Sebald was an admirer of other works than *The Investigation*, though this was to be a crucial text. He noted especially two books from the early 1960s, *Leave-Taking* and *Vanishing Point*. In the former, Weiss declared that his task was to observe and note down what he experienced. In a partly autobiographical work, the narrator engages with his failure to communicate with his parents and with his capacity for violence. He speaks of his self-chosen exile. The latter novel is again autobiographical and deals with the issue of exile, including the linguistic problems it poses, though the narrator embraces his extra-territoriality. He is disturbed, though, at the fate of a friend who died in a German uniform, not least because it reminds him that he himself perhaps had the capacity to become what repels him. For Weiss, the treatment of the Jews was a fictive concern before it became the subject of a documentary impulse. It was also a novel in which the threat of the Nazis is seen as deriving not from their difference from others but their similarity, a notion equally embraced by Hannah Arendt and Arthur Miller.

For Bertolt Brecht, the Holocaust did not offer itself up to aesthetic treatment. He found it difficult to envisage a form that could contain and express it. For Weiss, one answer was to set fiction aside in the name of a documentary presentation. Those who had published accounts of their time in Auschwitz had spoken as witnesses, offering autobiography as a guarantee of authenticity and a route into the seemingly inexplicable. Some, like Primo Levi, began writing in the camp. He completed his first book shortly after his return. Others relied on memory. They were limited, however, by the very thing which guaranteed their accounts' authority. They reported what they saw, what they experienced. Levi, for example, saw nothing of the main camp at Auschwitz. They walked with eyes lowered, because that was a survival mechanism. Of the Germans, they saw remarkably little (the SS was content to work through those who sought their own survival by cooperation). Still less were they personally aware of the detailed processes and procedures necessary to genocide. The larger picture was not only denied to them but was almost literally resistant to thought. What, after all, was there to understand? What logic, once detected, could begin to make sense of their daily distresses?

The guards themselves were the source of peremptory orders, arbitrary cruelties, systematised degradation. What they were not were people to be confronted with their actions, challenged, indicted, punished. That was a fantasy best not entertained. It was that process, however, which now began, nearly twenty years after the war's end, when those who had suffered were scattered across Europe and those who inflicted the suffering were seemingly secure in a forgetfulness which had seemed to have the sanction of the state no less than of personal necessity. Few had returned to boast of their time in the camps. They were no more inclined to remember than were most of those who seemingly miraculously escaped alive from a system whose function and reality was to make such an impossibility. Like their victims, they had begun the process of re-insinuating themselves into social life, in their case seeking grace without the necessity of confession. The Frankfurt trials ended this for some few of them, a very few.

The trials constituted one of those moments in which a judicial process mattered less for its ability to mediate between innocence and guilt than for its revelatory power. The Nuremberg trials had apportioned blame for a war conducted without quarter. A price had been paid by those incautious enough to have failed to avail themselves of escape into exile or simple anonymity. But these were those who had commanded the strategy. Beneath them were others who had facilitated, either with an inventive enthusiasm or with bureaucratic efficiency, the murderous schemes of those who had sought to reinvent not simply the map of Europe but the map of the human soul. The kidnapping and arrest of Adolf Eichmann in 1960 suggested that the net was now widening, that forgetfulness was not after all to be allowed to become a sanctioned policy. A subject that had slipped out of national and, indeed, international consciousness was, it seemed, now back on the agenda.

The Commandant of Auschwitz had been hanged. Dr Mengele had effected his own escape. There were others, though, who had burrowed down into the new Germany, resumed untroubled lives, prospered, thereby mocking those whose only hope had been that retribution must surely come though their own lives be forfeit. Now those who had performed the 'difficult task' of liquidating a race, or some few of them, were to be called before a German court and offered the justice they had denied to others. But what mattered beyond the findings was the exposure both of the facts of life in Auschwitz and of the mentality of those who served there.

The facts, of course, were known in a general sense, but there was no context of a national engagement with the past to give it meaning. The Holocaust stood as some impenetrable mystery best secured against the present when there were other priorities to pursue. What had been missing, too, was a dispassionate presentation, in a judicial setting, with the drama of the past summoned before the present and reported on by newspapers in Germany and around the world. The Frankfurt trials offered that. Sebald did not attend, reading about them instead in the *Frankfurter Allgemeine Zeitung*. Nonetheless, those reports de-stabilised him, shone a light on a past that had been obscure.

Those same reports would be drawn on by Peter Weiss in *The Investigation*, along with published accounts of Auschwitz that had begun to appear in the late 1950s. But, unlike Sebald, he had visited Auschwitz, in 1964. It was, he acknowledged, 'a place for which I was destined but which I managed to avoid'. It was also, though, a place that could communicate little to him beyond constituting the mise en scene of genocide. As he confessed, 'I have had no experience of this place, I have no relation to it, except that my name was on the lists of people who were supposed to be sent there for ever',[7] and that seems to have left a feeling of obligation. He visited not only the main camp at Auschwitz but also Birkenau and wrote of the experience. What he had not done was see those who had perpetrated the crimes confronted by their victims. Unlike Sebald, he had subsequently sat in the courtroom himself and watched as the Chief of Administration Karl Mulka, Dr Capesius, in charge of the pharmacy (who, with his fellow doctors Frank, Schatz and Lucas, had injected inmates with phenol), Herr Broad, of the Political Department, responsible for the personal killing of prisoners, and a dozen others were confronted by their accusers (in fact, there were twenty-two accused and four hundred witnesses). What drew him to the subject? Guilt, the guilt, he explained, of the survivor. He was another of those who had not died. The guilt was that of a German who had discovered an apparent immunity to which he believed he had no claim. In that sense he shared something with Sebald, who also looked at a past to which he was connected without understanding entirely what the nature of that connection might be.

On seeking to stage a work rooted in Auschwitz, he began, as did Hochhuth, by confessing the impossibility of capturing the place itself. This was to be a trial, in more than one sense. It was to be a reproduction of the actual trial, within the obvious limitations demanded by an event spread over time and involving large numbers of people. But it was also a trial in the sense of an experiment in deriving some sense of reality from an unreal situation, seeing past the evasions and denials which for the most part met those who had travelled so far to testify. As he explained, 'In presenting this play no attempt should be made to reconstruct the courtroom before which the deliberations over the camp actually took place. Such a representation seems just as impossible to the author as a representation of the camp on stage would be.'[8]

The sheer emotional power of the situation defied capturing. Indeed, his aim was to create a documentary theatre that was, as he explained, dry and emotionless. It was an impossible objective, though one he hoped to achieve through various distancing effects. Hochhuth had run the risk of melodrama, taking the action into the heart of darkness. Weiss offered testimony, believing that 'the central core of the evidence' could remain on stage, but testimony is anything but dry and emotionless, no matter the way in which it is delivered. Like Hochhuth, he shaped the exchanges into verse but unlike Hochhuth he resisted the temptation to extend the play as if sheer inclusiveness were the route to truth.

He hesitated between several titles: *The Camp, The Tribunal, Taking Evidence.* Evidence, indeed, is a crucial word. When Arthur Miller attended the trials he was struck by the imperfect memories of some of the witnesses as they tried to reach back into experiences that not only lay long in the past but contained a pain which part of them at least surely wished to forget. Forgetfulness, a feature of German society, in the trial was to be literal, though not, as it happens, in Weiss's play where the past must be laid before the judges both within and without the play and few ambiguities of this kind are permitted. He structured the play according to the pattern of Dante's *Commedia*, though where the *Commedia* moved towards salvation, Auschwitz was the denial of such. In doing so, he was not unique. Olaf Berwald recalls Arno Schmidt's 'Herrn Dante Alighieri', written in 1948–9 but not published until 1989, which draws a parallel between the *Inferno* and the Holocaust.[9] Primo Levi in Auschwitz had recited passages from the same work, even in the knowledge that this was no more than a device to distract.

Indeed, there is potentially a problem in importing into an account of the Holocaust a literary work, carrying with it, as it does, not merely aesthetic necessities but also a history of that work's own logic and coherences. Like the very structure of a trial, it is to propose a pattern, a form, a shape whereas what is at stake may precisely be an experience which lacked any of these things. Yes, there were procedures, logistical plans, a strict taxonomy that did, indeed, prescribe varying levels of hell to those who were the victims, but the impulse behind the elaborate mechanisms of mass slaughter was pre-rational, indeed in many senses irrational. Courtroom testimony is designedly purged of extra-legal components but the writer, even allowing for a self-denying ordinance that makes it necessary to restrict oneself to the words as spoken, not merely shapes the text but is tempted to locate it in terms of literary models which have associations of their own.

The Investigation was not so much a play as a political and social event. And it had a context. As Klaus L. Berghahn points out, there had been

> disturbing signs of continuity between the Third Reich and the Federal government ... Adenauer's personal secretary of the chancellery, Heinrich Globke, had been a commentator of the 1935 racial Nuremberg Laws, a fact that everyone knew, but no one bothered to notice. In 1962 the highest judge of the Federal Republic was exposed as a member of the Nazi judicial system, and the President had to dismiss him. That same year 143 high judges and prosecutors were forced into early retirement for

similar reasons, a special law allowing them to retire with full pensions. Slowly the repressed past was returning with a vengeance.[10]

The significance of the Frankfurt trials was both that in some way the judicial system should purge itself and that supposedly ordinary Germans should be called to account.

Weiss wrote it in 1964–5 as the trials unfolded. When it opened, in October 1965, it did so in fifteen theatres, in East and West Germany, simultaneously. By the year's end it had opened in more than thirty theatres in Europe. Within a year there were productions around the world. It was quickly filmed. The momentum established by the Eichmann trial, by Hannah Arendt's book, *Eichmann in Jerusalem*, and by Hochhuth's play was sustained by this seemingly dispassionate presentation of facts, this confrontation of victim and victimiser.

It was not in itself a polemic, beyond the fact that a prosecutor seeks to expose evasions, to give shape and form to the indictment. Indeed, the very notion of a trial presupposes the necessity for a defence counsel. Within the confines of this court it is legal justice that is enacted rather than a more profound justice as these few survivors speak for those who perished. The accused are not men who have pleaded guilty. They are present to announce their innocence, an innocence constructed out of denial. They deny that they were aware of the true extent and function of the camp. They deny that they individually bore any responsibility for it. If they are guilty of actions which might be construed as inhuman, then they performed those actions under duress or at the behest of those whose authority could not be challenged, more particularly in a time of war when obedience was as much a necessity of survival for them as for their accusers. The weapon of choice, inevitably, is memory.

Unlike Hochhuth, Weiss does not venture through the doors of the camp. It is not the camp itself that is in question, though the evidence laid before the court slowly establishes something of its reality. It exists only in so far as it can be described, elicited from those who must now put into words what was experienced in the

163

flesh. *The Investigation* is no more an unmediated text than the events at Auschwitz-Birkenau were unmediated. Not merely did Weiss have to select material from a trial lasting from December 1963 to August 1965, drawing directly on reports in the *Frankfurter Allgemeine Zeitung*, reducing nearly four hundred witnesses to nine, the number of judges and counsels to single representatives, he had to shape it into a coherent series of dialogues, redistributing words from one witness to another.

When a witness suggests that it is necessary to abandon the notion that the world of the camp is incomprehensible, he echoes Weiss's own view, even as the unfolding evidence seems to contradict this assertion. The very form of a trial suggests that a crime is susceptible of revelation and analysis, that irrational acts can be retrospectively located in a rational structure, that individuals can be held responsible for their actions. Yet everything about the camps suggests that this was and is not so. Within the camps all things were possible. The only structure was that provided by the necessity to murder on a scale beyond the means of the individual. There was a system, admittedly a system built on the irrational if you refused to accept the premises on which it was based. But why would you not accept it when it was national policy, when the leader had obligingly spelled out his intentions? The crimes against the Jews had always been presented as the product of historical, social, political logic. They were polluters of the gene pool, disruptors of social progress, secret plotters in a world-wide conspiracy. Their death was thus both necessary and justified. What followed was presented as no more than a process. After all, would it be more or less satisfactory to dispose of them individually? It was less satisfactory because the business was urgent and efficiencies were required if the national effort was not to be disrupted. Now, those who merely performed their duty were to be summoned before those who were themselves never tested, who lived in a secure world.

Yet in what sense could the play be said to be written by Weiss if his primary function was to be no more than an editor (and it was undeniably that)? Even so, as with Hochhuth's play, it is overlong, despite the fact that it condenses the legal proceedings. Played in its entirety it would last more than one evening. But as has been pointed out the play is not simply the product of legal proceedings. If *The Investigation* is structured on a trial it also shadows Dante's *Divine Comedy*, albeit in an inverted way since those suffering in hell did so because of sins committed whereas the Jews suffered for the sin of life. It is a dangerous strategy, metaphor and analogy potentially denying the specificity of the subject matter. Auschwitz, after all, was not *like* Dante's inferno. It was not *like* anything. That was its destabilising power. This was not some animated Brueghel, late period Goya, atonal music.

For all Weiss's Jewish identity, there is, as Robert Cohen has pointed out, something oddly unspecific about *The Investigation*. In a documentary play, he fails to document crucial details. The word Jew is not mentioned, any more, for the most part, than are those other groups singled out for the concentration camps, though the Soviet victims are mentioned, itself a political gesture on the part of Weiss whose own politics in the mid-1960s bled into the play, memories being shaped to serve present needs. Cohen recalls his comment that at one time the West Germans 'had allowed themselves to be chosen as a bulwark against Judaism, now they are a bulwark against Communism',[11] anti-Communism being the bridge between Nazi Germany and the successor state. *The Investigation*, in other words, might be focussed on the past and on the details of mass murder but Weiss was also concerned with a present in which continuity rather than discontinuity was of central concern.

The emphasis on the alliance between German industries and the camps, real enough, and emphasised, too, by Hochhuth, none-theless was not without its relevance to a writer whose politics were shifting towards the left and who increasingly saw capitalism as at the core of national and international problems. The companies which set up factories where they could draw on the labour of prisoners were the same companies that dominated the new Federal Republic. The Third Reich, Weiss implies, may have ended but it is not only the camp guards who have survived unscathed. Those guards now face some kind of belated justice. They are not joined in the dock, however, by those who benefited then and subsequently from those who laboured to the point of death. As Cohen points out, just before the play opened Weiss published an article in which he rejected his own bourgeois origins and the aesthetic experimentation that had characterised his early career. He did so in the name of socialism, albeit not that which he saw practised in East Germany. It was an intervention which threw a confusing light on his play and which led to suggestions that he was merely using rather than exploring the Holocaust, shining a light less on human depravity than on systems of government.

Aware of his own multiple identities, born in one country, living in another and with one parent Jewish and the other not, he was disinclined to see either victims or persecutors as historically determined. Each, he thought, contained the potential to become the other, though once again this sat uneasily with the specifics of the Holocaust. To be sure, Germans were on both sides in the camps. There were German Jews, German political prisoners, German homosexuals. Nonetheless, there was a clear hierarchy, which, in the case of Jews, made their German identity irrelevant, as they were presented as sly interlopers, contaminating Aryan identity.

In a series of 'remarks', which appear as a preface to the published text, Weiss explained his dramatic tactics. The trials themselves, he acknowledged, were 'loaded to breaking point with emotional power'. For his part, though, he wished to abstract 'only the central core of the evidence', which alone could remain on the stage. It is a slightly odd remark.

What, after all, was the central evidence from a trial lasting so long, and with hundreds of witnesses, and in what way would that be drained of emotional power? What he was after, he explained, was 'nothing but the facts as they came to be expressed in words during the course of the trial'. The personal was to be 'softened into anonymity', as the witnesses became exemplary figures which means, he explained, that they lose their identity as individuals and become what, in another curious phrase, he called 'little more than megaphones'. They were to express less their individual experiences than the experiences of many, 'at most indicated by alterations in voice and posture'. In part this acknowledged the processes of the camp, which had precisely stripped identity, denuding those who entered of their names, but it also served to resist an empathy which might serve to displace analysis with emotion, to distract from the revelation of process and the details of crimes justified as necessities.

The defendants, by contrast, retain their names, as they had in the camp, but, Weiss insists, 'it is not the bearers of the names who should once again be accused. They lend the author only their names, which here stand as symbols for a system which conferred guilt on those many others who never appeared before this court' (*The Investigation*, 10). In other words, here is a documentary theatre committed less to exposing individual guilt than to establishing what seem to be the crucial details of an indictment directed at more than those standing in the dock. For Weiss, it appears, these were not so much trials as a committee of inquiry and the fate of the few named conspirators less significant than an identification of underlying principles.

The prefatory remarks end with a final note: 'For the purpose of stage production an interval can be inserted after the Sixth Canto.' He was unconcerned at the prospect of breaking the emotional tension of the piece, not least because he wished to avoid a purely emotional response.

The verse – in fact literally prosaic in that he simply sets out prose statements in off-set lines which take no particular form – is one way in which he sought to control and contain the emotion. Few speeches are elaborate. The interrogative exchanges discourage elaboration. These are not Socratic dialogues. The accused frequently do no more than deny knowledge, insist that their own involvement was at best marginal.

Something of Weiss's motives becomes apparent in the fact that within the first few minutes he has begun to focus on the camps as an extension of German capitalism. The first witness is interrogated about the companies which established branches there: I. G. Farben, Krupp, Siemens.

It is a little difficult to know what Weiss meant when he suggested that emphasis on fact would relieve the emotional burden. Indeed, here, as in Claude Lanzmann's film, it is precisely the unemotional recitation of fact that generates the emotion. Witness 8 describes a guard's reaction to the birth of a child:

> While we were unloading
> A child was born
> I wrapped it in some pieces of clothing
> And laid it by its mother
> Beretzki came after me with the stick
> And beat me and the woman as well
> What are you doing with that shit
> He shouted
> And he kicked the baby
> And sent it flying 30 feet
> Then he ordered me
> Bring that shit over here
> And the child was dead. (25)

What he does not do is provide the emotion. Rather, as in a Hemingway story, he relies on the apposite detail to generate the emotion in the reader or audience. What the camp constituted was an alternative world in which new rules, practices, assumptions prevailed. As the female witness 5 explains:

> It was perfectly normal
> That everything was stolen from us
> It was perfectly normal
> That we stole the same things back
> Dirt wounds and pestilence all around
> This was perfectly normal
> It was normal
> That the dead were on every side
> And the immediate prospect
> Of one's own death
> Was normal
> The dying away of our feelings
> Was normal as was our indifference
> To finding corpses
> It was normal. (39)

Normal, too, were those who administered this antinomian world, normal in the sense of having come from and returning to a world in which such a place would have been unthinkable and the relationships between people would have been conducted with humanity and courtesy. Those who appeared at the Frankfurt trials were no less 'banal', to use Arendt's word, than that arch administrator of death, Adolf Eichmann. Nor were they easily distinguishable from those to whom they returned after the war and in whose company they flourished. One later worked as a nurse and was known as 'Papa Kaduk' by those to whom he administered and who were happy to praise him. The achievement of the Nazis was to have created an alternative universe in which normal values were inverted and the word normal therefore equally inverted.

Arthur Miller, who was present while the case of Kaduk was being considered, would be struck by the same truth. Until that moment he had never knowingly met a Nazi. In some way he had expected them to betray their inhumanity in their very beings. The greater horror was that they did not, that these had once been good neighbours, part of a society which prided itself on its civilities and cultivation and had seemingly slid with ease back into a society in the business of forgetting. To be sure, the camps offered a licence to the sadist as they also created sadists who went even beyond the inhuman orders they so readily obeyed. But the greater shock was the facility with which those who administered genocide became what they did and the necessity for those they oppressed to become what was necessary in order to survive. Guards and prisoners alike, standing in that Frankfurt courtroom, were confronting something more than the facts of persecution.

For the most part, Weiss abjures 'characters'. Figures are identified as witnesses. Incidents are described but not personalised, not least because his dramatic strategy is to compress many witnesses into a few. There is, however, one person identified, one story offered, that of a young secretary, Lili Tofler, who wrote a letter to a prisoner. The letter was found but even under torture she refused to name the recipient. She is granted the kind of autonomy and courage for which otherwise, it is suggested, there was no room and no time. She becomes almost a conventional tragic heroine, fully aware that she will be destroyed but finally remaining, like a Hemingway tragic hero, undefeated. Is this a sentimentality, in the context of the whole trial and, indeed, the whole play, or is this an acceptance that in the Brueghel-like picture of camp life, teeming with individual incidents, one, at least, suggested that it was possible to retain humanity? The truth is that there were such moments. Though survival, as those who survived later confessed, usually required the suppression of all normal instincts – the theft of food from those who would die without it, a defensive silence in the face of enormities – there were moments of mutuality and selflessness. Some later stressed the former, others the latter.

In dramatic terms, there is no plot, but in that respect it reflects the world of the camps in which time was suspended, each day survived being complete in itself, the future blocked off, the past irrecoverable except as unbearable irony. And though the actual trial resulted in sentences, the play has no denouement, no catharsis. Indeed it ends with a refusal on the part of the accused to offer precisely that and in doing so they stand as exemplary figures not of a retrieved past but of a disturbing present.

> I should like to emphasise again
> we did nothing but our duty
> even if it was often hard to do so
> even when we wanted to despair of it
> Today
> now that our nation
> has once again worked its way up
> to a leading position
> we should be concerned with other things
> than with recriminations
> These should long ago
> Have been banished from the lawbooks
> By the Statute of Limitations (203)

The final stage direction indicates 'Loud agreement from the side of the Defendants', who thus have the last words. In that sense the play exemplifies Weiss's conviction that the strength of documentary theatre lies in the fact that 'it reconstructs out of the fragments of reality a usable model for explaining present social conditions'.[12] But that, of course, implies an instrumentalist use of the Holocaust. Fragments of horror, he seems to imply, can be reassembled to form a different shape, to serve another purpose. Those indicted in the trial, as Weiss presents it, are thus not simply the accused but a contemporary society which ignores such crimes in the name of a model of society with which Weiss himself felt at odds. Memories are projected forward where they become weapons in a new war. The camps are presented as products of a particular society, as serving familiar interests, because society still retains that potential, and those interests still prevail.

Having himself been a participant in Nazi youth movements he was conscious of the ease with which the citizen could be enrolled in a suspect national cause which had absorbed yesterday's criminals. The play is in a sense unfinished because sealing off a historic injustice would serve only to conceal the truth that these events could not be separated from history as an unfolding story. Trials are conventionally seen as offering closure. Weiss's point is that though the camps were closed and the Nazis overthrown this did not eradicate the pressures which had given birth to them. He is aware the prisoners and guards could be interchangeable, acknowledging that possibility in himself. He is more interested in social and political forces. There might, he suggests, be an antidote to inhumanity: socialism. The countless millions, including many Jews, who died at the behest of Joseph Stalin made him vulnerable to attack by those who saw *The Investigation* as less a forensic study of the Holocaust than a piece of special pleading for a more amenable ideology. In a play that depended to some degree on specificities for its authenticity he avoided such specifics in the name of universality.

The trials themselves were a site of contesting memories but memories are in part shaped by perceptions. They carry the impress of interpretation. Those on trial affected forgetfulness, were ready to deny, but they also inflected their memories with their own assumptions, perspectives. Few confessed to or, it seems, felt guilt and there were those who thought the trials an unnecessary reminder of times best left unvisited. Weiss's drama was a conscious intervention in history. It was also, however, an intervention in contemporary society through the stress it placed not simply on the radical disruption that was the Holocaust but also on the alliance between Nazi ideology and capitalism, an alliance which stresses continuity. These were not memories of a past sealed off against process, unconnected with the present. Nor, however, was his interest in the Auschwitz trials without a personal dimension.

Sebald points out that Weiss, whom he describes as a 'rigorous moralist', had his early schooling in the brothers Grimm, 'a specifically German form of didactic cruelty'. He had thus been raised with images of 'the fantastic depiction of all imaginable punishments. These acts of mutilation and amputation', he added, 'can be interpreted as pendants to the categorical imperative of memory.'[13] He recalls Nietzsche's remark that 'we burn something into the mind so that it will remain in the memory; only what still hurts will be retained' (188). To Sebald, there was an emotional logic to Weiss's life and career. 'In his progress as a dramatist', he suggests, 'from grisly street ballad to his play on the lurid atrocities of the French Revolution, Peter Weiss surveys an area in which the horror figures of childhood and the leading figures of revolutionary government are all preparing a giant bloodbath together'. Yet along with this went an awareness that 'the grotesque deformities of our inner lives have their background and origin in collective social history' (188). Freud and Marx seem to edge together. Seen thus, his concern with the Holocaust is perhaps an extension of his disturbed fascination with cruelty as it also stands revealed as expressive of a social and political logic, rather than a free-floating and inexplicable terror.

Beyond that, he attended the Frankfurt trials as both a German and a Jew. For Sebald, his society had posed the question of which most directly defined him. Was he there as a victim or as a collaborator with the crimes laid out for inspection? What was most striking to Sebald was that Weiss edged towards the conviction 'that rulers and ruled, exploiters and exploited are in fact the same species ... Weiss's willingness to take this harvest of all moral obligations on himself raises his work far beyond all other attempts to "come to terms with the past" as the usual phrase runs' (190). The evidence for this lies in part in the fact that in the notebook on which he was working on *The Investigation* a number of the names of the Nazis, 'whether real or imagined', were a blend of the Jewish and the German. At the same time he observes that in 1964 Weiss also wrote in his notebook, 'How glad I am that I am not German', a statement which Sebald calls a deliberately 'facile exoneration', ironic in that its absoluteness contains its contradiction. Technically, he was Swedish. In all other respects he was German, German in his upbringing, German in the images, the values he absorbed. Why else the echo of his own name in the German prisoner forced to be complicit in murder by phenol, 'certainly incorporated into the text deliberately' (191)?

It was a dilemma to which he would return in his later *Trotsky in Exile* (1970), in which a German student confronts Trotsky with his earlier resistance to Jewish separatism: 'I am German by birth. With a Jewish stamp in my passport. My father's in Dachau. Once you were urgent against Jewish separatism. Are you still? For years German workers have been taught the virtues of international solidarity. Now they're helping to persecute Jewish families. What good is it to see ourselves as Germans, not Jews? We're now labelled a different race.'[14] Trotsky's reply, however, raises another disturbing ambiguity: 'The Jews ... have done their share in helping the rise of Fascism' (89).

His stress on the economic underpinnings of the Holocaust, on the organisation of genocide, was, it seemed to Sebald, in part a conscious attempt to neutralise what he saw as 'the subjective sense of personal involvement in genocide' (*On the Natural History of Destruction*, 191). It was also, though, offered as an indictment of his own times, indicating, as it did, 'that even now the economic conditions, considerations and forms of organization making genocide possible continued to operate' (191–2). Genocide was merely a logical extension of the exploitation of labour. 'Mass murder, after all', he observed, 'was no more than an extreme variation on the elimination of human beings by working them to death, as practised in Germany in the war years on a far greater scale than ever before in history' (192). In other words, what he admired was what Peter Brook would admire, Weiss's ability to situate events in a context wider than themselves.

For many, the Holocaust was hermetic, discontinuous with human history and nature alike. It stood as unique, unsusceptible of analysis, a mystery not explicable, merely acknowledged, recorded, recited. Weiss saw its real nature as lying in its continuity. *Marat/Sade*, Peter Brook remarked, was 'a corridor of echoes – and one must keep looking front and back all the time to reach the author's sense' (6). That was no less true of *The Investigation*. In *Marat/Sade* he reaches back to the French Revolution, having the Marquis de Sade describe a time in which

> We condemn to death without emotion
> And there's no singular personal death to be had
> only an anonymous cheapened death
> which we could dole out to entire nations
> on a mathematical basis
> until the time comes
> for all life
> to be extinguished[15]

In *Discourse on Vietnam*, he looks forward, as America commits itself to continue a savage war whose historical antecedents he is anxious to establish.

The invocation of Dante, meanwhile, was on the one hand an echo of the extremes of suffering detailed in his work and on the other a reflection of that desire to imagine salvation, albeit one denied by a seemingly resistant human nature. The frustration of that desperate hope is reflected in Weiss's play in the ironic laughter of the defendants. But there is another aspect to Dante. In *Trotsky in Exile* he insists that if the *Commedia* was in part a comment on the ruling class of Florence in the thirteenth century, a historical document, its real force lies in its connection with the present. This work by an exile transcends the time barrier. So too, it seems, does the Holocaust.

Peter Brook, writing in the context of his production of *Marat/ Sade*, praised Weiss for his skill in placing an action at a distance so that it could be judged objectively. Ostensibly that is what he does in *The Investigation*, except that, despite the setting of a courtroom, it is difficult to see that objectivity is either the intent or the effect. That, though, is not precisely what Brook meant. It is not a case of weighing facts and arriving at a verdict. From the beginning, after all, innocence is not a credible proposition. The judgement, rather, lay in the possibility of relating the events to a wider world. To Brook, theatre is 'made up of the unbroken conflict between impressions and judgements – illusion and disillusion', which, he adds, 'cohabit painfully and are inseparable' (6). In a good play, he suggests, 'the intelligence, the feelings, the memory, the imagination are all stirred' (5). Judgement thus depends not on a balance of guilt and innocence but on a balance, or admixture, of different modes of apprehension. That is what is offered in *The Investigation*, in which memory is stirred and shaped into accusation.

5   Arthur Miller: the rememberer

'What I got out of the Holocaust', Arthur Miller once remarked,

> was that memory was being destroyed forever. But if one looks
> at it from a distance, the Holocaust, dreadful and terrible and
> significant as it was, was only one part of a wider phenomenon.
> Count the people who have been killed in wars in this
> century ... Think of the memory that has gone. I often times
> think of that ... Maybe there were six people among the tens of
> millions who could have saved the world ... some philosopher
> who could have illuminated the whole universe ... Maybe
> one's function, a writer's function, in part anyway, is to
> remember, to be the rememberer.[1]

For a writer who throughout his life depended on memory as
the raw material for his drama, who saw the past not as so many
discarded presents, with no organic logic or moral relevance, but as an
informing part of present and future actions, to walk down the path of
history was not a retreat but a means of illuminating those actions.
Besides, to be Jewish, whether religiously practising or not, was to be
unavoidably aware of voices from the past, some insisting that he
remain true to his heritage, others crying out against a terrible fate.
Arthur Miller's plays are full of ghosts, in the Ibsen sense. Always
convinced that the chickens will come home to roost, like Willy
Loman, in *Death of a Salesman*, he was constantly drawn back in
search of the moment of betrayal.

There is a sense in which Miller's journey to that Frankfurt
courtroom, in 1964, in which a representative but limited number of

former camp personnel were called to account (though it was the third most significant trial, only twenty-two accused appeared to answer for their crimes), began in rural Poland some eighty years earlier when his father left for America to join the rest of the family. They were escaping the regular pogroms of the age and seeking a prosperity unlikely to come to them in the stetl of Radomizl. They carried with them a faith which in the ensuing decades became diluted, as their memories of that other place thinned to transparency. They continued to celebrate the regular rituals and the thirteen-year-old Arthur underwent his barmitzvah but secular necessities and the pragmatism of the new country slowly eroded convictions once seemingly bred in the bone. And when, as a teenager, he was introduced to Marxism, religion seemed something more than an irrelevance. He married outside the faith to a fellow Marxist and never reclaimed the religion of his grandfather and, to a lesser extent, his father.

Yet he did not wholly sever his links to that history and when as a young writer he was asked to outline his beliefs he insisted that he remained 'culturally' Jewish, with the obligations that that seemed to carry. When Israel was created he responded with enthusiasm, even giving a speech at a national rally. He was present when Andrei Gromyko, in New York, declared the Soviet Union's support for the new state.

Miller did not serve in the Second World War. A high school football injury prevented it. His brother, a fellow Marxist, did serve, and honourably. Miller had also failed to go to Spain in the 1930s, though a fellow Michigan student, whom he drove to New York to board a ship to Europe, did so and died. There was an undischarged debt. He sought to pay it in part through the patriotic radio plays he wrote for Cavalcade of America and a series called 'The Doctor Fights', which celebrated the activities of doctors throughout the military. He also wrote a script for a wartime movie called *The Story of GI Joe*, and though virtually none of his material made its way onto the screen he did publish what was in effect the diary of his time visiting bases throughout America (*Situation Normal*), which reveals him as a man determined to find evidence of anti-Fascism in those who served. It was a largely fruitless search, though what he did find was a casual and pernicious racism. He was aware of the plight of the Jews in Europe. Indeed, in a revised college play from the 1930s (*No Villain* which became *They Too Arise*) there is a reference to this. His own grandfather had been especially perplexed since to him Germany had always represented the epitome of culture. In another early play, *The Golden Years*, written for the Federal Theatre of which he was briefly a member before Congress closed it down for alleged Communist subversion, he addressed what seemed to him to be the paralysis of the European powers when confronted by the crude assault of Fascism, displacing this into a drama about Montezuma's capitulation to Cortes.

What struck him most immediately, however, was a domestic anti-Semitism. He had encountered it in the 1930s when he was looking for a job and found many such closed to Jews. He wrote about it in a wartime melodrama, *Boro Hall Nocturne*, and then, in 1945, published *Focus* which, along with *Gentleman's Agreement*, published that same year, was effectively the first attack on a native anti-Semitism that had in truth been virulent throughout the war years. At the very beginning of his career, this represented a clear statement of his beliefs. He might be alienated from the Jewish faith but, like the protagonist of his novel (himself ironically not Jewish), he was determined to stake out his territory. This was the more striking given that when he had submitted his first play to Broadway (a revision of his college play about a strike in the garment industry in New York modelled very closely on his own family) he was told it was 'too Jewish'.

Later, he would be accused of creating Jewish plays in which the Jewish identity of the characters was denied. Willy Loman, in *Death of a Salesman*, based on his uncle Manny who lived across the street from the Millers on East Third Street in Brooklyn, it was said, was stripped of his religious identity. Given everything Miller had written to this point it is hard to agree, though the setting is plainly the Miller home. His earlier play, *All My Sons*, set in Ohio, had not called for Jewish characters, being based on a real incident which occurred in that state and which was the subject of a public inquiry. *The Crucible*, of course, was set in seventeenth-century New England while *A View from the Bridge* was set in the Italian community of Red Hook, on the Brooklyn waterfront. *A Memory of Two Mondays* featured a character clearly based on Miller himself, who for nearly two years had worked for an anti-Semitic autoparts company in Manhattan, but, a largely nostalgic piece, it found no space for concern with anti-Semitism. In the early 1960s, however, with *After the Fall* and *Incident at Vichy*, he would place Jews, and the Holocaust, at the centre of his attention. In part, he was responding to those same events that stirred others to confront experiences put out of the public memory – the Eichmann trial, Hannah Arendt's book, *Eichmann in Jerusalem*, the Frankfurt trials. In part, however, he was led to this subject by his marriage to his third wife, Inge Morath, whose own early life had been lived in the shadow of Fascism.

Concern with the past was always an essential element of Miller's sensibility, and memory a means of access to it. He consistently mined his own experiences and those of others. Invention involved working with the given. He hesitated for some time before writing his autobiography, *Timebends*, for fear that he would squander the material on which he relied for his plays. The past, however, was crucial in another sense. He resisted alike the idea of history as a force independent of human agency and an absurdity which saw humankind as a product of cosmic ironies. There was a native existentialism to his work which saw characters as a product of their own actions. In his plays past events have present consequences. It was what he had learned from the history of drama, from the Greeks, through Shakespeare to Ibsen, his primary models. Beyond that, it was the basis for his vision of a moral world in which guilt was finessed into responsibility. In *Death of a Salesman* Willy Loman travels into the past through memories which he filters in an attempt to understand his present failure. That past, however, is not separated from the present. His characters are their past, not in the sense of being wholly defined by it but in the sense that they carry it with them. His plays were about people who could not, in the end, walk away. For Joe Keller in *All My Sons*, as for the culture of which he is a part, it is the future that matters. He tries to deny responsibility for his past but memory constantly retrieves it. Memory thus becomes an agency of moral action even as it becomes the site of contention.

In *The Crucible* what is at stake, beyond the issue of innocence and guilt, is the question of reality. But the evidence presented is 'spectral', that is to say it is fantasies encased in memories, and in the 1990s Miller likened such evidence to the 'recovered' or 'false' memories invoked by those who brought retrospective charges of sexual molestation against their relatives. With no actual evidence, years having passed, courts had nothing more to measure than conflicting memories. In *The Price* a shared past turns out not to have been shared at all, each person reshaping it to serve their present needs, insisting on their innocence at the price of proposing the guilt of others, a theme equally of *The Crucible* and of *After the Fall* and *Incident at Vichy*.

Beyond this, the past exerted another kind of pressure. The Miller family in the 1920s were wealthy. Having clawed their way out of the Lower East Side, they lived in an eleven-room apartment just north of Central Park. They were the epitome of the immigrant dream. Then, in 1929, they lost if not everything, then nearly so. The chauffeur-driven car, the maid, the summer home at Rockaway, went, along with the apartment and they moved across the river, ending up in a small frame house on East Third Street in Brooklyn.

Around him he saw the fixities of life dissolve. He never forgot those years and returned to them in play after play. They had taught him what, as a Jew, at some level he already knew. Everything could be taken away. They taught him that there were human values too easily forgotten in the pursuit of a happiness often confused with material wellbeing. It was for this reason that, in memory, he returned to that period – in *After the Fall, The American Clock, Playing for Time, Broken Glass* – intent to dramatise the fragility of existence. If he insisted that the function of the writer was indeed to be a rememberer it was not because he was interested in writing historical dramas but because the past is carried in the blood, because to forget is to deny who we were, who we are and who we might be, because there are exemplary lessons and to fail to learn them may be to pay a price too great to bear.

Early in their relationship, Inge Morath took Miller to Mauthausen concentration camp. Why did she do so, she who had resisted the Nazis and might be thought free of guilt and responsibility alike? She did so because the memory of those times remained fresh and because she was about to marry a Jew. She was an Austrian (and Austria had given the world both Hitler and Eichmann) and she spoke German. As Miller put it, 'her mind kept sifting through a past with which she wished to make peace'.[2] She had first learned of the existence of the camps when Allied aircraft flew overhead dropping thousands of leaflets, the leaflets a young Rolf Hochhuth had been set to retrieve. They contained photographs of shoes, the piles of shoes left behind by those who had gone to their deaths, the shoes which appear as a leitmotif in Sebald's work.

Now, as they drove through the countryside, past people who failed to raise their heads to see who was passing, Miller contemplated the fact that they must have done the same as Jews were transported to the camp, adding, 'Nor could I blame them altogether, and that was the troublesome part. I inevitably wondered what I would have done in their place, powerless as they were to intervene – if indeed such a thought had ever entered their heads' (523).

Mauthausen (where once, to celebrate Hitler's birthday, three hundred Jews were shot at two-minute intervals) was not then a place of pilgrimage or tourism. A watchman allowed them in. They walked around, the watchman acting as a guide. They saw the stone slab, with a curved cradle where a person's head could be rested, and the funnel to allow the blood to flow. Here gold teeth were knocked out. They saw the barracks and the stone cairn marking the spot where a Russian general had been forced to stand in sub-zero temperatures while water was poured over him until he died in a block of ice.

Afterwards, they retreated to a café below the camp. Inge's eyes had brimmed with tears throughout the visit. 'The builders of this place', Miller subsequently remarked, 'and the indifference we saw about us now – to say the least – had destroyed her youth and laid on her for the rest of her life a debt that she did not owe and could never pay and yet carried always, because of her humanity. It was a mystery' (524). It was that sense of indifference that took Miller and Morath to the Frankfurt trial where one of the witnesses, though not while the Millers were there, was Otto Dov Kulka, who as a child had sung in the children's choir at Birkenau, and played Beethoven's 'Ode to Joy' on a mouth organ. A decade and a half later, Miller would return to the business of music in Auschwitz.

They were there for only a day but more came out of it than an article for the *New York Herald Tribune*. He was struck in particular by the remarks of Fritz Bauer, the chief prosecutor who had fled to Sweden during the war and who had subsequently set himself to the pursuit of former Nazis: 'he was now a disillusioned man; it was not so much that the Nazi idea was holding on, he thought, but that people simply wished to avoid the past altogether, and certainly to deny its horrors' (525).

His own sense was that 'important though it is to memorialise the Holocaust lest it fade away, its inbuilt causation remained largely unexplored terrain for most people, who continued to nurture their fear of tribes and persuasions other than their own like something sacred'. The problem with 'identifying the universals in the Nazi condition', it seemed to him, 'was precisely that power and stupidity were so commonly joined in the world that there was something unremarkable about it, something lacking in explosive illumination' (526). Beyond that was a more profound dilemma for as the character based on Morath remarks in the shadow of the concentration camp in *After the Fall*, 'no one they didn't kill can be innocent again'.[3] The question is not merely to acknowledge what happened there but to know what to do with that knowledge.

The trip to Austria had an immediate effect. He was at the time involved in writing a play in which he endeavoured to come to terms with failings in his own life, the failure, in particular, of two marriages even as he was contemplating a third. He had been working on several aspects of the play for some years in a text which eventually split into two plays, *After the Fall* and *The Price*. Those elements traced back to the 1930s. What was new now was a realisation that the camps could be said to have a causal connection with the personal, social and political betrayals that he was otherwise intent to trace. He began to feel committed to the play, he later explained, 'because its theme – the paradox of denial – seemed so eminently the theme of Germany, and Germany's idealistically denied brutality emblematic of the human dilemma of our time'.[4]

When the play, *After the Fall*, was staged in 1964 its reception was dominated by the fact that it was seen as featuring the recently dead Marilyn Monroe. It was widely denounced for what was seen as its bad taste. It was, many critics claimed, not even an apologia but a self-justification. Certainly at its heart was a figure clearly based on Monroe and despite his denials there was no doubt that it was an exploration of his relationship with her. What was less noticed was that it was also an attempt to explore his relationship with his first wife and with his parents, and that it was concerned to forge a connection between personal failings and those evident in the domestic drama of the House Un-American Activities Committee, and the wider drama of the Holocaust. For those who did note the connection, the very disproportion was the cause of another sense of unease.

He had been led to write *After the Fall* some years earlier when he was asked to consider adapting Albert Camus's *The Fall* for the screen. At the heart of this novel is the moment when a man hears someone fall or throw herself into the Seine. He makes no move to save her, merely moving on. What, we are seemingly asked, do we owe one another? For Miller, though, involved as he was in the complexities of his relationship with Monroe, there was another question. What if Camus's protagonist had saved the girl? What, then, would have been the limit of his obligation? Miller, who had, in his own eyes at least, sought to rescue his then wife, as he thought, from her suicidal tendency, had been left dismayed both by her and his own capacity to draw a line, declare a limit to commitment. In the end, he fears, there is only one loyalty, to the self, and as his protagonist contemplates his life, and the times through which he has lived, he is afraid that that has, indeed, proved the ruling principle. Those who built the concentration camps, he muses, were glad of only one thing, that others and not they would be dying there.

Yet the issues of indifference, self-interest, the limits to human commitments, swirled around in his mind and eventually came together in the play, a contrapuntal piece about love and its withdrawal, loyalty and its abrogation, a desperate need and the failure to acknowledge yet alone meet it.

Death of a Salesman was to have been called *The Inside of His Head*, a reflection of the fact that much of the play was to take place in the protagonist's memories, as he searched restlessly for the cause of his own failure. It would, perhaps, have been more accurately applied to *After the Fall*, a memory play in which all the action is contained within 'the mind, thought, and memory' of the protagonist, Quentin, a lawyer who pleads his own case before the bench of his conscience in a play which raises the question of who is qualified to judge the actions of others if all are flawed.

The protagonist of Camus's novel is called a 'judge-penitent' and that would be an apt description of Quentin who is both accused and judge and whose memories constitute the evidence he lays before himself as before the audience. These are in part Miller's own memories and if the form of the play resembles a psychoanalytic session, with the subject reaching back into his own past, there is a sense in which the play served precisely that purpose for its author who was himself poised, uncertain as to how to proceed with his life.

Miller had spent several expensive years in analysis and was entirely familiar with its form and processes. Beyond that, its methodology precisely mirrored that of his own drama in which the past offered a clue to present circumstances not least because it inhered in that present to which it was causally linked. In *After the Fall* the characters are always present. They are not required to leave the stage. Their 'entrances' and 'exits' are prompted by recall. They simply 'appear and disappear instantaneously, as in the mind'. A National Theatre production of *Death of a Salesman*, directed by David Thacker and designed by Fran Thompson, used a revolve to bring characters, always present, into the foreground as Willy Loman's memory activates them. The dialogue in *After the Fall*, Miller insists, 'will make clear who is "alive" at any moment and who is in abeyance'. The formulation is an interesting one. In memory, the distinction between life and death is blurred. The effect, Miller suggested, 'will be the surging, flitting, instantaneousness of a mind questing over its surfaces and into its depths' (11). Against a grey background, drained of colour, those memories flame brightly.

The Holocaust was a late addition to the play, which opened in January 1964. Rising above the set and dominating the stage, Miller indicates, 'is the blasted stone tower of a concentration camp. Its wide lookout windows are like eyes which at the moment seem blind and dark: bent reinforcing rods stick out of it like broken tentacles' (11). In his opening speech Quentin invokes his meeting with a woman, in Germany, only months before. She is the reason for the play's existence. Tempted to marry her, he is forced to trace back through his life to account for the failed relationships in his past, as if he dare not start again without coming to terms with the denials and betrayals that he trails behind him.

And what is true on a personal level is true, too, on a public level for a fundamental concern of the play is how it is possible for life itself to continue after the reality of the camps has been exposed, the denials and betrayals which have come close to unstitching the fabric of social life and the substance of human connectiveness. The connection between the private and the public is made when individual acts of betrayal prompt the lighting of the concentration camp tower. In justification of what some saw as a disturbing disproportion he insisted that everything begins somewhere, that evil is not an abstract force but human nature writ large.

The solution to which the play moves is, in effect, announced early on by Holga, the character modelled on Morath:

> One day the house smells of fresh bread, the next of smoke and blood. One day you faint because the gardener cut his finger off, within a week you're climbing over the corpses of children … What hope can there be if that is so? I tried to die near the end of the war. [*she rises, moves up the stair toward the tower*] … I dreamed I had a child, and even in my dream I saw it was my life, and it was an idiot, and I ran away. But it always crept back on my lap again … And I bent to its broken face, and it was horrible … But I kissed it. I think one must finally take one's life in one's arms. (30–1)

Inge herself tried to die, climbing on the parapet of a bridge to kill herself, but was restrained by a wounded soldier returning from the eastern front. The play is not without its sentimentality if also its disturbing truth. 'Is the knowing all?' asks Quentin. The death of love, the burning of cities, the shadow of the camps all teach that 'we are very dangerous!' that we encounter one another 'not in some garden of wax fruit and painted trees, that lie of Eden, but after, after the Fall, after many deaths' (120). The mannered language suggests a substitution of rhetoric for analysis. The knowledge of imperfection, it seems, is enough. There is nothing to do but renew faith. With this insight, Quentin goes to meet Holga and his troubled thoughts fade to blackness.

Where he was criticised for exploiting Monroe's death, the real problem of the play comes from the fact that it was written in the moment he had discovered a personal redemption that made reconciliation with his own life both necessary and possible. Extended to a metaphysical principle it seems less than adequate. The camps become of a piece with all other acts of betrayal, to be accepted for what they are, evidence of human failing, before moving on. Critics saw the play as written in the shadow of Monroe's death. Its real problem was that it was written in the bright light of his new life with Morath. The question of indifference is sidestepped. It remains a play of genuine force and complexity but memory, which serves to bring so much evidence before the bar of consciousness, is bequeathed to darkness. Those who have filled his life remain, a final stage direction tells us, 'endlessly alive' but they have been assigned their place in a pattern which satisfies Quentin because he needs no more of them than their blessing. The camp tower is no longer lit as if its meaning, too, had been exhausted in the telling.

After the Fall opened the new Lincoln Center Theater and despite the air of scandal accompanying it proved so successful with audiences that a further play was commissioned. Fresh from the Frankfurt trials, he now tackled the Holocaust more directly, not by setting his play in the camps, but by entering the anteroom to this horror. *Incident at Vichy* is set in a place of detention in Vichy France. It was inspired in part by his memory of a story told to him by his former psychoanalyst, Rudolph Loewenstein, who had hidden in Vichy before the Germans moved in. It concerned a Jewish analyst who had been arrested with false papers but was saved by a Gentile he had never seen before who took his place. In part it owed something to a friend of his wife's, an Austrian prince called Josef von Schwarzenberg, who had refused to cooperate with the Nazis and spent much of the war in France engaged in menial work.

Not the least of the ironies associated with the play, however, was that when it was produced in England he found it necessary to explain the nature and significance of the SS, just twenty years after the war. It would go on to be banned in the Soviet Union, largely, it seems, because of its focus on Jews at a time when the Soviet Union's anti-Semitism was becoming the subject of international protests, including from Miller who in that same year, 1965, took on the Presidency of the international writers' association, PEN, at a time when culture was being enrolled in Cold War battles. His involvement in PEN was one further evidence of his wife's influence. She had always been fascinated with Russia and was anxious to go there. The Soviet Union, meanwhile, was keen to open back channels to the West.

Sitting in the Frankfurt courtroom, like Peter Weiss he was particularly fascinated by the figure of 'Papa Kaduk', who at Auschwitz had a habit of randomly shooting prisoners but who, after the war, had subsequently gone on to establish a reputation as a gentle nurse. Like Weiss and Sebald Miller was struck by the fact that while these events had been taking place in Auschwitz and the other camps, ordinary Germans, like the members of the jury, had been going about their daily business either oblivious to or wilfully ignoring what was occurring and apparently having no memory of it or interest in the subsequent revelations: 'while this was happening they were shopping, putting their children to bed, going on picnics on sunny days ... while mothers like themselves and children no different from their own were forced to undress, to walk into a barren hall, and breathe the gas which some of the defendants now sitting here carefully administered'.[5] Beyond this, like Weiss he noted considerable opposition to the trials as if the stirring of such memories were at odds not merely with new national priorities but even with human decencies.

In the article he wrote about the Frankfurt trials, in many ways a revealing and disturbing piece, Miller was concerned with two things. Firstly, he was exercised by the possibility of a revived Nazism, a fear born out of a suspicion of Germany that would continue when the Berlin Wall came down, he being by no means certain that a unified Germany would be good for the peace of Europe. What 'makes the German to this day an enigma to many foreigners', he explained, 'is his capacity for moral and psychological collapse in the face of higher command' (65). The problem of the trials, as it seemed to him, was that 'they are being called upon to identify with the victims when their every instinct would lead them to identify with the uniformed, disciplined, killers'. The German soul, he insisted, 'is caught in the same airtight room with theirs – the part that finds honor and goodness and decency in obedience' (67). The authoritarianism of the German, Miller suggests, had once been leavened by a Jewish scepticism which had humanised it. Genocide had thus both been a result of the German character and compounded it. The German, it seemed to him, writing in 1964, was paralysed, a word that he had used with respect to the behaviour of the West when talking of *The Golden Years* and that he would use again in *Broken Glass* in 1994.

Only secondly was he concerned to explore the wider significance of the violence being exposed by the trial. How, like George Steiner, he wondered, could a country of such culture, such technological and scientific excellence have committed such crimes? And beyond that, what is it in man that makes such things possible? Throughout his career Miller drew on the figure of Cain, and did so again now in his essay on the Auschwitz trials. Given freedom, the son of Adam and Eve committed murder. It did not start in Auschwitz. 'So the question in the Frankfurt courtroom spreads out beyond the defendants', he insisted, 'and spirals around the world and into the heart of every man. It is his own complicity with murder, even the murders he did not perform himself with his own hands. The murders, however, from which he profited if only by having survived' (67–8). Those last five words, of course, had a special relevance, and not only for a Jew like himself, immune to everything but the accusation he levels against himself, which he had levelled in *After the Fall* and which he would level again in *Incident at Vichy*.

In his essay he begins to reach out beyond this courtroom, invoking the existence of the atomic bomb, an instrument of mass murder. A year later he would be taking a lead in the opposition to the war in Vietnam, as did Peter Weiss, suggesting that his new play could be said to have a bearing on that, too.

After publication of his article he received hostile mail, unsurprisingly especially from Germany. He was accused of demonising an entire people rather than distinguishing the guilty from the innocent. He would be similarly accused in relation to *Incident at Vichy*, one critic invoking Karl Jaspers's *The Question of German Guilt*, which warned against categorical judgement of a nation. He was guilty, it was said, of willingly characterising an entire people, ascribing to them modes of thought and behaviour. Miller's point, however, was precisely that the guilt extended beyond the accused. In 1997, Daniel Jonah Goldhagen, to an equally fierce critical response, published *Hitler's Willing Executioners: Ordinary Germans and the Holocaust*, in which he insisted that guilt did extend in this way not least because 'the perpetrators, "ordinary Germans", were animated by a particular *type* of anti-Semitism that led them to conclude that the Jews *ought to die*'.[6] There was, in other words, a history, that he documented, which made the inexplicable explicable, and which provided the fertile soil for Nazism that, far from resisting, Germans embraced. Germans were, he repeated, 'fundamentally anti-Semitic' (63).

Incident at Vichy is set in Vichy France in, it appears, 1942. A number of men have been rounded up by the police and are held in a 'place of detention'. One by one they are summoned for interrogation. At first, they are unclear why they have been arrested but it is increasingly evident that what is at stake is their Jewish identity, or, in one case, their gypsy identity. Those not so identified are given a pass and allowed to go free. They leave through a door which leads to the street and freedom. The police action has netted a seemingly heterogeneous collection of people but, finding themselves thus gathered in, they try to understand their situation, to prepare their defences, pronounce their innocence. The German officer who presides plainly finds his task distasteful but justifies himself, challenging his prisoners to evidence a selflessness which he is not himself willing to display.

The corridor has a single guard. The possibility of escape seems to exist, though we later discover that there were other guards beyond. Nonetheless, the question of acquiescence hangs in the air, something that disturbed Miller as it did Bruno Bettelheim. Interestingly, there is an account of a woman who found herself in a similar situation, not in France but in Lithuania. She, too, was rounded up and held with others, though they knew their likely fate as those in Miller's play do not. She resolved to escape and, allowing others unknowingly to distract the guard, walked out of the door. In the words of Lawrence L. Langer, who recounts the story in his *Holocaust Testimonies*, she is evidence not of communal resistance but of the 'solitary struggle of the impromptu self to stay alive', which in her case meant that she 'must of necessity isolate herself from her fellow victims',[7] as she did from her own mother, who was unwilling to join her. She was followed by the Lithuanian guard, who asked her why other Jews had gone unprotestingly to their deaths. He finally let her go. For Langer, the bravery of the gesture is inevitably tainted by its necessary selfishness as memory of it is shadowed by the breaking of family loyalties. Thus even courage becomes contaminated and memory 'is thus the reverse of redemptive, as the witness plunges into a buried past to rescue the private truths of the event we call the Holocaust' (157).

Having read so many survivor testimonies, with their evidence of inhumanity, Langer rebels against those who insist on seeing survival as evidence of a triumph of the human spirit. 'The ease with which the self adapts its identity to a surrounding situation', he insists, 'threatens the notion that spiritual *value* is the primary incentive for human conduct. Hence many Holocaust commentators cling to a grammar of heroism and martyrdom to protect the idea that the Nazi assault on the body and spirit of its victims did no fundamental damage to our cherished belief that, even in the most adverse circumstances, character is instinctively allied to the good' (162). Thus he even attacks Martin Gilbert, whose harrowing book, *The Holocaust*, with its detailed accounts of horrors, nonetheless ends with an encomium to the human spirit seeing survival itself as a testimony to this. For Langer, this is simply at odds with the truths carried forward by memory, a mythology to be preferred to the radical insights offered by testimony. Survival, he suggests, was more often to do with the suppression of spiritual value, the denial of loyalty, a retreat into the self, a suspension of those supposedly defining characteristics of humanity.

Yet, pitched against this are other stories. Tzvetan Todorov recalls the story of a woman, Mrs Tenenbaum, who had obtained a pass which permitted its holder to avoid deportation. She gave the pass to her daughter and then committed suicide to ensure that her daughter would accept it. That young woman lived a bare three months more, though in that time knew happiness. He highlights another story, that of a young woman who joined her mother on the journey to Treblinka rather than let her go alone. Loyalties, it seemed, were not so easily broken.

For his part, Miller creates a character in the person of Prince Von Berg for whom survival proves intolerable if it can only be purchased by indifference to others, though that itself, of course, could be presented as a form of self-concern. That it is not so is a measure of the fact that for all his insistence that good and evil 'are not compartments but two elements of a transaction' (*Echoes*, 72) he is still drawn to the necessity of identifying redemption. And what of the man whose survival is gifted to him? Of necessity he accepts the guilt which is a consequence of allowing another to die in his place. The question for Miller, outside rather than within the play, is 'what he makes of his guilt, having survived'. Besides, he notes, we are all survivors to the extent that when others die we are left, regretting the loss but quietly relieved and even satisfied at our own survival. In Miller's words, 'death, when it takes those we have loved, always hands us a pass' (73).

Incident at Vichy was set in the antechamber to the camps, not the camps themselves and though we, the audience, know their fate the characters do not with any precision. Yet there is no doubt that there is a selection going on and no doubt in their minds, finally, it seems, that the opposite of freedom is suffering and death. This, however, is Arthur Miller and not Kafka or Samuel Beckett, nor is this

Sartre's *Huis Clos* in which hell is other people. Miller's interest, in the play, lies in the one just man who justifies human existence and not the ironies of salvation won at the cost of human values. In *After the Fall* he had confessed that there were limits to selflessness, that we live after the fall and can continue only in the knowledge of a flawed humanity. The Holocaust had existed only as metaphor, a floating signifier, some ultimate extension of personal betrayals. Now he was concerned to explore the possibility of genuine selflessness, and there is such a man in *Incident at Vichy*, who on being given his free pass hands it to a man whose life, it is assumed, would otherwise be forfeit. Having declared that the unthinkable crimes of the Nazis have 'paralysed' everyone, he, himself, overcomes that paralysis.

As Miller explained in an essay in the *New York Times Magazine* to accompany the production (*Echoes*, 70), quoting Hermann Broch, 'And even if all that is created in this world were to be annihilated, if all its aesthetic values were abolished ... dissolved in scepticism of all law ... there would yet survive untouched the unity of thought, the ethical postulate.' He does, however, add a rider to this: 'What is dark if not unknown is the relationship between those who side with justice and their implication in the evils they oppose' (71). He was thinking, he explained, of the situation in Germany while acknowledging its extension to the United States. Indeed, he seems to have written this piece precisely to insist that the wartime setting was a function of plot and not theme.

Those who watched a woman stabbed to death outside their window in the Queens borough of New York City and did nothing were, he pointed out, of a piece with those who had stood aside twenty and thirty years before and watched the slow unwinding of genocide. Those whose sense of self-worth came from their contempt for 'the Negro' shared something, he suggested, with those who had derived theirs from the distance between themselves and the Jews. If there was a sense in which he was intent on insisting on the relevance of his new play to audiences who might not necessarily be drawn to a work about Jews in the Second World War, he was also underlining a truth of all his plays set in the past.

His was never an antiquarian interest. It was precisely the connection between past and present that concerned him, each period informing the other, and though in the person of the self-sacrificing Prince he seemed to be creating a selfless individual, in the course of the play he comes to understand the extent of his own compromises. For Miller, that was substantially the central issue in the play, something underlined by his observation of the Frankfurt trials in which German acquiescence had been as much on trial as those summoned before the court from their comfortable postwar existences.

As he remarked, 'Without for an instant intending to lift the weight of condemnation Nazism must bear, does its power not become more comprehensible when we see our own helplessness toward the violence in our own streets? How many of us have looked into ourselves for even a grain of its cause? Is it not for us – as for the Germans – the others who are doing evil? ... We do not have many wills, but only one; it cannot be continuously compromised without atrophy setting in altogether' (71).

In 1965, even as he looked back to 1942, he was already committing himself to a new cause. At his alma mater, the University of Michigan, he attended one of the first teach-ins against the Vietnam war and in his *New York Times* article suggested a direct connection between that war and the moral thrust of *Incident at Vichy*. Who 'among us', he asked, 'knew enough to be shocked let alone protest, at the photographs of the Vietnamese torturing Vietcong prisoners, which our press has published? ... There is no way around this – the prisoner crying out in agony is *our prisoner*' (74). Once again, he invoked the figure of Cain. For Cain's cry of 'Am I my brother's keeper?' however, he substituted 'Am I my own keeper?' (75). The problem, he suggested, is the difficulty of detecting 'our own hostility in our own actions' (74).

Incident at Vichy, then, takes an aspect of the Holocaust and presents it as a metaphor and there were those who objected precisely to that fact. Its sheer availability for co-option was seen as a denial of its unique nature. The risk was that a generalised human tendency towards violence, an acknowledgement of an inherent self-concern, a dehumanisation of the Other, would serve to vitiate the particular guilt of those who had proved innovators in cruelty and enthusiastic exponents of mass murder. Vietnam was not *like* the Holocaust, nor was the American treatment of African Americans analogous to the German treatment of the Jews.

There are other risks in *Incident at Vichy*. The sheer arbitrariness of the redemptive gesture implicit in Von Berg's offer of a free pass can seem little more than a testing of the proposition which underlay the Holocaust itself and which Camus explored in *Caligula*. If all things are possible then arbitrary good is no less available than arbitrary evil. This is evidence not so much of a moral system as of simple contingency. In a sense it is a play which explores available interpretations of behaviour as of history. These are exemplary figures for Miller as in another sense they were for the Nazis. Gathered here, awaiting their fate, are Jews, a Communist (who, like Peter Weiss, sees Fascism as a product of capitalism), a businessman, an actor, an aristocrat. They constitute a society and each member of this arbitrary society attempts to interpret the seemingly implacable fate which confronts him by applying different interpretations of experience, but religious conviction, political loyalty, adaptability, accommodation all prove equally irrelevant because what they confront has nothing to do with belief, reason or pragmatics. There is no more appeal against this fate than there is against death itself. Despite his invocation of Hermann Broch, there seems little space for the 'ethical postulate'.

There is also a hint of self-doubt on Miller's part, surely, in his acknowledgement that neither the actor, Monceau, nor the amateur musician, Von Berg, can secure immunity through their art, both theatre and music having been commandeered by the Nazis for whom art could be enrolled in their cause, an accompaniment to slaughter. Indeed, Miller has Von Berg use disturbing images to describe them. They are, he insists, 'poets ... striving for a new nobility, the nobility of the totally vulgar ... Their motives are musical, and people are merely the sounds they play.'[8] In a literal sense, this looks forward to the screenplay and play he would write, based on Fania Fénelon's book, *Playing for Time*, her account of life as a member of the Auschwitz-Birkenau orchestra. It is an acknowledgement both of the

Nazis' attempt to perfect the administration of death as though it were an art form and the inutility of art, indeed the complicity of art in the face of such presumption. And where does that leave Miller's own play?

Among those vacuumed up by the Vichy police are an old Jew and a gypsy, manifestly what they are and hence in some sense the standard against which the others are to be judged, what they wish most desperately to deny being. Their status as victims, though, is not to be taken as evidence of their innocence. As Miller has the most articulate of the group observe, 'Each man has his Jew; it is the Other. And the Jews have their Jews' (288). It was a remark that led some to suggest that in generalising prejudice he was generalising guilt and hence going some way to withdrawing the indictment that surely should be levelled.

In Auschwitz-Birkenau, in 1944, a Sunday concert was staged in the spring sun. A female singer performed an aria from *La Bohème*. This was followed by a rendition of *The Charge of the Light Brigade*. The audience was appreciative. During the course of the performance, however, a young woman ran towards the barbed wire behind them and grasped the electrified fence, writhing from head to toe. The audience – members of the SS – and the musicians watched as a second woman tried to release her, only to be electrocuted in turn. The music continued. A third woman ran forward with a wooden stool and endeavoured to lever them free. Silhouetted against the brightness, 'the crooked bodies formed grotesque swastikas'.[9] The two women were taken away to the sound of music from *The Merry Widow*. The concert was such a success that members of the orchestra were rewarded with an egg, between them. In the men's camp, Primo Levi listened as another orchestra played 'Rosamunda', a polka recast to accompany the slave labourers as they marched out to work. Like any army, Levi remarked, 'they needed an orchestra to march them quickly and regularly to work'.[10] Nor did music necessarily humanise the players. A musician from Amsterdam, Josef Lessing, became a kapo and one of the most cruel. A violinist, he strutted around with a truncheon, beating those who at other times listened to his music.

If *Incident at Vichy* approached the Holocaust obliquely, *Playing for Time* stepped inside the concentration camp itself. In 1980, he was asked to write a screen adaptation of Fania Fénelon's account of her time playing the piano in the orchestra in Auschwitz-Birkenau. He later adapted it for the stage. Oddly, there is no reference to either in his 1987 autobiography, *Timebends*, perhaps because it was accompanied by controversy as the central role was given to Vanessa Redgrave, well known for her support of the Palestinian cause and therefore, unjustly, accused of anti-Semitism by some. Eventually, even the diminutive Fénelon, four feet eleven, herself raised objections, disturbed by the notion of being played by an actress considerably taller than herself. The controversy continued for some months in the press while Miller received hostile letters at his Connecticut home. There was talk of advertisers boycotting it. Even the filming was not without its problems, though when it was transmitted it was well received.

It was thirty years after her release from Bergen-Belsen, where she and others had been marched from Auschwitz in November 1944, that Fénelon sat down with Marcelle Routier to write *Playing for Time*. She had, she explained, to 'get over the camps' before she could write, 'thirty years of silence during which I tried to forget the unforgettable'. She wrote, she explained, to exorcise memories of the orchestra having 'never left the camp' (ix). Those with whom she had shared that time – and the book begins with a reunion of two of them – had taken different paths. As Marcelle Routier explains, 'Forgetfulness has helped them in various ways; the dimming of memory has enabled them to survive' (vii). They gather, though, to retrieve what they can, uncertain 'which part of life in the camps the others might have decided to forget' (vii), as though forgetfulness were a matter of choice. By contrast, Fénelon, we are told, is 'a person of merciless recall', and it is that assertion which is in part the book's claim on our attention.

Fania Fénelon, whose real name was Goldstein, and whose number at Auschwitz was 74862, was a Parisian nightclub singer who worked for the Resistance. Like so many others, she felt immune entertaining German soldiers and walking the streets of her own city.

Early in 1943 she was arrested and sent to Drancy prison, a holding centre, before, nine months later, being sent to Auschwitz.

Playing for Time is a book and not an oral witness and that is immediately apparent in the language. The cries of girls are described as 'needle-sharp fragments, little scraps of broken mirror' which sink 'razorlike' into her brain (3). Where oral testimonies are often tentative, fragmented, delivered in a simple un-metaphorical language, written accounts tend to reach for a different language. There are times when that language seems to blunt the immediacy of memory as if it were necessary to shape emotional responses, but aesthetic choices can distort, as if it were necessary to charge language with a kinetic force not inherent in the events described. Memories are teased out, shaped into a narrative when what was lacking in the camps was precisely a narrative, a sense that there was a motion towards or away. Drama has the advantage of stripping out description, re-instituting the primacy of speech.

Fénelon's is not a story of privation as compared to most accounts of Auschwitz-Birkenau. She was assigned to the women's orchestra led by Alma Rosé, daughter of the first violinist of the Vienna Philharmonic Orchestra and a niece of Gustav Mahler. The members of the orchestra had what most of the inmates did not – warmth, showers, pleasant accommodation, free access to toilets – while lacking what they did – lice. They were the privileged. Yet they, too, lived on sufferance. In the world of the camp no one knew if he or she would live to see the next day. Of the twelve hundred who had arrived on Fénelon's train, only one hundred had not been immediately taken to the gas chambers. She learned the lesson that all had to learn. As the air filled with the smell of burning bodies, 'I had to remain indifferent – indeed to take no notice. To what kind of heaven', she asked herself, 'should one turn to pray for this kind of insensitivity?' (60).

Nonetheless, there is something strange in Fénelon's question, 'Would there be enough survivors from the orchestra for the truth to emerge, or would all that would be known come from some few survivors of the camp who had cast a shocked glance in our direction and retained, in all good faith, only a subjective vision reflecting their feeling of the moment: envy, jealousy, anger, bitterness, or black humour?' (155). In what sense would the memories of those lacking the admittedly suspect privileges of the orchestra members be subjective, deformed by envy, jealousy etc., and those of Fénelon and the others objective? What truth could be captured by those who suffered but did so less, by those who played stirring marches, but not by those men and women who marched out to a labour that would kill most of them?

The answer in part lies in their privileges. On one occasion they are allowed out for a walk in the woods, accompanied by two guards. They are not dressed in the striped uniform of the camp. It is a unique moment but as they pass a peasant Fénelon observes of her that she 'would doubtless say, later, that we hadn't been as badly off as all that ... That's what eye-witnessing is all about' (202). And, indeed, this is part of the problem of eye-witnesses. They report what their eyes witness. To see is not to understand. An action or event becomes exemplary for lack of a context, for want of full knowledge. Miller would resolve this in part by accommodating the musicians' experiences to those others, and be attacked for doing so.

In part what is being claimed by Fénelon, however, is precisely a different sense of time. Though rehearsals might be day-long, these captive musicians were not subject to the same physical and mental extremes as those others for whom surviving the moment was the overwhelming need. Their work was not designed to break them. Their day had a rhythm of its own determined not simply by arbitrary rules, to which they were indeed subject, but by the necessities of their art, which preserved its own internal rhythms. They might be forced to play their instruments but those instruments, and the music they played, constituted a resource. Even as they were forced to entertain those who imprisoned them, they could find within the music an alternative world, even a source of beauty. They were fed the same food as others but were rewarded, from time to time, with parcels from 'Canada', where goods taken from those about to die were available. They traded in the covert markets and were allowed a latitude denied to others. How, then, was their truth to be given primacy?

In *Playing for Time* Fénelon displays a remarkable memory. Indeed, in the introduction to her book she claims never to have forgotten anything. In the camp she could recall the stories she had read in Corneille, Racine and Molière and retell them to her fellow prisoners. She kept a notebook, though it is hard to believe it could have been as detailed as her thirty-year-old memories suggest. Even so, her recall of conversations is surprising as, thirty years after the event, she remembers an encounter with the orchestra's leader which extends over six pages, much of it reconstructed dialogue, accompanied by descriptions of gestures which would sit more comfortably in a novel – 'her voice became gradually warmer, less harsh and metallic', 'Alma gave a throaty little laugh', 'She fell silent, her face expressionless', 'Her nostrils flaring, Alma was trembling with indignation and retrospective anger', 'Her jaws tensed, contracted, she clenched her fists' (111). It is not that this is inauthentic – authenticity being a primary claim – but that what is being offered here is not simply witness, uninflected evidence, but a story, or series of stories.

Each member of the orchestra has such a story. One is a Party member, looking for some future apotheosis, another is a woman who finds consolation in a love affair with a fellow musician, still another is a weak-willed individual who offers herself to the guards in return for food. And there are stories beyond the orchestra's barracks. In the summer of 1944, Mala Zimetbaum, formerly of the Belgian resistance, and her lover Edek, from the Polish resistance, for a while stand as an image of hope for all of them, indeed all those in the camp (the same story is told by Primo Levi in *The Drowned and the Saved*, who recounts it, he explains, because he 'would like the memory of it to survive').[11] They escape, but are brought back and killed (Levi recalls that she cut her wrists with a razor blade on the gallows and slapped her executioner's face with her bloodied hand, resulting in her being trampled to death, details not included by Fénelon), locks of their hair being preserved to this day in the Auschwitz museum. Fénelon is, indeed, assembling an orchestra of characters rooted in the chilling reality of camp life but shaped, too, by her and her collaborator Marcelle Routier.

Presiding over the orchestra was Lagerführerin Maria Mandel, a beautiful SS officer, whose beauty the women find particularly disturbing so at odds is it with her role. Dr Mengele would also prove personally attractive. At other times, though, SS men, and the kapos placed in charge of them, appear what they are, their features distorted and grotesque, their response to music crude and uncomprehending. This is a world, in other words, that is impossible to read. Survival depends upon pleasing those who are the source of the threat. To bring tears to the eyes of Mengele, who shed no tears over those on whom he experimented or those he sent to the gas chambers, is seen as a triumph of their musical skills because it may guarantee the continuance of the orchestra and hence their lives. They are so many Sheherazades. When the architect of the Final Solution, Heinrich Himmler, arrives, everything must be done to please him. The music which sustains their inner lives must be deployed to give pleasure to a man responsible for the death of their families.

Fénelon and the other women ended up in Bergen-Belsen where death was delivered via phenol injections. Here, she later realises, she was within yards of the dying Anne Frank, different stories coming together, the chain of different memories momentarily touching. Her account ends with a summary of the subsequent lives of those with whom she spent her time in Auschwitz-Birkenau. It is, for the most part, a story not merely of survival but of triumph. She herself died of cancer, in Paris, in 1983.

What, then, does Arthur Miller make of this, first as a screenplay and then a stage drama, losing, as he necessarily does, the voice of Fénelon, whose memories these are, whose editorialising in part conditions not merely what we see but how we regard what we see? Her book was written, she explained, as an act of exorcism. It is dedicated to her fellow survivors. She writes to lay ghosts to rest, to drive out the images which come to her at night because, as she explained, 'I'm still there, I've spent every night of my life there, for thirty years.' She does not think of it, 'it' she explains, 'thinks *for* me' (ix). In his screenplay, Miller gives Fania a motive not apparent in the original text, in which Fania had set herself to forget: 'We must', she says in the camp, 'have an aim. And I think the aim is to remember everything',[12] a conviction underscored in the screenplay by an invented character who charges her with this responsibility.

For Miller, it was initially no more than a commissioned work, swiftly completed. Where Fénelon and her fellow musicians performed for their masters so, in a different sense, does Miller, though what for her and her fellow musicians was a necessity of survival, for him carries a commercial and aesthetic imperative. There are compromises at the heart of the artistic enterprise, an issue implicit in *Playing for Time* but which he was to explore in greater detail in a late play called *Finishing the Picture*. In the screenplay, he spells it out indicating that Fania, performing for Mengele and the camp Commandant, should be seen 'staring at the ultimate horror – their love of music', an irony underscored when Miller gives that Commandant Himmler's actual words as he thanks her for music that will be a consolation which 'strengthens us for this difficult work of ours' (58). More immediately, here was an experience to be inhabited and presented without Fénelon's mediating presence. The published version of the screenplay presents *Playing for Time* as 'Arthur Miller's Drama of the Holocaust', at first glance a dubious claim. Whose story, after all, is this? Her memories, seen through thirty years of troubled dreams, become his crafted drama, shaped first for the screen and then the stage. But her memories, too, are shaped in collaboration with an author scarcely innocent of the demands of narrative.

Fénelon's book opens with a preface by Marcelle Routier which tells of a reunion between Fénelon and two of those who had suffered with her. Fénelon's own account begins in Bergen-Belsen, with her liberation, then switches to her arrival in Auschwitz, then briefly moves back to her detention in Drancy. The screenplay, however, begins as she entertains German troops in a nightclub, a foreshadowing of the later scenes in which she would again perform for the enemy. What had been a free choice was to become a requirement. The action then switches immediately to the cattle trucks on which she and others are proceeding towards Auschwitz, each individual picked out by the camera. They drink from a nearly-full bottle of water which is then seen empty as we move forward in time and the ordered scene that had marked the beginning of the sequence gives way to disorder, anarchy and death.

The train comes to a halt and the selection begins, though Miller places Mengele – not yet arrived in Fénelon's text – on the platform, conducting affairs. And here is the first hint of Miller's intent in his adaptation. Beyond the special circumstances of this group of women, the essence of whose story differs radically from that of the generality of those sent to the camp, he is concerned to explore the broader reality of Auschwitz. While insisting that the camera 'memorialises the faces' of those on the train as they are taken to their death, and invests even the abandoned clothes of the dead with the personality of those who wore them (a shoe, for example, is to be seen worn by an individual and not simply as an object), he is looking to the broader issues.

When the women are taken into the reception block in the book they undress and see handbags and jewels on a nearby table. In the screenplay there are 'hundreds and hundreds of valises, stacks of clothes, piles of shoes, bins of spectacles, false teeth' (15). Oddly, a chess set and compass highlighted in the sequence on the train as belonging to a young boy and a chess player have also made it into this room, though there would have been no time for them to do so since they belong to those taken away to the gas chambers in the selection. Seeing them, moreover, prompts Fania to turn towards the crematoria with a fearful understanding which can as yet have no basis since she believes the others on the train to be secure having been carried off on trucks marked with red crosses. In a desire to individualise the victims, to stress Fania's connection with rather than separation from the other victims, and no doubt also in a desire to bring forward the knowledge that will shortly terrify her, he asks the viewer to understand that symbolic truth has primacy.

The desire to individualise is something more than a writer's wish to paint a vivid portrait. As Miller notes: 'From time to time, one or more of the secondary characters will emerge in the foreground of this story in order to keep alive and vivid the sense that the "background group" is made of individuals. If this film is to approach even an indication of the vastness of the human disaster involved, the minor characters will have to be kept dramatically alive even in shots where they are only seen and don't have lines' (33).

At the same time, he is anxious to make his protagonist a representative figure. Thus Fénelon, never required to do hard labour, is pictured doing such, along with her companions. Her friend Marianne (Miller strangely changes the 'Clara' who figures in Fénelon's account to 'Marianne') has a camp number that is more than a quarter of a million higher than Fania's, as if he wished to collapse different times and prisoners into one. The story of a bizarrely aberrant group is to be made to stand for those who in fact had looked upon them with contempt and suspicion. Miller does, indeed, it seems, wish this to be his drama of the Holocaust.

In his screenplay, Miller has a resource not available to Fénelon: simultaneity. As Mengele is shown listening to Fénelon singing 'a smoky, very Parisian ballad', something that does not occur in the book, but a means of Miller linking Fénelon's performances for the German military in Paris with those which she gives in Birkenau, his face is first superimposed on hers and then seen as he directs deportees emerging from a freight car to right and left, death or life. Flames reflect orange light on his face, he who never approached the crematoria. Ironies are underscored. In contrast to the book, the orchestra is shown playing as the transports unload.

Miller also introduces a character of his own, Shmuel, a prisoner, an electrician, of whom he says, he is 'perhaps deranged, perhaps extraordinarily wise' (46). This wise fool reappears from time to time, having seemingly recognised in Fania someone to whom he can entrust a task. When he comes across her averting her eyes from the violence he insists, 'You have to look and see everything, so you can tell him when it is over', the he, it seems, being God. It is a writerly gesture, the more so when the women are finally liberated from Bergen-Belsen where they have been taken and Shmuel appears in a barn door. The light behind him, we are told, 'contrasts with the murk within the building and he seems to blaze in an unearthly luminescence. He is staring in a sublime silence, as now he lifts his arms in a wordless gesture of deliverance, his eyes filled with miracle, and turning he starts to gesture behind him ... A British soldier appears beside him' (145). It is a curious elevation of the physical into the metaphysical, a desire to colour redemption with a transfiguring grace which owes nothing to Fénelon's account, though she had herself been in a delirious state due to typhoid. Here, though, there is no question of us seeing through her eyes. The gesture is Miller's and there is much in the screenplay that is.

The screenplay underscores elements present in Fénelon's book but which are also fundamental themes of Miller's plays and essays. Both Mengele and the Nazi woman whose enthusiasm for the orchestra sustains it are presented as beautiful. For Fania, that is the essence of the problem. 'We are the same species. And that's what's so hopeless about this whole thing' (62). And in a speech not in the original book, but an echo of *Incident at Vichy*, Miller has Fania declare, 'I am sick of the Zionists-and-the-Marxists; the Jews-and-the-Gentiles; the Easterners-and-the-Westerners; the Germans-and-the-non-Germans; the French-and-the-non-French ... I am a woman and not a tribe!' (78–9). This is a speech echoed elsewhere in Miller's work and anticipated in the observation that 'the Jews have their Jews'. In an echo of *After the Fall* Fania tells a fellow musician that she will survive 'and everyone around you will be innocent, from one end of Europe to the other' (100), later remarking that 'we know a little something about the human race that we didn't know before' (124). They meet, in other words, after the fall.

The script is informed by the postwar debates about the responsibility of the Allies that were to be found in Hochhuth's play but were not part of Fénelon's book. Thus a Catholic remarks, 'When I first came here I was sure that the Pope, the Christian leaders did not know; but when they found out they would send planes to bomb out the fires here, the rail tracks that bring them every day. But the trains keep coming and the fires continue burning. – Do you understand it?' (100). The answer offered by another member of the orchestra is that 'They don't want it to seem like it's a war to save the Jews' (128).

The film ends with the reunion described in the preface to Fénelon's book but now we are told on one page that thirty-five years have passed, when in fact thirty years have done, and a page later that they had not met for thirty-three years. In the play version this becomes more than forty years. Miller was once asked of *Death of a Salesman* when it was set only for him to confess that he was unsure, never having had a clear grasp of time. That proves true here as yesterday and today begin to blur and the final camera direction indicates that the camera should pull back so that 'we resume the normality of life and the irony of it; and now we are outside on the avenue, the bustle of contemporary traffic; and quick close shots of passersby, the life that continues and continues ...' (150).

Miller begins the play version with Fania addressing the audience directly and, as he indicates, there was to be no attempt at realism. He was happy to dispense with a set, with changes of locale made in full view of the audience. Even the constricting barracks were to be presented symbolically. When the women's heads are shaved, he suggests bald wigs or simply cloths to cover them. Costumes were to be picked from the floor in full view. In general, he indicated, 'there is no need to "naturalize" changes of costume or scene; everything can be done in full view and should be since the play, in one sense, is a demonstration, a quality that need in no way be disguised'.[13]

The notion of a demonstration suggests a degree of detachment on the part of the audience which is plainly at odds with the action. The presentation, however, is a response to the paradox whereby the 'truth' of the past is to be approached via the lies of art, even an art supposedly rooted in the real. And in this play, of course, art is compromised because it concerns those whose survival depended precisely on a compromise expressed through their art, an art that is amoral, carrying, it seems, no values, available for co-option, a background noise to genocide. These musicians are capable of seeking protection inside music but that music is interrupted by the sounds of killing as if art were in fact an evasion, the comfort to be taken in the face of death, and this has implications beyond the special circumstance of the Holocaust.

In a play which confesses to the suspect nature of art, the exposure of theatricality becomes a necessary acknowledgement of complicity. The cinema invites the viewer to submit to images which overwhelm. The theatre perforce confesses to its facticity. The play is a 'demonstration' in that it insists on a detached observation of fact and process.

The speed with which victim becomes oppressor is clear when Marianne is placed in charge of her fellow musicians and becomes a sadistic kapo only to be stripped of her position on their liberation and assaulted by those she had brutalised. This, too, is a 'demonstration'. Fénelon told her story to exorcise her demons, to lay memories to rest. Miller, requested to adapt her work, appropriated those memories to shape an accusation and offer a confession, a confession of confederacy. At one moment Fania declares herself half Jewish, with permission from the bureaucracy cutting her yellow star in two. When she reinstates the other half she is claiming an identity not fully her own, as Miller's Lawrence Newman had done in *Focus*. She is aware, however, of the ambiguity of her gesture since she rebels against that tribalism of which she was a victim.

No one in Fénelon's memoirs, or in Miller's screenplay or play, is innocent. How could they be when they have seen what they have seen and done what they have done? To have survived is to have done what was necessary in order to survive. At the time anxiety and guilt were displaced by necessity. Later accounts have the air not simply of evidence presented for the judgement of successive generations, but of guilt, spoken aloud in order to relieve the pressure of repression.

This is not, of course, to suggest any equivalence between those whose power led to fundamental human betrayals and later to denials of responsibility and those whose weakness necessitated acts only justified by extremity. It does, however, suggest a gulf between Fania Fénelon, whose ambiguous memories took so long to move from word to page, and Arthur Miller, for whom her work was to be valued at least in part for what it told of the human capacity to betray, a truth which reached out beyond the confines of Auschwitz-Birkenau and Bergen-Belsen.

In Miller's case the Holocaust had become a source of fascination, in part because of his own ambivalent relationship to his Jewish identity, which he alternately embraced and rejected, at least as an exclusivist creed demanding unquestioning loyalty and spiritual submission. But his real interest lay in what it had to say about the human animal whose predilection for violence had been identified in the Jewish and Christian Bible and whose history seemed to challenge Enlightenment values. His plays repeatedly reached back because he saw less evidence of progress and transcendence than of repetition, a wilful refusal to learn not simply the lessons of the past but the capacity of human beings to deny what they are and what they are capable of being. When he pulls the camera back at the end of the film version it is not because the action is over, the issues resolved, memories dragged into the light and exorcised, but because they are not.

Miller seems to have wished Fénelon to be representative even knowing, as he did, that she was privileged. For him, the project soured precisely as others announced proprietary rights over these experiences, defending them against him for what they saw as being the liberties he took and angry that an actress should have been cast whose politics they assumed to be at odds not simply with their own but also with the spirit of the camps. It was as if to support the Palestinian cause would be to sanction a renewed genocide, oblivious to Fénelon's own resistance to exclusive categories and Miller's still more rigorous rejection of them.

Miller called the Holocaust the 'watershed of our history'. *Playing for Time*, he suggested, completed the theme of *After the Fall* and *Incident at Vichy*. In other words, he saw it in the context of his own work and not simply as a film turned play. At its core, he explained, he saw 'the anomie and paralysis before the knowledge of mass destruction'.[14] He was drawn to it because 'the same questions haunt us'. For Fénelon it was the past that was unfinished business. For Miller, it was the present.

And there it might have rested were it not for the fact that former members of the orchestra dissented from the 'merciless recall' of Fania Fénelon and what they saw as the distortions of Arthur Miller. What was in dispute was the version of the past offered by Fénelon; what was challenged was both her version of that past and the central role she seemingly ascribed to herself. We are all the protagonists of our own dramas and *Playing for Time* is constructed out of Fénelon's memories. Perhaps it is hardly surprising, therefore, that she became the redemptive force. 'If it hadn't been for you ...' declares Irene, one of the survivors, not finishing the remark; 'if you hadn't been there', announces Anny, 'we would never have held out' (viii). The leader of the orchestra, Alma Rosé, by contrast, is described by Fénelon in altogether less enthusiastic terms. That was not, however, how others recalled it and when, in 2000, a biography of Alma Rosé appeared, written by Richard Newman, with Karen Kirtley, the balance shifted somewhat.[15] Memories, it seemed, were in conflict.

In his book *Holocaust Testimonies: The Ruins of Memory*, Lawrence L. Langer poses a key question when he asks, 'To whom shall we entrust the custody of the public memory of the Holocaust? ... Candidates' he observes, 'abound, all in search of a common goal: the detour that will, paradoxically, prevent us from being led astray. All', though, 'are in thrall to what Maurice Blanchot calls the "impossible real". All approach a limit beckoning them across Blanchot's "perilous threshold". With the exception of surviving victims', he suggests, 'all are witnesses to memory rather than rememberers themselves. They have an "unstory" to tell' (39).

But why the exception for 'surviving victims'? Do they not, in Blanchot's words, have 'an unstory' to tell, reshaping memories or simply staging a drama of which they are the protagonists? Those who survived to write their accounts have unstories to tell as they endeavour not merely to recall what was suppressed, sometimes unconsciously so, but to shape such fractured memories into coherent and understandable narratives. To enter narrative is to enter the history of narrative. To enter language is to enter a history of language. And which former self is to be uncovered now for others, that hard, protected, embattled self with its fierce concentration on its own needs as opposed to others, or that other self which used to function in a world in which selflessness was a virtue?

As Langer rightly says, 'a memoir still abides ... by certain literary conventions: chronology, description, characterization, dialogue, and above all, perhaps, the invention of a narrative voice' (41). That narrative voice is a controlling one which, as in a novel, predisposes the reader to certain assumptions about the narrator and hence those others with whom she/he has dealings. For the novelist, this can be a conscious source of irony (as in Willa Cather's *My Ántonia* or F. Scott Fitzgerald's *The Great Gatsby*); for the memoirist

208

it serves to place the narrator at centre stage, as others are moved to the wings. When Fania Fénelon wrote *Playing for Time* it was not only the story of an orchestra. It was her own story and she, therefore, was at the centre.

Alma Rosé, the leader of the orchestra, is the source of a necessary but forbidding authority in Fénelon's and Miller's accounts. She is on the periphery of the world they choose to stage. In the postwar world, however, her brother recalled an encounter in an outdoor market. A woman overheard his name and asked if he was related to Alma, who had played at Auschwitz. She was one of three Slovak sisters who had been in the camp. 'Your sister saved the lives of many Jewish girls' (10), she insisted. The sisters had not been members of the orchestra.

Fénelon's account of Alma Rosé was plainly not the whole truth. The concerts they staged, the woman in the marketplace explained, had been the source of hope for many. Indeed it turned out that many camp survivors challenged aspects of Fénelon's account. As Richard Newman points out, Anita Lasker-Wallfisch, cellist in the orchestra and later a well-known musician, publicly denounced the 'fantasies' set forth in *Playing for Time*. In particular, she and other members objected to the harsh version of Rosé it presented and which she characterised as 'an offensive portrait' (11).

Alma Rosé was born in Vienna in 1906, of Jewish heritage on both sides of the family, though her parents married in an evangelical church. Her father was a violinist: concert master of the Vienna Opera and Philharmonic Orchestra and for six decades leader of the Rosé Quartet (Rosé was a stage name. He was born Rosenblum). Her mother was Gustav Mahler's younger sister. In the 1930s, Alma Rosé led a women's touring orchestra. On one occasion, in 1935, as Richard Newman points out, she performed some twenty-five miles from what would become Auschwitz-Birkenau, where she would die. She married a Czech musician, a marriage that would give her a Czech passport which later proved useful. The marriage ended in 1935 and there were suggestions that for a musician anxious to succeed in Germany a Jewish wife had become something of an inconvenience. The Nuremberg laws of 1935 forbade marriage between Jews and

German citizens. He was not German but the implication was clear. He and his family later insisted that the divorce had no connection with events in Germany. However, after the war he was fined by the Czech authorities for fraternising with the Nazis.

Following the Anschluss in March 1938, Rosé's father was dismissed from the Philharmonic. By May, the Nuremberg laws were extended to Austria, which became part of the Third Reich. That August, Rosé's mother died. She had grudgingly converted to Catholicism to help her brother's career (which had been subject to Habsburg requirements), while her husband had become a Protestant. Such manoeuvres were of utility under the race laws. Rosé then fled to England, along with her father. There was no work for her there, however, and, fatally, she decided to go to Holland, where she could perform. She was still there when German forces moved in, in May 1940.

Alma Rosé attempted to escape through France, armed with a prussic acid capsule, but was arrested in Dijon and taken to Gestapo headquarters. From there she was moved to Drancy, in the north-east of Paris, from which 76,000 Jews would be deported (15). It was known as the 'antechamber to the death camps'. It was January 1943. She left on 18 July. Fania Fénelon arrived at Drancy in April 1943. In other words, two famous musicians were there at the same time, over-lapping by three months. Yet not merely was Fénelon unaware of this but no mention occurs in her book of the fact that she and Rosé had shared the same experience.

Of those on Rosé's transport, 128 children were gassed on arrival. She herself was assigned to the notorious Block 10 at Auschwitz I, where experiments were conducted on young women and girls. While there, she asked the *Blockälteste* (block senior), Magda Blau, for a violin. Astonishingly, she received it and against orders performed for her fellow prisoners. After the war, Richard Newman recorded Magda Blau as remarking, 'Alma had been the light at the center of one of those small glimpses of humanity, courage, and decency between the inmates, an individual whose behavior and performance – in spite of the pressure from the Germans – made life a little more bearable' (225). It was portraits of Rosé such as this that would lead some to challenge Fénelon's account.

The senior officer of the women's camp at Auschwitz II, Birkenau (named for the birch trees which grew there), on a site some three kilometres from the main camp, was Obersturmbahnführerin Maria Mandel (hanged in 1948), one who is shown in Fania's account seizing a young child from its mother and then surrendering it for gassing. She wished to establish a women's orchestra to match the men's orchestra in the main compound which had been established in 1941 with non-Jewish personnel. A second men's orchestra had been formed the following year at Birkenau. The women's orchestra was initially led by Zofia Czajkowska, also known as Tchaikowska, who in Fénelon's account is seen in largely negative terms but was more favourably remembered by others. Certainly, she seems to have shown both energy and talent in assembling the orchestra. To her, therefore, went some of the credit for the survival of Jews. One such, Hélène Scheps, a Jewish violinist from Belgium, recalled the 'miracle' that occurred when a well-dressed, 'civilized-looking woman' approached her as she emerged from the humiliation and terror of the reception process: 'An angel had come to take me by the hand' (232). Though given to anger, Tchaikowska was described by another camp inmate as a 'fine lady'. It was she who aided the transfer of power from herself to Rosé.

In *Playing for Time* Fénelon recalls a fellow musician as saying of Tchaikowska that she was 'a solid peasant type ... completely unpredictable, stupid and hysterical ... fuelled by spite'. People such as her, she says, 'have to please the Nazis in order to survive ... They've ended up thinking like Nazis, feeling that they too are a master race' (133). It was Tchaikowska, though, who added Polish folk songs to the repertoire, songs which deeply affected the sick and the dying. Nonetheless, it was the arrival of Rosé that transformed the orchestra. She professionalised it, but she would also do what she could to rescue people.

When a woman falsely claimed to be able to play the accordion, Rosé trained her to save her life. Rosé also seems to have set herself to employ Jews in the face of suspicion of such a policy. Though she knew that she relied on the support of the Nazis, it was not for them that she played. In the words of a young percussionist, Hilde

Grünbaum Zimche, 'Alma believed that if we perhaps survived this period, we could prove we could build something in the camp, and survival would be proven worthwhile, and perhaps we could continue [to perform] with the same group of people after the war. In my opinion, she didn't believe we played for the Nazis but [that] we played for ourselves in order to survive. She also knew the orchestra had to be good or we would be liquidated' (*Alma Rosé*, 246). She constantly improved conditions, making demands of the camp administration. For the Polish Anita Lasker-Wallfisch, 'she commanded an absolute and total respect from us, and by all appearances, from the SS' (251).

Oddly, Fénelon has Rosé remark that 'My father, who was first violinist in the Berlin Opera orchestra, had a privileged position, and the coming of the Führer didn't harm us at all ... We were part of a minority that the Nazis kept for themselves. My father's quartet was well known throughout Europe. Stories of arrests and deportations seemed things in another world. They didn't affect me or even interest me ... And my arrest cut me off from it completely' (*Playing for Time*, 112). This seems to be wrong in every particular. Did Rosé lie or was Fénelon's total recall not total after all? What is disturbing about this reported statement by Rosé is that it feeds the model of her that Fénelon seemed anxious to develop. If it was a memory, it was demonstrably false and this is a problem with testimony. The Director of the Yad Vashem archives has said that 'Many were never in the places where they claim to have witnessed atrocities, while others relied on second-hand information given by friends or passing strangers.'[16]

In the person of Alma Rosé, perhaps, it is possible to see a resolution of the paradox whereby SS officers could be moved by music as of the dilemma of the musicians in giving comfort to their destroyers. For her, the SS were an irritant, albeit with the power of life and death. Their approval might be crucial but that was not what she found in music, which was something more than a bargaining tool. It was even something more than mere escape. It was an invitation to excellence. What she heard was not what her oppressors heard. She served the music rather than the music serving her. It existed, Rosé insisted, in 'a sphere where we could not be touched by the degradation of concentration camp existence' (*Alma Rosé*, 262).

According to Lasker-Wallfisch, 'Alma had turned the orchestra into a camp institution of considerable standing long before Fania arrived as a singer' (261), though Fénelon was crucial as an orchestrator and remarkable for her prodigious memory of musical scores. But there was no doubt as to who was the more important. Speaking after the war, Hélène Scheps insisted that 'Alma saved our lives ... If Alma hadn't been there, we wouldn't be here' (262).

Among the objections of survivors to Miller's film version was the poor playing of the orchestra. In fact they had worked hard to perfect their sound. Interviewed subsequently, they insisted on the beauty of their music. The crematorium was a hundred yards away and the selections would eventually take place a bare fifty yards away, but in the face of death, and with their own lives threatened, they worked, in the view of many of them, to create something more than a functional soundtrack to murder. Lasker-Wallfisch denied that the other prisoners spat at them, an accusation to be found in Fénelon's account, though there were certainly those who resented their privileges.

Among Fénelon's statements that were subsequently challenged was her assertion that Rosé had beaten the girls and defended herself by insisting that the German conductor Wilhelm Furtwängler had done likewise, that she was a woman without a heart. Richard Newman quotes Otto Stresser, an archivist of the Vienna Philharmonic, as denying that Furtwängler had ever struck anyone and doubting that Rosé would have suggested otherwise (272). A member of the orchestra had no memory of her beating people but did recall the penalties she exacted on those she regarded as failing in their responsibility to the orchestra and the music.

Unsurprisingly, memories were inexact and conflicting. There were, for example, those who recalled them playing during selections, while others denied it. But there is a consistency to Fénelon's version of Rosé, as a significant but not entirely likeable or central figure. She was vital to the orchestra, but so, too, was Fénelon herself, who claimed Rosé as a confidante. When Rosé was told that she was to be released, Fénelon writes that she chided her for her willingness to entertain the Wehrmacht, identifying this as an aspect of her German identity, forgetting, seemingly, that she was Austrian and had been arrested as a Jew. Rosé's response is that at least her 'friend' Frau Schmidt (an internee described by Fénelon as 'the Führer of Canada') was pleased, inviting her to a private dinner. Newman reports Zafia Cykowiak's denial of this supposedly close relationship. She insisted that 'Fania and Alma were not that close ... In fact, despite Fania's gifts as a musician, her driving ambition and schemes were often at odds with Alma. There is no doubt that Alma respected Fania for her professional musicianship, but I cannot imagine her as a confidante' (298). Others denied that such a release would even have been possible. The supposed private dinner was in fact Frau Schmidt's birthday celebration, attended even by members of the SS. When Rosé fell ill and died after this Fénelon suggests that it was thought to be the result of jealousy by Schmidt, who herself wished to leave and could not stand the idea of someone else doing so. She cites Schmidt's disappearance as plausible evidence of this. In fact she was also admitted to the hospital with similar symptoms. Both, it seems likely, suffered from botulism.

When Rosé died members of the orchestra were permitted to pay their respects. But here is another discrepancy between the memories of survivors and Miller's film version. As Newman puts it, 'Orchestra survivors to a person have said that the death scene in *Playing for Time* blasphemes the realities of Birkenau. The film ludicrously showed Mengele placing Alma's violin on her breast, a detail and fact not attributable to Fania's account' (303). It was not the only complaint levelled at the film. Among other objections, it was pointed out that Schmidt was a Sudeten German prisoner and not an SS woman.

However, the real venom was reserved for Fénelon's account. When it was published, it prompted fierce rebuttals. Lasker-Wallfisch denounced the 'preposterous distortions of the truth about everyone who took part in this "drama"' (323). Helena Dunicz-Niwińska claimed that it was more of a novel than an eye-witness account, a view, Newman tells us, shared by several others. Yet another survivor described it as 'garbage or worse' (323). When the film appeared, Lasker-Wallfisch complained that

> In the film Fania Fénelon emerges as the moral force who bravely defied the Germans and held members of the orchestra together, while the conductor, Alma Rosé, is depicted as a weak woman who imposed cruel discipline on the orchestra for fear of the Nazis and who was heavily dependent upon gaining Fania's approval. It just wasn't like that ... Fania was pleasant and talented, but she was not as forceful as Alma, who helped us to survive. She was the key figure, a woman of immense strength and dignity who commanded the respect of everyone. (323–4)

Fénelon's account, Newman explained, struck many survivors as 'fanciful' and 'even wildly invented'. Her contempt for Poles, Slovaks, Czechs, Germans and German-speakers distorted the memoir while her remark that she felt a woman under the gaze of Mengele was regarded as offensive and absurd. She remained a member of the orchestra less to protect them than herself. Among 'the most derogatory distortions of Alma's attitudes', he claims, 'was Fania's depiction of the near-hysteria of the orchestra' as they prepared for the arrival of Reichsführer Heinrich Himmler, architect of the concentration camps. In fact, Newman points out, 'Himmler never visited Birkenau after 17–18 July 1942.' Fénelon's account is thus an invention.

So, the claim that she 'has forgotten almost nothing' (*Playing for Time*, vii) seems wide of the truth. But what are we to make of an account which another orchestra member invites us to regard as little more than a novel? In so far as it is offered as witness, memory is set against memory as memory is set against recorded fact. Memories do conflict. One witness recalled Auschwitz as devoid of birds; another recorded being struck by the presence of birds, a normality so at odds with what went on in the camp where people could only wish to fly away. These were different people at different times. In the case of *Playing for Time*, however, we are confronted with a group of people who shared an experience but are at odds over key aspects of that experience.

This was not the last time Miller would revisit this period. With *Broken Glass*, in 1994, however, he travelled back in part through his own memory. He had long recalled a strange figure from his youth, a man who habitually dressed in black as though, in Chekhov's words, in mourning for his life. Along with that went a separate but equally compelling memory of a woman who lost the use of her legs for no reason that doctors could identify. He could, however, see no dramatic potential in such memories until they came together in a play with which he returned to 1938 and Kristallnacht. Why then? In part, perhaps, it had something to do with developments in Europe. On the one hand he had seen signs of a revival of neo-Nazism, but along with that had gone convulsions in Yugoslavia which meant that as the play was in rehearsal what was being called 'ethnic cleansing' was once again happening at the heart of Europe. Just as he had been struck in the 1930s by the paralysis affecting the western powers, so, now, the paralysis of the woman in his play emerged as a primary metaphor in a work in which the central character, Phillip Gellburg, wrestles with a Jewish identity to which he is hesitant to commit himself. That dilemma has effectively paralysed Gellburg's relationship with his wife. Seeing no connection between events in Europe and himself, he has also allowed the connection between him and his wife to atrophy. For her part, his wife now has a justification for her inaction. She is no longer capable of action.

When a Jew, whose parents had been deported to Poland the previous year, assassinated a German diplomat in Paris, propaganda minister Joseph Goebbels approved attacks on Jews across Germany. On 9–10 October, SA members killed some one hundred Jews and carried thirty thousand off to concentration camps. Hundreds of synagogues were burned or destroyed. The glass windows of seven and a half thousand Jewish owned stores were smashed. Nor was this the action of the few. Daniel Jonah Goldhagen, whose book, *Hitler's Willing Executioners: Ordinary Germans and the Holocaust*, as its title implies, was designed to dispel the notion that anti-Semitism was exceptional, points out that the day after Kristallnacht, one hundred thousand Germans turned out for a rally in Nuremberg to hear the anti-Semitic diatribe of Julius Streicher. Alfons Heck, a member of the Hitler youth, later pointed out that after Kristallnacht, 'no German old enough to walk could ever plead ignorance of the persecution of the Jews, and no Jews could harbor any delusion that Hitler wanted Germany anything but *judenrein*, clean of Jews'.[17]

At the time, just out of university and intent on launching his career, Miller himself failed to register the enormity of events in Europe. He, too, was negotiating his Jewish identity, aware of the hesitation of American Jews to be too strident in their views. No wonder that betrayal and denial, both markers of the Holocaust for Miller, became primary themes of his work. Perhaps his disastrous first play, *The Man Who Had all the Luck*, in which a man is obsessed with the fact that he prospers while others suffer, carries something of Miller's own sense of guilt. It is possible, after all, that he tracked back through time to the Holocaust precisely because he was aware that his own immunity was the result of contingency and that that bequeathed him a responsibility. Miller was not a practising Jew but he knew all too well that that would not have granted him immunity had his family remained in Poland and a knock come on the door.

In his play, Sylvia is obsessed with photographs in the newspapers which show elderly Jews being humiliated. She feels this so acutely that it becomes of a piece with her personal dilemma, married to a man, Phillip, who seems to feel nothing acutely, taking pride in his employment by a company known not usually to employ Jews and in his son, who is making his way in the army despite the prejudice that exists there. This might make it seem that he celebrates his Jewishness, but in fact he finds its burden more than he can bear. Both husband and wife have been in denial and as a result have come to a crisis. The play ends, however, with a limited recovery by both, in the case of Phillip on the edge of death.

Miller's private memories become linked in the course of the play to public memories about an event thousands of miles away. Two traumas become one. He is not suggesting an equivalence, merely, as in so many of his plays, searching for a correlative. As shells landed on Sarajevo, he staged a play in which the bonds which should connect begin to dissolve, and two Jews are confronted with the meaning of their Jewishness.

It was not Miller's last comment on those times. In his one-act play *Clara* a Jewish detective offers the lesson he learned from the camps: 'That day in 1945 ... When they first showed those pictures of the piles of bones ... the bulldozer pushing them into those trenches, those arms and legs sticking up? That day I was born again ... and I'll never let myself forget it. "Do it to them before they do it to you. Period."'[18]

In 2002, he published a story set in 1936 in which a Jewish tap dancer meets Adolf Hitler. He escapes with his life. Miller never did quite escape his feelings of an ambiguous Jewish identity. He was not directly connected to events in Europe. He lost no family members, was secure and prospered. Yet he repeatedly returned to those times as if they contained a vital clue to something more than the obscenities of the camps. His distrust of the Germans – and he was disinclined, as we have seen, to see responsibility as being limited to the Nazis – did not imply that he saw the Holocaust as unique, though he acknowledged its profound significance. Beneath its particularities, he saw an abrogation of human responsibility, a denial of connectiveness, a betrayal of fundamental values whose stain spread out beyond that time and that place. His work acknowledged the void beneath the apparent securities of the quotidian but it also asserted the possibility of constructing a meaning seemingly evacuated from a life whose contingency could otherwise seem profoundly dismaying.

Memory was not merely the mechanism of recall, snapshots of an unconsidered past. Nor was it an uninflected witness to a lost time. It underpinned the notion of causality and hence of a morality that could hold individuals and societies responsible for their actions. For him, we contain the past and memory is the sword flourished in the face of denial.

6   Anne Frank: everybody's heroine

Though it took some time for the Holocaust to make its way onto the stage, there was one notable exception, a play based on a diary written by a young German girl who spent over two years in hiding in Holland. Her name was Anneliese Marie Frank. Her story was not a product of memory, at least not the story told within the pages of her diary. It was a contemporaneous account, though even she went back to refine it somewhat. But the ending of that story, an ending not part of the diary or the eventual stage presentation, is a product of the overlapping memories as those who travelled with her or encountered her as she was sucked ever deeper into the abyss of the camps, tried to recall those moments in later life, reading back through a knowledge of her new-found significance. In some sense the later story would seem to annul if not the diary then the mood and resilient confidence of a girl whose imagination and emotions pulled her towards the future, who was confident of her own inner strength and the possibility of some ultimate triumph.

For many, her account would contribute the most affecting and accessible approach to the Holocaust. For others, it would offer a misleading source of sentimentality, not because it failed to tell a deeply moving story of someone at the beginning of her life, unaware that there would be no tomorrow, but because it enabled the reader to celebrate her life precisely because we are spared the appalling squalor, pain and despair she would come to know and which linked hers with the fate of others who were not allowed the period of remission granted to her, being sped to their deaths without even temporary respite. Still others looked, largely in vain, for evidence of a sustaining Jewish faith. Peter Novick recalls the curious comment of Israel Gutman of Yad Vashem: 'Anne Frank is unlike many of the Jewish young people in the communities of Eastern Europe. The Dutch girl is not an organic part of Jewish national life and a Jewish atmosphere.'[1]

Aside from the fact that she was not Dutch (though, ironically, wished to become such, perhaps thereby playing into the hands of those who would later find her such an ambiguous emblem), she was, apparently, to be retrospectively eased out of her symbolic role as an image of those children destroyed in the Holocaust. This was a view seemingly endorsed by Lawrence Langer, a respected Holocaust scholar. As Novick has pointed out, forty years after the publication of the diary, and still more its adaptation into play and film, the Franks 'became the representations of the Holocaust that nearly everyone who writes on the subject loves to hate' (117). The 'universalism' celebrated in the 1950s came to be seen as the betrayal of a specifically Jewish experience; the celebratory tone at odds with the horrors not only of her untold story but more particularly of an experience that, with the decline of anti-Semitism in America, became, Novick suggests, the new core of a resistant Jewish identity. Some even thought that the diary did not belong in the Holocaust section of bookstores – itself an innovation of the late twentieth century – or, indeed, in the Holocaust story itself. Some, indeed, flirted with the idea that it might have been better if the diary had not existed or if the Franks had chosen some other solution to their dilemma than hiding away in their 'secret annexe'.

Such arguments, however, carried little weight with those many people belatedly alerted to the horrors of the camps and for whom the story of a doomed young girl proved a means of access if not directly to those horrors (and the indirection constituted part of the appeal) then to the human nature of what was lost. A child thrown alive into the oven, such as would be described by Elie Wiesel, stuns the mind. It is a blunt, impenetrable truth, intransitive in its absoluteness. A young girl full of hope, learning to live and love, and whose fate was known to all her readers but not herself, creates a sense of irony, pathos, tragedy, empathy, more easily accommodated, more easily assimilated. It might also seem to open the doors to sentimentality, inviting the reader, in the words of warnings sometimes offered before the results of football matches are announced to those who do not wish to know, to 'look away now'. But there it is – an account which ends with an ellipsis, from the Greek *elleipein* meaning 'to leave out'.

Anne Frank's memory was kept alive not merely by her story, told in print and on the stage, but by a physical memorial. An office and warehouse in Amsterdam, and more particularly its annexe, became the site for pilgrims anxious to visit what became a Holocaust shrine, indeed one of the most popular such. The question, however, was what that shrine memorialised. Even as for many it came to represent the millions who died in the camps, and more especially the children whose lives were forfeit before they were fully underway, there were others who contested, sometimes bitterly, not merely the representations of that life but also the legitimacy of the Frank family as a template for that suffering. If the past was to be remembered it was not this past.

The first attempts to place what became *The Diary of Anne Frank* were not successful. Publishers fought shy of it, in at least one case because of the frankness with which its author had discussed her burgeoning sexuality. Her father, Otto Frank, however, continued his efforts. Extracts from the diary first appeared in *De Nieuwe Stem* in 1946 and the Dutch edition, with some cuts, was published in 1947 in a print run of 1,500 copies. Meanwhile, a German edition was prepared. This differed in certain key respects, as a critical edition prepared by the Netherlands State Institute for War Documentation spelled out in 1989, so that subtle, and not so subtle, differences occur which mean that different audiences read slightly different versions of the text.

The German edition concealed the fact that the family spoke in Dutch during their period in hiding, rather than their native German, while 'the Dutch sentence, "he ended up looking like a giant and he was the worst fascist there was", was rendered as "watching him grow into an invincible giant". The Dutch: "And, indeed, there is no greater hostility than exists between Germans and Jews", became in German: "And there is no greater hostility in the world than between *these* Germans and Jews!" ... The rule that people in the Annexe were required "to speak softly at all times, in any civilized language, therefore not in German", became ... " ... All civilized languages ... but softly!!!" ',[2] though this seems to be a change also made in other editions. With a similar logic, 'heroism in the war or when confronting the Germans' became in the German translation 'heroism in the war and in the struggle against oppression' (173). A gap, in other words, was opened between those responsible for the Franks' plight and the German people in general. A particular Anne Frank was on offer, one approved by her father, who accepted these changes as being in the spirit of his daughter. The family, he insisted, had had many German friends. Nor should it be forgotten that they were themselves German. Nonetheless, his perspective is substituted for that of his daughter, who chose not to narrow responsibility.

The German edition finally appeared in 1950, with a print run of 4,500. It took five years for the paperback edition to appear. The first English and American editions came in 1952, the same year that Arrigo Vita was undertaking the Italian translation down the corridor from Primo Levi, six years after Otto Frank had started trying to secure publication of his daughter's diary in Holland and after ten American publishers had rejected it. These editions reinstated material cut from the Dutch edition, especially material of a sexual kind, while intruding a passage which does not exist in the original: 'The Germans have a means of making people talk' (74), which certainly has a British sound to it. In other words, though only to a very minor degree, each country's publishers modified the text to serve their own interests or to reflect what they assumed to be the sensibilities of their readers.

Nonetheless, after a slow and tentative start, the diary had begun to find a readership, a readership which expanded with the play in 1955 and the film in 1957, in which year the Anne Frank Foundation was established to maintain the premises at 263 Prinsengracht where the family had hidden and which today welcomes over half a million visitors a year. For nearly half a century now, schoolchildren around the world have been introduced to the subject of the Holocaust by way of the diary.

Yet the story ends before the family are captured. What we see is a young girl growing towards womanhood, angry, sometimes, with her mother, falling in and out of love, exploring her sexuality, recording the fears and hopes of a family following the progress of the war on the BBC, detailing long days and nights in the fragile security of their hideout. The ultimate plight of the Jews is reported by the young author but not seen directly. Despite the Franks' situation, the tone is largely optimistic. Anne, whose ambition it is eventually to become a writer, slowly matures in that role. The book ends with an entry in which she accuses herself of being uncharitable but commits herself to 'trying to find a way of becoming what I would so like to be, and what I could be, if ... there weren't any other people living in the world' (699), an ironic conclusion given her immediate fate.

The shock is that, despite the huge popularity of this book, indeed in some senses because of its popularity, it has for some become a symbol of all that is wrong with a certain kind of Holocaust writing. Here, it is suggested, is a young girl whose Jewishness appears not to sink down into her, to be a resource. Certainly she insists that 'Surely the time will come when we are people again, and not just Jews', but she never renounces that identity, even while asking, like Arthur Miller's Gellburg, in *Broken Glass*, why such a burden should accompany that identity:

> Who has inflicted this upon us? Who has made us Jews different from all other people? Who has allowed us to suffer so terribly up till now? It is God who has made us as we are, but it will be God, too, who will raise us up again. If we bear all this suffering and if there are still Jews left, when it is over, then Jews, instead of being doomed, will be held up as an example. Who knows, it might even be our religion from which the world and all peoples learn good, and for that reason only do we have to suffer now. We can never become just Nederlanders, or just English, or representatives of any country for that matter, we will always remain Jews, but we want to, too. (600)

The book necessarily stops short of everything that makes the camps what they were. In focussing on the individual lives of a group of people, and one person in particular, we are reminded of what was lost, of truths obscured by the sheer numbers of those who perished, but we are also saved from staring directly into the light of a dark sun. When told by her mother to think of all the misery in the world and be thankful that she is not suffering it, Anne's response is to observe, 'My advice is: "Go outside, to the fields, enjoy nature and the sunshine, go out and try to recapture happiness in yourself and in God. Think of all the beauty that's still left in and around you and be happy!" I don't see how Mummy's idea can be right, because then how are you supposed to behave if you go through the misery yourself? Then you are lost ... He who has the courage and faith will never perish in misery!' (520). The fact is, of course, that Anne did perish in misery, but that lies outside the diary and until long after its publication was unknown in its details. The first entry in her diary was made on 12 June 1942, and the last on 1 August 1944, three days before the Grüne Polizei burst into the 'Secret Annexe'.

Anne's father, Otto, was born in Frankfurt and served in an artillery regiment in the First World War. In 1925 he married Edith Holländer, from Aachen. Their first daughter, Margot, was born in 1926 and Anneliese in 1929. Otto had been involved in banking but when he came to Amsterdam it was as owner and director of a company selling fruit products, especially pectin, though he later diversified, trading in herbs, chemicals and pharmaceuticals.

Undoubtedly, the Franks could have escaped to England or elsewhere but Otto convinced himself that Dutch neutrality would be respected, as it had been in the First World War. When it was not he still stayed. Then, in 1940, a German decree called for the Aryanisation of Jewish firms. Otto contrived to nominally pass control to non-Jewish colleagues, believing, it seems, that it would be possible to wait out the war. There followed a series of anti-Jewish laws which, among other things, forced the transfer of his two daughters to a Jewish school. By 1942 it was clear that the family was in danger and he tried to secure their right to leave the country, but failed. Jews began to be rounded up and in July 1942 Margot received a summons to report for work in the 'East'. It was plainly time to act. Giving the impression that they were leaving for Switzerland, in fact they entered the 'Secret Annexe' of the company's warehouse, where they would be sustained by their friends. They were joined there by the van Pels family, and later by a dentist named Fritz Pfeffer (though Anne Frank changed their names to van Daan and Dussel, the latter meaning 'fool'). Some 25,000 Jews went into hiding in the Netherlands, though few as entire families. For a time, the Franks seemed to have escaped their likely fate.

Anne had been given a diary for her thirteenth birthday, in June 1942, and the first entries date from that time. It became not only a place to keep a daily record but somewhere she could write about her feelings, her hopes and frustrations. She created a correspondent called 'Kitty' and addressed her innermost thoughts to her. In July 1942, in a section (one of many) not included in the original publication, she described the restrictions under which the Jews had laboured:

> Jews must wear a yellow star; Jews must hand in their bicycles; Jews are banned from trams and are forbidden to use any car, even a private one; Jews are not allowed to do their shopping between three and five o'clock, and then only in shops which bear the placard Jewish Shop; Jews may only use Jewish barbers; Jews must be indoors from eight o'clock in the evening until 6 o'clock in the morning; Jews are forbidden to visit theatres, cinemas and other places of entertainment; Jews may not go to swimming baths, nor to tennis, hockey or other sports grounds; Jews may not go rowing; Jews may not take part in public sports. Jews must not sit in their own or their friends' gardens after eight o'clock in the evening; Jews may not visit Christians; Jews must go to Jewish schools...(226)

In October, she acknowledged the likely fate of those being rounded up. She knew that arrested Jews were taken to Westerbork, in the province of Drente, and then sent on. The Franks were avid listeners to the BBC, which in June had referred to gassings in Poland. Anne wrote: 'If it is as bad as this in Holland whatever will it be like in the distant and barbarous regions they are sent to? We assume that most of them are murdered. The English radio speaks of them being gassed' (273). Later she notes, more accurately than she could have known, 'Hungary is occupied by German troops. There are still a million Jews there, so they too will have had it now.' Elie Wiesel was one of them. She was thirteen when she wrote the first entry and fifteen when she wrote the last.

In Germany, meanwhile, on the eastern outskirts of Berlin, another fifteen-year-old girl, Liselotte Günzel, was keeping her diary. On 22 November 1943, the RAF bombed the city. She wrote, 'The whole inner city is said to be a heap of rubble. Friedrich[strasse], [Unter den] Linden, Leipziger Strasse, Alex[ander Platz], everything destroyed, Auntie K. bombed out. My school burned out, can't go there anymore.' In what even Goebbels admitted was an inferno, 1,132 tonnes of high explosive and 1,331 tonnes of incendiary bombs had been dropped: 3,758 people were killed, 574 were missing and half a million were homeless. On 29 December, having spent hours in the cellar of the family home as bombs shook the building, she wrote, 'We have one advantage over people from earlier generations ... we have become acquainted with mortal terror. Then everything falls away from a person; all the whitewash, everything apart from God that was most sacred in my life left me when death stretched out his finger toward me (I would never have believed it).'[3] Anne Frank was not the only talented young girl privately registering the horrors of the war. It was August 1943 before she learned that Jews were assuredly being murdered in the camps and April 1944 before she wrote of 'the whole Nazi brood, these war-criminals and Jew-murderers' (306).

Anne Frank's diary is as remarkable a document as readers have always taken it to be. Its power undoubtedly comes from the fact that while the war constitutes the background, and the possibility of detection governs her life, what is most striking is the portrait which slowly comes into focus of a young girl growing up, discovering her sexuality (at one stage she confesses to being sexually attracted to other girls), at odds with her mother, suffering the usual teenage irritability, developing an idealistic vision of the world and her potential place in it. It is possible to watch her slowly maturing sensibility and a parallel maturity with respect to her writing. She has, she solemnly tells herself, 'grown wise within these walls' (515), she who suffered occasional bouts of depression but who struggled to understand herself and her world even as her access to that world was so severely circumscribed.

It is because we are permitted an intimacy denied to everyone else – we read the diary to which only an imagined husband was to have been granted access – that we feel her fate as acutely as we do. We develop a confederacy, a feeling of protectiveness, that leaves us, eventually, as impotent to intervene as all those who had to watch as those they cared for were taken away. In other words, it is a book that enables the reader to understand something of the guilt contingent on that helplessness.

The reader, however, is privy to an irony that the author could not know as she wrote. The very gap between Anne's tremulous discovery of her 'boundless desire for all that is beautiful and good' (518), and the squalid and terrible fate which awaited her is known to the reader but not the writer and that is what makes the most naive of statements so painful to bear. Having come to the conclusion that there is 'in people simply an urge to destroy, an urge to kill, to murder and rage', and that 'until all mankind without exception, undergoes a great change, wars will be waged, everything that has been built up, cultivated, and grown will be destroyed and disfigured', she none-theless insists that she does not despair because 'I am young and strong and am living a great adventure ... I have been given a lot, a happy nature, a great deal of cheerfulness and strength. Every day I feel that I am developing inwardly, that the liberation is drawing nearer and how beautiful nature is, how good the people about me, how interesting and amusing this adventure! Why, then, should I be in despair?' (628–9).

Just two weeks before they were discovered she wrote, 'I have lots of courage, I always feel so strong and as if I can bear a great deal, I feel so free and so young! I was glad when I first realized it, because I don't think I shall easily bow down before the blows that inevitably come to everyone' (690).

They were betrayed. By whom? After the war a series of investigations were carried out, at first perfunctorily but after the Nazi hunter Simon Wiesenthal identified the officer in charge of the raid, former SS-Oberscharführer Karl Josef Silberbauer, with more thoroughness. The most likely candidate was a warehouseman, W. G. van Maaren, who had been hired in the spring of 1943 and who was guilty of a series of petty thefts from the building. He had been suspicious that someone was hiding there and certainly when the raid came the largely Dutch police made their way directly to the hiding place. Nothing was directly proved and he was never indicted.

It is impossible to know what changes Anne might have made in her diary had she survived, and we know her penchant for revision since she had already begun the process before she was taken from her refuge. Indeed, in the 1994 edition of the *Anne Frank Magazine*, Laureen Nussbaum points out that Otto Frank's suggestion that 'Apart from very few passages, which are of little interest to the reader, the original text has been printed' is at best disingenuous. In fact, beginning in May 1944 Anne revised her early spontaneous entries, in ten weeks filling three hundred and twenty-four pages with rewrites which offered Otto a choice between the two versions and, effectively, between two Annes, as she revisited her younger self. It is possible, therefore, to be over-protective of a text that was as it was in part precisely because she did not survive. Her experiences in the annexe were first written down, then revised by herself, by her father after her death and finally by her translators. We know what she included, not what she decided to omit. Anais Nin remarked of her own diary that 'The only person I do not lie to is my journal. Yet out of affection even for my journal I sometimes lie by omission. There are still so many omissions.'[4] The Anne Frank who now exists in memory is a product of various mediations. She is apparently shared by millions, that sharing being part of her appeal as if she brought together those who might otherwise seem divided by language and history. That it is a factitious unity, however, is the cause of something more than unease. For some it is the cause of affront.

Cynthia Ozick records the case of Cara Wilson, a Californian born in 1944, the year Anne had been seized and taken to Auschwitz, who conducted a correspondence with Otto Frank. As a twelve-year-old, she had unsuccessfully auditioned for a part in a projected Twentieth Century Fox film of the diary. Thereafter, she identified with Anne, but on a level so disturbingly trivial as to be the cause of dismay, the more so since Otto Frank himself, good-hearted but naive, seemed to welcome the relationship. In 1995, she published a book, *Love, Otto*, which recorded their exchanges. What Cara Wilson seems to have registered was a young girl anxious for her father's attention, jealous of her sister, and subject to the usual tensions of teenage life. What she seems wholly to airbrush out is the circumstance of Anne Frank's life. Tattoos, she reports in a letter to Otto, are all the rage, quite as if she were oblivious to the significance of tattoos to those entering Auschwitz-Birkenau. While claiming an identity with her role model, she seemingly failed to understand, and cared nothing to understand, why Anne Frank was important. In seeing her as her contemporary she was happy to annihilate history. This mattered, Ozick suggested, not because this young, and then no longer young, woman was aberrant but because she embodied precisely a desire to appropriate Anne for reasons of uplift and support that endorsed a denial of the darkness against which she stood, the darkness which eventually swallowed her and others. Anne was being remade into a Valley girl.

If the problem began with the initial editing and continued with its translation and presentation in various countries, it seemed to reach a climax with its dramatisation, a process accompanied by law cases and bad faith. The play version of the diary, though it would go on to be immensely successful and win the Pulitzer Prize, did not have an easy ride to production. The American journalist Meyer Levin, who had reviewed the diary for the *New York Times Book Review*, and was the author of a radio programme about it, was granted the rights to dramatise it by Otto Frank. Nor was he without qualifications. In 1945, as a war correspondent, he had been among the first to enter Buchenwald, Dachau and Bergen-Belsen. He had, Cynthia Ozick points out, assisted survivors to reach Palestine and was the producer of two films about their struggle to reach the putative homeland. In 1950, he had published *The Search*, which explored aspects of the Holocaust and its impact on himself.

He now secured Otto Frank's agreement that he should write a dramatised version of the diary and seek out a producer. He did so in the course of the following six months but when he submitted it to Cheryl Crawford, formerly of the Group Theatre, she, acting on the advice of Lillian Hellman, rejected Levin's text, a version which supposedly stressed Anne's Jewishness and concern with Jewish issues (though since his version is subject to an injunction it is impossible to be sure). Ozick is inclined to blame Hellman's anti-Zionism, seeing this as a function of her Stalinist commitments, though other producers also rejected the play. The rights then passed to Kermit Bloomgarden, who had worked on Arthur Miller's plays, and he commissioned Frances Goodrich and Albert Hackett (in fact husband and wife), successful screenwriters with MGM.

Levin responded by taking out an advertisement in the *New York Post*, only the beginning of a campaign that would eventually end in the law courts, an undignified process in the context of a work written by a young girl anxious to tell her own truths about the world. The Hacketts themselves wrote no fewer than eight versions before one was finally accepted.

When it was staged it was an immense success, though a Paris production, David Barnouw reports, was blocked by the US State Department, who judged that it might prejudice Franco-German relations (80). Once again, German sensibilities were to be protected.

Levin now brought a case against Otto Frank and Bloomgarden to the Supreme Court of the State of New York, claiming to be the victim of a breach of contract. The lawsuit failed but that was not the end of Levin's attempt effectively to claim ownership of the dramatic rights. A settlement was made but Levin persisted, even having his own version produced in Israel by an army theatrical company. In a subsequent book, fittingly called *The Obsession*, he claimed that his version had been rejected because it was 'too Jewish', despite the fact that, as Novick has pointed out, his own initial reviews of the diary had themselves praised the fact that it transcended what he called the 'sectarian circle' and celebrated the human spirit. Its Jewishness, it seemed, had intensified with the passing of the years until he was defending not so much the diary as his own desire to re-invent it as a holy script of the Jewish experience. He was particularly enraged that the adaptation was in the hands of non-Jews.

In fact, whatever the deficiencies of the play it did not do much violence to the essence of a diary that itself placed little stress on Jewishness, though the director had urged less emphasis on her admittedly tenuous faith and the playwrights did intrude a comment on the fact that Jewish suffering was of a piece with the suffering of others. At the same time, by its very nature, the play was bound to deviate from the diary. As Brooks Atkinson notes in an introduction, it 'is virtually an independent work ... The diary is subjective. But Mr. and Mrs. Hackett have had to create a play that takes an objective point of view toward a group of people of whom Anne is only one, and not necessarily the pivotal one.'[5]

The difference, of course, is crucial. The diary is, indeed, Anne Frank's understanding of the world. It and she change significantly with the passage of time. She is a writer, developing her skills of observation and expression. Her view is not that of others and it is precisely the refraction of events, often insignificant in themselves, through her sensibility which constitutes the book's claim on our attention. In the play, the situation remains. These people, to whom we are introduced and whose anxieties, petty and profound, we observe, are to be offered up to a fate they can barely imagine. But that is only one aspect of the work that Anne Frank herself hoped might one day be opened up for other eyes, if only those of her imagined husband. She was simultaneously a young girl for whom the diary was a confidante, a young woman growing towards maturity, and a writer discovering and developing her craft. In the play, the Hacketts become impersonators of Anne's voice. This is not, like Peter Weiss's play, a documentary precisely respecting the testament offered. It is a drama in which Anne is part of the ensemble and in which her voice is no longer her own and her testimony hence no longer her possession.

The play does include a number of voiceovers ostensibly from Anne's diary, but oddly these are simple inventions. Otto Frank, for example, begins by introducing an entry from 6 July 1942. There is no such entry and the entry we are offered is fallacious. Indeed, though the text is careful to identify the precise dates of entries, none of the speeches thus identified comes from the actual diary, the apparently authenticating voice being merely a fictive device. Indeed, even the moment when the diary is presented to Anne takes place in the secret annexe rather than on her thirteenth birthday, before the family went into hiding. It is hard to see why this was thought to be a good idea. The precision of the dating is surely offered as a guarantee of truth. Its speciousness is thus not merely surprising but self-defeating. Another entry, for example, is specifically identified as dating from 1 January 1944. Again, there is no such entry. Anne's final voice-over in the play takes place immediately after the police raid. In fact the last entry came three days before the arrest. This Anne wishes to be a dancer or singer. By this stage in her life, Anne Frank wanted, more than anything, to be a writer, hence the significance of the diary.

What we are left with is a play about a group of people struggling to get on with one another in straitened circumstances, aware of an external threat, along with a burgeoning love affair between Anne and Peter, the young man with whom she shares her time in the attic. What we are left with is a celebration of human resilience. What we do not have, and perhaps cannot have, is the diary simply transposed to the stage. Anne's life is no longer her own. She is one character among many.

The play continues beyond Anne's death, Mr Frank returning at the end of the war, a day after receiving confirmation of his daughter's death. But the play ends, or almost so, with Anne's disembodied voice sounding out: 'In spite of everything, I still believe that people are really good at heart' (174). The final line is given not to her but to her father, who confesses his shame that he lacks such a generosity of heart.

It was a line that would annoy some, precisely because it seemed evidence of a desire to turn the terrible death of a young girl into a piece of Cheeryble cheeriness. The fact is that she was, of course, optimistic, that until the police burst into their hideout her diary is full of encomiums to the natural world and her sense of her own possibilities. It is true that she belatedly acknowledged human depravity, to an extent that might have seemed surprising to those forgetful of what she had already suffered as a Jew, but this knowledge is balanced by her own resilience, a youthful enthusiasm. That tension is the source of a nearly disabling irony felt less by Anne herself than by those reading her work.

For Garson Kanin, the director, however, this was to be a Broadway product, uplifting, amusing, sentimental and, so far as possible, ethnically vague. Ozick quotes Kanin as saying that he wanted something 'spirited and gay', and suggesting that 'Hebrew' would 'simply alienate the audience' (85). He wanted to avoid the play becoming 'an embarrassing piece of special pleading ... The fact that in this play the symbols of persecution and oppression are Jews is incidental' and thought that Anne's own emphasis on her Jewish identity 'reduces her magnificent stature'. Seemingly oblivious to the reason that Anne was trapped in a hidden room in Amsterdam from 1942 to 1944, before being dragged away, he wished, it seems, to transform her life into a coming-of-age story in which a young girl triumphs, in her heart, if not in actuality, a romantic victim dying in the bloom of life with a declaration of faith in humanity, guiltily endorsed by her distraught father. Kanin had, he explained, 'no desire to inflict depression on an audience' (86). As Ozick points out, so little did Kanin seem aware of the meaning of what he was producing that in the role of Anne Frank's mother he cast Gusti Huber, a former member of the Nazi Actors Guild who earlier in her career had denounced non-Aryan actors.

Ozick and others had their own agenda, their own interpretations. If Anne was capable of stressing her Jewishness she was equally capable of insisting on other identities, of recognising a wider conflict. If her father and then the Hacketts had chosen to produce their own version of Anne, then Levin and, in a different way, Ozick had their own. Who owns Anne Frank? In a sense only Anne Frank, but she was not granted the time or circumstance to complete her story. What we have is not the story of Anne Frank, only the story she chose to tell before her eyes were opened and then closed, before the suffering which led to her death in Bergen-Belsen.

For all her optimism, what lay ahead, and what was slowly revealed, was not merely death but the breaking of her spirit as she was confronted with the evident truth that people, or those who had control over her life, were not good at heart. For those final months, however, we no longer have a young girl's naive understanding of life to rely on. Instead, those months have to be reconstituted through a chain of memory. At first the links in that chain seem secure enough but as the family's journey through the camps began so there were fewer and fewer sightings. The particular significance of Anne Frank, meanwhile, was only established with the appearance of the diary and many of the witnesses were not approached for some forty years.

The women whom Willy Lindwer interviewed for a documentary film in the 1980s, were at first unable to talk about their experiences. At points their accounts differed from one another. Some already knew the Franks, others did not. They had all been through appalling experiences and this other family, with its young girl, were on the periphery of their own lives as they were increasingly driven back on themselves, living defensively, securing their survival, closing down certain channels to the world in order to get through each minute, hour, day. Anne Frank had been one among many and her life not charged with a special significance. Now, the witnesses were asked to go back along the line of their memories and filter out those moments when they had glimpsed one girl among many, even one they knew, and place her at the centre of recall.

Of the 25,000 Jews who went into hiding in the Netherlands, one third fell into German hands, the Franks among them. They were taken from the Prinsengracht. Two of their helpers were arrested, one being released because of illness, and returning to run the Franks' business, the other escaping. The Franks were taken to the SD (Security Service) headquarters and then a prison before being transferred a few days later to Westerbork, the detention camp in the province of Drente. Between the summer of 1942 and the autumn of 1944, eighty-five trains left Westerbork, sixteen for Sobibor and sixty-six for Auschwitz.[6] Because they were accused of a crime, rather than being rounded up simply as Jews, the Franks were kept in the disciplinary barracks. What we know of the rest of Anne's life comes from a series of memories, some of them fragmentary and even contradictory. It is as though we see her proceed to her death through a series of flashlit but damaged photographs.

It was at Westerbork that Anne was seen by Janny Brandes-Brilleslijper, who had been sent there with her sister and set to breaking up batteries. It was hard and dirty work but they were not brutalised. Life was tolerable, though there was always the knowledge that their names could be called for the next transport east. She did no more than register the Franks' existence.

Rachel van Amerongen-Frankfoorder, who had worked in the resistance, also ended up working on the batteries:

> In the 'S' barracks I ... met the Frank family ... Otto Frank
> came up to me with Anne and asked if Anne could help me ...
> She was really so sweet ... gay and cheerful ... After a few
> days, I think that she, with her sister and mother, landed in the
> battery department, because almost all the women went
> there ... You didn't have to go outside – in the rain or in the
> mud .... I think Otto Frank was eager to arrange that for Anne.
> That's the reason that he came to me with Anne – not with his
> wife and not with Margot. I think that Anne was the apple of his
> eye ... It was a lovely family. (92–3)

The Franks were also seen by Bloeme Evers-Emden, a Jewish girl who had been in hiding:

> In Westerbork, the first family I met was the Frank family
> whom I had known from school. We exchanged stories of some
> of our experiences of being in hiding. Afterwards we saw each
> other regularly. I think – although I don't know it for certain any
> more – that I saw Margot at the tables where we worked on
> batteries. (119–20)

Lenie de Jong-van Naarden, in her mid twenties, met the Franks for the first time. Her husband made friends with Otto and she with Mrs Frank: 'She worried a lot about her children. She was always busy with those girls' (144). Ronnie Goldstein-van Cleef, a resistance member who had been betrayed, also met the Franks for the first time. Her view of them was somewhat different. 'The Franks were pretty depressed. They had had the feeling that nothing could happen to them. They were very close to each other. They always walked together. I didn't have much contact with them; we greeted each other' (176).

These are memories hedged about with uncertainty – 'I think she landed in the battery department', 'I don't know it for certain any more' – and with a degree of contradiction – Anne was 'gay and cheerful', the family 'lovely', yet 'pretty depressed'. There is an eye-witness report that Anne and Peter were seen together and that they seemed radiantly happy. If so, it was a brief respite and a faded love had been re-ignited since in the diary they had drifted apart.

The Frank family stayed in Westerbork for a month. Trains left for Poland every Tuesday. On 3 September 1944 they were put aboard the last transport to leave the Netherlands, the advancing Allies now being a mere hundred and twenty miles away. There wcre 1,019 people on board.

Janny Brandes-Brilleslijper was in the same wagon as the Franks but she had no contact with them, instead holding onto her own sister, separated, as they were, from her parents. Under the pressure of the journey people were already ceasing to treat one another with respect. Lenie de Jong-van Naarden was also in the wagon, with its straw covered floor and bucket for a toilet:

> Mrs Frank had smuggled out a pair of overalls, and she sat by the light of the candle, ripping off the red patch. She must have thought that without that red patch they wouldn't be able to see that we were convict prisoners ... Many people, among them the Frank girls, slept leaning against their mother or father ... It was simply a death train. People died [while] under-way, and there were many who were dead when we arrived. I believe that we were in those cattle cars for two days and nights. (147)

At Auschwitz, they were ordered out of the wagons and the terror began. They survived the selection. It was presided over by Dr Mengele. Five hundred and forty-nine others did not, including all children under fifteen. Anne's fifteenth birthday had been three months earlier. The women were marched to the Birkenau camp, where they were put into barracks 29, while Mr Frank stayed in the main camp. Elie Wiesel, returning to Birkenau after the war, remarked that 'The beauty of the landscape around Birkenau is like a slap in the face: the low clouds, the dense forest, the calm serenity of the scenery.

The silence is peaceful, soothing. Dante understood nothing. Hell is a setting whose serene splendor takes the breath away.'[7] Was it a fluke of nature, he asked himself, that what he called the 'theoreticians and technicians of collective horror carried out their work surrounded by beauty, not ugliness'? These, though, were his feelings as he stood many years later. At the time, for him, as surely for Anne Frank, it was the barbed wire, the noise, the terror that predominated. There was, in his memory, no sky, merely flames.

Lenie de Jong-van Naarden, was one of the few who later reported on the fate of the Frank women.

> In the period that we were in Auschwitz – about two months –
> Mrs Frank tried very hard to keep her children alive, to keep
> them with her, to protect them. Naturally, we spoke to each
> other. But you could do absolutely nothing, only give them
> advice like, 'If they go to the latrine, go with them.' ... You
> might walk in front of an SS man by accident, and your life
> would be over. They simply beat people to death. It didn't make
> any difference to them. A human being was nothing. (153)

They were set to dragging rocks from one end of the camp to the other. Ronnie Goldstein-van Cleef recalled daily life, with its work, roll calls and humiliations. Five women shared a single cup, taking three sips each of the liquid that was called coffee but tasted vile. But that cup might have been used during the night as a toilet and then washed out in suspect water: 'Anne Frank also stood in the same group with me often, and we used the same little cup and passed it to each other' (183). Anne, she explained, 'was very calm and quiet and sometimes withdrawn ... We stood there for hours. After a time, Anne developed a rash. She had scabies and was sent to the hospital block. Margot went with her.'

Lenie de Jong-van Naarden explained, 'The two sisters stayed with each other, and the mother was in total despair. She didn't even eat the piece of bread that she got' (155). The two women, who stole food, dug a hole under the barracks and passed bread through to Margot. In the hospital, the girls began to withdraw from others. Ronnie Goldstein sang for them. After a time, she explained, 'The

Frank girls looked terrible, their hands and bodies covered with spots and sores from the scabies. They applied some salve, but there was not much that they could do. They were in a very bad way; pitiful ... There wasn't any clothing ... We were all lying there naked, under some kind of blankets' (192). Also in the camp were the Hungarian Jews, of whom Anne had written. In his barracks, Primo Levi had watched their arrival. He worked briefly with them, one telling him that when their convoy had arrived the SS made them take off their shoes and walk barefoot on the jagged stones of the railway bed.

Anne and Margot were moved on to Bergen-Belsen as the Russians advanced at the end of October. Their mother did not accompany them. She stayed in Auschwitz and died on 6 January 1945. Bergen-Belsen had originally been one of the better camps. It was technically not a death camp but by the time Anne Frank arrived conditions had deteriorated. Of the 125,000 Jews who ended up there, 50,000 died. With little accommodation, they were required to live under canvas but in early November a fierce storm blew the tent away, leaving the women exposed until they could be moved into what had been a shoe workshop. Both Margot and Anne caught typhus.

Hannah Elisabeth Pick-Goslar later recalled an encounter with Anne:

> Anne came to the barbed-wire fence ... The fence and the straw were between us. There wasn't much light. Maybe I saw her shadow. It wasn't the same Anne. She was a broken girl ... She immediately began to cry, and she told me, 'I don't have any parents anymore.' I remember that with absolute certainty. That was terribly sad because she couldn't have known anything else. She thought that her father had been gassed right away ... I always think, if Anne had known that her father was still alive, she might have had more strength to survive, because she died very shortly before the end. (27–8)

She had nothing to eat, was cold, with few clothes. When, later, Pick-Goslar tried to throw food over the fence to her, another woman stole it.

Rachel van Amerongen-Frankfoorder recalled, 'The Frank girls were so emaciated. They looked terrible. ... They had those hollowed-out faces, skin over bone. They were terribly cold ... You could really see both of them dying. They showed the recognizable symptoms of typhus – that gradual wasting away, a sort of apathy ... until they became so sick that there wasn't any hope ... Look, I didn't pay any special attention to them because there were so many others who also died.'

As Janny Brandes-Brilleslijper noted, 'Anne was sick ... but she stayed on her feet until Margot died; only then did she give in to her illness. Like so many others, as soon as you lose your courage and your self-control ...' (73). Brandes-Brilleslijper recalled that

> she had such a horror of the lice and fleas in her clothes and that she had thrown all of her clothes away. It was the middle of the winter and she was wrapped in one blanket ... Two days later, I went to look for the girls. Both of them were dead! First, Margot had fallen out of bed onto the stone floor. She couldn't get up anymore. Anne died a day later. We had lost all sense of time. It is possible that Anne lived a day longer. Three days before her death was when she had thrown away all of her clothes during dreadful hallucinations. (74)

'Maybe I saw her shadow', 'I didn't pay special attention to her', 'it is possible that Anne lived a day longer' – certainty is seldom a characteristic of memory, even when the rememberer believes it to be. In the context of the camps, time was distorted. In the dark surrealism of Belsen the real was itself problematic. Revisited decades later, events are liable to rearrange themselves. Nonetheless, these few fragmentary accounts intersect in their portrait of Anne's squalid death and the collapse of that confident self proclaimed by the fifteen-year-old such a short time before, unexposed as she had then been to the inhumanity to which she had been able to give a name but not a face.

Mrs van Pels, Mrs van Daan in the diary, died approximately three or four months later, having been transferred to Bergen-Belsen and then on to Theresienstadt. Her son Peter, whom Anne had believed herself to love, was taken on a death march and died in

Mauthausen in May. Of the eight who remained hidden for so long before betrayal rendered them into the hands of their enemies, only one survived, Otto Frank. He had lost everyone, though he clung to the hope that his daughters had survived until finally he learned the truth from one of those who had witnessed their end. Publication of the diary thus became a way of memorialising. It contained the voice of Anneliese, as, ironically, the play would not. But the play, while deviating from the original, sent people back to the book, as to the place where they had hidden in fear and hope between 1942 and 1944.

In 1997, Cynthia Ozick published an article in the *New Yorker* in which she asked, 'Who Owns Anne Frank?'[8] Noting the textual changes that had taken place in the course of its history, she argued that almost everyone who had approached the diary with the well-meaning intention of publicising it had contributed to the subversion of history. She complained about the conversion of Anne into usable goods, suggesting that it might be better if the diary had been burned rather than treated as it had been by its various adapters. Miep Gies, who had assisted the Franks and who discovered the diary, once remarked that if she had read it she would have burned it as being too dangerous to those it named. Ozick remarked, 'It may be shocking to think this (I am shocked as I think it), but one can imagine a still more salvational outcome: Anne Frank's diary burned, vanished, lost – saved from a world that made of it all things, some of them true, while floating over the heavier truth of named and uninhabited evil' (87).

The diary, she pointed out, was not the genial document it was represented as being. It is punctuated with an awareness of what was going on beyond the confines of their refuge and because it lacks a conclusion cannot even be said to be the story of Anne Frank. But, most significantly, she claimed that in the fifty years since its first publication it

> has been bowdlerized, distorted, transmuted, traduced, reduced;
> it has been infantilized, Americanized, homogenized,
> sentimentalized; falsified, kitschified, and, in fact, blatantly
> and arrogantly denied. Among the falsifiers have been the
> dramatists and directors, translators and litigators, Anne

Frank's own father, and even – or especially – the public, both readers and theatergoers, all over the world. A deeply truth-telling work has been turned into an instrument of partial truth, surrogate truth, or anti-truth. The pure has been made impure – sometimes in the name of the reverse. Almost every hand that has approached the diary with the well-meaning intention of publicizing it has contributed to the subversion of history. (78)

That process had begun with Otto Frank's suppression of aspects of a diary that failed to coincide with his own sense of its possible function.

Readers, meanwhile, had brought their own falsifications to bear. How, after all, she asks, could they come to the diary 'without having earlier assimilated Elie Wiesel's "Night" and Primo Levi's "The Drowned" (to mention two witnesses only), or the columns of figures in the transport books'? To do so is 'to allow oneself to stew in an implausible and ugly innocence' (78). It is a stringent requirement. It is necessary, it appears, to educate oneself in the details of the Holocaust before it is possible to read what is admittedly not a Holocaust book for fear it will be taken as an adequate account not only of genocide but of the life that is supposedly at its centre. The ellipsis which ends the diary was provided not by the editor but by Anne Frank herself. What she could not have known was the force of that ellipsis, never to be completed because her life, like those others who she imagines but does not know while at the Prinsengracht, would take her places she could not imagine. Ozick wishes the reader to provide what is not there, indeed insists that that absence must be filled. We must go where the text does not.

Anne's is an innocence that clearly sticks in the throat, for Ozick insists that 'the diary's most celebrated line (infamously celebrated, one might add) – "I still believe, in spite of everything, that people are truly good at heart" – has been torn out of its bed of thorns' (81), not least because two sentences later Anne speaks of the world transformed into a wilderness and an approaching thunder that will destroy her and her family as it has destroyed the millions. Ozick seemingly forgets that even then Anne insists that she must hold onto her ideals and that the day may come when she will be able to realise them.

Anne Frank's innocence is neither implausible nor ugly because she did not know what would invalidate it. We can know, and that is what leads Ozick to be so pitiless in her refusal to allow easy consolation. What she objects to is the translation of a girl's innocence into our wilful ignorance: we see her life as exemplifying a human spirit precisely and calculatedly denied by the processes as much as by the existence of the camps. But Ozick was not alone in her objections. Hannah Elisabeth Pick-Goslar, Anne's Jewish friend, present at her dying in Bergen-Belsen, also objected to the stress laid on the 'good at heart' sentiment. Ozick, however, even takes exception to the objective of the Anne Frank Foundation and its International Youth Centre because its declared objective, to foster 'as many contacts as possible between young people of different nationalities, races, and religions', seemed to her 'a civilized and tenderhearted goal that nonetheless washed away into do-gooder abstraction the explicit urge to rage that had devoured her' (81). The last part of that sentence is hard to unpack. In what sense was it the urge to rage that destroyed Anne Frank? It was not rage that killed her but malevolence of a kind that even she could not imagine, who had matured enough to follow the reports which made their way into their fastness. The fact that she could not was in part a measure of that humanity to which readers cling, and not entirely without cause. Anne died. Others survived. The torment, after all, ended, at least in its particular form. The Nazis were not finally allowed the prerogative of defining human nature.

If Cynthia Ozick challenged Otto Frank's editorial interventions, the excisions and amendments of translators and what she saw as the wilful reductiveness and distortions of the play, she did not challenge the Frank family itself or see them as representatives of a false consciousness. Bruno Bettelheim did. First in *Harper's* magazine, in 1960, and then in his book *Surviving and Other Essays*, he launched a pitiless assault. The very success of *The Diary of Anne Frank*, so fixed in the public mind and memory as a story of human resilience, was to him evidence of

the power of the desire to counteract the realization of the personality-destroying and murderous nature of the camps by concentrating all attention on what is experienced as a demonstration that private and intimate life can continue to flourish even under the direct persecution by the most ruthless totalitarian system. And this although Anne Frank's fate demonstrates how efforts at disregarding in private life what goes on around one in society can hasten one's own destruction.[9]

Nor was this merely a general point, though his reaction to the Franks was indeed part of his developing thesis and anxiety with respect to what he saw as Jewish passivity. It was an assault on the decision by Otto Frank to try to secure his family, as a family, on his failure to draw the logical conclusion from his circumstances, to escape or to fight.

Having confessed that it would be wrong to 'take apart so humane and moving a story', that is precisely what he then chooses to do, provoked by what he sees as the uncritical response to the diary itself and to the play and the film based upon it. The acclaim which that story, in all its forms, received seemed to him primary evidence of a desire not to remember but to 'forget the gas chambers' and glorify a retreat into a private world. To eulogise their decision to go into hiding as a family was to ignore the fatal nature of that decision, the acquiescence it implied, the refusal of a wider responsibility to resist and rebel. Even Anne is not exempted from his criticism since she, too, simply wished to go on with life as usual. The fact is, he insists, her fate was unnecessary and senseless.

Family life was inimical to survival. Their insistence on staying together thus made them more vulnerable while their psychology was such that they even failed to provide an exit from their hiding place. Failing that, they 'could have provided themselves with some weapons had they wished. Had they had a gun, Mr. Frank could have shot down at least two of the "green police" who came for them ... Even a butcher knife, which they certainly could have taken with them into hiding, could have been used by them in self-defense.' And here comes a comment which links the fate of the Franks with Bettelheim's wider concerns: since, with the exception of Otto, they were all to die anyway, 'they could have sold their lives for a high price, instead of walking to their death' (248–9). He comes close to saying that their deaths were their own fault. Indeed, surely he does say such. He certainly says that they were evidence of a passivity that a subsequent generation of Jews found baffling, a theme picked up elsewhere in his essays.

Otto Frank, he concedes, might not have been willing to kill those who wished to murder him but surely he would have been willing 'to kill those who are bent on murdering not only them but also their wives and little daughters' (249). Having just affirmed Mr Frank's courage ('one must assume that Mr. Frank would have fought courageously' (249)), he effectively accuses him of cowardice, being, it seems, unwilling to defend the defenceless. He also criticises the whole family because 'instead of supporting each other's ability to resist the demoralizing impact of their living conditions', they 'bicker with each other over trifles' (252). Otto Frank's decision to teach his children academic subjects, meanwhile, was 'erroneous' in that it took the place of teaching them how to escape.

He hastens to insist that his remarks are not intended 'as a criticism of the Frank family' (249), though it is hard to see them as anything else, but as a reaction against 'the universal admiration of their way of coping, or rather not coping' (250). However, he then proceeds to identify those who chose a different course and by resisting either survived or sustained a notion of survival. He, too, objects to the ending of the play and movie, so at odds, as it is, with our knowledge of Anne's fate. If people 'are really good at heart,' he suggested, then we 'can afford to forget about Auschwitz' (250). The emphasis on family life, meanwhile, was an invitation to disregard 'Nazi racism and tyranny in general ... even if one is Jewish'. The reason the play and film were loved by millions was 'because while it confronts us with the fact that Auschwitz existed, it encourages us at the same time to ignore any of its implications. If all men are good at heart, there never really was an Auschwitz; nor is there any possibility that it may recur' (251).

It is not, though, simply that ringing affirmation that he objects to. His whole essay is predicated on his bafflement that for the most part Jews seemed to have gone to their deaths without resistance. In truth, it was something that also puzzled Arthur Miller, but in Bettelheim's case the Frank family's continued commitment to the idea of a private life at a time when the very idea of civility and privacy were in the process of collapse was not simply an error, it was evidence of an inertia which in turn was a symptom of a death instinct.

The journey from Anne Frank, writing in her diary, to culpability for the destruction of the Jews is so immense as to seem – and indeed be – absurd. It is evidence, though, not merely of the significance she had assumed in the public memory, but also of the uses to which she had been put. To her father, the full extent of her sexuality and her hostility to her mother had to be muted. For the German translator, with Otto's connivance, the anti-German sentiments had to be toned down. For Levin she was to be a Jewish icon, for the Hacketts and the play's director a symbol of human resistance and triumph, for Bettelheim an embodiment of bad faith and, ultimately, of that denial which was itself evidence of a death instinct.

In 1962, Bettelheim returned to the Franks, reprinting the essay in 1990. He had not relented. Again, while insisting that he had no quarrel with the Franks, he proceeded to quarrel with them for their 'ghetto philosophy', for trapping themselves in a room with no exits, literal or symbolic, and to suggest that the concern for Anne and her family was evidence of the fact that 'We seem to find human grandeur in submitting passively to the sword.'[10] There was one person, though, from that household who he professed to admiring: Miep Gies, who had sustained the family in their years in hiding at considerable risk to herself and her family and who, nonetheless, thought she had not done enough. Oddly, given his views of the Franks and the diary, he praises her for protecting the very privacy against which he had railed, which alone had made possible the writing of the diary. Without her, no diary. 'Her courage, her humanity, and her decency give us all hope for humanity' (213). She, after all, acted. But she was not Jewish.

Primo Levi was not an admirer of Bettelheim or his essay on the Franks. Levi, too, had failed to leave when he might but 'emigrating meant overcoming an enormous potential barrier: to crawl out of our hole. Where we had family, affection ... It wasn't easy and to criticize

the Frank family for failing to act differently is superficial ... It may
be that sticking together was a dangerous choice, but it was also the
only way to preserve some semblance of life as it was before.'[11]
Bettelheim had had his own experience of the concentrations camps.
Indeed he served a year in one. But this was before the killings began.
He emigrated to the United States in 1939, secure against the threat
that had been faced by the Frank family. Nonetheless, he was not
immune to the pressures about which he had written. In 1990, he took
his own life.

The question of who owns Anne Frank was raised in another
sense in 1979, when Philip Roth published *The Ghost Writer*, a novel
in which a Jewish writer, Nathan Zuckerman, is attacked by his
fellow Jews, much as Roth himself had been, for having written
stories which they see as reflecting badly on the Jewish community.
He is told that he should see the Broadway production of *The Diary of
Anne Frank*. His parents add their voices, afraid that people will
believe that his refusal to do so will imply that he dislikes the Jews. 'I
didn't see it', he confesses, 'I read the book. *Everybody* read the book.'
When he is asked if he liked it he replies, 'How can you *dis*like it.'

He then meets a young girl who claims to be Anne Frank, who
had survived Belsen, travelled to England, where she changed her
name, and then moved on to America. She had, she explained, known
nothing of her father's survival or the publication of the diary but on
discovering the fact of both, rather than call her father she had written
off for the Dutch edition of the book and then later attended the play
where she had sat 'amid the weeping and inconsolable audience'.[12] It
was an experience she found unbearable. As she explained,

> It wasn't the play ... It was the people watching with me.
> Carloads of women kept pulling up at the theatre wearing fur
> coats, with expensive shoes and handbags ... it was the women
> who frightened me – and their families and their children and
> their homes. Go to a movie, I told myself, go instead to a
> museum ... The women cried. Everyone around me was in
> tears. Then at the end, in the row behind me, a woman
> screamed, 'Oh, no'.

After this, she decides that she must remain silent because if she revealed the truth 'they would have to come out on the stage after each performance and announce, "But she is really alive. You needn't worry, she survived, she is twenty-six now, and doing very well"' (123).

Specious or not, and the girl seems to have laid claim to the identity of Anne Frank as a means of gaining significance, of attaching herself to history, as perhaps did those who read the diary and saw the play, she raises an interesting question. What if Anne Frank had not died and her diary had been simply another survivor's story with an addendum explaining what she subsequently suffered and her eventual redemption, would readers and audiences feel that they had been deprived of a death, that the unique appeal of the diary had been undermined? Is it the romantic appeal of a young girl's death that gives it its force? The tears in the theatre would not have been shed if a programme note had reassured those who came in part to shed those tears.

Beyond that, there was, as Zuckerman points out, an irony in a Jew being urged to show his solidarity by attending the play in that the diary shows less a religious family sustained by their faith than a group of people for whom religious ceremonies seem to have had little more significance than the raising of spirits. Anne speaks of praying but is given a New Testament by her father for Chanukah, admittedly to the disapproval of his other daughter. In other words, the diary and the play achieve their success not because of the acknowledged Jewishness of this family who are, of course, pursued and killed for being Jews, but because they, and she in particular, are seen as representative of a suffering mankind, almost drained of a religious particularity. And since this was still the version of the camps on offer at the time of its publication, it played to the then current account of what would only later be seen as the Holocaust. Anne, in Roth's book, refracted through Nathan Zuckerman's account, is 'only dimly Jewish', but

> that was the point – that was what gave her diary the power to make the nightmare real. To expect the great callous and indifferent world to care about the child of a pious, bearded

247

father living under the sway of the rabbis and the rituals – that was pure folly. To the ordinary person with no great gift for tolerating even the smallest of differences the plight of that family wouldn't mean a thing. To ordinary people it probably would seem that they had invited disaster by stubbornly repudiating everything modern and European – not to say Christian. But the family of Otto Frank, that would be another matter! (144)

The Anne Frank of Roth's novel decides to remain silent about her identity because to do otherwise would be to destroy the effect of the diary. It would 'never be more than it was: a young teenager's diary in her trying years ... something boys and girls could read along with the adventures of the Swiss Family Robinson' (145). And if she had survived, then her declaration that 'people are really good at heart' would have done battle with the story of decline and despair. The diary, she comes to believe, is justified because it is a memorial, because it preserves her family as they had been before they had been destroyed, eliminated, and if them then those others whose fate they shared. And perhaps the particularity of a Jewish plight, a minor theme of the diary, would yet force itself on the consciousness of those who believed they mourned the death of a girl, much like their own daughters, sisters, even lovers.

This surviving Anne, who calls herself Amy, has chosen a new identity not to deny her past but to prevent herself being defined by it, in truth the problem for many survivors who are invited to become that aspect of their history. Now, she finds herself wanting the tears of Christians, wanting their unfocussed love even as she is aware of the indulgence it represents. She wants to use those tears to wash away the debasement she believes herself to have suffered. Yet she also knows that if she were to announce her survival one result would be to betray her book and another would be to pass into the possession of other people and no longer be simply her own self.

In Roth's fiction there comes a moment when Anne Frank seems to become merely Amy, a young woman in search of a story for her life. But some of the issues raised in *The Ghost Writer* are real enough. Was the gift Anne Frank offered the world her death and would we, as we imagine, have reached out to prevent it? Were those attempts to soften the German edition themselves evidence of a desire to read the diary not as an account of the persecution of a Jewish family but as the plight of a family struggling against evil, against a kind of determinism? And who was Anne Frank – the young girl who interprets herself to us, increasingly conscious of the image she generates, or the one who moved towards death, glimpsed, if at all, only by those who struggled to recall her decades later when she had already been re-invented by her readers, recalled by those whose own necessities determined what they saw as well as what they subsequently chose to remember?

Nor was this the only example of Anne Frank being incorporated into another work. In 1992, the Polka Theatre for young people in London commissioned a play from the Jewish writer Bernard Kops. Following a poll it had emerged that the two subjects to which they were most attracted as epitomising the human spirit were Helen Keller and Anne Frank. Kops chose Anne Frank in part because there was a chain of memory connecting him to her. His father had left Holland for London at the beginning of the century but never became financially secure. With the approach of the war, like the Franks he was determined to reach Holland, believing that its neutrality would be respected, but failed when no one would lend him any money. As a result, they lived while their Dutch relatives died. But there was another connection.

Among those who were with Anne Frank in Westerbork was the Dutch Jewish writer and translator Rosie Pool, also known for her studies of African American poetry. She worked in the Resistance and initially escaped from Westerbork, subsequently smuggling herself back in order to organise resistance. It was she who had translated Bernard Kops's first play, *The Hamlet of Stepney Green*.

Kops repeatedly visited the Franks' attic. As he explained of his play, '*Dreams of Anne Frank* is not a dramatization of her [Anne's] diary. Rather, it is an original way of focusing upon the girl, to bring alive that unquenchable spirit and show how she managed to be creative in the darkest of times. To write the play, I went to the facts of her life for the spine of reality and to my imagination for the subjective matrix, the foundation of my drama.'[13] What was to be on offer, in other words, was that ennobling and uplifting Anne to which others had objected. It was not, however, simply the Anne of the diary. His was to be a 'total imaginative creation'. All the events and dialogue were 'imagined and subjective' (154). Memory, he insisted, 'has no absolute chronology', so that he felt free to invent. Indeed, he has Anne remark that 'time is a mystery. What has happened is happening again ... memory has no continuity' (177). He was, he confessed, interested in '*my* Anne' (155), and that meant giving himself licence to free her from her constraints, permitting her to speak directly to Winston Churchill, assassinate Hitler, go ice-skating, marry Peter, though by the end of the diary it is clear that this would have been far from her thoughts. It was a play with music (Anne sings, 'Fate gave me a yellow star' (166) while Mrs van Daan, Mrs Frank and Margot sing a version of the Andrews Sisters' 'Mother, may I go out dancing' (190)). The house is given a voice. Neither time nor space constrain. She can, as she claims, travel in her mind.

Ironically, though his strategy is to diverge from the diary, in fact he is more scrupulous in quoting from it than the Hacketts had been. When he has characters identify the date, in contrast to the Hacketts' adaptation the dialogue is genuinely sourced from the appropriate entries in the diary. On the other hand he seems intent to have a religious sensibility infiltrate the text as though to address those complaints levelled by some that Judaism had been evacuated from both diary and play.

The play ends, or almost so, with Anne's remark that 'Just as my world opens, it closes. Just as I stop being a child, I stop being' (201–2). We hear the wail of a train. The cast now all wear yellow stars and then undress to reveal prison clothes. Anne is left alone on the stage reciting a prayer. She dances and invokes the possibility of future peace. The play concludes with a speech by Otto Frank in which he celebrates the diary and what it stands for but confesses he would swap it in an instant for the living daughter who wrote it.

In 1998 the play was performed in Mostar, Bosnia, to accompany an Anne Frank exhibition. It was acted by children from Sarajevo. Also from Sarajevo was Zlata Filipovic, a thirteen-year-old girl who had kept her own diary of her experiences there as the city was bombarded by the Serbs.

Nor was this the last time that Anne Frank would be appropriated by a dramatist. In *The Model Apartment*, by the American playwright Donald Margulies, Lola, a Holocaust survivor, recalls a young girl, with eyes like shiny black marbles, who at Belsen, and at her suggestion, had kept a second diary. This is that second diary that critics of the original's disturbing optimism had implicitly longed for. 'All I care about', Lola recalls Anne Frank as saying, 'is people should see what I write and know the truth and remember. I want people to remember' (247).[14] According to Lola, as she died of typhus so she dictated the book. But, as she says, 'Who knew what she would mean to the world' (248), and the diary was lost.

The Model Apartment is scarcely a realist text. Lola's daughter, now in her late thirties, is a mentally disturbed and grotesque woman, half sister to a girl who had died during the Holocaust. The same actress plays both roles, the thin lost girl, the grotesquely fat sister, resentful at the homage paid to the dead sister: 'I'M ALIVE. I CAN'T HELP IT I WASN'T EXTERMINATED!' (255). She is resentful of the role in which she has been cast, the burden she is required to bear, 'stuffing all those dead people inside me' (256). Her parents have moved to Florida in part to escape her and what she represents. In the penultimate scene she has to be restrained and is taken away in an ambulance. The play ends with their dead daughter, recalling the Jewish ceremonies that the family had once shared before their lives were deformed by what happened to them much, presumably, as Anne Frank's would have been had she survived to write that second diary, to live on as a survivor and not a victim, her life transformed by the fact of survival and hence drained, as it would have been, of a certain significance that came with her death. Death, after all, was the apotheosis that retrospectively flooded her life with meaning.

Anne Frank, though, was not the only figure resurrected from the diaries. In a subsequent work, both Otto Frank and the would-be adapter of the diaries Meyer Levin received a letter from a man who claimed to be Peter van Pels, the young man who shared the secret annexe with Anne. The same man stood up at the trial in which Levin sought to sue Otto Frank. This was not, though, the real Peter van Pels but the product of the literary imagination of the novelist and journalist Ellen Feldman. In 1994, she visited the Anne Frank House and heard a guide state that Peter had been the only one hiding in the annexe whose fate was unknown. In fact the statement was erroneous, but by the time she discovered this the idea for a novel had been born. *The Boy Who Loved Anne Frank* was published in 2005 and is another act of appropriation. It was also, however, a book that explored many of the issues implicit in such acts.

Peter van Pels has survived to arrive in the United States as a displaced person. Ironically, and somewhat incredibly, he immediately encounters the son of another inhabitant of the annexe, the dentist who had sent his son away on the *Kindertransport* before himself going into hiding. Peter denies all knowledge of the man's dead father as of the Franks. Instead of memories, he confesses, he has instincts and these lead him in the direction of caution and denial. In a New York with Dutch origins, he feels no need to change his name, implicitly attaching himself to one history the better to suppress the truth of another. In particular, he denies that he is a Jew, Ellen Feldman taking her cue from a passage in the diary in which Peter is quoted as saying that life would have been easier as a Christian. And, indeed, Feldman scatters her text with quotations from the diary in part to authenticate her fictions which inevitably infiltrate that diary as it becomes mere back story and in part to raise questions about authenticity. In some ways, indeed, this is a postmodern novel, with stories within stories, fictions and facts commingling.

Peter was, he claims, born again on his arrival in America. He wishes to exist in the present even as the past presses on his psyche and flashes of memory break through his defences. The past is, anyway, vague to him. He recalls an event in which a Jew on a train had been beaten only to realise that it is not his memory but the memory of a story: 'not remembering because the story did not belong to me, though somehow in the retelling and reimagining it had become mine'.[15]

In America, Peter meets two Jewish sisters. One refuses to marry him when he insists he is a gentile. He marries the other, concealing the truth of his past and his Jewish identity alike. There is, however, a price to be paid. He all but loses his voice, doing so, he later realises, when he saw his wife reading Anne Frank's diary, whose very existence came as a shock. At first, he himself resists reading it, even attempting to throw it away, as he had his own past. When he does, though, he is angry at her portrait of his parents and the changing of the names of those who had shared her time at the Prinsengracht. For his part, he arranges to have his concentration camp tattoo removed from his arm, only to change his mind when he learns that the same surgeon had removed a tattoo from the arm of an SS officer. However, with the past nonetheless erased, all moral distinctions are, it seems, expunged and with it, as Arthur Miller had asserted, all moral responsibility. There is plainly a struggle going on in Peter's psyche.

Meanwhile, he is squirrelling away money against the day he and his family may have to flee, this being a truth that survives even as he attempts to deny the past. Sometimes, indeed, he finds himself snatching his children up with a knife in his hand as if to protect them from a danger that has become himself.

His life becomes more fraught when his wife goes to see the stage version of the diary. She brings home what she claims is an understanding of certain things, though what she has learned from such an experience seems to him contestable. How can art, factitious, artificial, subject to its own aesthetic and, indeed, financial demands, pretend to offer truth? 'I was not going to tell her', explains the protagonist, 'that sitting in a theatre for two and a half hours watching actors pretend to be hungry and frightened and doomed was not going to help her understand me. I loved her for not understanding me' (146). Here, then, is a fictive character inspired by a long-dead person explaining the inadequacy of art to approximate to truth in a novel in which the concealment of truth is a central necessity to that same protagonist. Ellen Feldman sets up a series of refracting mirrors until the reader is placed in the situation of recoiling from one fiction in the name of another.

Here is a novel that contains a critique of its own processes in which the author seems on the one hand to want to have her cake and eat it while on the other suggesting the fraudulence of her own conceit (Philip Roth sidesteps a similar paradox by making his character a subtle fraud). She also uses the novel to rehearse arguments about the diary. The protagonist's wife responds to the play because it celebrates the 'triumph of the human spirit', precisely the grounds on which it was rejected by its critics, until she becomes aware of the controversy involving Mrs Frank being played by a former star in Nazi Germany. Accordingly, Madeleine van Pels decides to organise a boycott, a plan frustrated by her husband who wishes to avoid public attention.

For Peter's part, what offends is the work itself. All over America, he observes, multiple Ottos 'stumbled into stage set annexes to discover their daughters' diaries and Anne and Peter fell in love, and a dozen different versions of my father, tall, short, fat, thin stole bread out of my mouth' (165), the latter an incident added to the play to solve a perceived problem in the second act. The original figures are pluralised, commodified, re-invented, made available to those who seek the displacement of suffering into sentimentality. Shelley Winters, who played the role of Mrs van Pels in the film version, put on forty pounds to play the part: 'She was eating her way into my mother's character, like a tapeworm' (167).

Inevitably, the film follows the play and Peter's wife goes to see it. She returns with what he calls 'an air of tender distraction'. It was 'more than sorrow for the poor bastards she had seen impersonated on the screen', he suggests. 'It was longing. She wanted to know what it was like to suffer, for a while' (169–70). Within her fiction, in other words, Ellen Feldman rehearses precisely that anxiety about the attraction of works about the Holocaust that disturbed so many of those for whom its secret must be shared in the knowledge that such sharing is not only the root of compromise but a surrender of any ability to police its reception.

Eventually, the protagonist also sees the film, finding his own role and that of Anne's reduced to that of 'clean-cut American kids, even if they were supposed to be German Jews hiding in Amsterdam' (172). He watches affronted again by the scene in which his father steals bread, offended by this appropriation of his father for fictive purposes even as he himself is evidence of just such an appropriation.

The film, he learns, had originally extended the action to Auschwitz but the ending was changed when it became apparent that audiences would not accept it. The story, it seemed, must end with Anne still alive, her subsequent death being no more than the source of regret. 'That was what the audience wanted', Peter thinks, 'The triumph of the human spirit ... The reassurance that in spite of everything, of people going to their deaths in their millions merely for the accident of their birth, of other people willing and eager to pry gold fillings from their mouths before they shovelled them into ovens, of ghoulish experiments on un-anaesthetised individuals in the interests of medical science, of an entire people's bloodthirsty complicity to cleanse the world of another entire people, in spite of all that, human beings are good at heart' (173–4).

By this point Peter van Pels can no longer sustain the fiction of his American identity. Memories begin to break through and he grows increasingly fearful that he might kill his children in order to protect them. He visits a synagogue and confesses to a man for whom the information seems to have no significance. He writes to Meyer Levin who replies insisting that Otto Frank is a self-hating Jew. He writes to Frank himself who in turn threatens him with lawyers if he persists in his claims. Finally, he appears at the trial in which Levin sued Frank and stands up publicly to announce his identity, only to be expelled from the court. The man who had denied his Jewishness is himself denied.

Sent by his wife to see a psychiatrist, he discovers that some of his memories are false and that the self he has finally decided to embrace has itself been infiltrated by other people's memories. His story is that of others.

The novel ends as he and his wife return to the Prinsengracht as others go to the Holocaust Museum in Washington DC. There, visitors are given the identity card of someone lost in the Holocaust, inside the front cover of which is a statement: 'This card tells the story of a real person who lived during the Holocaust,' an ironic claim in a fiction about a character modelled on a real person. Back in Amsterdam, meanwhile, Peter and his wife watch as a German couple photograph their daughter alongside a statue of Anne Frank. 'Smile', they say. 'My God', comments the protagonist, 'have they no memory?' (261).

And what if Anne Frank had survived in fact rather than fiction? What would her attitude have been towards the diary she kept and the young girl whose thoughts are to be found there? Decades later, another young girl found herself hidden away from the life she knew, though this time she was dragged there by a homicidal paedophile. Sabine Dardenne, half starved, raped and sexually abused, spent eighty days chained by the neck in a Belgian cellar. At any moment, she knew, she could be killed. She was twelve years old, a year younger than Anne Frank when she began her very different incarceration. When she was released she was determined not to be defined by what had happened to her, resented those who wished to preserve an image of her as a suffering young girl. She received letters attacking her for refusing to share. The trial aside, she resisted attempts to appropriate her suffering, resisted, too, those who wanted her to tell her story until in 2004 she chose to do so in order, she explained, to relieve the pressure of other people's demands on her. She, too, kept a diary, indeed diaries, during her time in the cellar, but as she explained, 'Those diaries, I can read them 15 times and they're still not me ... They're a 12-year-old girl who was once me.'[16]

Anne Frank did not survive to resist appropriation, to explain that she was no longer continuous with the girl she had once been. She is ours because she was not able to insist that she was her own self, resistant to being defined by what had happened to her rather than what she willed. Despite her protestations, it is hard to believe that Sabine Dardenne is as untouched by her experiences as she suggests, though she remains insistent that the past is done with, that she will not remain hostage to it as she was once held hostage by a man as contemptuous of the sufferings of others as those who once broke into that secret annexe in an Amsterdam house. Dardenne, who chooses not to dwell on memories of what was, was rescued as Anne was not. Dardenne is a living woman. Anne is not and has become a symbol. Had she survived would she have acknowledged her younger self but insisted of her diary, as Dardenne has of hers, that 'they're not me'?

In a letter that she wrote to her father on 5 May 1944, and not made available in full until 2006, she drew a portrait of herself as a girl no longer. She was, she insisted, independent in body and mind. Her self-doubts and problems had been set aside. She no longer needed a mother. She was ready to go her own way, to follow the path that seemed right to her. She was a fourteen-year-old only in age. The battle, she explained, was over. She was strong and accountable only to herself. Less than three months later, she and her family were betrayed. Less than a year later, she was dead.

Primo Levi commented on the fact that a single Anne Frank attracted more emotion than the myriads of those who suffered as she did but whose image remained in the shadows. It was, though, he conceded, inevitable. Pity is attracted to individuals as horror, he might have said, is prompted by the suffering of the many. In a 1979 interview, he handed the interviewer his poem 'The Girl-Child of Pompeii'. It tells of a young girl caught in the eruption and unearthed later clinging in death to her mother. She is a memory preserved by the ashes rather than being rendered into them. The preservation of Anne Frank took a different form but her pain too was captured and held in a terrible suspension, the more terrible, perhaps, because death did not come in an instant. She lived long enough to turn her youthful hopes to ash:

> In this way you stay with us, a twisted plaster case,
> Agony without end, terrible witness
> To how much our proud seed matters to the gods.[17]

7   Jean Améry: home and language

How much home does a person need? Not to the same
degree ... that our mother tongue proved to be hostile, did
the foreign one become a real friend. It behaved and still
behaves in a reserved manner and receives us only for brief
formal visits. One calls on it, comme en visite des amis, which
is not the same as dropping in on friends. La table will never
be the table.

Jean Améry, At the Mind's Limits

Without a mother tongue, a person has a defect.

Aharon Appelfeld, The Story of a Life

W. G. Sebald begins his consideration of Jean Améry with a quotation
from that author's *Lefeu oder der Abbruch* (Lefeu or Demolition): 'Let
my unhappiness burn and be extinguished in the flames.'[1] It was an
indication of Améry's forlorn intent simultaneously to permit his
suffering to be known and to see it consumed in its own expression. It
was Améry's restraint that impressed, a restraint sometimes presented as a casual irony, but it was his insistence on confronting what
others chose to forget which compelled Sebald's attention and respect.

George Steiner, whose family escaped from Europe to safety
(only one or two of the Jews in his French *lycée* survived),
contemplated what it was not to have died, or to have survived after
seeing into hell: 'not to have known how one would behave at the
midnight of history, not to know and yet to meet from time to time
those who behaved magnificently and do not even want to talk about

it – those who have been to the frontier of their own selves – leaves
one with a feeling of, I would not call it envy, but a certain ache of
unknowing. It is ambiguous. I feel ashamed and not ashamed of such
feelings.'² That confusion of feelings, that sense that there are those
who have been to the edge and discovered the limits of themselves
even as they saw other limits transgressed to the point that even the
senses were to be distrusted, is wholly understandable, as is the
admiration for those whose reticence about their own experiences is
taken as a mark of their own tensile strength. The sense that there is
some undisclosed secret, however, a perverse privilege in the
extremity of suffering, is harder to accept.

Those few who returned carried back a desolate message which
they hesitated to utter, unwilling, even unable, at first to break the
silence that was a product of a certain awe or even some ultimate tact.
It was as if news of such a degrading experience were indeed so
shaming as to demean those already demeaned. It is hard, though, to
know quite what is meant by behaving magnificently. There were
such, and we know the story of some few of them. There were still
more, however, for whom survival was not a priority but the only
priority. One of those Jews set to drag dead bodies to the pyres spoke of
locking himself up inside himself, as if there were some secret place
to which even he was granted no access. Time enough later, if there
were a later, to find the key, to allow that world to be recreated, at
least in language, though the difficulty of doing so is clear enough.
Anyone who has watched survivors face a film camera and simply try
to recall the details they now feel obliged to retrieve, as a duty to those
who died, is to see those memories begin to well up until speech
becomes impossible and only tears may be eloquent. Yet the obligation
invariably wins out. A message must be scratched on the stone for
others to read despite the inadequacy of words to approximate
experience. It becomes necessary to remember because news must be
transmitted to the future. One who set himself to remember, albeit
two decades on from the events he recalls, was Jean Améry.

A primary function of memory, according to Steiner, is the
necessity to avoid a second death. He has spoken of a discipline he
practises which is also a commemoration. He stands in front of

memorials, 'the ninety-six thousand names on one wall in Prague', for example, and sets himself to memorise a block of ten names, 'and I say to myself that perhaps by doing this I am not only honouring them but trying to say to them, "Look. There is not going to be the second death, the total ash: somewhere you are present in other human beings." And I think that is worth doing. In Hebrew we call it the *kaddish*, the prayers for the dead. It seems to point to the history of a people always in motion, always in danger, and trying to have a passport made up of the past' (177). The survivors who offered witness did so to avoid such a second death.

Jean Améry was born in Vienna in October 1912, the son of a Jewish father and a fervently Catholic mother. His name, though, was not that under which he would later be known. He was Hans Mayer. The family lived in Hohenems, a small town in the state of Vorarlberg in western Austria. His father died in the war, in 1916. After his father's death, he and his mother moved into the country, where she managed an inn, before returning to Vienna. His father's family had lived in Austria for two hundred years. They were thoroughly assimilated. His great-grandfather had been fluent in Hebrew but that fluency disappeared along with their religion. Améry was nineteen before he became aware of the Yiddish language, though he had no sense of a cultural heritage or religious conviction. But his memories were not of Judaism and no one, he insists, 'can become what he cannot find in his memories'.[3] It is true that it was as a Jew that a tooth was knocked out at university (where he studied literature and philosophy), by a Nazi long before Hitler came to power, but it was in 1935, when he read the details of the Nuremberg laws in a newspaper in a Vienna coffee house, that he became Jewish, though in no real sense was he any more Jewish than he had been half an hour before. The laws might not yet apply to him, as an Austrian, but he knew he would not be immune.

In recalling this moment years later, in an essay instructively entitled 'On the Necessity and Impossibility of Being a Jew', he denied that he was seeing this moment refracted through his experiences at Auschwitz. He asks the reader to believe that he could already hear the death threat as he read that newspaper. Had he not once seen a photograph in a magazine with a banner declaring 'No one shall go hungry, no one shall freeze, but the Jews shall die like dogs'? From this moment onwards, he insists, he felt like 'a dead man on leave', aware that the Jew was invited to assimilate such a view of himself as a preparation for what must appear as a fate, a destiny. Everywhere he looked, everything he heard, insisted on his necessary exclusion. Step by step the Jew was to be detached from the everyday normalities which constituted his grasp on the world and if he was a contaminant in the present so he had been in the past. He had lived on sufferance and must now die as a natural logic of his nature. His fingers were to be prised from the present and past alike for he was a product of historic process, a pariah for a reason.

The dilemma for Améry was that he had become something he had never believed himself to be in anything but a technical sense. As Sartre remarked, 'The Jew is in the situation of a Jew because he lives in the midst of a society that takes him for a Jew.'[4] Améry found himself caught in a paradox. He did not believe in the God of Israel, knew little about Jewish culture and his earliest memories were of walking through a snow-covered village to midnight mass at Christmas. Yet he knew that the family's neighbours regarded them as Jews and on one level it was a description he accepted without regarding it as definitional. It was one part of his mixed inheritance, though not one he regarded as an adequate description.

With the Nuremberg laws, however, what others thought became what was. He was obliged to contradict memory. In his own words, at that moment he felt 'promised to death'. Later, in describing his feelings he unambiguously used the word 'we' of the Jews, even as he was confessing to the ambivalence he felt towards a faith which in truth he did not share, not earlier, not later. He acknowledged the truth of Sartre's observation in *Anti-Semitism and Jew*. He was in part the invention of those who would destroy him. His knowledge of himself, the product of memory and inner convictions, was simply trumped by the assertion of those with the power to define reality. Guilt was not a matter to be weighed in the balance. It was a birthright. Jews were offered another version of the past that relied not on their memories but on the constructions of those who wished to consolidate a new view of history that would make themselves its apotheosis. They may have projected the Reich a thousand years into the future but they felt the need to reach back into the past to justify their prophecies, and the past they claimed left a racially pure breed of men and women moving through time until they should reach the point at which the mongrel, the inferior, would acknowledge their dominance. Nor were the Nazis pure inventors of this battle for supremacy. Without centuries of anti-Semitism they would have had poor soil in which to scatter the seeds of their enmity.

As a result of the Nuremberg laws, Améry was asked to go back to his beginnings and reconstruct himself as one doomed from birth. As he was to discover in Auschwitz III, Buna-Monowitz, in the new hierarchy there was no one lower than the Jew. Even the most degenerate criminal ranked higher. Even the Poles 'who had been thrown into the camp after the ill-fated Warsaw insurrection ... despised us unanimously' (*At the Mind's Limits*, 88). And that judgement, enforced by the Germans, had, he realised, the sanction of a world unmoved to protest or intervene.

The only response, he argued, was to accept one's fate while rebelling against it, to reject the false hope which lay in denying the legitimacy of the sentence pronounced, as if it were at odds with the spirit of a nation temporarily cowed by brutalism, or a world which failed to act only out of ignorance, and revolt. At first that took the form of joining a Resistance movement which even he acknowledged to be amateurish and misguided in its immediate objectives. Later, when he was no longer free to act, he had to discover some other way not simply to survive, though that was the imperative, but to do so with some moral core intact. It also took the form of accepting his identity as a Jew, no longer permitting himself any equivocation or ambiguity as if the fate offered to Jews might not be appropriate to him and, by inference, was perhaps to them. It took the form of action, even when that action seemed insignificant and self-defeating. Thus, in Auschwitz, struck in the face by a Polish professional criminal set over him, he struck back. That he was immediately severely beaten was beside the point. The punch had reassembled a dislocated self.

Austrian anti-Semitism now found a focus. Almost as an act of resistance, Améry chose to marry a Jewish woman in 1937, though the moment that Austria became part of the Third Reich on 12 March 1938, whatever tenuous hold they had on their world was lost. Everything changed, uniforms, the emblems on municipal offices, even, he explained, the menus in restaurants. The ground seemed to move. They fled to Belgium in January 1939, making their way along smugglers' routes in thick snow. They were accompanied by an old Jew, this being their new identity, Jews forced to flee. They were picked up by a truck and eventually made their way to Antwerp, sending a telegraph message to their family in schoolboy French confirming their arrival. They had, however, done more than enter another country. They had entered another history and another language. They had just fifteen marks and fifty pfennigs, which they now exchanged for what then seemed to them to be foreign currency. Thus began their exile, and in German, he later recalled, exile is linguistially related to misery: the word for misery is *Elend*, whose etymological root means 'another land'.

Thus, too, began a series of lessons in what it was to lose one's home, though he had lost it long before he trudged through the snow towards the Belgian border. It is true that in a sense he had chosen exile, but the decision had not been his to make. He had already been an exile before he left. After the war, Germans would be expelled from the east and lose all their possessions, a livelihood, a place in which to root their memories. He had lost that but he had also, he insisted, lost a people and a language. Those with whom he had been raised had gone on to be informers, bullies, or simply to embrace a new faith which not merely excluded but vilified him. He had lost a country because that country had been taken from him. It was not his to feel homesick for. The past no longer acknowledged him. He had been erased from it. His homesickness, as he confessed, now became an alienation from the self. He no longer had a language to inhabit. Indeed, he insists that the moment it was decreed that Jews could not wear the folk costume he had worn from his childhood, he ceased to use his dialect. Even his name, Hans Mayer, which he had always heard with that dialect colouring, was drained of all substance. Memories of his region were now rendered ironic.

Even his ancestors were retrospectively dispossessed and were thus carried into exile by their descendant. Suddenly, the wandering Jew seemed more at home than him if only because centuries of dispossession had created a kind of familiar environment. 'Next year in Jerusalem' was less an announcement of immediate expectation than an expression of shared faith, pronounced in the knowledge that others were simultaneously intoning this hope masquerading as certainty. It was not a faith he could embrace.

But it was language that lay at the heart of his dilemma. The émigré German writer (such as Thomas Mann) not only continued to deploy the language but could claim to be its protector, the true voice of a Germany that had temporarily degraded words along with social form, ethical behaviour, political values. In Belgium, for Améry, there was never any question of making such a claim. The true exiles 'knew that they were outcasts and not curators of an invisible museum of German intellectual history' (45). In time he would find cultural models but even then he felt the need to anchor himself in 'village and city streets'. A true internationalism, it seemed to him, 'thrives only in the soil of national security', and that was precisely what he had lost. 'One must have a home', he insisted, 'in order not to need it' (46). Where, after all, he asks, would James Joyce have been without Dublin, Joseph Roth without Vienna, Proust without Illiers? Memory is in large part a matter of place.

In Belgium, he found that he could not read the code. What did a gesture mean, the smile of an official? He was himself living in a world whose signs were 'as inscrutable ... as Etruscan script'. Home meant so much more than location. It was a key to possession of what he called 'the dialectics of knowledge and recognition, of trust and confidence' (47). It might be that time would construct a new world, restore a lost sense of security, facilitate an easier decoding of daily experience, but even then it seemed to him that this required an intellectual effort.

It was a point made by Max Sebald, who explained of himself that even writing a letter in English, after more than thirty years of working in Britain, was a conscious process, never having become purely instinctual. Somewhere, buried not so deep, was an alternative linguistic world, a cultural interference pattern. There is, Améry insists, no 'new home' (48). Home will always mean childhood and youth and that home has a language. To lose that is to lose the self. The absoluteness of that loss should already have been apparent when the Nuremberg laws were passed, but even then the possibility of escape did something to nullify this. When German troops entered Belgium in 1940, however, that tenuous connection seemed irrevocably broken. Now, Germans – and indeed Austrians – were the enemy and he became part of the Resistance.

On one occasion, as he and his group were planning a surreptitious poster campaign, they were interrupted by their downstairs neighbour who came to complain about their noise. He was an SS officer. But what most disturbed Améry was that he spoke in his own dialect (there is a similar incident in Sebald's *Vertigo* as drunken revellers, shouting out 'unsavoury things', provoke a stab of fear, immediately before the narrator (Sebald?) loses his passport, proof of his German identity). For a second, Améry was something more than a compatriot. He found himself almost convinced that if he spoke to him their shared past would wipe out the truth of his representative brutality. That he could not deploy that dialect, and replied only in a stuttering French, marked for him the completeness with which home had become nothing more than enemy country. It was not that he had lost his country but that, he now realised, it had never been his. The assumption that it was was exposed as a misunderstanding, hence the power of the photograph in Sebald's *The Emigrants*, of a Jewish family in lederhosen confidently claiming an identity of which they would be calculatedly deprived. He and his kind had been actors believing their performances to be the thing itself. Homesickness could only be an unearned pretension, surrendered to, on occasion, but illegitimate, a self-deceit of a kind usually only permitted in dreams.

Language did not just crumble away, piece by piece, as Günther Anders had suggested it must for those forced to operate in other languages, it shrank, narrowed by the compulsive revisiting of obsessive subjects. Cut off from an organic connection, it began to atrophy. To read the official German press, meanwhile, was to find oneself confronted by a vocabulary at odds with one's own plight. Of what nationality, for example, is an enemy bomber? 'The meaning of every German word', he confessed, 'changed for us, and finally, whether we resisted or not, our mother tongue became just as inimical as the one they spoke around us' (53). In a similar mood, Aharon Appelfeld would speak of 'German – the language of those who murdered my mother' and ask 'how does one go back to speaking in a language drenched in the blood of the Jews?' (112).

Améry's flight to Belgium, and the tense optimism of his time with the Resistance, provided only a temporary reprieve. In July 1943 he was arrested by the Gestapo. He was at the time carrying a mimeographed pamphlet declaring 'Death to the SS bandits and Gestapo hangmen!' which hardly left much room for discussion. What surprised him was that those arresting, and subsequently questioning and torturing him, seemed no different from anyone else. There was no mark of the Beast. He was taken to Gestapo headquarters and assured that if he offered up the names of his fellow resistance members he would be placed in a military prison and thus avoid the ministrations of the SS. He explained that he knew nothing except aliases and had been led to their houses only at night, a reply that was partly prepared and partly true. It did not prevent a fist in the face and at that moment his reality began to change. Certainly, nothing in his life had prepared him for this. In some curious way, curious because he had already anticipated its likelihood, this blow seemed a breach of trust, of the belief that life was conducted according to certain agreed principles. Nonetheless, he discovered to his surprise that the blow acted as its own anaesthetic. Certainly, he had not felt obliged to capitulate. What followed was what they had threatened. He was driven the twenty-five kilometres from Brussels to Fort Breendonk, a First World War fortress now turned into a small concentration camp.

It was, however, as a member of the Resistance that he was arrested, not as a Jew. He was still in the business of distancing himself from an identity forced on him by others. What followed was an attempt to elicit the information he was presumed to possess. And what also followed was torture of a kind that made a fist in the face a mere courtesy. For Améry, looking back, what distinguished the

Third Reich's attitude from that of other regimes around the world was that its torturers tortured because they were torturers. They did so 'with the good conscience of depravity' (31).

In his essay on torture, he went out of his way to abbreviate his description of his own suffering. Nonetheless, he is obliged to offer the bare details. His arms were tied together behind his back and he was suspended from a hook in the ceiling. There was, he explained, 'a cracking and splintering in my shoulders that my body has not forgotten until this hour. The balls sprang from their sockets. My own body weight caused luxation; I fell into a void and now hung by my dislocated arms, which had been torn high from behind and now twisted over my head' (32). He offers no description of the pain. It was, he says, what it was. There were no words that could capture it. His feelings, he explains, 'mark the limit of the capacity of language to communicate' (33), and that was a primary problem for the witness. It is not merely that language is inadequate to the task of communicating extremes of experience but that it acts to pull such experiences into the realm of civilised discourse. The fact of pain can be recalled (and here he is reaching back in memory twenty years) but not its somatic reality. A brutal and arbitrary assault loses its extra-linguistic shock the moment it is shaped by the regularities of grammar and syntax, contained by words whose approximations can come close to denying what they seek to express.

He had another problem in that the language in Breendonk and, subsequently, Auschwitz, was German, his own language, though so denatured and crude that Primo Levi suggested it 'scorched his mouth'.[5] What would follow in the years ahead took him further into this world without words. Under torture he became simply a body, a physical being and nothing more. Torture, he confessed, leaves its memory trace; it is 'ineradicably burned into him, even when no clinically objective traces can be detected' (*At the Mind's Limits*, 34). Twenty years later, he explained, he was 'still dangling over the ground by dislocated arms, panting and accusing myself' (336). And one element of that trace is the knowledge that torture drove out mind and imagination. Enlightenment values were simply turned off like a light switch.

As it happened he had no information to offer and bizarre though it seems he was still tenuously part of a rational world in which his torturers sought information and when none was forthcoming eventually realised as much. He had not remained silent. He had spilled forth information. He simply invented it to stop the pain. Had he possessed what they sought it was entirely probable he would have offered it up. He acknowledged that others would not and did not, and pays homage to Jean Moulin, who knew everything about the Resistance and told nothing.

What Améry remembered those years later was an alternative world, coherent in its incoherences, a world that required only submission. Past experiences offered no leverage. In recovering his time in the camps he became a kind of anthropologist reporting on alien mores, rituals drained of meaning but within whose arbitrary rules he had been obliged to live. The difficulty was one of translation. To explain the nature of torture it would be necessary, he suggested, to turn torturer and transform the reader into his victim. The displacement of pain into the word 'pain' of necessity denied its essence. Still more, the memory of pain exists on a different plane to the thing itself.

What, then, did torture do? It stripped the individual of any connection with the world. 'Whoever has succumbed to torture', he insists, 'can no longer feel at home in the world.' It is as though he accuses himself, and others like himself, of complicity. 'The shame of destruction', he says, 'cannot be erased' (40). He is an exile in a more profound way than he who simply walks through the snow to cross a boundary. He is no longer at home in the world.

From Breendonk he began his journey to the camps and on his way noted the dispassionate glances of Germans as the cattle trucks stopped at stations to unload the dead. It was a further stage in learning that he no longer had a home in the world, that there was no longer a connection between him and those with whom he would have felt a natural affinity as he grew up, an affinity now revealed as illusory. He would go to Buchenwald, Bergen-Belsen and other camps before spending a year at Auschwitz-Monowitz. His wife died while he was incarcerated. After liberation, he returned to Brussels where he married again and survived through his journalism, writing about anything but his experiences in the camps. Primo Levi wrote his memories immediately on his return. Améry did not, though they did not leave him.

For Sebald, Améry's significance lay in part in the contrast between his desire to retrieve and the postwar German state's desire to deny. His essays, written in the 1960s, are pitched against an indifference that was itself a shadow of that which had facilitated the horrors of the camps. History was not to be a closed book reassuringly placed on a library shelf. It was a process, a product of decisions made or not made. He set himself to witness not as a historian intent to fill in the white spaces of knowledge nor yet simply as a polemicist, but as an engaged citizen for whom the past was organically connected to the present which was in part its product. For Améry, the wound was never to be healed. It was a product of a disease not to be cured by compensation, forgetfulness, denial, gestures of reconciliation that would permit effortless continuance, as if a shrug of regret might be sufficient to dispose of the past.

At the time he began to write he was the unwelcome guest at the party, the forgotten relative revealing family secrets. He recalled the Nazi flag, a blood-red cloth with a black spider on a white field waving from the most remote farmstead when others wished to suppress such memories as if they held a mystery best not revisited, a nightmare from which they had awoken to a bright new day.

Looking back from a postwar world, not unnaturally he asks whether this sense of being at home in a place or a language has not been superseded by a new cosmopolitanism, only to insist that such a cosmopolitanism is liable to have shallow roots. Placed under pressure the individual needs to turn somewhere, an idea of a transcendent internationalism being unlikely to fit the bill. We need, he insists, the fact of 'living with things that tell us stories' (57). This is a process which he chooses to call 'remembering'.

The very word sends him spinning back from such specula-tions, which for the moment have allowed even him to forget his main theme – the Third Reich and the loss of home it engendered not only in him but in countless millions. At first, he confesses, loss of the past had seemed compensated for by a hope in the future. With the passage of time, however, and for those no longer so young, memory becomes an ever more critical component of identity. And soon, his situation would change. Ahead of him in his narrative lies the erasure of the self through torture, deportation, and life in a numbered barracks with a number tattooed on his arm. Ahead of him lies an identity determined by the brute power of a camp guard and a system constructed with the sole purpose of eradicating him and those who were taken to be his kind. The past, meanwhile, 'had been retracted by society' (59). He existed only in the present.

The Holocaust was, he agreed, the existential reference point for Jews but to have experienced it directly was to have attained an ambiguous but undoubted privilege. Others could empathise but they were like blind men speaking of colour. Only those who had been taken to the edge could report on what they had discovered there. His dilemma was that he was a Jew without religion, without tradition, without a community, without a history, without messianic hope. He was a Jew by virtue of Nuremberg and Auschwitz, by virtue of the number tattooed on his arm. He was a Jew by virtue of not being allowed to be something else, a status which nonetheless he must affirm and make his own. He was a Jew by virtue of containing within himself not merely the memory but the fact of catastrophe, that and a surviving fear: 'Every morning when I get up I can read the Auschwitz number on my forearm, something that touches the deepest and most closely intertwined roots of my existence; indeed I am not even sure if this is not my entire existence.' Every day, he declared, 'I lose my trust in the world' (94).

To pass another on the street and exchange polite words is to be reminded that that person, or one like him or her, would have looked the other way as he was dragged away to torture and death. A gap had opened up that he could not believe would close. The irony is that the moment his past was denied, stripped from him, annihilated, he had become a Jew. The anti-Semite had created him but he had also created himself, a complex fate, the more so since he could take no consolation from the comforts available for the religious.

After the war, Europe was on the move, sometimes voluntarily, often as the result of compulsion. Survivors made their way home or, like Otto Frank, father to Anne, unable to adjust to familiar places stripped of familiar faces, moved on in an attempt to escape memories which could only breed pain, irony, regret. They settled in new countries but carried those memories with them, acknowledged or not, recalled or not, now refracted through the prism of a new language not necessarily receptive to or easily expressive of experiences suffered in an alien culture. Grasp on a new culture could never be entirely secure.

To Eva Hoffman, the importance of emigration in the biography of survivors and their children has been oddly underestimated.[6] Remote in space and time, they often now felt that that other life was discontinuous with their new selves. There was even, for some, a sense of shame at the price paid for survival, not merely guilt at having survived but guilt at what had been necessary to bring that about. Even in Israel there were those who treated survivors with disdain, David Ben Gurion believing that the survivors represented the worst elements in Jewish society, compromised by the necessities that led to their survival. The dead, meanwhile, were accused by others – Bruno Bettelheim chief among them – of a passivity amounting to confederacy with the killers. To have lived or to have died was to be accused of bad faith. Meanwhile, the world was anxious to move on.

For the next twenty years Améry neither returned to Germany nor addressed a German readership, writing instead for Swiss publications. Then, in 1964, he gave a radio talk on the subject of Auschwitz called 'Encounter of the Intellectuals with Auschwitz'. It was in part this that led him to write *At the Mind's Limits*, originally entitled *Beyond Guilt and Atonement*, a title whose very absoluteness reflected his unyielding stance.

As he explained in the 1966 edition, after twenty years of silence, he had been led to write his first essay on his experiences in the Third Reich by the Auschwitz trial in Frankfurt, the trial attended by both Peter Weiss and Arthur Miller and which proved so influential with Sebald. During those twenty years, he explained, he had neither forgotten nor repressed what he called the twelve years of German fate. He had, he explained, been 'in search of the time that was impossible to lose'. He had hesitated 'at the threshold of verbal expression'. He had no wish to add to what had now begun to be a growing pile of documentary work. What he aimed to do was offer 'a phenomenological description of the existence of the victim' (xiii). Only later did he feel the need to add a qualifier – the *Jewish* victim. With calculated irony he identified a German audience 'who in their overwhelming majority do not, or no longer, feel affected by the darkest and at the same time most characteristic deeds of the Third Reich'. He would, he explained, like to relate a few things that had perhaps not been revealed to them.

Eleven years later he wrote another preface, looking back on this experience through a history of continuing brutality in the world. He had written not of the human condition in his book but of the inhuman condition and he found this scarcely any better. Nonetheless, while explaining his alarm at the rise of a new anti-Semitism and his distaste for the Left's appropriation of the word 'Fascist' to apply to any right-wing regime, he decided to change nothing. Time had moved on but not in relation to the camps and the issues they raised. He confessed to being no closer to understanding why such events had occurred among a people of 'high intelligence, industrial capability, and unequalled cultural wealth' (vii), while rejecting those explanations which would propose Auschwitz and Treblinka as products of German intellectual history, late capitalism, economic crisis. History, it seemed to him, was helpless precisely because this was sui generis. The camps remained 'a dark riddle' (viii). No light entered them and none left. What he offered, therefore, was not analysis or explanation but testimony.

He was aware that there was no honour in being a victim. He felt impelled, he explained, simply to describe though that is far from what he proceeded to do. He had no desire to elide hangman and victim with some specious notion of reconciliation. The 'moral chasm' was to remain open. His aim was enlightenment, not clarification or classification since that would seem to imply resolution, the filing away of yesterday as though it had become a completed history. He was anxious above all that remembering would not, as he put it, become 'mere memory' (xi). What happened, he acknowledged, happened but that it happened could not simply be accepted. It was necessary always to rebel against the fact and against a present that was content to dismiss such experiences as incomprehensible. He wrote with passion because what he wrote about demanded no less, always aware, however, that his account would be regarded as inadequate to its subject, that in some bizarre way it might be seen as normalising the radically abnormal. He might have been concerned to write about the confrontation, as he put it, between Auschwitz and intellect but intellect was not to become a means of incorporating it into a rational account, as if its very procedures implied a coherent meaning at the heart of horror.

In Auschwitz, it seemed to him, the intellectual was especially dispossessed. None of the resources on which he was accustomed to draw proved of any utility. Culture had simply been appropriated from Riemenschneider down to Beethoven and Novalis. Where those with practical skills might find some position which could offer limited protection in the camps, the intellectual was liable to find himself reduced to a physical labour for which he had precisely not prepared himself. Survival depended on physical strength.

He recalls searching out a famous philosopher only to receive grunts where he had looked for evidence that the intellect has its own sustaining resources. His own attempts to recuperate snatches of verse, to remember lines by Hölderlin, came to nothing, lines committed to memory sending back no echoes in this place, not least because intimate friendships were not possible, each locked within himself, not least because those lines came back from another time and place from which he had been excommunicated. Words could be recalled but the context drained them of meaning, though memories of Thomas Mann's *The Magic Mountain* did momentarily lift his spirits. Home, language, history, culture, were suddenly ungrounded.

In this place there were no subtle discriminations. The only things that mattered were the brute distinctions pronounced by the ideology which prevailed. Where he looked for consolation he found only irony. Indeed, it was looking for consolation that made the intellectual especially vulnerable to that irony. This, after all, was the essential component of the absurd in a place where hope was cynically deployed – with talk of work leading to freedom, cleansing 'showers', carefully positioned Red Cross trucks – as a tactic in the wider strategy of death. Not only were people killed but they were mocked for those very human qualities that made such a death seem inconceivable. Indeed, it was the inconceivable nature of what they did that was to be the chief protection of those who waded in blood. No one would believe because what was done was unbelievable.

In a curious way, the reality of Nazi Germany was linked to the elimination of the Jews, who had not merely fallen under the wheels of history but been destined to play their role in the coming into being of the Third Reich. The Nuremberg laws came instructively early as if they gave a sudden energy to the new order. Nor was it enough that the Jews should be removed in the present. They had to be retrospectively eliminated. Their culture was to be destroyed, the archives scoured and wiped clean. Their children had to be reduced to ash so there could be no future. And when the Reich that was to have lasted a thousand years collapsed after little more than a decade, the camps in which so many had died were destroyed, largely to conceal evidence of what was thus acknowledged as a crime, as, of course, it had not been before, but also because this was part of that elimination of all signs that Jews had lived and died, that they had ever existed.

Améry entered the camps without that consolation of ideology or religion that could in some way make sense of suffering. He felt no envy for those who embraced such consolations. Yet he did envy their calm and strength and the transcendence that enabled them to preserve a threatened individuality since they retained an alternative home, a wider community from which they were never completely separated. His dilemma was that he had no such community, except the enforced recognition that he suffered because he was identified as part of those others. He was a detached intellectual made aware that the intellectual tradition to which he laid claim was no longer his.

Here, people died to music. The German romantic view of death he had ingested was here stripped of its meaning. As he remarked, 'No bridge led from death in Auschwitz to *Death in Venice*' (16). Hesse,

Rilke, become meaningless. The aestheticising of death becomes impossible, indeed death itself, merely deferred moment by moment, assumed less importance than the quality of the soup which would ensure another day's survival. There was no purpose in reaching beyond the real along a line of abstract thought or language liberated momentarily from its concrete immediacy. Time shrank to a point. 'Nowhere else', he insisted, 'was reality so real.' Philosophical declarations 'no longer meant anything. We didn't require any semantic analysis or logical syntax to recognize this' (19). Beauty, knowledge, death itself, all became meaningless. There was no wisdom to be acquired here, no moral improvement. And when it was over it became immensely difficult to re-enter language and trust its assumptions.

There was, though, something carried away and that was the conviction that 'the intellect is a *ludus*'. This in turn led to a loss of arrogance. He quotes a fellow Austrian, Karl Kraus, as saying that, 'The word fell into a sleep, when that world awoke' (20). And if the essays Améry would go on to write suggested that the word itself might be awakened, the very style of those essays, ironic, detached, even in describing his own sufferings, suggests that it would never be completely resuscitated. 'The word always dies', he remarked at the end of his most famous essay, itself a bare twenty pages long, 'where the claim of some reality is total. It died for us a long time ago. And we were not even left with the feeling that we must regret its departure' (20).

Jean Améry was not so much a witness as an analyst, a polemicist, a philosopher. He did suffer. He did offer witness. That, though, was not his primary purpose. He set out to understand not the mind of his oppressor, opaque in its absoluteness, nor even the nature of anti-Semitism, but the impact on the self of what he and others suffered. These events, after all, had taken the mind to its limits. They had broken language, dispossessed the individual of something more than home. They had seemingly negated memory, re-presented it as a false claim on experience to which he had no legitimate claim. He was, indeed, de-legitimised as a person. He existed only to become the anti-matter in a myth. He was not even a sacrifice on the altar of

Nazi ambitions, for that would be to grant him a role and hence significance. The irony was that it was not so much his birth that rendered him a Jew. He was declared a Jew and must thereafter struggle with what he called the necessity and impossibility of being a Jew. He came to feel like the only sane man in an asylum in which his sanity was an irrelevance. Nothing about him is Jewish except his determination to declare solidarity with other Jews, not on the basis of religion, culture or history, but of a shared threat. It becomes the foundation of his dignity, his freedom, his humanity, his sense of reality. He is a Jew, he explains, only in fear and anger, not in belief. Nor is this a metaphysical state. His argument is not with God but with men. Concern with the absurd is a kind of game. He is dedicated to the literal and the real and with living out the tension between the necessity of being a Jew and the impossibility of being one, between being a victim and refusing such a designation. He did not exist, he realises, until he became a Jew, albeit a Jew who would not be recognised as such by many of his fellow Jews.

Not merely did his pre-1935 self become an unreality, its memories not erased but simply crossed through, but life after 1945 became equally unreal. In a world whose talk was of progress, with its Declarations of Human Rights, its democratic constitutions, he reverted to a truth symbolised by the numbers on his arm. If the camp had seemed surreal, now everyday life did in that people behaved as if the truth of the camps had been learned, instead of being consigned to a receding past, receding in significance as well as time. He had lost his trust in the world and could only learn to live with that radical distrust. He lives alone, he explains, with his Jewish faith which is not a faith but simply a foreignness he has learned to embrace. As a result, his is a conversation with the world which can never be entirely open because he possesses a knowledge he can never never fully articulate or, if articulate, communicate.

Améry was close kin to Arthur Miller's fictional character in *Focus*, a non-Jew whom others identify as Jewish and who finally accepts a Jewish identity because not to do so would be to become confederate with his oppressors. In the end his Jewish identity is a question of solidarity. It mattered more to him, he confessed, than his love of literature. Without that, he explained, he would still be a human being. Without a feeling of solidarity with the threatened he would be a fugitive from reality, a reality he had learned not only like but through a blow to the face. Anti-Semitism may be an abstract noun but there had been nothing abstract about it.

The 'dramaturgy' (his word) of anti-Semitism still existed within the larger drama of Jewish history. His anger becomes the basis of his Jewish identity, solidarity the foundation stone of his shared apprehension of threat. His problem, he acknowledges, is to exist in the tension between fear and anger. He confesses to a 'trace' truth in accusations of bitterness. He is not, he accepts, good at gestures of magnanimity. On the other hand, he is not incapacitated by this dilemma. He exists in the world, reads books, listens to music and if he had become more responsive to injustice and violence in the world, he had not, he insisted, become an obsessive, unable to function as an individual. His consciousness of the camp, his memories, do not lead him to metaphysical angst, to fashionable concerns with the death of God. His concern is social and political.

Yet, beneath such speculations, he was alone with his memories, alarmed at signs of a revived anti-Semitism and thirty-three years after his liberation from Auschwitz, on 17 October 1978, he committed suicide in a Salzburg hotel, swallowing poison. Despite their disagreements over Judaism and Améry's description of him as a 'forgiver', his death greatly affected his fellow survivor, Primo Levi, who now began to translate *At the Mind's Limits* into Italian. He wrote to a friend:

> Suicides are generally mysterious: Améry's was not. Faced by the hopeless clarity of his mind, faced by his death, I have felt how fortunate I have been, not only in recovering my family and my country, but also in succeeding to weave around me a 'painted veil' made of family affections, friendship, travel, writing, and even chemistry.[7]

By implication, Améry lacked such protections. Survival is so much more than merely not to have died. For some, its burdens proved insupportable. Nonetheless, suicides are, as Levi confessed, mysterious and his own suggestion that Améry's was not seems presumptuous, not least because he, himself, would later take the same decision. The supposed protections of family, friendship, travel, writing would ultimately prove inadequate for him. And if the wartime experiences of both men may not have been a principal cause of their deaths, it is difficult to believe that somehow the shadow of that time had not lingered. In the end, memories released as witness or therapy may defer to memories which lead back to some ultimate darkness. In the view of his widow, Améry, who was the author of a book, *On Suicide* (published in 1976, two years before his death), which justified the taking of one's own life, chose suicide as a 'path to freedom'.[8]

For Primo Levi, Améry, whom he characterised as his companion and antagonist, was a 'political combatant who enlisted because of the disease that plagued Europe and threatened (and still threatens) the world; that of the philosopher of the spirit, which in Auschwitz was absent; that of the diminished scholar from whom the forces of history have stripped away country and identity'.[9]

Primo Levi, who devoted an entire chapter to Améry in *If This is a Man*, recalled the incident in which Améry had struck the Polish man who had aimed a blow at him but suggested that while in part admiring it, it stood as evidence if not of a false path then of one that could later lead to a cul-de-sac. In *The Drowned and the Saved* he remarks:

> 'trading punches' is an experience I do not have, as far back as I can go in memory; nor can I say I regret not having it ... go[ing] down onto the battlefield ... was and is beyond my reach. I admire it, but I must point out that this choice, protracted throughout his post-Auschwitz existence, led [Améry] to such severity and intransigence as to make him incapable of finding joy in life, indeed of living. Those who 'trade blows' with the entire world achieve dignity but pay a very high price for it because they are sure to be defeated. (109–10)

Ironically, given his own later fate, he added, 'Améry's suicide, which took place in Salzburg in 1978, like other suicides allows for a nebula of explanations, but, in hindsight, that episode of defeating the Pole offers one interpretation of it' (36). It is a severe judgement, as though resistance were itself the source of self-destruction. Levi's own suicide is subject to the same nebula of explanations but his remarks on Améry suggest his consciousness that the damage wrought by the camps could not easily be annulled not least because it had the power to restructure the self, define it even through its oppositional necessities. Nor was he himself immune to anger.

Primo Levi learned that Améry had accused him of being 'a forgiver', in particular because he had showed some sympathy for Ferdinand Meyer, a German whom Levi had encountered in the I. G. Farben works at Auschwitz, and with whom he carried on a postwar correspondence in which the German seemed contrite. Améry characterised Meyer's letters to Levi as a 'soul striptease', redolent of 'metaphysical *Schmus* baby pap'.[10] He was wrong about Levi. That he should level the accusation, however, says something for his own attitude. Levi remarked, 'Améry calls me a "forgiver". I don't consider this either an insult or praise but an imprecision. I am not inclined to forgive ... because I know of no human act that can erase a crime. I demand justice, but I am not able, personally, to trade punches and return the blows.'[11] But, he added, 'If I too had seen the world collapse upon me; if I had been sentenced to exile and the loss of national identity; if I too had been tortured until I fainted and lost consciousness and beyond, I would perhaps have learned to return the blow, and would harbour, like Améry, those "resentments" to which he dedicated a long essay full of anguish' (111).

Simon Wiesenthal once invited a number of writers to contribute to a volume in which they were asked to respond to the dilemma represented by his own story of the dying SS man who confessed that he had burned Jews alive and on his deathbed asked a Jew (Wiesenthal himself) for forgiveness, only to have the man walk away. What, they were asked, should have been his response? Améry's response was to say, 'Politically, I do not want to hear anything of forgiveness ... I refuse every reconciliation with the criminals, and with those who only by accident did not happen to commit atrocities, and finally, all those who helped prepare the unspeakable acts with their words.'[12] On a personal level it was immaterial. Forgiveness was a matter either of psychology or of politics. Psychologically, he could conceive of circumstances that made forgiveness possible. He was agnostic. But what mattered was the politics, the necessity to see that such events should not recur and in that context forgiveness was not possible. Wiesenthal's admirable function, it seemed to him, was not merely to remember but to search out and demand unequivocal justice.

Levi's reply to Wiesenthal was:

> You did well to refuse forgiveness for the dying man. What would your pardon have meant for the German or for you? Probably a great deal for the German (a purification which would have freed his religious conscience, all too tardily aroused, from the terror of eternal punishment). But for you I think it would have been meaningless – an empty formula – and consequently a lie. (343)

Améry and Levi were a deal closer than the former chose to believe.

Levi recognised Améry's dilemma. For Améry, according to Levi, 'being Jewish was simultaneously impossible and obligatory',[13] but being Jewish also meant rebellion. And so, Hans Mayer became Jean Améry, an anagram of his former name, one history, one language, being replaced with another, one set of memories cordoned off as though the product of another self. And then that identity in turn was replaced with a number.

Améry claimed not only to have known Levi but to have lived in the same barracks in Buna-Monowitz. Oddly, Levi, who laid claim to an indelible memory, could not recall him or his appearance, suspecting that Améry might have confused him with a fellow Italian, the artist Carlo Levi. Their misunderstandings, it seemed, were of long standing.

In his book on suicide, based on a series of radio talks, Améry contemplated not simply what he preferred to call 'voluntary death', which he thought an extraordinary act, but the state of mind of one contemplating it, time edging towards its end. And with no forward reality what but memory exerts its imperium, meaning now lying in the past? 'Memory, arrested in time, the memory of past times in the present', he explained, 'grabs its abundance closer and closer to itself until it is only a tiny, very heavy nucleus, a nucleus of the ego.' So many things have compacted themselves into any life, he insists, most profoundly trivial, that the nature of that ego is ambiguous. The trivial, indeed, seems to exert a greater pull than what might have seemed more profound – and interestingly, throughout *On Suicide*, there is only one reference to the camps. The 'lived time', he states, 'is still present, even if enclosed within in the most minute proportions. But it will no longer be present, because its irreversibility is actualized and made concrete: it is not death that pursues the suicide, but that the suicide snatches it to his breast, closing tight all the doors through which help could enter.'[14] The closing of the doors, however, may restore the self to itself. 'As far as I can see', he says, 'voluntary death … is nowhere recognized for what it is: precisely *free and voluntary* death and a highly individual matter that, to be sure, is never carried out without social reference, with which however and finally *human beings are alone with themselves, before which society has to be silent*' (97).

Yet what is this self, thus seemingly summed up by its termination? Interestingly, he offers a confession of the fallibility of memory, and of the interpretation of memory, which lies at the heart of that self. 'What I experienced in 1919 [he himself was born in 1912] – my entry into elementary school, the immediate results of the collapse of a proud empire – became false in the light of 1930, became true in the perspective of 1940, and is once again a lie when I direct my eyes to it today. Was I already deceiving myself at the moment of my experience', he asks himself, 'and am I deceiving myself now at this hour? Am I making my yesterday just as much an untruth as my present and is perhaps what has passed only wrong as a consequence of the light of the lie I see it in today?' Most crucially, he concedes that the 'certainty of a false and dishonest life, of lying to the world and to oneself, exists for everyone who reawakens in memory what is over and done with in one's life' (147–8).

So, this man, who spoke of 'the deceptive magic of memory',[15] for whom the recall of what befell him in Auschwitz was of central moral importance, simultaneously and obliquely announces his ambiguous relationship to the man who had once suffered and his resistance to being defined by anything but the shimmering infinitude of experiences which were both true and false, marginal and central. Voluntary death, he suggests, involves 'an absurd intoxification of freedom'. What it must not be is a simple submission, a capitulation to process. This is not, he insists, the would-be suicide of a concentration camp inmate (and here is his sole invocation of the camps) who relinquishes his intent in favour of another day of degradation. Death may be welcomed in the name of 'dignity, humanity, freedom. And so death becomes life ... And now negation all at once becomes something positive.' However, crucially, he adds, 'But the survivors are right: for what are dignity, humanity and freedom in preference to smiling, breathing and striding?' (On Suicide, 152–3). And here is the heart of his dilemma.

Tzvetan Todorov, in his book on moral life in the concentration camps, *Facing the Extreme*, observes that 'the difference between choosing death and submitting to it is enormous; it is the difference that separates human beings from animals. In choosing one's death, one performs an act of will and thereby affirms one's membership in the human race.'[16] He wrote in the context of the Jewish plight in the Warsaw ghetto. Even then, however, he made a distinction. Adam Czerniakow, president of the Jewish Council established by the Germans, took his own life when he learned that the residents of the ghetto were to go to Treblinka. He did so out of a sense of his own powerlessness, oddly adding in his suicide note that he hoped it would show others what to do. But this suicide, private, was seen by many as a sign of weakness. Later, Mordechai Anielewicz, young commander of the ghetto rebels, also seems to have taken his own life, a symbolic gesture appealing not to those around him but to history. To Todorov, therefore, it was not enough for such gestures to indicate the dignity of the subject; they had to contribute to the welfare of others. Otherwise, suicides, he suggests, potentially serve only themselves. They begin and end with the self. They are expressions of an act of will but to what ends?

What, then, are we to make of Améry's decision? Was he no more than a deferred victim? Was he taking control of his life by ending it? Was it a defeat or a victory? Were these even questions he would himself have been able to answer?

He ended his book on suicide on an equivocal note that can, perhaps, stand as an epigraph for a man who here debates with seeming objectivity a fate that he would so soon choose to make his own:

> Things don't go well with potential suicides and haven't turned
> out the best for suicides. We ought not to deny them respect for
> what they have done and left undone, we ought not to deny
> them concern, especially since we ourselves do not cut such a
> splendid figure. We look lamentable, anyone can see that. And
> so, subdued and in an orderly manner, with lowered heads,
> we want to offer a lament for those who departed from us in
> freedom. (153)

When Nathaniel Hawthorne's Hester Prynne died her tomb-stone was engraved with the scarlet letter she had once been forced to wear as a mark of her humiliation but which she had transformed into a badge of honour. Jean Améry is buried in the Zentralfriedhof in Vienna. His grave is covered with ivy. His Auschwitz number is engraved on his tombstone.

But this was not quite the end of Jean Améry. Just as there would be those writers who would seek to resurrect, at least in fictive terms, Anne Frank, and even the young man with whom she shared her hiding place, so, in *The Golems of Gotham*, Thane Rosenbaum would bring back not only Améry but also those others who had survived the camps but chosen subsequently to end their lives. The central character is a writer, both of whose survivor parents had taken their own lives. His daughter creates a golem through whom the dead are brought back. So, in modern-day New York, Améry and Primo Levi (who fell from the third floor of his apartment building), Paul Celan (who drowned himself), Piotr Rawicz, author of *Blood From the Sky* (who jumped in front of a train), and Tadeusz Borowski, who wrote *This Way for the Gas, Ladies and Gentlemen* and who gassed himself, appear, along with Jerzy Kosinski (drugged and suffocated), who suffered, Rosenbaum suggests, from survivor envy, and who was never in the camps but nonetheless was seen as throwing a dark light on their world. They argue with one another, adopting the position in death (or its near equivalent) that they had once done in life, though all unite in deciding not to invite along Bruno Bettelheim, dead by his own hand in 1990 but too much of an antagonist, with his obsession with Jewish passivity, to be welcome. They even encounter a very much alive Elie Wiesel on the street, though he is unable to see them, and regard him as perhaps the last of their kind.

The novel is in part comic, as they set about making New York amenable by banning smoke of any kind, abolishing tattooing, stopping the overcrowding of trains. Yet it is also a serious consideration of those who bore witness yet died at their own hands. The steel trap of Levi's memory snapped shut, we are told, from reflecting too long and too much but 'some survivors had no choice but to respond to their near-death experience by producing art. Whether it was for themselves, their lost families, or the world did not matter, just that it had to be done. The Nazis demanded it, even if inadvertently so.'[17] At a time when the world has moved on, without many signs of improvement, and when the survivors no longer survive, one of the dead insists, this story 'has to be told and retold, in many different ways. There have to be more tellers, and many more listeners ...' (266). And what is to be done when 'indifference and amnesia begin to rule the world' (294), when a mere gesture is seen as sufficient?

> A visit to a museum, the reading of one book, sitting through a single film, one dinnertime conversation, and it has all been digested, mastered, and taken in – and then we're on to the next thing. Humanity is all about rebuilding, all in the process of evolving – one seamless march forward no matter who gets trampled underneath. And yet the most consistent but detested movement of them all is the unsurrendered retreat, the chastened doubling back to the unsolved crime scene. (294–5)

Jean Améry was one of those who chose to double back. Nor was his death a surrender.

8   Primo Levi: from the darkness to the light

In July 1941 Primo Levi graduated from university. He received an illuminated parchment on which was written 'in elegant characters that one Primo Levi, of the Jewish race, had been conferred a degree in Chemistry summa cum laude. It was therefore a dubious document, half glory and half derision, half absolution and half condemnation'.[1] Already, he was being reminded that he lived on sufferance, inhabited a parallel universe. Yet it was some time before he felt the blade twist. Indeed in the autumn of 1942 he and his friends went to the theatre and to concerts, spent their time discussing the plays of Eugene O'Neill and Thornton Wilder, playing intellectual games, falling in love. As to what was happening 'during those same months in all of Europe occupied by the Germans, in Anne Frank's house in Amsterdam, in the pit of Babi Yar near Kiev, in the ghetto of Warsaw, in Salonika, Paris, and Lidice ... no precise information had reached us ... Our ignorance allowed us to live, as when you are in the mountains and your rope is frayed and about to break, but you don't know it and feel safe' (129).

On 11 April 1987, Primo Levi left his apartment, walked across the landing and fell forty-five feet down the stairwell of his apartment building as his grandfather had once jumped to his death out of a window. He, who had dissuaded others, such as fellow survivor Marcello Franceschi, from committing suicide, had evidently chosen to take his own life forty-two years to the day after liberation from Auschwitz. As he had remarked of Jean Améry, there is no penetrating the mind of a suicide. Levi had been suffering from depression and the cause may have been more immediate than memories of a distant

285

time, but the irony remained and it is tempting to feel that the experiences he had struggled to exorcise through his books had finally overwhelmed him. Asked why those in the camps, with every justification for immediate and overwhelming despair, did not commit suicide, he replied that animals do not commit suicide. Ending one's life, he implied, required thought. By 1987, he had had plenty of time to think.

Primo Levi was a survivor who went on to offer witness. For many, he was the paradigm of such, recalling in detail what he and others suffered and shaping those experiences, those observations, into a lucid and accusatory prose. Survivors of traumatic events, he observed, are divided into two well-defined groups: 'those who repress the past *en bloc*, and those whose memory of the offence persists, as though carved in stone ... I belong to the second group. Of my two years of life outside the law I have not forgotten a single thing. Without any deliberate effort, memory continues to restore to me events, faces, words, sensations, as if at that time my mind had gone through a period of exalted receptivity, during which not a detail was lost.'[2]

In his first book, *If This is a Man*, he seemed unequivocal but as the years passed so he became sharply conscious both of the necessity for witness and the fallibility of those, like himself, who stepped forward. 'It is possible', he conceded, as he drew on this material to write stories, 'that the distance in time has accentuated the tendency to round out the facts or heighten the colours: this tendency, or temptation is an integral part of writing, without it one does not write stories' (11). Nonetheless, the necessity to speak out was irresistible, not least because there had been those determined that none would survive to bear witness. In the preface to his *The Drowned and the Saved* he recalls, as did Simon Wiesenthal, the message from those responsible for genocide. Those who entered the camps, clinging at least to the thought that one day retribution would follow, were told:

> However this war may end, we have won the war against you; none of you will be left to bear witness, but even if someone were to survive, the world would not believe him. There will

perhaps be suspicions, discussions, research by historians, but there will be no certainties, because we will destroy the evidence together with you. And even if some proof should remain and some of you survive, people will say that the events you describe are too monstrous to be believed; they will say that they are the exaggerations of Allied propaganda and will believe us, who deny everything, and not you. We will be the ones to dictate the history of the Lagers [camps].[3]

This was what, in a telling phrase, Levi called 'a war against memory' (18). Against this could only be pitched the memories of those who, by chance, cunning, adaptability, did survive. At the same time, he acknowledged the case for silence. As he explained in *The Drowned and the Saved*, those who experienced the camps were divided into two distinct categories, with, as he said, rare intermediate shadings: 'those who remain silent who feel more deeply that sense of malaise which I for simplicity's sake call "shame", and those who do not feel at peace with themselves, or whose wounds still burn' (121). He was one of those whose wounds still burned. They speak, he explained, because their imprisonment has proved definitive, because they have survived it and because they feel the necessity to do so as members of an ambiguously privileged confederacy. But what then? And so he includes a health warning. 'An apology', he announces, 'is in order. This very book is drenched in memory' (21). Everything would depend upon memory but Levi felt obliged to confess to its fallibility.

The Germans might have destroyed the gas chambers and crematoria; they might have incinerated the records so meticulously kept and now meticulously disposed of, but memory itself was subject to entropic forces. 'Human memory', he acknowledged, 'is a marvellous but fallacious instrument ... The memories which lie within us are not carved in stone; not only do they tend to become erased as the years go by, but often they change, or even increase by incorporating extraneous features' (11). Lacking a true knowledge of the alphabet of memory, its language, the processes whereby it is laid down and 'with what pen' it is written, we are at a loss to know what weight to give it. Some mechanisms, he accepts, 'are known which falsify memory' and since these include trauma, repression, abnormal conditions of consciousness, along with 'interference by other "competitive" memories', it seems clear that the camps were not the ideal environment for accurate recording or subsequent recall. As he remarked, 'I intend to examine ... the memories of extreme experiences, of injuries suffered or inflicted. In this case, all or almost all the factors that can obliterate or deform the mnemonic record are at work' (12). With time, memories began to fragment, the pieces reassembling themselves according to principles not necessarily presenting themselves to the conscious mind.

Among those who were 'the bearers of secrets' were those themselves responsible for depravity, but they would forever remain silent or transform what they remembered to come into alignment with subsequent psychological, social or political needs. What might have been becomes what was. Such people, as he says, weigh anchor from the truth, no longer necessarily aware of what that truth might have been, the invented slowly acquiring the patina of conviction. How could the owners of the German company Topf of Wiesbaden, which designed and manufactured the crematoria for the camps, continue to trade under the same name after the war, making crematoria for 'civilian' use (as if those who had died in the camps were anything other than that), unless they had a startling capacity to deny memory? On the other hand, a story frequently repeated, he points out, retouched here and there, recited, often begins to have a perfection of form if not of accuracy. Memorials, ceremonies, create a new context for old memories. With the passage of time memories become 'blurred and stylised' (8), influenced by information derived from the evidence of others, or even from stories, fictions whose power lies precisely in their seeming veracity.

That was a special problem even for those who survived, for those who might wish, like Levi, to speak on behalf of others. It is, he accepted, 'natural and obvious that the most substantial material for the reconstruction of truth about the camps is constituted by the memories of the survivors', but who were they and what did they see? Such accounts, he insists, accounts such as his own, had to 'be read with a critical eye'. Seemingly paradoxically, he suggests that 'For knowledge of the Lagers, the Lagers themselves were not always a good observation post.' It was impossible for any one prisoner to gain a sense of the whole, not least because each was enclosed by his or her own immediate experience and because its logic was so alien. Testimonies, anyway, came not from the generality of prisoners but from what he called the 'exiguous minority', those who secured some privileged position, who 'never fathomed them [the Lagers] to the bottom' (6). The very privilege, albeit provisional and not dependent on ultimate compromise, falsified what was reported. The only ones who knew could never report. And since the privileged were often the political prisoners their reports were liable to be freighted with certain assumptions. As he observed in *The Drowned and the Saved*,

> we, the survivors, are not the true witnesses ... we are those who by their prevarications or abilities or good luck did not touch bottom. Those who did so, those who saw the Gorgon, have not returned to talk about it or have returned mute ... They are the rule, we are the exception ... We who were favoured by fate tried, with more or less wisdom, to recount not only our fate, but also that of the others, the submerged: but this was a discussion on behalf of third parties; the story of things seen from close by, not experienced personally. (63-4)

He could not be sure, he confessed, whether he and others like him wrote out of a sense of moral obligation to those who died and hence could not themselves bear witness, or 'in order to free ourselves of their memory' (64). Why the latter? Because of a sense of guilt, the guilt not only of having survived when others did not, but of the compromises necessary in order to secure that survival, the good luck, even, that chose them over others.

Levi wrote *If This is a Man*, he explained, in Italian for the Italians, for those who did not know or did not wish to know. He had memories of himself when young having to dress in the uniform of a Fascist youth organisation (just as a future Pope in Germany was dressing as a member of the Hitler Youth) and on a postwar radio programme chose the Fascist hymn as a reminder of that fact. He had learned the meaning of fascism. Others had not. But in a sense the true target of the book was the Germans. It was a gun aimed at them. It was to be a settling of accounts. It was also to be an attempt to understand those who carried out the crimes, and those who stood aside and watched with no evident desire to intervene even to the extent of offering a glass of water or a crust of bread to those in extremis. 'Almost all', he observed, 'though not all, had been deaf, blind and dumb: a mass of invalids surrounding a core of ferocious beasts. Almost all, but not all, had been cowardly' (138). He then recounted the gesture of a German who was prepared to allow him into an air-raid shelter, as if this one gesture of human solidarity would serve to highlight the otherwise near total suspension of humanity. After the publication of his first books he engaged in correspondence with a number of German readers. It was an awkward experience and one for which his fellow prisoner Jean Améry had no time. Yet he was, he confessed, disinclined to love his enemies.

In some ways it is ironic that Levi's name should be so intimately connected with the Holocaust, not least because he thought the term singularly inappropriate, its Greek derivation suggesting a burnt offering to the gods. Despite the fires that lit the sky over Auschwitz, there was never any sense that the slaughter served anything beyond Nazi policy. The only gods to appease were those who chose to locate the Jews in terms of their own myth of racial superiority. Yet it is Levi's words that are to be found on the Italian block at Auschwitz, a place that he thought the Poles were appropriating to their own memories and which, like Sebald, he feared was at odds with aspects of its own past. How, he wondered, could there be cafeterias at Auschwitz? Nonetheless, the sign which bears his words implies his acceptance of a particular role in using memory and memorials as a warning.

> Visitor, observe the remains of this camp and consider: whatever your nationality, you are not a foreigner here. Ensure that your journey was not in vain, that our own deaths have not been in vain. For you and for your children, may the ashes of

Auschwitz serve as a warning. And may the dreadful fruit of hatred, whose traces you have seen here, not grow again – not tomorrow, not ever.[4]

'It was my good fortune', he insisted, 'to be deported to Auschwitz only in 1944' – the opening words of what became one of the most famous of the books to emerge from the Holocaust, *If This is a Man*. For the words 'good fortune' and 'Auschwitz' to be contained in the same sentence is to suspect irony. There is none. Primo Levi did, indeed, arrive at the camp when the killing had moderated somewhat. He was there for eleven months, and when he returned to Italy his family were all alive, though of the 650 Jews originally deported with him (his figure; others put it at 489, 193 of whom were gassed immediately on arrival)[5] he was only one of three to return. According to Ian Thomson, Levi's biographer, many of the Italians thought the train en route for Auschwitz was bound for Austerlitz. What W. G. Sebald might have made of that!

His story of his time in Auschwitz is bleak but there are others far more so. It added, he confessed, nothing as an account of atrocities. He did not write it to accuse, though accusations shape themselves from what he describes. Nor was he inclined to see the *Lager* as wholly unique, separable from the rest of history. It was, he said – and Arthur Miller would say the same and be attacked for it – 'the product of a conception of the world carried rigorously to its logical conclusion'.[6] The same essentially could be said of those in the camp who decided to collaborate, to become the agents of their oppressors in order to win some sliver of advantage. These, he insisted, had existed in all times and in all places when the conqueror ruled and decisions had to be made as to how to respond to absolute power. Even so, his book, ignored at first and gathering significance only with the years, was a product of an overpowering need to speak out because the 'story of the death camps should be understood by everyone as a sinister alarm-signal' (15).

It was born not in the post-war world but in Auschwitz itself. He even kept notes there, only to destroy them lest they be found. He did so out of a need 'to tell our story to "the rest", to make "the rest" participate in it' (15). That impulse, he admitted, was violent, to the point of displacing other necessities. On his return he would accost fellow passengers on trains, to tell them what some were ready to hear but what to others sounded like the ravings of a madman. Later he was fond of invoking Coleridge's Ancient Mariner, who had a similar compulsion to accost strangers and tell them his tale. Before that, however, his books had one other function, though linked to the first. It was a matter of 'an interior liberation' (15). He had written the chapters, he explained, not in logical order but in the 'order of urgency', his own and that which should be felt by those he assumed might wish to hear. He was not, though, a supplicant. If he wrote like the narrator of Coleridge's poem or Melville's *Moby Dick* out of a necessity to tell his story, he was also capable of uttering a cold curse on those 'who live safe / In your warm houses' and who fail to listen to the tale he tells not because it is his but because it could, as he had himself discovered, so easily be theirs:

> Consider if this is a man
> Who works in the mud
> Who does not know peace
> Who fights for a scrap of bread
> Who dies because of a yes or a no. (17)

Meditate, he insists, on the implications of the fact that this came about, 'carve' the words in your heart, repeat them at the rising of the sun and its setting, repeat them to your children or yourself, suffer the disintegration of that secure life with what it has to tell about what he called, and this time surely with an admitted irony, 'a quiet study of certain aspects of the human mind' (15). The poem was originally called 'Psalm', but became 'Shemà' ('hear' or 'listen' in Hebrew). It was written while the Nuremberg trials were underway. It was an accusation and an imprecation.

When he returned to Italy, after a painful journey, within a matter of months he wrote his record of that time. It began with his escape from Auschwitz, freshest in his mind, then moved backwards. Six publishers refused the book before it was finally accepted early in 1947. Meanwhile, he was working as a chemist, a job which prevented his attending the trial of Auschwitz commandant Rudolf Höss as a witness.

If This is a Man was published in October 1947, with a Goya etching on its cover. It did not do well, though a young Italo Calvino did hail it, in part for its author's skill at characterisation. Two and a half thousand copies were printed before his publisher went bankrupt. It sold 1,500 copies. The book disappeared, in part, as he speculated, because people were busy mourning those they had lost. They were all about the business of reconstructing themselves no less than their society. He, himself, was inhibited from speaking, believing that he lacked the skills, until a photographic exhibition on the subject of the camps was staged at which he was persuaded to speak. It was the beginning of another career. Then, in 1958, the book was republished and found its readers, in Italy and around the world. Its success led to a writing career which included not simply his Auschwitz books but science fiction stories, a novel about a Jewish partisan group (*If Not Now, When?*) and an autobiographical work (*The Periodic Table*).

Speaking in 1983, Levi confessed that his writings were like a form of artificial memory. He was, he remarked, developing a case for the prosecution, not a call for revenge but an act of witness. He was aware, however, of the problems of his form. 'No matter how hard you try', he explained, 'a written portrait never reproduces the person. Complicated factors get in the way, like failing memory, unknowing idealization, for good or ill, or even knowing idealization, because sometimes we take a person and try our best to make a "character" out of them.'[7]

He denied, for the most part, doing this in *If This is a Man* but in truth the writer in him was there from the start. Speaking in 1984 he confessed that the book had worked 'as a sort of "prosthesis", an external memory set up like a barrier between my life today and my life then'. Yet at the same time, even as he confesses to reliving events through his words, he admits the inadequacy of those words to capture them and here is the difficulty with witness and, indeed, memory. As he explained,

being in prison ... generates a curious effect by which the days as you live them seem eternal but as soon as they are over they collapse into an instant because they have nothing in them. The past is compressed, thinned, it has no depth. I think this is hard to render, because memory works in precisely the opposite way: the single clamorous terrifying episodes, or conversely the happy moments, prevail and invade the canvas, whereas as one lives they are a part of totally disintegrated reality. (251)

In other words, it is only partly that memory selects, that the past in memory is not the past in fact. The problem is that even the experiences from which the mind will later select are themselves distorted at source. What he calls the 'technicolour' prevails over the 'grey'. The stretches of boredom or prolonged work cede to the rarer moments in which some feeling or encounter stands out from the continuity of nullity even as the latter constitutes the heart of camp life. Though the memory may trawl up apparently insignificant details from the depths, it is defeated by sameness, the unrelenting and sustained fear masquerading as habit which slowly crucified so many and which sinks out of sight and consciousness, like any continuous sound or sight.

Who was Levi? He was born in 1919 into a Jewish community in Turin. His father was an engineer. At university he read chemistry, something that would prove to be crucial in the camp. For four years before his arrest he, in common with Italy's other Jews, was subject to the racial laws. In 1938, his sister, like the Frank daughters in Amsterdam, was dismissed from her state school to be taught in a Jewish school. He graduated in 1941 and by 1943 had joined the Resistance operating in the mountains. By the end of the year Mussolini was prepared to embrace Hitler's genocidal solution to 'the Jewish problem', and Jews were made subject to immediate arrest and the loss of all their property.

In January 1944 Levi and his band of disorganised irregulars were discovered as the result of betrayal by a fellow Italian. As he explained it subsequently, at that time 'I had not been taught the doctrine I was later to learn so hurriedly in the Lager: that man is bound to pursue his own ends by all possible means, while he who errs once pays dearly.'[8] Their shared idealism, unregulated by shared competence, had left them vulnerable. The lesson of the camp, he later found, was to be one not of mutuality and self-abnegation but of the strategies necessary to survival and what those strategies might mean in terms of a conception of human capacities and values. The memories he carried from Auschwitz were memories not merely of pain, deprivation and abasement but of a new conception of humankind, though in truth his own account allows for a certain mutuality even in the face of suffering. For the moment, though, he was one of a band of people brought together by a common commitment but about to enter an unimagined world.

Rather than run the chance of execution as a partisan, he identified himself as a Jew and after time in a prison camp was sent, on 22 February 1944, to Auschwitz, though the text he was to write carries no hint of his Jewishness. God had seemingly turned his face away. He was there until the Russians liberated the camp the following January. On his last night in the detention camp, he was with a young woman, Vanda Maestro, a student who had been a year ahead of him at university and whom he loved. She would die in the gas chamber at Auschwitz in October.

On their arrival they went through the process so familiar by now but a shock to them. They were tattooed, thus breaking a Mosaic law, stripped, shaved, reborn. Levi's new name was *Häftling* (prisoner) 174517. Even that number, identifying him as a recent arrival, carried with it a sign of vulnerability. Had he but known it, he now had a life expectancy of three months, though life was not what anyone could anticipate in this place. He was assigned to Auschwitz IV, which provided slave labour for camp III, Buna-Monowitz, the site of a factory, still under construction, to produce synthetic rubber. The camp was, he later discovered, effectively 'rented out' (his phrase) to I. G. Farbenindustrie, the chemical company, which paid between four and eight marks a day for each slave labourer, not of course to the workers but the SS.

The camp was presided over by Richard Baer, an SS major, but the camp hierarchy meant nothing to Levi. It was 'an imperium of night and fog whose structure we did not know'.[9] While the whole Nazi machine was dependent on men such as Baer, they flourished because 'the National Socialist message found an echo precisely in the Germans' traditional virtues, in their sense of discipline and national cohesion, their unquenched thirst for primacy, their propensity for slavish obedience' (86–7). Writing in 1960, he found little changed: 'Anyone who takes them to task for the dreadful events of recent history rarely finds repentance, or even critical consciousness: much more often he encounters an ambiguous response, in which are intertwined a feeling of guilt, a desire for vindication, and a deliberate and impudent ignorance' (87). This was the silence that oppressed W. G. Sebald. It was a silence increasingly broken by those who now wished to bear witness, though Levi himself did not wait until 1960 to record his experiences.

Despite Levi's insistence on the selfishness essential for survival, he nonetheless records moments of solidarity. Italians were likely to favour Italians. Friendships were formed, though one of the inmates later observed that 'You put up a protective shell that excluded everything that did not personally help you to survive.'[10] Nonetheless, he was one of three friends who clung together, even sharing the food which became an obsessive concern. Later, Elie Wiesel would resist Levi's seeming emphasis on what was often presented as a necessary survival mechanism or proposed by what he called the 'technicians of death'. 'Everyone for himself, they told us. Forget your parents, your brothers, your past, or else you will perish.' What happened, he insisted, 'was the opposite. Those who lived only for themselves, only to feed themselves, ended up succumbing to the laws of death, while the others, those who knew whom to live for – a parent, a brother, a friend – managed to obey the laws of life.'[11]

Auschwitz was another planet with its own arbitrary laws and lores. Levi began to jot down details of what he saw, writing in a notebook given to him for analytic chemistry, he being one of the very few selected to work in a laboratory. But, as he well knew, the act of writing was itself the source of danger. He later confessed that his notes never extended beyond twenty lines. He would, he realised, have to rely on his memory.

In seeking to talk of his experiences in Auschwitz, indeed in the face of those experiences at the time, Levi came up against those same limits to language identified by so many survivors. He became aware 'that our language lacks words to express this offence, the demolition of a man'. On his arrival at the camp, 'with almost prophetic intuition, the reality was revealed to us: we had reached the bottom'.[12] It was necessary to learn the language of the oppressor, to read the codes, acknowledge the laws and prohibitions, no matter how arbitrary they might be, if there was to be any hope of survival. Those who did not became the *Muselmänner* (literally 'Muslims'), the 'drowned', the non-men, the divine spark extinguished, too empty, he suggested, to really suffer. It would sound painfully dismissive, as if he could be sure that such retained no inner life, locked away, cryogenically suspended until some future resurrection, were it not for the fact that other survivors have spoken in the same terms. Survival itself, all knew, might be a matter of sheer chance but it might also be the product of a strenuous effort or a shrinking of the self into its own confines.

There was another strategy, he acknowledged, that carried its own annihilating implications. If it was possible to negotiate for oneself a task serving those who ran the camp, there was if not immunity then at least a limited respite. But what conclusions could be drawn from the Jews who chose this route? They, he explained, 'form a sad and notable human phenomenon, inevitably setting themselves apart, an alienation for which history could perversely be said to have prepared them. In their persons converge present, past and atavistic sufferings, and the tradition of hostility towards the stranger makes of them monsters of asociality and insensitivity' (96–7). He is close here to embracing Steiner's suggestion that in some senses Jewish exclusiveness was taken to a logical conclusion by the Nazis, who took them at their word.

The meaning he chose to derive from the camp, however, went beyond questions of private tactics or sectarian histories. The offence was altogether more profound. At the moment of his release he contemplated the Germans who seemed to lack a sense of shame, the shame 'that the just man experiences at another man's crime; the feeling that such a crime should exist, that it should have been introduced irrevocably into the world of things that exist, and that his will for good should have proved too weak or null, and should not have availed in defence'.[13] The doubtful privilege of his generation, he declared, was 'to grasp the incurable nature of the offence ... It is foolish to think', he added, 'that human justice can eradicate it. It is an inexhaustible fount of evil; it breaks the body and the spirit of the submerged, it stifles them and renders them abject' (188). It prompts, he suggests, hatred and a desire for revenge. Not the least significant aspect of Primo Levi is that he succumbed to neither.

In one sense, he was lucky. As a chemist, he had his value. He was selected to work in a laboratory inside the plant designed to produce synthetic rubber (not the least irony of which being that it never produced anything). This gave him access to those who were neither prisoners nor guards. A certain human commerce was possible, along with commerce of another kind. He mended a puncture for a German lab technician and received a hardboiled egg and four sugar lumps in return. She also whispered to him that 'Christmas will soon be here', an odd remark to address to a Jew but, to him, a human gesture whose impact was disproportionate. As he explained, decades later, he was 'not trying to make excuses for Nazi Germany. One human German does not whitewash the innumerable inhuman or indifferent ones, but it does have the merit of breaking the stereotype' (*Moments of Reprieve*, 92). Going back in memory he was not trying to balance the scales but was allowing space for other memories to seep through. Nor was she the only German to make a human gesture though in truth such moments were marginal and trivial in the context. The interest, however, lies in the obligation he feels to register such moments without underscoring the irony implicit in them.

Ironically, and unknown to him, at this same time and in the same place another human gesture was being offered. A British sergeant, with the inappropriate name of Charles Coward, bribed an SS man to allow him to substitute the bodies of dead civilian workers for Jews, some four hundred of whom were smuggled out as a result of his actions. Levi's survival, though, depended in part on two people. One was Alberto, who would not return from Auschwitz and whose mother would give money to a confidence trickster who would feed her with consolatory stories about her dead son. The other was Lorenzo Perrone, a bricklayer from Fossano, who was skilled in acquiring food and who always shared with Levi. Levi would write about him in *If This is a Man* and then, many years later, in *Moments of Reprieve* when, with his death, he felt free to address the past more directly, no longer constrained by discretion, no longer obliged to modify his memories.

He met him in June 1944. Lorenzo was not a prisoner but allegedly a voluntary worker (in fact forcibly transferred from an Italian firm in France). As a result, he had a certain freedom not granted to Levi and at risk to himself set about sustaining his new friend through the theft of food. Lorenzo was what was supposed not to exist in the camps – a man of pure altruism. On 1 January 1945, with the Russians approaching, the Germans disbanded the Italian camp and Lorenzo set out by foot to make his way home. Years later, Levi felt free to tell the truth of his end. This spontaneously good man was never able to settle into civilian life and took to drink. He died alone in a hospital, as Levi says, 'of the survivors' disease' (160). He 'had seen the world, he didn't like it, he felt it was going to ruin. To live no longer interested him' (159). He was, in short, a virtual suicide but without him Levi would possibly not have survived.

When at last the camp was liberated by the Russians, it became necessary to learn civility again, to step into an airlock before returning to a life that could, however, never be the same again. As he explained, 'Suddenly your neighbour was no longer your adversary in the struggle for life but a human being who was entitled to be helped. This really was a kind of reawakening for us. Our sensitivity and willingness to help others was being born again in and around us.'[14] Even so, there were still limits. As he and his friends shared their food in the camp after the liberation, when the guards had fled, they ignored the cries of many dying in the adjoining barracks. What else was there to do? If they shared, they would all die. The lessons of the camps were not unlearned as yet.

The journey home would justify a second book. In some senses he replicated the journey of many others, who sought to reach a home that would never be the same again, memories having been laid down in the mind to come tumbling out in nightmares that some would suffer for the rest of their lives. It was when he arrived that he learned of the death of Vanda Maestro. It did not cut as deep as it would once have done. As he explained, 'Nevertheless I knew with extreme clarity that I would suffer later for her death' (206). For the moment, memories of her were swallowed in those other memories, yet to be assembled into a meaningful form, yet to be processed and under-stood, yet to stand out against the smother of daily indignities, violences, despairs.

He reached home on 19 October 1945. He went unrecognised by the concierge. He was not the man who had left. One fifth of Italian Jews had died. There seemed no triumph in having survived, indeed along with anger went a sense of shame. In 1986 he explained to his biographer, Ian Thomson, 'I had the sensation that I was living ... but without being alive' (221). He could not sleep. As for his fellow Italians, they seemed to have new priorities. After a time, some of the traitors were forgiven in the name of a new Italy. Old enemies were replaced with new as Soviet Communism was seen by some as a saviour and others as a primary threat. It was in 1947 that Arthur Miller went to Italy and noted the survivors of camps, so many wraiths waiting for passage to Israel but meanwhile with no apparent connection to anyone else.

Though the initial text of *If This is a Man* came quickly, he began to shape it. The story that he repeated to so many people, including strangers, gradually began to assume a form. It became a conscious narrative, with a plot and what in a fiction would have been characters. He changed the names of some of those in the camp as he did in the book with which he eventually followed it. He also changed their nature to the point that some of them would protest. As Ian Thomson points out, 'With endless retellings he was refining the subtle plays of suspense and pacing that would hold a reader's attention on the page' (224). He himself claimed that it was written without 'even a hint of literary worries'. If there was 'literature there', he declared, it was 'unwelcome, an intrusion'. Yet it was in fact a text with conscious allusions to literature, and not simply to Dante (he described forced labour as 'Dantesque'). A conversation about Dante was to feature in his book but it would not be remembered with such clarity and significance by the person with whom he had held it (though, ironically, this conversation was one of the few episodes in his book whose authenticity he had been able to verify, a curious admission in a work of witness).

Memories of the camp, in other words, were being overlaid with other memories, literary memories which themselves contained other meanings, analogous to but not coincident with those he sought to retrieve and, having retrieved, shape. There are references to Manzoni and others. His interest in social Darwinism took him to Jack London where he could find a perfect paradigm for that battle for survival that had characterised the camp.

Even in the camp, cultural memories were of vital importance to him. He would, he explained, have given bread and soup – the literal lifeblood of the camp – to rescue such memories in that they made it possible to 'to re-establish a link with the past, saving it from oblivion and reinforcing my identity' (*The Drowned and the Saved*, 112).[15] Memory, in other words, was a primary constituent of the self, a protection against those who would reduce him to a number and declare the irrelevance of his life and the insignificance of his past. He badgered others to see if they could contribute anything to re-establishing his connection to literature and science and, indeed, part of his argument with Améry would be over the interpretation of the word intellectual, which, to him, included the scientist no less than the writer. At the same time, however, he acknowledged that reason, art and poetry were irrelevant to the task of deciphering a place from which they were banned. They might be of momentary utility but did not help in orienting oneself or in understanding the chaos. In the end, he suggests, they were best abandoned, along with thoughts of home and family, or at least relegated 'to that attic of memory where all the clutter of stuff that is no longer useful for everyday life is deposited' (115).

He was aware of the limitations of the intellect in such a situation. There was, after all, little point in trying to understand that which did not offer itself to understanding, or explain the inexplicable. Despite his hunger for literature, he was also aware of the fundamental irrelevance of literary assumptions. Both he and Améry, he realised, came at death through memories of literature. In Auschwitz, such were exposed as mere affectations. He was also alive to the fact that the intellectual – especially the German, he added – tends to become an accomplice of power.

In *The Drowned and the Saved*, with its references to Dostoevsky and Manzoni, he accused the progressive French author Vercors, in his story *Les armes de la Nuit*, of 'aestheticism and literary treachery' while arguably dealing in just such a currency himself as he shaped his material. Memories, he confesses, assumed to be the guarantee of authenticity, begin to 'drift'. As he himself remarked of others,

> among the testimonies written or heard, there are also those that are unconsciously stylised, in which convention prevails over genuine memory: 'whoever is freed from slavery rejoices. I too was liberated hence I too rejoice over it. In all films, all novels, just as in *Fidelio* the shattering of the chains is a moment of solemn or fervid jubilation, and so was mine.' This is a specific case of the drifting of memory ... which is accentuated by the passing years and the piling up of the experiences of others, true or presumed, on the layer of one's own. (53)

But at the heart of the enterprise, nonetheless, was the necessity to remember. As he remarked, 'It's a miracle that I'm still alive and in good health, and reunited with my family. I've made a vow never to forget this, and I repeat it to myself every day like a prayer. Not that I thank Providence: if there had been a Providence, Auschwitz and Birkenau would never have existed.'[16] In a letter quoted by Ian Thomson, his close friend Jean Samuel, who had shared his time at Auschwitz, stated what would become the credo of many of the survivors: 'Whether we like it or not ... we are witnesses and we bear the weight of it' (240).

Writing thirty years after his time in the camp, Levi confessed that 'I find it difficult to reconstruct the sort of human being that corresponded, in November 1944, to my name or, better, to my number: 174517.'[17] He had become, in a sense, a stranger to himself. He had returned desperate to tell his story, writing what he called 'concise and bloody poems' (151), but was transformed by meeting the woman who would become his wife. His writing, he explained, 'became a different adventure, no longer the dolorous itinerary of a convalescent, no longer begging for compassion and friendly faces, but a lucid building, which now was no longer solitary ... Paradoxically, my baggage of atrocious memories became a wealth, a seed' (153). Memory thus becomes something more than retrieved event. It becomes a mechanism of redemption.

He was, then, soon to be married and around him Italy was beginning the process of renovation. He might be looking back to a time of darkness but his present was opening up. His memories were already subject to other influences. He may have begun to write with a certain despair and self-contempt as well as anger but these feelings were to some degree now moderated. He also saw himself as a writer, indeed in some senses primarily as a writer and as a result he wished to be something more than a witness.

Levi wrote his book immediately after the war. His body, his mind, still bore the marks of those eleven months. His fingers were still pressed to the Braille of a physical text. And whatever his changed circumstances, there was anger. In this first book, those rare occasions on which Germans offered him any help were excised. This was not to be a work in which he attempted to understand but only to document, while even that documentation was to be partial.

Later, he would amend it, adding figures he had excluded from the first edition, including one who seems in part to have been based on Otto Frank, Anne Frank's father, who he encountered in Auschwitz. Neither edition was accurate in all regards. He was, after all, a writer and shaped what emerged as his characters to serve other interests than merely the documentary. Nonetheless, in what became a preface to the German edition of the book he wrote, 'here I am today, 174517, able ... to speak to the German people and to remind them of what they have done, and to say to them: "I am alive, and I would like to understand you in order to judge you."' His primary purpose, he explained, was 'to bear witness'.[18] He was not, he insisted, inclined to accuse the Germans as a group, no matter his later observations.

Levi followed his book about life in the camp with *The Truce*, which documented his long journey home in 1945. Perhaps because time had gone by (he wrote it seventeen years after the events to which it refers) his memories were now more subject to amendment, his book even more clearly shaped into literary form. He even added material he had picked up from a woman he met. Once again, a number of those he ostensibly featured in the book complained of his fictionalising of them. As he confessed to one of them, 'the words and adventures I attribute to Cesare have been liberally recreated, interpreted, and, in part, invented' (303). For a man who had originally set out to bear witness, this was a curious admission. When he later added details, in *Moments of Reprieve*, with Cesare's permission, he confessed, 'It may be imprecise in some details because it is based on two memories (his and mine), and then over long distances human memory is an erratic instrument, especially if it is not reinforced by material mementoes and is instead spiced by the desire (again, his and mine) that the story be a good one' (*Moments of Reprieve*, 144).

Another, who found himself portrayed as cynical and obse-quious, not to mention eleven years older than he had been, was mortified. Levi later asked himself whether the events in his book had really happened feeling, sometimes, that he had written a novel. When he published *The Periodic Table*, once again there were those who complained of distortions of their lives, appropriated, as they were, as characters. Some never forgave him. He even distorted the figure of a German chemist with whom he had had a long correspondence after the war and who had made friendly gestures towards him in Auschwitz. It would, he explained, be more effective if he were presented as a shameless ex-Nazi, surely a curious statement. Clearly the writer now superseded the witness.

The Truce did far better than *If This is a Man*, though the latter now acquired a different life, first as a radio play, produced in Canada by CBC and in Italy by RAI, and then as a stage play, described by Ian Thomson as a patchwork of scenes from the book put together by Pieralberto Marché. The staged version finally opened in November 1966. It was a considerable success with audiences but was seen by most critics as inferior to its source.

His literary career, however, occurred in the interstices of his life as a chemist, a role in which he took pleasure when it involved laboratory work but not when it called for management skills. Meanwhile, he suffered from recurrent depressions, hesitating to trace these back to Auschwitz, though on occasion suggesting that their roots might lie in his Jewish identity, which prompted a further sense of unease.

For some time, he had chosen to speak about his experiences in schools. In his own home, however, his children would hear nothing of it. It proved unbearable for them to see their father in terms of such events and since children tend to internalise fears it is tempting to think that they heard something of their own potential fate in these stories from another time and place.

The Truce did not appear until 1963. As he explained, he felt he had settled his account and fulfilled his civic duty to bear witness and so had stopped writing for a decade and a half. *The Periodic Table* followed in 1975, though he continued to have difficulty finding a publisher, in Britain seeing it rejected by twenty-seven publishers. Then came *The Wrench*, three years later, and his novel *If Not Now, When?* in 1982. In 1986, with *The Drowned and the Saved*, he returned to the implications of the camps and offered a darker version of the future than he had done in *If This is a Man*.

In *The Drowned and the Saved* Levi reminds us that reality 'can be distorted not only in memory but in the very act of it taking place' (19). In other words, the seemingly objective fact, later to be recalled, is transformed even as it occurs, denial rushing in to fill the space left by despair and an unbelieving sense of shock. Consoling myths, ideological convictions, refract truth through the prism of fear and desolation. The actuality to Levi was 'a thousand sealed-off monads, and not the solidarity for which one hoped', or the too neat division between 'we' and 'them'. Solidarity dissolved in the face of compelling needs. For the most part, the camps did not create saints, victims who rose above their persecutors by virtue of their suffering. They degraded and co-opted those who quickly understood that accommodation was necessary to survival. Prisoners entered what Levi called 'the grey zone', grey in that it is a denial of a black and white morality.

It remains necessary, though, to distinguish victims from murderers. Levi was not well disposed towards those (like Arthur Miller) who suggest that we are all victims and murderers. He had, he explained, no interest in whether 'in my depths there lurks a murderer' for the fact is that he was a victim and did not murder. In common with millions of others, however, he was reduced to simple physical needs which generated their own necessities.

The most extreme cases were those of the *Sonderkommando* (virtually all Jews), the Special Squad who were special in that they oversaw the process of shepherding the victims to the gas chambers. It was they who then stripped the dead bodies, cut their hair, removed their gold teeth before feeding them into the ovens, later raking their ashes out. The activity won them a three-month reprieve before they in turn were fed into the crematoria. By definition, few survived to bear witness and those that did were often silenced by their shame and guilt. Some details, however, did survive through diary pages 'written feverishly for future memory' and then buried like time capsules secured against a time when judgement would be made. Levi refused to condemn such men.

In some ways it is significant that Levi should choose to translate Franz Kafka's *The Trial*, the Kafka whose own sisters died in the camps. Its description of a man condemned to death without cause or explanation was too close to his own experience for the parallel not to insist upon itself. The process of working on the book, however, seems to have triggered another depression, the Escher-like world of Kafka stirring memories that his own books had in part sought to exorcise. He wrote of 'an atavistic anguish, whose echo one hears in the second verse of *Genesis*: the anguish inscribed in everyone ... of a deserted and empty universe crushed under the spirit of God, but from which the spirit of man is absent: not yet born or already extinguished' (*The Drowned and the Saved*, 65). This is close to that terror felt by the figure described by Nabokov in his autobiography, the young man appalled by his own absence from creation. The second verse speaks of the earth 'without form, and void', a darkness 'upon the face of the deep'.

There are moments in Primo Levi's work when the camps, or the frightening depressions from which he suffered, seemed to overwhelm him, as in this passage in which Creation is already encoded with its reversal, an un-peopled world less pregnant with life than suffused with the stench of death. A crime has been committed whose potential should have stayed the hand of any God contemplating peopling the earth, and yet the fact that God plainly saw that potential was evident in the story in the fourth chapter of Genesis which saw a brother kill a brother, a story which also obsessed Arthur Miller.

Yet another part of Levi wanted no truck with an idea that would see all bear the mark of Cain, which was not the mark of the murderer but God's sign that the murderer should be left unmolested – a warning, a threat, a prophecy. Auschwitz, after all, was not the casual product of an absent God. It was constructed by men who were embedded in history and who came to power with the enthusiastic support of many and the acquiescence of others, who did not act when they might have done. There was, in other words, a politics, a sociology, a psychology to the Holocaust which was not an eighth plague directed at the chosen people rather than their oppressors. And would it happen again? Quite possibly. He wrote *The Drowned and the Saved* after Cambodia but before Rwanda. At the time, he thought that memory, still fresh with blood, would prevent its recurrence in Europe. Even as he wrote this, however, he was no more than a few years removed from the genocide, or ethnic cleansing, in the former Yugoslavia.

His attraction to Kafka came, he explained, not merely from his prescience but from the fact that he existed in some senses at the other end of the spectrum from himself. 'In my writing', he explained,

> for good or evil, knowingly or not, I've always strived to
> pass from the darkness into the light, as ... a filtering pump
> might do, which sucks up turbid water and expels it
> decanted: possibly sterile. Kafka forges his path in the
> opposite direction: he endlessly unravels the hallucinations
> that he draws from incredibly profound layers, and he never
> filters them. The reader feels them swarm with germs and
> spores ... His suffering is genuine and continuous, it assails
> you and does not let you go: you feel like one of his characters,
> condemned by an abject and inscrutable, tentacular tribunal

that invades the city and the world ... capable at this point only of suffering.[19]

Of *The Trial*, he remarks, 'I, a survivor of Auschwitz, would never have written it, or never in that way: out of inability, or insufficient imagination, certainly, but also out of a feeling of shame before death that Kafka did not know, or, if he did, rejected; or perhaps out of lack of courage' (108). The book's final sentence, ' ... it was as if the shame of it must outlive him', seemed not at all enigmatic to Levi. Joseph K is ashamed, Levi suggests, at having struggled and at the same time at not having resisted, of wasting his life in pettiness, of surviving when he might have taken his life in his own hands by ending it. He is ashamed because the tribunal which destroys him 'is in the end a human, not a divine, tribunal: it is composed of men and made by men, and Joseph K with the knife already planted in his heart is ashamed of being a man' (109).

Levi set his face against the notion of incommunicability, even though within the camp he had learned the deformation of language. Part of his memories, he confesses, were blank magnetic tapes which simply recorded without understanding scraps of foreign language, its tone, volume, pitch. Those memories were stripped of meaning, Babel fragments. They were recorded in the belief that they must encode meaning but with no comprehension as to what that meaning might be. He was unable even to distinguish between a curse and a banal enquiry. Words simply became associated with activities without ever becoming attached to them. This was what he called 'useless' or 'paradoxical memory' (74), even as it might have been playing a role in a mechanism of survival. His conscious mind could not fathom it; he only knew that survival depended on becoming fluent in the brute utterances of those who determined the smallest things.

Yet at the same time, in the years that followed Levi had to believe in the possibility of communication. In the great continent of freedom, he insisted, 'freedom of communication is an important province' (81). He rejected those literary and literary critical movements which saw discourse as a self-mocking and doomed enterprise unable to penetrate an irremediable solipsism. For him, communication was an imperative. Silence, proposed by some out of a sense of irony and by still others as a mark of respect, served nothing, he thought, beyond its own essential ambivalence. Nothing comes of nothing. In the camps there had been a wilful refusal to communicate. The popular name for the truncheon with which people were beaten was 'the translator'. Violence was the only universal tongue. After the camps, the truth had to be spread, no matter how flawed the language, how inadequate the vocabulary, how strained the syntax. Yet there were certain linguistic memories. Levi subsequently became aware of the coarseness of his German pronunciation but made a decision not to change it for the same reason that he chose not to have his tattoo removed from his arm. Both were a form of memory.

What were the memories he carried? Levi explained. They took the form, in the first days, of 'an out-of-focus and frenzied film', shot in black and white, with, he added, sound but not a talkie (73). Later he would remember pieces of words, acoustic gestures, and begin the process of looking for meaning within the chaos.

In the 1980s, Levi had put his career as a chemist to one side and wrote a series of stories, based on those he had known in the camp. These were never, he explained, 'the persecuted, the predestined victim, the prostrate man' (*Moments of Reprieve*, 10) to whom he had dedicated his first book and about whom he 'had obsessively asked ... if this was still a man' (10). Instead, the stories focussed on 'moments of reprieve' (10). The sense of shock, it seemed, had finally abated. In November 1986, he wrote that Auschwitz was no longer the 'Ground floor' of his memory. The camp had disappeared from his dreams. Five months later, he was dead. Had his dreams returned?

Elie Wiesel was clear. He rejected the idea of depression. This simply did not fit into his narrative of the camps. His death must be the final act of a tragedy. Levi was 'a man who never ceased to battle the black angel of Auschwitz'. Could this be 'reduced to a banal nervous break-down',[20] he asked. He repeated the point in the second volume of his autobiography, *And the Sea is Never Full*. An American novelist, he explains, 'publishes an article that shocks quite a few of us. He says that Primo's friends should have urged him to get treatment, a good therapist could have cured him. This is a typical banalization. Here we have existential evil, the lifelong incandescent wound of a soul, reduced to a nervous break-down common among writers whose inspiration becomes blocked, or among men of a certain age' (346). It is a remarkable statement, combining a stunning self-assurance with casual insult. He apparently knows why Levi died while others were dismayed that he had not had the help that perhaps he needed. For Wiesel, who disagreed with Levi on more than Israel, who thought him 'too severe' with survivors (347), too much of a leftist, erroneous in proposing the existence of a 'gray zone' in the camps which he, Wiesel, chose to interpret as an assertion that every inmate was guilty, nonetheless wished to see Levi's death as a kind of martyrdom. Levi, he believed, felt guilty, guilty of failing to communicate a central truth. He had died in despair because no one would listen. Memories had killed him because those memories could not adequately be communicated. Wiesel proposes a narrative into which Levi, it seems, was required to insert himself, even in death.

That Levi chose to take his life on the anniversary of his release from Auschwitz, if, indeed, he did, was itself surely a sign of another release that he sought. Like Jean Améry, with whom he was in part at odds but who was close kin by virtue of their shared experience, he died at the age of sixty-seven. It is tempting to suggest, as many did, that the camp had reached out to claim him, the date of his death suggesting a connection. But he was also a clinically depressed man and though his wartime experience was clearly a part cause of this, depression creates its own internal logic, its own prison cell from which death can at time seem a release. There is finally no definitive explanation of his decision to plunge down that apartment staircase. But the weight of memory can prove unsupportable and perhaps it did for him, a survivor who never really survived if we mean by that that he could walk free of his experiences and feel no shame or guilt, no obligation to the dead or to those who might one day find that history repeating itself.

Nor, it should be remembered, are the experiences of those who found themselves confronted with the possibility of immediate death, trapped in a world not of their own invention, so remote from the experiences of all. Certainly the particularities of the Holocaust can be shared only through witnesses who bring us the news of the unimaginable, but, as Levi explained in an essay about Chaim Rumkowski, leader of the Litzmannstadt ghetto, like Rumkowski 'we too are so dazzled by power and money as to forget our essential fragility, forget that all of us are in the ghetto, that the ghetto is fenced in, that beyond the fence stand the lords of death, and not far away the train is waiting'.[21]

In 2004, almost sixty years after Levi's release from Auschwitz, the South-African-born British actor Antony Sher adapted *If This is a Man* for the stage. He was doubtful about doing so, not believing that it was possible to present concentration camp inmates on stage or screen in a conventional manner. There had, he knew, been a film of *The Truce* while Levi himself had co-written a stage version of *If This is a Man*, with Pieralberto Marché, staged in the same year as the Italian publication of Weiss's *The Investigation*, 1966. This, though, had not been published. For him, however, there was another problem. Beyond difficulties of adaptation lay the attitude of the family, which at first resolutely refused permission for an adaptation, though in fact Sher had already written a draft when he sought that permission. 'Is he', Sher asked of Levi, 'public property? Is he ours or is he theirs [the family's]?'[22] As with Anne Frank, it seemed, the question was one of ownership.

The stage play was effectively to be an abridgement, but this in turn raised questions. He resisted the idea of setting the action in the camp, of wearing the striped prisoner's clothing, though these had been used in Levi's own play which was set in Auschwitz. The play itself, though, was to be as close to Levi's work as possible. In the end, he estimated, 98 per cent of the material came from *If This is a Man* while the remainder was drawn from *The Truce* and *Moments of Reprieve*, with elements from Levi's interview with Philip Roth. He chose to make the figures of Albert and Lorenzo, who had helped sustain Levi in the camp, more central: it was Lorenzo after whom Levi had named both his son and daughter.

The problem of staging was to be solved by focussing on the Levi who wrote the book, concentrating on the postwar figure, soberly dressed, calm. Indeed the power of Sher's performance was to lie precisely in its reticence and restraint, which mirrored that of Levi. It stood in odd contrast to Sher himself, who in the book he wrote about the experience of writing the play (*Primo Time*) is almost a parody of the sensitive actor, prone at any moment to burst into tears, visit his therapist, assemble good-luck charms and emote about personal relationships. How much greater the achievement, therefore, of being able to contain his performance so that he reflected the observational clarity of Levi. With the advice of his director, he denied himself the emotional colour with which he was initially tempted to flood certain moments.

To prepare himself for the one-man show, Sher went to Auschwitz, trying, as he explained, to stir life out of dead ashes. He visited Levi's school, university and factory in Turin and, although discouraged by Levi's family, even the place where he fell to his death. Nor was the text alone sufficient. In order to reach some physical understanding of the privations which Levi underwent he submitted to various exercises. Thus, in order to gain some appreciation of what it had been like to be shut in a cattle truck and sent to the camp he was driven around London in a closed vehicle, while being abused by German-speaking actors hired for the purpose. He slimmed himself down.

These were all, of course, mechanisms to enable him to inhabit the man he would perform. It is difficult, however, to read his account without being struck by the sheer disproportion between three quarters of an hour in a National Theatre vehicle and spending days in a cattle truck, without water or toilet facilities, uncertain as to destination, uncertain whether you are to live or die. But perhaps this is to do no more than underline that difficulty of approaching the experience to which he had confessed at the beginning of the project. Levi's book becomes a performance, lasting an hour and twenty-seven minutes. Just as a written account differs from individual testimony, so a performance differs from a written text. A theatrical performance can never be anything but that.

When Antony Sher stepped onto the stage of the Cottesloe he did, indeed, step onto a stage. What followed were lines culled from Levi's work but what the audience saw had been shaped by designers, costumiers, lighting technicians, a composer, musicians (there was music, both recorded and live), a director. Sher relied on computer-controlled lighting, sound effects (minimal, but there). He stood before the audience in greasepaint performing Primo Levi but incontrovertibly Antony Sher, an actor, as it happened, who had recently made a comic film in which he played the role of Adolf Hitler. He had had to learn his lines and deliver them in a certain way to an audience who had bought their tickets for the evening, read the programme and been invited to turn their mobile phones off so as not to spoil what was manifestly a performance no matter how moving this legerdemain should turn out to be.

Sher's account is partly to do with the production and partly with his personal battle against what he called 'the Fear', a stage-fright which had begun to disturb him and which included the fear of forgetting his lines. So, this play about remembering was presented by a man in fear of forgetting. In the end, the family approved Sher's text and the production proved successful, but the experience of Auschwitz had now been processed through Levi's memory, through his own reshaping of those memories into a book, and thence into a performance whose text was edited and performed by a homosexual, Jewish actor from South Africa for whom this was a one-person show whose stress, by his own choice, was on two redemptive figures to whom he wished to give primacy.

Levi's depressions may indeed have been spawned by the Holocaust. He was, after all, one among many who chose to take their own lives. What there cannot be is certainty. What there cannot be is a sense of indignation at the idea, advanced by some, that he might have been saved by treatment. Wiesel was one of those who rejected such a possibility. For him, Levi must be a victim, to be reclaimed from their disagreements in death as he could not be in life. For a man who is adamantly opposed to the appropriation of other people's lives, Wiesel comes close to an act of appropriation himself, as, of course, did Thane Rosenbaum in bringing Levi back, at least as a ghost, into twenty-first-century New York in *The Golems of Gotham*. In another sense, perhaps, so did the British novelist Martin Amis, who, in *Time's Arrow* (1991), not merely chose to write a novel about Auschwitz but initially planned to use Levi's phrase, 'the nature of the offence', as his title. It is retained as a sub-title.

313

As he explained in an 'Afterword',

The offence was of such a nature that perhaps we can see Levi's suicide as an act of ironic heroism, an act that asserts something like: My life is mine and mine alone to take. The offence was unique, not in its cruelty, nor in its cowardice, but in its style – in its combination of the atavistic and the modern. It was at once reptilian and 'logical'. And although the offence was not definingly German, its style was. The National Socialists found the core of the reptile brain, and built an autobahn that went there. Built for speed and safety, built to endure for a thousand years, the *Reichsautobahnen*, if you remember, were also designed to conform to the landscape, harmoniously, like a garden path.[23]

Thomas De Quincey once described an ironic reversal of time whereby 'If once a man indulges himself in murder, very soon he comes to think little of robbing, and from robbing he comes next to drinking and Sabbath-breaking, and from that to incivility and procrastination.'[24] Amis's novel was based on a similar conceit: the reversal of time. The concentration camp thus became a place of healing. The dead were brought back to life. Gas pellets were removed from the gas chambers, the bodies began to move. And over all this presided doctors, and one doctor in particular, Mengele. For those, like Elie Wiesel, who thought the experience of Auschwitz necessarily resistant to the fictive impulse, this would surely be a repellent idea. Amis was not without his own doubts, having disliked the intrusiveness of William Styron's *Sophie's Choice*: 'I hated that book. Primo Levi talks about the dangers of literary lechery when writing fiction about the Holocaust and I think that *Sophie's Choice* commits that sin, and many others.' He had, he confessed, written his own book terrified by what George Steiner might say and astonished that he should have found his way to this subject given that 'I was perhaps the least qualified living writer to do it.'[25] It was territory, he confessed, that he would previously have felt inhibited from entering.

Nonetheless, it seemed to him that by reversing time he was ironically displaying Auschwitz as the Germans insisted it was, part of their plan to cure the state, 'something good, something palliative, something efficacious. I don't think', he added of his own approach, 'that is a trick.' It was precisely the morally inverted world that was Auschwitz which he wished to stage, though even he felt a certain inhibition the moment he imaginatively entered the camp. 'When I get to Auschwitz in the novel', he explains, 'imagination ends. I don't make up anything about Auschwitz. All those things that I report happened, including, for instance, at the Euthanasia Centre, the party given in celebration of the five thousandth victim, the victim being present, dead in a paper hat and a paper bib. Everything is true. I didn't dare make up anything about that, about Auschwitz and the road to Auschwitz' (36).

Acknowledging the danger of the enterprise, he nonetheless insisted on its legitimacy:

> I think if a writer feels justified in going somewhere then he
> must go there. I am a complete exceptionalist. I do believe
> that the Holocaust was like nothing else, for several reasons;
> for instance, it was an entirely unprovoked mass atrocity.
> Perhaps for the first time in history there was a state murder
> of children. Children have been murdered by the state before
> but not with manifests and timetables, and not by the
> trainload. It is like nothing else but ... no subject has an
> 'out of bounds' notice on it. (37)

Time's Arrow deals in satire, in what Amis himself calls 'indirection, savage dramatic irony' (41). The reversal of time creates that irony. Thus the prisoners march forth to work and as a result are released back onto trains which return them to their cities of origin. *Arbeit macht frei* thus becomes literally true instead of standing as a taunt and a deceit. The dead, retrieved from the gas chambers, are re-equipped with hair, spectacles, spinal braces. Work is carried out on their teeth:

> Entirely intelligibly, though, to prevent needless suffering, the
> dental work was usually completed while the patients were not
> yet alive. The *Kapos* would go at it, crudely but effectively,

with knives or chisels or any tool that came to hand. Most
of the gold we used, of course, came straight from the
Reichsbank ... The bulk of the clothes was contributed by the
Reich Youth Leadership. Hair for the Jews came courtesy of
Filzfabrik A. G. of Roth, near Nuremberg. Freightcars full of it.

(*Time's Arrow*, 129–30)

The elision of genocide and capitalism stressed by Peter Weiss
is here underscored by a simple shift of time scales while Mengele's
miracle of withdrawing phenol from dead bodies, thus giving them
back their lives, dramatises the fact that he and the other doctors who
presided over the death camps had themselves reversed their normal
functions as they murdered those who their training had insisted they
must protect.

Perhaps there was a reversal of time for Primo Levi, too, in
those last moments. In trying to understand his death, his son
directed people to read the conclusion of *The Truce*, where Levi
described a recurring dream in which everything that is secure
collapses. He finds himself alone at the centre of a grey and turbid
nothing. He is back in the camp. All else has been a deception of the
senses. He hears again a voice bark out a command: '*Wstavàc*'. Get
up. His response, his son suggests, was to do the reverse. Down he
plunged, stepping out of a fervid dream into a final peace.

Perhaps it was not suicide. He claimed that the dreams no
longer came and denied a link between his depressions and his time in
Auschwitz, though the Chief Rabbi of Rome, on the tenth anniversary
of Levi's death, disclosed that he had received a telephone call from
him ten minutes before he died in which he had declared that he could
not go on with life, saying that every time he looked at the face of his
dying mother he remembered the faces of those at Auschwitz. It is
possible, though, that his anti-depressant drugs induced dizziness and
that he did no more than reach out for the low banister. Maybe we
resist such a banal but entirely plausible explanation because we want
to believe that his story ended not with an arbitrary accident but a
logic which takes us back to the moment of trauma. We know, after
all, that so many others took their lives when time seemed to have

redeemed them, as if they had fulfilled the duty they had set themselves, run the race to the end and now asserted that their lives were truly their own to sustain or conclude. Levi, it is pointed out, left no will, except that of course he did. He bequeathed the world his books and the truths they told and whatever the cause of his death its manner served less to conclude a story than send us back to its beginnings, to an experience that could never be exhausted in the telling.

9   Elie Wiesel: to forget is to deny

Adolf Eichmann was remembered by one generation as a balding man sitting behind a glass screen in an Israeli court, having been kidnapped and flown to Jerusalem. His trial played its part in stirring old memories, in urging those who had remained silent to speak. Another generation remembered him in his prime. He was the man who had planned and executed genocide. He arrived in Budapest in March, 1944, and within weeks had arranged for the deportation and slaughter of four hundred thousand Jews. The operation was efficient, systematic and it swept up a young boy and his family, one family among many, and carried them to Auschwitz. To Eichmann, such people were invisible beyond numbers in a ledger. Their removal and extinction was a task that he carried out with rigour and a certain pride in his own effectiveness. That boy, however, had a name. He was Elie Wiesel.

'If there is a single theme that dominates all my writings, all my obsessions', wrote Elie Wiesel, born in September 1928 and fifteen therefore when his world collapsed, 'it is that of memory – because I fear forgetfulness as much as hatred and death. To forget is, for a Jew, to deny his people – and all that it symbolizes – and also to deny himself.'[1] It is not simply a question of remembering the events of the Holocaust. He insists that the Jew should remember 'that you were a slave in Egypt. Remember to sanctify the Sabbath ... No other Biblical Commandment is as persistent. Jews live under the sign of memory ... To be Jewish is to remember – to claim outright to memory as well as our duty to keep it alive' (9–10). Where Jean Améry and Primo Levi sought and found no respite or resource in their faith,

Wiesel placed his at the centre of his work and life. For him, the need to remember was an imperative for those who needed to survive as a people. Memory was the source of Jewish strength, fusing the past to the present, the individual to the group.

Yet when it came to writing his memoirs it seemed that memory was to be patrolled in the name of taste, decency, the very Jewish people who seemingly demanded the necessity for recall. So, he confesses, 'I must warn you that certain events will be omitted, especially those episodes that might embarrass friends and, of course, those that might damage the Jewish people. Call it prudence or cowardice, whatever you like. No witness is capable of recounting everything from start to finish anyway. God alone knows the whole story.'[2] It is an oddly cavalier statement. Beginning with minor matters of discretion he broadens out to acknowledge not only that a witness has a limited perspective but that in some senses the truth is unknowable because in the possession of God. Given the crucial status he gives to memory its editing becomes potentially destabilising, its partial nature a threat to a larger truth to which he also commits himself, the necessity to remember everything.

'I do love them, the Jews of my town', he explained, 'the Jews of the ghetto. That's why I glorify them in my writings – and I make no secret of it. Unlike some of my colleagues, I refuse to dwell on ugliness and abjection. My characters are not sexually obsessed or pathologically greedy ... The enemy had heaped enough abuse on these Jews without my adding to it ... I shall not act as their detractor, but as their *melitz yosher*, their intercessor' (66–7). If he is to be a witness, it seems, he is not to be a disinterested one. His memories are to be crafted according to certain moral imperatives having to do with upholding an idea of the decency of the victims. Certain truths are not to be engaged with. There is a higher necessity than simply recording everything he saw.

If he does not see through a glass brightly he does, at least, see himself as occluding certain facts which do not serve the truth he wishes to delineate, though in fact ugliness and abjection do form an essential part of his testament. Indeed a gap manifestly opens up between his declared objective and the seemingly ineluctable demands of testimony. Nevertheless, he was ready to absolve the Judenrat and the Jewish police in the ghetto, even considering Chaim Rumkowski, who ruled with autocratic power in the Łódź ghetto, a victim of oppression along with the Jewish kapos who ruled in the camps. In his view 'all Jews were victims' (66).

He was also hesitant to speak of his sister, 'scorched by a darkened sun' (71). She was gassed at Auschwitz. She was to remain his secret, a secret kept even from his own family simply because he found it almost unbearable to think of her, let alone to allow those thoughts to make their way into words. Some memories, it seemed, were not to be shared, not least because the pain of doing so was to recreate the condition of absolute loss which was to be respected but which also could not serve his higher purpose.

Nonetheless, for all his caveats and conscious evasions, he regarded memory as central. He belonged, he explained, to a generation 'obsessed by a thirst to retain and transmit everything. For no other has the commandment Zachor – "Remember!" had such meaning' (15–16). He acknowledged that memory could prove 'voracious and intrusive', that it could, despite his insistence on strategic omissions, 'shine a merciless light on faces and events', but nonetheless felt that it was necessary to 'say "No" to the sands that bury words and to forgetfulness and death' (16). At the same time, an abyss, he confessed, began to open up between the child he once was, and whose experiences he would seek to retrieve, and the man he became.

Wiesel was born in Sighet (official name Sighetul Mármaţiei) in Transylvania, originally part of the Austro-Hungarian empire, subsequently part of the Kingdom of Greater Romania. By the time he left it was a Hungarian city. Its name had changed from Máramarossziget in his father's time (when it was in Greater Romania), to Sighetul Mármaţiei, at the time of Wiesel's birth, and to Máramarossziget again, the latter following the re-drawing of the borders of Poland, Hungary and Romania by Stalin and Hitler. He recalled having to learn the Hungarian national anthem overnight, the Romanian national hymn having been abandoned.

At home, the family spoke Yiddish but also German, Romanian and Hungarian. In the stores he would often hear Ruthenian,

Ukrainian and Russian. It could be a complex fate to be born in central Europe but always there was a unifying faith, perhaps the more important given the contingent nature of national identity. Wiesel, like his family, was of the Book. He was drawn, indeed, to Jewish mysticism.

When Hungarian troops arrived, the population was at first enthusiastic but in 1941, as Wiesel recalled, a thousand 'foreign' Jews were expelled to Polish Galicia, now under German occupation. One man, Moshe, the beadle, who was to appear in *Night*, returned to reveal that those expelled had been murdered, their naked bodies being buried in ditches. He was not believed. A man had borne witness and people refused to accept his testament. It was a first and formative lesson for Wiesel.

For some time, the Jewish community remained largely untroubled. Admittedly, in 1943 news that the Warsaw ghetto had rebelled arrived, as did information about its destruction. In his own home his mother wondered at such irresponsibility when they should simply have waited out the war. No rumours of the Holocaust penetrated Sighet. Life continued much as ever until, on 19 March 1944, everything changed. The Germans crossed the borders. Even so, things did not seem so bad. They did not know that in Budapest Adolf Eichmann had arrived to organise their annihilation.

Now, they were required to wear yellow stars and those restrictions on Jewish activities familiar elsewhere in Europe were imposed. The Hungarian army and police began to enforce those restrictions with enthusiasm, as they would implement Eichmann's plans. Still, the Jews of Sighet were ignorant of what lay in store. Later, Wiesel would condemn those, including American Jews, who failed to inform them and hence indirectly encouraged their passive acceptance of the orders that would mean their deaths. Even when the Germans encircled the Jewish area, creating a ghetto, or, rather two (a smaller one being established nearby), those thus contained believed they would be saved by Soviet troops who would free them. There was even a sense of relief since they would no longer have to deal with the sullen resentment of those others who had always treated them with suspicion. They organised themselves, became a Jewish republic, except that this republic was constructed over a void. They were disabled by hope, the hope that Steiner insisted was sustained to the very doors of the gas chambers, a hope encouraged by the Germans anxious to maintain acquiescence, a hope that was the basis of an irony deeper than that planned by those who took pleasure in reassuring the damned.

Finally, in May 1944 it was announced that all Jews would have to report for transportation. It was an order that stirred a more ancient memory than those of life in this polyglot, ever-changing community, a memory of exodus. Once again the Jews were to be moving on, though it was clear that this was not an escape. Everything had to be left behind. The process of eroding memory had begun. Old ties were to be broken.

As the first Jews were shipped out so they left everything behind, scattered on the ground or in their houses. Some picked up what was thus abandoned only themselves to abandon them as their time came. The world, Wiesel explained, began to contract as the country became a city, 'the city a street, the street a house, a house a room, the room a sealed cattle car, the cattle car a concrete cellar where ...' (74). The ellipses are his. The logic of the final contraction was made clear to them all at last.

The Wiesels had been offered an alternative. Their Catholic maid had proposed to hide them away in a country cottage. She had slipped through the cordon around the ghetto to urge them to escape. Not knowing their fate, they declined on the grounds that a Jew should not be separated from his community. Not even the children could be left behind since that meant breaking up the family, the family that would be separated on their arrival at Auschwitz-Birkenau. They missed another warning. A Hungarian policeman who had assured them he would warn them of danger knocked on the blocked-up window. By the time they responded he had gone. Wiesel only learned of his mission after the war.

Once at the station they were loaded eighty to a cattle wagon. He later claimed to recall every hour, every second of the journey not least because this was the last time he would see his family. His memory 'gathered it all in' (76). In his autobiography, he insists that a structured social life soon asserted itself. In *Night*, by contrast, he suggests that they were free of social restraint, young couples copulating in front of those who chose to ignore them. In both books he recalls the woman who screamed hysterically, claiming to see a fire burning ahead of them, a fire invisible to them until days later they arrived at Auschwitz.

They soon realised that they were not staying within the boundaries of Hungary. They were stripped of whatever items of value they might have preserved. Eventually, they arrived at Auschwitz where immediately Wiesel was separated from his mother and sister at an imperious wave from Dr Mengele. Advised by a prisoner, he and his father lied about their age and were marched off past a pit in which babies were being burned. It is worth pausing a second to re-read that sentence which fails so completely to communicate the reality concealed behind so simple a statement of fact. Even his attempt to elaborate displaces pain and shock onto a lyrical prose which denies the essence of what it purports to describe. In that moment, and the night that followed, memories were laid down even as faith was stripped away: 'Never shall I forget that smoke. Never shall I forget the little faces of the children, whose bodies I saw turned into wreaths of smoke beneath a silent sky. Never shall I forget those flames which consumed my life forever. Never shall I forget that nocturnal silence which deprived me, for all eternity, of the desire to live. Never shall I forget those moments which murdered my God and my soul.'[3] Such thoughts, though, came later. At the time the need to survive blotted out that perspective as it blotted out awareness of a resistance movement in the camp or the war news which filtered down. Nor, according to his autobiography, had his faith been destroyed. He continued to pray, to recite the Talmud, to celebrate, as far as he could, Jewish festivals. Doubts and revolt came later.

Indeed, his continued faith perplexed his fellow Auschwitz survivor, Primo Levi. 'He had seen too much suffering', Wiesel explained, 'not to rebel against any religion that sought to impose a meaning upon it.' By contrast, he himself had seen 'too much suffering to break with the past and reject the heritage of those who had suffered' (83). Beyond that, Wiesel seems to imply that Levi's views may have been shaped by a certain privileged treatment. 'He was a chemist', he explained, or perhaps complained, 'I was nothing at all. The system needed him, but not me. He had influential friends to help and protect him; I had only my father. I needed God, Primo did not.'[4]

He never, he insists, rejected God even while rebelling against his justice, his silence, his absence. His argument with God was within the faith. Perhaps it is not surprising that there were those who chose to treat such a stance with suspicion, not least given his own account of the hanging in the camp of a young child. For his part, it was perhaps necessary to accept the pain of faith rather than relinquish that faith. As he remarked, to 'proclaim one's faith within the barbed wire of Auschwitz may well represent a double tragedy, of the believer and his Creator alike' (84). By what seems an inverted logic, it becomes necessary for man to pity God.

What is it that he remembers of his time in Auschwitz? Desertion, certainly, but also, it seems, a continued faith which like all faith seems to derive its energy precisely from its seeming illogic. And in his case he had the example of his father, who never abandoned his faith and in clinging to it asserted his own memory of generations for whom suffering was never taken as proof of their own abandonment by God. Memory was thus a consolation, a denial of the principle of the camps that each man was on his own, though he himself describes sons pleased at the thought of the death of fathers whose weakness was a threat to their own survival. Such a feeling had fluttered across his own soul but loyalty can be a product of guilt as much as of conviction. Which it was in his case is never entirely clear.

In his autobiography he asked himself what kept him alive. 'Was it the will to testify – and therefore the need to survive ... Did I survive in order to combat forgetting?' The answer was that 'such questions did not occur to me. I did not feel invested with any mission. On the contrary, I was convinced that my turn would come and that my memories would die with me' (80). What motivated him was the presence of his father. It was the mutual support of father and son that brought him through and which so nearly brought his father through as well.

Nonetheless, once in the camp, thoughts even of those closest to them 'no longer touched even the surface of our memories' (*The Night Trilogy*, 45). They spoke of them but no longer had any concern for their fate. They existed in a half-world. An SS officer instructed them as to their future memories, should they survive: 'Remember this', he told them, 'Remember it forever. Engrave it on your minds. You are at Auschwitz ... Here you have got to work. If not, you will go straight to the furnace. To the crematory. Work or the crematory – the choice is in your hands' (47). This was their initiation. Immediately afterwards his father was knocked down for asking where the toilets were. Wiesel did not move. He had learned his first lesson.

From Birkenau they moved to Auschwitz I and here there was a speech of another kind, this time from the Polish prisoner in charge. 'Have faith in life', he insisted, 'Drive out despair, and you will keep death away from yourselves. Hell is not for eternity ... Help one another. It is the only way to survive' (50). For those who would later suggest that survival depended on selfishness this speech offered a different model and, indeed, even those memoirs that seemed to advocate self-interest are replete with evidences of the contrary. For Primo Levi it was Lorenzo. In *All Rivers Run to the Sea*, Wiesel recalls a young Hungarian Jew who confesses to a minor infringement of the rules in order to save his uncle from a beating and who dies as a result. 'I remember, I remember', Wiesel intones as if this were part of some religious rite. He stored it all 'unconsciously', he explains, though he claimed to remember only the victims and not what he called the hangmen.

In his study of the moral life of the concentration camp, *Facing the Extreme*, Tzvetan Todorov entitles one of his chapters 'Caring' and details cases in which selfless acts seemed to have redeemed those facing the eclipse of all human feeling. Sometimes this took the form of sacrifice, of a refusal to deny; sometimes it was a matter of sharing a morsel of food, fortuitously discovered or stolen, theft being a virtue as well as a necessity so long as it was not from fellow sufferers. Wiesel's Polish prisoner, however, was removed from his post. He was too humane.

Yet a certain hardness grew, a protective carapace, so that when a young Pole from Warsaw is publicly hanged, by prisoners rewarded with two plates of soup, Wiesel is moved but in retrospect remembers finding the soup excellent that night. That detail, so easy to suppress, stands out in his memory because memory is also the source of accusations. Yet he also remembers another hanging. The electric power station at Buna was blown up and responsibility traced to a Dutch Oberkapo. He was hanged along with his angelic-looking child assistant – though some of the children were crueller than their parents, one, Wiesel reports, beating his own father. The child took half an hour to die. The prisoners were required to parade past him. 'Where is God now?' a man cried out. The answer sounds in Wiesel's mind: 'He is hanging here on this gallows.' That night 'the soup tasted of corpses' (72).

For many, reading that passage, Wiesel was announcing the death of God. It was, the author insisted in his autobiography, a blasphemous interpretation. 'I have never', he asserted, 'renounced my faith in God.'⁵ Yet in *Night*, a book which he asserted was the foundation of his work to which everything else was a mere commentary, he recalls his despair not of man but of God on the eve of Rosh Hashana, the beginning of a new year. 'How could I say to him', he asks, '"Blessed art Thou, Eternal, Master of the Universe, Who chose us from among the races to be tortured day and night, to see our fathers, our mothers, our brothers, end in the crematory? Praised be Thy Holy Name, Thou Who hast chosen us to be butchered on Thine altar?"' (*The Night Trilogy*, 74). God stood accused. On Yom Kippur, the Day of Atonement, he refused to fast, not because to do so would be ironic in a camp in which most were starving, but because he 'no longer accepted God's silence' (76). His later protestations of faith seem hollow in the face of a cold anger rooted in immediate experience.

Thirty-six years on from his experience in Auschwitz, he seems to deny the radical despair that infected him as the ceremonies of his faith were conducted in the face of what seemed to be evidence not merely of its inutility but of its collusive betrayals. Yet even now, in his autobiography, he declares 'I will never cease to rebel against those who committed or permitted Auschwitz, including God. The questions I once asked myself about God's silence', he declares, 'remain open.'[6] In the second volume of his memoirs he returned to this moment, to his denial of loss of faith, now declaring that his affirmation of faith had prompted resentment among the secular.

And was memory always a good? Two days before the advancing Russian troops liberated those left behind in the infirmary, Wiesel and his father decided to leave it, believing that they would be liquidated (in his memoirs, *All Rivers Run to the Sea*, it is given as nine days). Instead they joined first a march and then a train journey to another camp, Buchenwald. The march turned into a run, lasting days. And as they ran, a Rabbi, beloved by everyone, asked Wiesel if he had seen his son. The man was weak and had been falling behind. Wiesel explained that he had not, only subsequently to remember that he had. The son had seen his father weakening and falling behind and instead of staying with him had chosen to lengthen his stride. It seemed to Wiesel, suddenly, that he had been trying to abandon a father who had become a burden: 'I had done well', Wiesel comments, 'to forget that' (*Night*, 97).

Sometimes, it seems, forgetfulness is a moral virtue. The event, however, was also a lesson, should he need one, in his responsibility towards his own father as for four days and nights they travelled in snow and ice in open cattle wagons across Germany, Wiesel stopping his father from being thrown out when it was presumed he had died. Yet even now there was a contrary lesson from a fifteen-year-old boy and his father. The latter had hidden a small piece of bread. His son felled him to the ground and snatched it. The man died, only for his son to search him for more food before himself being set upon and killed.

Of the hundred who boarded the train, just a dozen disembarked. Their ultimate destination? Buchenwald. Now his father fell ill and he received the standard advice to look out for himself: 'Don't forget that you're in a concentration camp. Here, every man has to fight for himself and not think of anyone else. Even of his father. Here, there are no fathers, no brothers, no friends. Everyone dies for himself alone' (115). Wiesel confesses to wishing he were free of his father, the father who died on 29 January 1945, having been ill with dysentery and then struck a violent blow by an SS officer. His son was not with him. 'There were no prayers at his grave. No candle was lit to his memory. His last word', Wiesel wrote, 'was my name. A summons to which I did not respond ... And, in the depths of my being, in the recesses of my weakened conscience, could I have searched it, I might perhaps have found something like – free at last!' (116). Thereafter, every January he recalled that January, pain and guilt intermixed.

Is *Night* perhaps less a book of witness than a confession? Is its inspiration not so much accusation (save self-accusation) as guilt? His memory is pitiless. He was, we have to remind ourselves, fifteen at the time he lived through these events, but he makes no concession to that fact.

The period after his father's death – some two and a half months (a time, as we know from other accounts of the final days of Buchenwald, of great privation) – is a blank, not because he remembers nothing but because he chooses to remember nothing. His father's death seemed to be the true end of the story. He himself was transferred to the children's block but it is as if time had stopped. Eventually, the camp commander announced that the camp was to be liquidated and that evacuation would begin. In the end it seems likely that it was the Jews and not the camp who faced liquidation, a fate they only escaped because the resistance organisation took up arms. That same evening, the Americans appeared. Days later, Wiesel fell ill with food poisoning and nearly died. He had survived but when he stared in a mirror it was a corpse that stared back. A child had become less a man than a golem. Fifteen years went by before he chose to publish his book. What was his motive? Speaking of another former prisoner he remarks, 'He, too, has devoted his life to defending the survivors' (*All Rivers Run to the Sea*, 91), thereby identifying his own avocation. His memories, then, are not random. They serve a cause.

He notes that according to the Midrash there is a place called 'secret' and that when God is sad he goes there to weep. 'For us', says Wiesel, 'this secret place lies in memory, which possesses its own secret' (105). It is a gnomic remark that suggests the degree to which the most profound of questions about the human capacity for ingenious evil and the Divine capacity for an apparently disinterested withdrawal remain mysteries. The one prompts an anguished admission of possibility become fact. The other can only be addressed through faith, which by its nature acknowledges the limits to understanding, indeed demands the suspension of rational inquiry in the name of a transcendent submission. For Primo Levi, that demand was an affront, a metaphysical version of that obedience demanded of those who found themselves the victims of a secular power which seemed to rule over its own kingdom.

For Wiesel, despite the revealing contradictions of his accounts, as God is alternately accused and seemingly absolved, the ultimate abandonment of God is an impossibility as if it would stand as a confirmation of God's abandonment of man. There is no justification for Auschwitz or Treblinka and he resists a theology that would permit such. Yet he leaves in place a God with no need to justify himself to man, a God to be pitied as a witness to suffering, the working out, as it seems, of a law of unintended consequences. If God was offering a lesson it was unclear what that lesson might be beyond the opacity of the Godhead.

And where does memory function in this? It is, in part, the evidence presented before the court not only of Wiesel's own conscience but the conscience of the world, apparently in abeyance as babies were thrown into blazing pits and innocents were hanged and left to die for thirty long minutes. Memory is the place he, too, goes to weep but the act of public recall is evidence that this is something more than a closed loop in which he endlessly replays personal trauma. The subject is obsessive but memory is not a product of self-lacerating guilt.

On his return from the camp, he lived alone in Paris, distrustful. Then he took up his studies, including biblical studies. He did not find adjustment difficult. He was reunited with surviving members of his family. His ambition, meanwhile, was to become a writer. The obvious subject was to hand, albeit a subject that he had felt unable to communicate to others: 'I could write my memories of the camp, which I bore within me like poison. Though I never spoke to anyone about this, it weighed upon me. I thought about it with apprehension day and night: the duty to testify, to offer depositions for history, to serve memory.' After all, what, he asked, 'would man be without his capacity to remember?' For him, memory was a passion no less powerful and pervasive than love. What does it mean to remember, he asked. 'It is to live in more than one world, to prevent the past from fading and to call upon the future to illuminate it. It is to revive fragments of existence, to rescue lost beings, to cast harsh light on faces and events, to drive back the sands that cover the surface of things, to combat oblivion, to reject death' (150). But the truth was that he was not ready. He was suspicious of the very vocation he sought. Neither was he ready to share his memories, to shoulder what he would later come to believe was a responsibility.

Nor, at that time, did he feel there was a language to hand. After all, he recalled, the Zohar (an ancient series of Kabbalistic books) spoke of the exile of words, the gap which opens up between experience and the language which attempts to express it. Words thus become obstacles. As he put it, 'words broke my spirit. I had no confidence in them, for I sensed what I would later come to feel with greater certainty: Human words are too impoverished, too transparent to express the Event' (151). They lacked the depth, the profundity, even perhaps the profanity to reflect such a truth. The question, as it seemed to him, was whether it was the teller who lied or the words. He quotes the Hebrew poet Bialik as saying that 'Words are whores. Decked out in their finery, they offer themselves to the first passerby.' For his part, Wiesel insisted that without Yiddish, the literature of the Holocaust would have had no soul: 'I know that had I not written my first account in Yiddish I would have written no others' (292). Yiddish reached back beyond the camps. It was an assertion of continuity in the face of those who would have terminated tradition, history, memory itself.

That, however, raised another problem. If Yiddish was to be the language of memory how could it encompass what it was necessary for him to say? There was, in other words, a compromise at the heart of the venture. Was he to be true to language or event? This might all have seemed pretentious were it not for the fact that so many survivors confessed to the inadequacy of language when it came to describing their experience of the camps. Not merely did such places generate their own deformed language but it was perhaps the redemption of language that it should prove inadequate to the task of encompassing what happened there.

There were other subjects that did not intimidate him in the same way. Indeed he became a journalist, in which guise he travelled widely, including a visit to Israel to which he felt a special loyalty, though it was on this trip that he was tempted by suicide, as he had been earlier when he was living in Paris, with no clear sense of direction or purpose, a time, he explained, when his self no longer seemed to belong to him. For a while he doubted everything but his memories, even though he could as yet see nothing to do with them. Nonetheless, memory 'was protected by the dead who inhabited it'. Their presence seemed more real than his everyday surroundings. And even when that insistent pressure faded it was, he felt, because he had as yet done nothing with the fact of his survival. He was in a double bind. Few seemed interested in hearing from such as he while he lacked the vocabulary and perhaps the distance to do justice to his experiences. When he did finally do so he would be a man of thirty trying to re-inhabit the mind and sensibility of a fifteen-year-old.

From 1948 to 1951 Wiesel studied literature, psychology and philosophy at the Sorbonne. He took pleasure in learning French. It would be ten years before he wrote his memories of the camps. He did so in a book whose original title was *And the World Has Remained Silent*, an accusation levelled at others but also at himself. It did not find a ready publisher, appearing first in Spanish in Buenos Aires, where doubtless it could be read by the odd German smuggled out to freedom after the war. It was an encounter with François Mauriac, however, that eased his way in France. In 1958 the book appeared as *La Nuit* (Night), the title by which it is now known, and he had begun what would be a lifetime commitment. Everything he wrote thereafter, novels, plays, autobiographies, circled around his wartime experience as he tried both to testify and explore the dilemmas thrown up by an experience which he felt obliged to regard as hermetic, even as he felt obligated to regard it as communicable. Why else break one's silence? As the years passed, his memories did not fade. They became if anything more insistent as he extended his feelings of obligation in the direction of Israel and the defence of Jews everywhere. If any politician forgot the centrality of the Jews in the camps, he was on his feet protesting, writing to the press. If any attacked Israel, he detected an anti-Semitism disguising itself as politics.

What is a memory, however, and how is it to be communicated? There is a shape to *Night*, of necessity, but that shape was not formed by his experience of Auschwitz. Rather his experience of Auschwitz had to be located in a literary form. Nor can the imagination be wholly laid aside. He himself has said that 'the real and the imagined, one like the other, are part of history; one is its shell, the other its core. Not to recognize this is to deny art – any form of art – the right to exist.'[7] Yet he is also profoundly suspicious of fiction as a contaminant. Every word of *Night*, he insists, is true. Yet even truth must be presented in a form and with a narrative drive which is not that of the camps, where the arbitrary ruled, where time condensed into a moment or extended into the shadow of death.

Night has the form of a bildungsroman. We watch as a boy grows in wisdom, albeit wisdom of a terrible kind. In the heart of darkness, it is a love story, a love story which tells of the fierce attachment of a father to a son and a son to a father, an attachment far deeper than normally defines such a relationship in that each of them was trying to keep the other alive, each willing to sacrifice everything for the other, even in the face of a temptation to do otherwise that at times was all but irresistible. It is an act of witness, but what is witnessed is not simply brutality and depravity. It is something other. And that something other, though part of the story, also creates a tension with that story.

Wiesel began, in time, to see his responsibility as extending beyond his own testimony. His function was, in part, he accepted, to 'limit the trivialization of memory'.[8] He even raised the question of whether silence might have been a preferred option rather than expose what he called the mystery of Auschwitz to 'profanations', though he also invoked the Talmud, which declares that 'Silence easily becomes acquiescence' (7). Memory, in other words, became a battleground and he increasingly found himself engaged in disputes with those who sought to bring the story of the Holocaust to a wider audience, indeed even with a man dedicated to securing justice for the dead – Simon Wiesenthal.

In particular, he dismissed novels, films, television series which seemed to him to reduce the Holocaust to soap opera, to capitalise on the sufferings of the dead, to sacrifice fact to sentiment. In an essay called 'Trivializing Memory', in his significantly entitled reminiscences, *From the Kingdom of Memory*, he writes that Auschwitz 'defeated culture; later, it defeated art, because just as no one could imagine Auschwitz before Auschwitz, no one can now retell Auschwitz after Auschwitz. The truth of Auschwitz remains hidden in its ashes.'[9] Still less could it be captured in popular media.

In his memoirs, he reproduces in full his attack on the television series *Holocaust*. The attack, he insisted, was a duty. The production was untrue, 'offensive, cheap ... an insult to those who perished. And to those who survived' (*And the Sea is Never Full*, 117). The mere fact of fictionalisation played into the hands of those who thought the Holocaust no more than a fiction. Meanwhile, the old canards about Jewish passivity were once again invoked, as they had been in the Eichmann trial. To him, even the victims were heroes. Meanwhile, the series was full of egregious errors. Characters were implausibly implicated in all aspects of the Final Solution, the Jewish family at its centre being required to go on a journey round various concentration camps while the German officer who is made to stand for those who planned and executed the genocide implausibly pops up at every historically significant moment.

He objected, in particular, to the intrusion into the gas chambers themselves. Special effects and gimmicks deformed the privacy of a moment that could not be and should not be recreated. In short, the Holocaust was not simply another event, capable of being fictionalised. It was unique and its mechanical reproduction damaged that uniqueness as the aesthetic and commercial values of the media took primacy. The fact is, he asserted, 'You may think you know how the victims lived and died, but you do not. Auschwitz cannot be explained nor can it be visualized. Whether culmination or aberration of history, the Holocaust transcends history ... The dead are in possession of a secret that we, the living, are neither worthy of nor capable of recovering' (121).

Such a view, of course, leaves the writer, the director, the actor nowhere to go. But he goes further than this. The problem is not simply that any form of fictionalisation must fall short of the reality, must distort by accommodating it to the norms, expectations, modes of presentation of the particular art form, but that the experience itself resists such incorporation because, as he says, the Holocaust was 'The ultimate event, the ultimate mystery, never to be comprehended or transmitted.' Anything must be in bad faith. As he remarked, 'It was easier for Auschwitz inmates to imagine themselves free than for free persons to imagine themselves in Auschwitz' (122). Not to have been there is to disqualify oneself. The Holocaust, he insisted, 'is not a subject like all the others. It imposes certain limits. There are techniques that one may not use, even if they are commercially effective. In order not to betray the dead and humiliate the living, this particular subject demands a certain sensibility ... and, above all, faithfulness to memory' (168).

It followed, of course, that he was bound to reject *The Night Porter*, a 1974 film by Liliana Cavani, along with William Styron's *Sophie's Choice*, and he did so even though the result was a breach with Styron which has still not been closed. He was disappointed with *Ghetto*, a play about the Vilna ghetto by the Israeli playwright Joshua Sobol, and said so, feeling it his duty to patrol the subject as though he had been appointed a guardian of the flame. Unsurprisingly, here was another damaged relationship. Sobol insisted that *Ghetto* was based on fact but this alone seemed no defence to Wiesel. By giving more prominence to certain facts rather than others, it appeared to him, Sobol had made his play a lie. Beyond anything, however, what he objected to was the fact that the play presented Jews in an unfortunate light. Some were seen as defeated and seduced by the enemy. There was black marketeering and prostitution. If it was a reality, he objected, it was a very limited one.

In other words, this protector of memories was a protector of certain memories. As a witness he was a partial one. As a moral guardian he was no less so. He attacked *The Winds of War*, based on

Herman Wouk's novel, though this time claiming that the author understood his need to object. More surprisingly, and despite his preference for documentary, which of course precisely privileges the survivors, he took issue with Claude Lanzmann's film *Shoah*, which he tells the reader he had initially helped with his *Times* review. While acknowledging its achievement he once again objected to intrusion into the gas chambers.

He was not, he asserted, claiming presumptive rights to the subject. Anyone, he said, could write on any subject and on any individual. There is, he confessed, no 'game preserve'. Having said so, however, he insisted that 'no one, myself included, is authorized to speak on behalf of the dead, no one may appropriate their memory' (123). There were, he thought, suddenly all too many people who thought they had the right to speak about the Holocaust, to decide who deserved to write, who was sentimental, who should be read, and who should not, quite as if he had not done exactly the same thing, the difference being, of course, that he was a survivor and those others were not.

Quite the most surprising argument he found himself embroiled in, however, was with the Nazi-hunter Simon Wiesenthal, whom he suspected, among other things, of jealousy over the Nobel Prize which was awarded to him in 1986. Wiesenthal, he says, coveted the prize. At the heart of the disagreement, besides an obvious personal antipathy on both sides, was, it seemed, Wiesenthal's belief that Wiesel was interested primarily in the Jewish survivors, rather than extending his concern to gypsies, Poles and others. He was, Wiesenthal remarked, a chauvinist and as such an opponent of his own concern that there should be a true brotherhood between all victims. For his part, Wiesel chose to note Wiesenthal's apparently cordial relations with Albert Speer and Kurt Waldheim. Neither man emerged from this dispute with credit. Wiesel regarded the premise of Wiesenthal's *The Sunflower* (his story of the dying Nazi's search for absolution from a Jew) as absurd and repeats gossip which he claims to have derived from Mossad, the Israeli secret police, to the effect that his rival had interfered with Israeli attempts to capture Mengele and was a self-regarding braggart.

The bitterness of this dispute – and there were others – suggests something more than a disagreement over emphasis. There is, Wiesel's denials notwithstanding, a territoriality about it. What Wiesel presents as a duty is also a privilege. Attitudes to Israel, of which Wiesel was a staunch supporter, may also have played a part. Yet there was a dispute too about the past, about numbers – they disagreed over the number of those dying. Indeed, plainly both men found their lives in some sense determined by that past. They were survivors who had emerged from the camps with different impera-tives. Neither was prepared to forget. In the case of one this led to a relentless pursuit of the killers; in the case of the other it resulted in a desire to celebrate the victims and the country to which they had fled, which represented not only a homeland but a denial of accusations of Jewish passivity.

For both, memory was a motivating force, though Wiesel was not unaware of the ambiguities, problematics, insecurities associated with memory. In the second volume of his autobiography, now fifty-five years removed from his wartime experiences, he was ready to pose a number of crucial questions: 'Does memory become richer, or does it shrink as man leaves his early experiences farther and farther behind? What makes it surge back? How does one follow its upheavals? And how does one assimilate the traces it leaves behind?' He is, he admits, fascinated by everything that touches on memory, including what he calls its mystical force, but confesses that 'Memory desires to encompass everything, but it merely illuminates fragments.' He then asks himself, 'Why this recollection rather than another? And what happens to all that I have already forgotten? And then: what is the relationship between individual memory and collective memory? Which enriches the other, and at what cost?' He then says something curious. 'More than history, it contains Truth.' Without it life would have no meaning. It was an essential component.

So, memory is simultaneously ambiguous and unknowable and an essential key to existence, in particular, he says, to writing and teaching. It is by its nature limited in perspective and yet closer to Truth (his capitalisation of the word implying a transcendent rather than contingent force) than history.

336

The emphasis on memory, however, is not itself a product of those who survived and stood as witnesses. Even as the events unfolded there were those who saw themselves as laying down the foundation for memories as they desperately recorded what they saw. In the Warsaw ghetto, Emmanuel Ringelblum gathered a committee of one hundred. Together, Wiesel insists, 'they became the memory of a besieged Jewish community' (104) even as they struggled to assimilate what was happening. Even the *Sonderkommandos*, whose job it was to burn the corpses, wrote, as we have seen, for the future that would one day travel back on their memories and buried their diaries where they could and where they were later unearthed. The argument is thus not about the necessity to remember but the nature of memory, how it operates, what is recalled and what forgotten or denied, what relationship it has to the whole. Auschwitz was not one place nor yet was Birkenau. It depended on the date of your arrival, your state of health, your previous profession, your utility, your sensibility, those alongside whom you lived, those who by chance were set over you, the time of year, your politics, religion, nationality, whether you came alone or with your family and whether that family died, immediately, or whether they survived to challenge or uphold family loyalties.

Nor is memory only a matter for those who suffered. While insisting that he does not believe in collective guilt and that the children of killers are children and not killers, Wiesel does assert that they must be held responsible for the memory of their elders' crime. And certainly Albert Speer's children felt that responsibility as did the children of many others.

Wiesel's 1990 collection of reminiscences *From the Kingdom of Memory* is in part an explanation of his desire to write, born out of the necessity to witness but expanding into fiction and drama. Having survived, he felt the need to justify his life and since he had a story to tell he felt obliged to tell it. Not to tell that story, he explained, was to betray it. The problem was in part one of language, which fell so short of experience, and in part one of finding a way to voice what seemed to draw a veil around itself and demand a respect that could perhaps only be paid through silence. Such events seemed to demand a primeval language yet the language deployed has to speak to those who knew nothing of what so disabled the witness.

Wiesel, however, a man admittedly somewhat given to the portentous, insisted that 'I owe the dead my memory. I am duty-bound to serve as their emissary.'[10] The problem is that language conceals as much as it reveals, its associations, its order, its communicative essence at odds with what must be engaged. Though he deals in words, he distrusts them, even as he acknowledges that language was the beginning of creation, the prefigurer of creation, the means of invoking and celebrating a godhead. It is the carrier of memory, the means of sharing memory. He recalls that in the Hasidic tradition mankind was saved at the time of the flood not by the ark alone but by eloquence, the Hebrew word *teva* denoting both 'ark' and 'letter'. Their faith, after all, would be inscribed in a book; and though the Nazis took special pleasure in forcing their Jewish captives to defile that book in the most literal of ways, that did not erase the words written there. He recalls a Talmudic legend which tells of the Romans wrapping a rabbi in the sacred scrolls and setting them on fire. When his disciple asked him what he saw he said, 'I see the parchment burning but the letters are floating in the air' (29).

If Wiesel's arguments with God took place within a faith so, too, did his arguments with language. He recalled the banal words, the coded evasions of those who planned and enacted genocide – 'final solution', 'special treatment', 'relocation'. In this new vocabulary people became 'things' or worse. Did that betoken shame, on the part of those who seemed to feel none, the need for secrecy, on the part of those who claimed to take pride in their actions, a sense of irony, a black humour? Somewhere between the word and the thing fell the shadow, and that shadow covered those who deployed this language as well as those who suffered: no matter that their suffering would not make its way into words until later, when memory would decant itself into a language purged, so far as possible, of impurities. For some, like the Nobel Prize-winning German Jewish poet Nelly Sachs, it was impossible to pronounce certain German words. For those such as Wiesel himself the struggle was to make words work. Do we remember in images, he might have asked himself, or in words, and if in images then how could those be shared, translated, deciphered except through a vocabulary forged for another human universe than that which prevailed in Birkenau or Treblinka?

Yet, for him, Auschwitz becomes the beginning and the end. Everything before and after has to be explained in terms of that place and what happened there. It is part of what he calls his inner landscape. He is concerned to bring back those who were taken away, aware, however, that for the Jew time has a different feel, as in a very different sense it did to the Nazis who at Treblinka built a fake railway station to reassure those about to die, and set the hands of the station clock permanently at 6 p.m. Past, present and future are part of the same experience. Abraham is a present as well as a past fact. To be a good Jew, he explained, precisely meant living in more than one period. What else are the festivals which punctuate the Jewish year but a bringing together across time and space of those who derive their identity from continuity, the very continuity the Nazis set themselves to disrupt? His novels, as he has explained, all feature a Hasid, a child, an old man, a beggar, all those who have been persecuted and pursued. He offers them, as he says, shelter within his fictions.

Memory, he insists, is a means of exorcising the ghosts hovering over Jewish history. Reconciliation was only available through memory. 'Does it also involve pain? I welcome it. I think of the children – walking slowly, almost peacefully, toward the flames – and I am grateful for the pain that links me to them' (200). In his Nobel address, in 1986, he restated his basic creed. 'Without memory, our existence would be barren and opaque, like a prison cell into which no light penetrates, like a tomb that rejects the living ... for me, hope without memory is like memory without hope ... the opposite of the future is not the past but the absence of past' (238–9).

Yet he also concedes that it is human to forget and that 'forgetting helps us to go on living'. The Talmud itself, he confesses, states that without forgetting 'man would soon cease to learn. Without the ability to forget, man would live in a paralysing fear of death' (243). Only God, he concedes, must remember everything. The problem is to balance these equal necessities. In Wiesel's work there is no balance. For him a central figure was Job, not Jewish but in some sense bearing the impress of a Jewish experience of suffering yet retaining faith: 'Because I remember, I despair. Because I remember, I have the duty to reject despair' (248).

It is hard not to detect a sense of hubris in Wiesel. It is as though his role of witness has raised him up to become a moral arbiter. It is in the end not enough to remember unless memory be a spur to patrol the world looking for slights against the Jews or Israel. This begins with the camps where he detects those who would appropriate Jewish suffering and hand it back to the world universalised, stripped of its particularity. It continues when he upbraids President Reagan for seeming to honour the SS along with the Wehrmacht in a memorial service and breaks with President Mitterrand when details of his suspect past, involving Vichy and friendship with a French Chief of Police who had organised the deportation of the Jews, are revealed. It is not that he is in the wrong but that he is so determined publicly to be in the right. In the second volume of his autobiography he details these and other breaches of what he considers something more than decorum. So powerful is the past that everything must be strained through its narrow mesh.

The Holocaust exerts a gravitational pull on Wiesel. He has himself spoken of the temptation while writing his novels of being rushed back to the shadows, restrained only by his belief that the Holocaust and fiction are incompatible. When he appears in Thane Rosenbaum's *The Golems of Gotham* he is treated by the other survivors, now dead by their own hands, as the last of his kind. It was a possibility that Wiesel himself envisaged and it was not one he relished. As he told an interviewer, 'Somewhere in my novels I have tried to imagine being the last survivor. I do not want to be that survivor. I'm afraid of that survivor, of his vision. I'm afraid of the madness that would invade him, weigh upon him, to have so much knowledge, and to know that, with him, all this knowledge will go down, will go out.'[11]

For Elie Wiesel, the Holocaust was essentially a Jewish disaster and one not to be processed through fiction, though he himself wrote novels which circled around it. But there were other witnesses who while observing the Jewish plight were not themselves Jewish and who did choose to record what they saw through fiction, albeit fiction virtually indistinguishable from fact. One such, who, like Jean Améry and Primo Levi, Anne Frank and Elie Wiesel, spent time in Auschwitz, began to write virtually immediately after his release and, like Améry and Levi, evidently came to find life insupportable, one in a long line of those who survived only to find survival ultimately impossible to bear.

'Tadeusz Borowski opened a gas valve on July 1, 1951. He was not yet thirty.'[1] Jan Kott chose to begin his account of Borowski with an implacable fact that seemed in some sense a logical extension of a scarred life. Born in Zhitomir in the Ukraine in 1922 of Polish parents, Borowski had been four when his father was sent to a labour camp inside the Arctic Circle to work on the White Sea Canal. His crime was to have involved himself in a Polish military organisation during the First World War. Borowski was eight when his mother was deported to Siberia. He himself was taken in by an aunt and was twelve before his parents returned, his father having been exchanged for Communists imprisoned in Poland. They moved to Warsaw. Here, he began to write, publishing his first volume of poems in mimeograph form in 1942, three years into the German occupation of a country in which the occupiers enforced strict censorship. They were published in an edition of 165 copies and were bleak, ironic, as he stared into a future rushing towards him. A few weeks after publication of the poems both he and his fiancée were arrested by the Gestapo. They spent two months in prison before, in April 1943, they were sent to Auschwitz. On 4 April the last Aryans had been selected for the gas chambers. They arrived on 29 April. His camp number, tattooed on his arm, was 119198. He was twenty-one.

Neither of them were Jewish and hence they were not rushed to the gas chambers. At first he was set to labour, but after an illness was made an orderly. Later, he would be sent to Dachau by way of a camp outside Stuttgart. Both of them survived. On 1 May 1945, the camp was liberated by the Americans but he then spent four months in a displaced persons' camp on the outskirts of Munich where he began to write his short stories. These included 'This Way for the Gas, Ladies and Gentlemen' and 'A Day at Harmenz'. They appeared in Poland before he did. He returned by way of Bavaria and Paris, arriving in the now Communist country in May 1946. His fiancée was in Sweden but she returned and they were married. Two years later he became a member of the Party, publishing two volumes of stories.

In 1949 he went to Berlin, as Kott explained in an introduction to the 1976 publication of Borowski's stories, to work in the Press Section at the Polish Military Mission in Berlin. It seemed as if he were content to lend his talents to the Party. Two years later he was dead, three days after the birth of his first daughter (though he had been involved in a relationship with another young woman for some time). It was his third attempt to end his life. Kott draws attention to the fact that he died only weeks after a friend, in whose apartment he and his then fiancée had been arrested by the Gestapo, had himself been arrested and subsequently tortured by Polish Security. It was as if this closed the circle. There seemed no escape.

As Kott observes, his had been a European story of abandonment, displacement, moral entropy. To an extent that story is certainly a recognisable one, involving transportation, hard labour, trauma. Yet in certain crucial respects his story is not that of Améry, Levi or Wiesel. He was a witness but he viewed the world of Auschwitz from an entirely different angle. Because he was not Jewish he had certain crucial privileges, beginning with the fact that he was not fated to die. He might be killed because of some infraction but he would not be gassed and incinerated by virtue of his race or religion. Indeed, he did not suffer the deprivation of those others. Working in 'Canada', being responsible for cleaning out the cattle wagons which delivered their victims to the station, he had access to food, drink, clothing. That his short stories should be seen as classic works of Holocaust literature might thus seem strange. His memories were not those of others. His perspective was not that of the doomed. What earns him his position is not even the unflinching manner with which he describes the horrors he observed. It is that he is pitiless with respect to himself, that he is unblinking in implicating himself in a process from which he was in some undeniable if distorted way a beneficiary. Because he was fed and clothed as a result of those brought to this place to die, when the transports ceased to arrive with regularity he found himself lamenting their non-appearance. Because thousands had died, he had not.

The narrator of three of the stories bears his name, or variations of that name. He resists the temptation to distance himself from responsibility. If these are fictions, the gap between fact and invention seems to have closed. He is not about the business of consolation. Kott quotes a review which Borowski wrote of another book about camp life. 'The first duty of Auschwitzers', he insisted,

> is to make clear just what a camp is … But let them not forget that the reader will unfailingly ask: But how did it happen that *you* survived? … Tell, then, how you bought places in the hospital, easy posts, how you shoved the 'Moslems' [prisoners who had lost the will to live] into the oven, how you bought women, men, what you did in the barracks, unloading the transports, at the gypsy camp; tell about the daily life of the camp, about the hierarchy of fear, about the loneliness of every man. But write that you, you were the ones who did this. That a portion of the sad fame of Auschwitz belongs to you as well. (22)

That is precisely what he does in his stories which are less stories than slivers of autobiography, a kaleidoscope of moments, dark images whose tone is captured in the title of one of them, later taken as the title of the English-language collection – *This Way For the Gas, Ladies and Gentlemen*, though he himself chose to entitle another edition *A World of Stone*. 'Harden your heart to stone', says Camus's character in *Caligula*, 'it's what He has done.'[2] Beyond Camus, it is tempting to read Beckett back into this world: 'The end is in the beginning and yet you go on. Perhaps I could go on with my story, end it and begin another ... Dig my nails into the cracks and drag myself forward with my fingers.'[3]

'This Way for the Gas, Ladies and Gentlemen' begins with what could be a parody of Eden. In this place everyone is naked, men and women, drained, it seems at first, of sexuality. Perversely, this appears to be a place of plenty. The narrator is eating fresh white bread, along with bacon. Others eat sardines and tomato salad. There is evaporated milk. He and his companions speak of the immediate possibility of champagne, shoes, a shirt. He receives regular mail from home, being distressed when no letters arrive for two months – this in contrast to the Jews who can neither send nor receive mail unless as part of some fraud to deceive relatives. What kind of place is this, then? Yet just below them, on wooden bunks, are nude men, smelling of excrement. A rabbi intones from a prayer book. 'Let him rave', says one of those eating, 'They'll take him to the oven that much sooner' (32). Life and death lie side by side. The physical gap between those with and those without is small but they could be inhabiting different universes.

The protagonist, it transpires, is one of those required to clear out the arriving transports and seize the goods of those on their way to the gas chambers. These are taken to 'Canada' where they are sorted through, but in the process it is possible to take what the Reich does not require, what the Reich does not regard as its due, its property. This is a story, in other words, about those who, because of their background, did not die, but who depended on a steady flow of Jews and others to secure their own well-being. And Tadeusz Borowski was one of them. This story was not simply witness, it was confession, at first on behalf of himself but eventually on behalf of mankind in that an emerging political consciousness ultimately defers to an absurdist view as the implications of the camp expand out into a world whose contingency stands suddenly exposed.

When a train approaches they are required to run to meet it. Those arriving find a 'cheerful little station, very much like any other provincial railway stop' (33). From the German point of view this is offered as a momentary reassurance, like the trucks marked with red crosses. It is a means of control, of preventing panic, though its irony is of a piece with a place in which human instincts are inverted. Those from Canada offer their own reassurances to the terrified men and women who tumble, exhausted, from the cattle trucks but only because it is 'the camp law: people going to their death must be deceived to the very end. This is the only permissible form of charity' (37).

A little further down the line is where 'they load freight for Birkenau: supplies for the construction of the camp, and people for the gas chambers. Trucks drive around, load up lumber, cement, people' (33–4). In this place people are freight. Trucks are given more agency than those they carry. Later, trucks are described as starting up, quite as if they were animate, in control of their own destiny. The SS officers, meanwhile, discuss their families as they await the families they will break up, some to die immediately, others later. They stroll 'majestically'. They are 'majestic' (36). The words are the narrator's. He is, in truth, closer to them than to the doomed he will shortly confront.

And when the train arrives, he and his fellow prisoners are required to climb on board and remove dead children he himself describes as 'naked little monsters with enormous heads and bloated bodies' whom they carry 'like chickens, holding several in each hand' (39). Yet even as he deploys the reductive language of the camp, as he tries to harden his heart to stone, he finds himself wracked with contradictory and largely inexplicable feelings. 'Are we good people', he asks, not because he is confederate with the Germans but 'because I am furious, simply furious with these people – furious because I must be here because of them. I feel no pity. I am not sorry they're going to the gas chamber' (40), the 'them' being Jews who, perversely, become responsible for their own deaths. He feels in a limbo. 'I am not sure', he thinks to himself, 'if all of this is actually happening, or if I am dreaming' (41).

When another train rolls in and is unloaded, a woman tries to join those marked for a temporary reprieve by pretending she is not the mother of the child who tries to follow her, calling out to her, begging not to be abandoned. To the approval of an SS man she is struck by a Russian prisoner who shouts at her, 'you bloody Jewess! So you're running away from your own child! I'll show you, you whore!' Woman and child are both thrown on to the truck to be taken away and gassed. Moral affront is taken by a man with no moral sense and who himself lives only on the whim of those who see him as an agent of their own power. It is scarcely surprising that the narrator has lost his sense of the real, that he now feels a rising terror and runs away, hiding from his pursuer, even then watching as a one-legged young woman, shouting in pain, is thrown on top of a pile of corpses while a young girl runs round and round in a circle until she is knocked down and shot. He vomits before retreating to his barracks where he lies and consoles himself with the thought that 'others may be dying, but one is somehow alive, one has enough food, enough strength to work ...' The ellipses are Borowski's own. Ellipses, it seems, are a mark of Holocaust literature.

The thought has something of a mantra about it, a means of blanking out thought. Yet even as he offers himself this spare consolation he thinks of those who arrive expecting everything, not knowing what awaits them, not knowing they will die and that experienced professionals 'will probe into every recess of their flesh, will pull the gold from under their tongue and the diamonds from the uterus and the colon' (48). By contrast, the SS seem 'dignified, businesslike'. For several days, he confesses, 'the entire camp will live off this transport' which, by universal consent, 'was a good, rich transport' (49). Language, it seems, is mutating.

Written so soon after the events it describes, as Borowski was held in a displaced persons camp, this 'story' seems hardly to have had time to be processed through the memory. Indeed, though offered as a fiction it is indistinguishable from the accounts offered by those who sought to bear witness, who wrote what they saw precisely because it defied belief. The space between writer and narrator figure appears to have been all but closed. Many wrote of the compromises necessary to survival. Borowski acknowledges something more. Primo Levi would write of his luck in being sent late to Auschwitz but Borowski had several advantages, if the word could be said to be appropriate to anyone sent to that place. He was not Jewish. He did not have to fight for food or clothing. He knew that if disease did not kill him, or an SS officer exercising his absolute power, he would survive. But he knew, too, that his survival depended on the death of others, that a slackening of the killing rate would threaten his well-being and that survival was thus morally tainted. The story's title is a sardonic reminder of the circus of death in which he was required to play the role of clown. Here the surreal was real.

The second story composed while he was at the camp near Munich, 'A Day at Harmenz', seems more clearly crafted. It opens with a lyrical invocation of the natural world, the setting against which the harsh daily drama of work was conducted:

> The shadows of the chestnut trees are green and soft. They
> sway gently over the ground, still moist after being newly
> turned over, and rise up in sea-green cupolas scented with the
> morning freshness … The trees form a high palisade along the
> road, their crowns dissolve into the hue of the sky … The grass,
> green and velvety, is still silvered with dew, but the earth
> steams in the sun. (50)

The word 'green' appears three times in the first ten lines. It stands in contrast to the burned bones dumped by a truck, and the blood-stained bodies of the men who labour to lay railway lines or clear ditches. Nonetheless, though the action is punctuated with pointless acts of violence and by threats, for the most part this is a story of what seems a normal day in an abnormal world, as the men avoid what work they can, keep an eye open for the kapo and still more the passing SS and haggle between one another over food or articles to trade. Loyalties are forged, broken, re-forged. A woman in a nearby farm slips them food, especially Ivan, who has plainly caught her eye, though she has to watch him beaten when he accepts the blame for the stealing of a goose.

Once again, the narrator, Tadek, wants for nothing, even passing his food to others. He is vulnerable, as are they all, to sudden and irrational denunciations, but to an extent he is an observer.

A selection threatens but there is never any sense that it will involve him. There are Jews amongst them, one a man called Becker who, at a previous camp, had had his fellow Jews beaten and even hanged his own son for stealing. "'I'll tell you this in parting'" Tadek remarks,

> 'I sincerely hope that you, along with your scabs and sores, go straight to the chimney!' ... 'You know the story about the wolf ...' I smiled spitefully at my own wit and walked away humming a popular camp tango called 'Cremo'. The Jew's empty eyes, suddenly void of all content, stared fixedly into space. (55)

It is difficult to know what to make of such a passage. If Tadek is a character, he also seems close kin to Tadeusz. (In Polish, 'Tadek' is the diminutive form of 'Tadeusz'.) The casual cruelty implied by a 'wit' that turns on the total vulnerability of the one and the at least limited immunity of the other stands exposed by the writer himself. There is no self-accusation in the text. The story alone shapes that accusation. Yet later in the story he hands the man food, the gesture almost neutralised by the language with which the offer is made: '"Okay, Jew, come on up and eat. And when you've had enough, take the rest with you to the cremo" ... I looked at Becker. His eyes were half-closed and, like a blind man, he was vainly groping for the board to pull himself on to the bunk' (80–1) – just as Beckett's character would speak of dragging himself forward with his fingers. These are the final words of the story which thus ends with the plight of the condemned Jew, as it does with the moral equivocation of a man who hardens himself against what he sees even as he makes a gesture that might seem to suggest the survival of feelings that otherwise no longer seem to have a place in this distorted world.

A defining characteristic of Borowski's work lies in this sudden change of direction, a kind of vertigo that is the product of his privileged condition and the hopeless fate of so many, the pastoral beauty of his surroundings and the brute fact of slaughter. In 'The People Who Walked On' he once again describes eating well and receiving mail, as though obliged to repeat the news of his privilege. In his world doctors dress wounds, rather than simply supervise genocide. Everything that is missing from those other eye-witness accounts to which we have accustomed ourselves, is here supplied, though he knows, and explains, that this tenuous civility exists over a void. In the middle of the night, as lamps glow, suddenly 'there would be a burst of flame above the wood ... and terrible human screams'. His 'body trembled and rebelled' (85). He describes the building of a soccer pitch, with green lawns and vegetable gardens, only to explain that between two throw-ins in a match three thousand people had gone to their deaths. For him, the cold mornings 'meant merely a refreshing pause before a hot summer day'; by contrast, the women at Birkenau, twenty yards away, who 'had been standing at roll-call since five in the morning, turned blue from the cold' (85–6). Was Anne Frank among them? Were Fania Fénelon and Alma Rosé? In a later story he describes the rest of the camp standing to attention while 'we, the lucky spectators from another planet, lean out of the window and gaze at the world' (100).

Yet what he sees has the same admixture of beauty and horror that seems to have characterised his experience in the camps. Thus he recalls a young woman and her mother who were forced to undress preparatory to being killed. The young woman was so beautiful that it transfixed the Oberscharführer who was to lead her to her death. What followed was a bizarre admixture of tenderness and cruelty. Telling her to be brave, he held her hand with one of his own and with the other covered her eyes. 'The sizzling and the stench of the burning fat and the heat gushing out of the pit terrified her. She jerked back. But he gently bent her head forward, uncovering her back. At that moment the Oberscharführer fired, almost without aiming. The man pushed the woman into the flaming pit, and as she fell he heard her terrible, broken scream' (96). The narrator adds nothing because there is nothing to add. 'Your memory retains only images', he confesses (97). One of these was of this young woman, head bent forward, standing over the flaming pit: beauty, ugliness, life, death fused in a single image.

Borowski's fiancée, arrested at the same time as him, ended up in the Frauenkonzentrationslager at Auschwitz and he was able to write to her. 'Auschwitz, Our Home' effectively reproduces one side of that correspondence and in the process, like 'The People Who Walked On', describes life in the camp. Her present reality he can imagine but his most vivid memory of her is of the back of her head seen at Gestapo headquarters, an ironic echo of the young woman who plunged into the flames. He cannot recall her face. Memory is not a simple recording device. It registers images according to a logic beyond interrogation.

The irony now is that he is training as a medical orderly in a camp in which doctors are at the heart of a conspiracy against those they are sworn to tend to. In barracks number 10, the experimental block, where Fania Fénelon briefly found herself, women are injected with typhoid by 'a man in a green hunting outfit and a gay little Tyrolean hat decorated with many brightly shining sports emblems, a man with the face of a kindly satyr. A university professor' (108). As ever in his work green is simultaneously a sign of hope and death, the flash of silver a marker of cruelty, shining, as it does, from the immaculate uniforms of those who preside over chaos.

The camp has its entertainments. There is an orchestra; there are boxing matches. There is even a brothel available to those with any influence. There is a green hedge along the wall, a strip of green lawn along the edge of the barracks but these are mere distractions and deceits. The truth glows in the sky. The truth is a fundamental impotence and absurdity. He recounts an occasion on which ten thousand men returned to the camp from a work detail, to the beat of a march. At that moment several trucks full of naked women arrived. They were on their way to the gas chambers and called out for help: 'And they rode slowly past us – the ten thousand silent men – and then disappeared from sight. Not one of us made a move, not one of us lifted a hand', not the Borowski who accuses himself along with his companions: 'us'.

For George Steiner, the Jews were victims of something more than Nazi depravity. They were victims of hope. Here, surely, was the root of Beckett's vision of a deep absurdity, born out of the refusal to accept a profound disorder, a lack of imminent purpose. Borowski found the same irony in the camps. 'We lived for a better world to come when all this is over', he wrote. 'Do you really think that, without the hope that such a world is possible, that the rights of man will be restored again, we could stand the concentration camp even for one day?' Yet he felt with equal passion that

> It is that very hope that makes people go without murmur to the gas chambers, keeps them from risking a revolt, paralyses them into dumb inactivity. It is hope that breaks down family ties, makes mothers renounce their children, or wives sell their bodies for bread, or husbands kill. It is hope that compels man to hold on for one more day of life, because that day may be the day of liberation. Ah, and not even the hope for a different, better world, but simply for life, a life of peace and rest. Never before in the history of mankind has hope been stronger than man, but never also has it done so much harm as it has in this war, in this concentration camp. We were never taught how to give up hope, and this is why today we perish in gas chambers. (121)

It is hard to find such a statement in the work of those others who set themselves to witness. For the implications of his statement extend beyond the circumstances which prompted them. Hope, he goes on to suggest, is a product of youth and not experience. Yet he also set himself to be a witness, to harness his memories. He himself wished to kill one or two men, he confessed, simply to throw off the concentration camp mentality, the effects of continual subservience, of watching people being beaten and murdered. He was sure, though, that he would be marked for life. Nonetheless, like Beckett, he was caught in the paradox of writing about unmeaning. 'I do not know', he wrote, 'whether we shall survive, but I like to think that one day we shall have the courage to tell the world the whole truth and call it by its proper name' (122). What that truth or that name might be is not immediately clear, beyond testifying to genocide. That he chose Communism is both explicable and dismaying given the depth and breadth of the gulags but he died before their extent was truly known, still hoping it seems, and hence still betraying himself with that hope. His memories were shaped to a purpose but what that purpose was beyond accusing is not clear. For the absurdity he describes can surely not be contained by the wire surrounding the Auschwitz camps as if that place were truly aberrant and the human instincts revealed there unique.

These are called stories, and they contain such, but they are surely not fictions in the sense of pure inventions. Everybody in the camps, he explains, told stories, sometimes from books, sometimes from life. This was a place full of Sheherazades. Usually those stories were set outside the camp but those are not the stories he chooses to repeat. The stories he records often have a point which lies less in the stories themselves than in the response they provoke. When a man recalls a Jew who had been forced to send his own father into the gas chamber but who subsequently retrieved family photographs from that father's coat pocket, Borowski adds, 'We laughed'. There is frequently something uncomfortable not only in the brutal directness of the events recalled but in the response of those among whom he counts himself. Whatever else he is concerned to do, absolving himself seems not to be on his agenda.

The stories within stories, meanwhile, slowly build a portrait of an increasingly unreal world. Indeed, at one point he observes that if 'the barrack walls were suddenly to fall away, many thousands of people, packed together, would remain suspended in mid-air. Such a sight would be more gruesome than the medieval paintings of the Last Judgement' (130). And that reference to art is a clue to his own sensibility as he professes to distrust and even despise a history of civilisation which forgets the many who were enslaved, tortured, worked to death, and celebrates those who thus earned time and privilege to write poetry and plays. No longer a Platonist, seeing the things of this world as a reflection of the ideal, he insists that there 'can be no beauty if it is paid for by human injustice, nor truth that passes over injustice in silence, nor moral virtue that condones it' (132).

In other words, he is expressing distrust of the very fiction-making process in which he is involved, the idea that suffering can or should be transposed into art, which perhaps explains the porous membrane between fact and fiction in his work. He is not about the business of transcendence and in this 'story' ('Auschwitz, Our Home') in particular, which presents itself as a letter, fiction-making defers to philosophical argument. It is possible to detect his move towards

Communism, not least in his account of how German industry was involved in the construction of Auschwitz (it settled, he notes, for 30 percent of its costs, evidently desperate to curry favour), benefiting from the availability of labour for the factories it established alongside the crematoria and beneath the smoke of burning bodies.

All of which is a little strange, perhaps, in what is supposedly a letter to his fiancée but this 'Letter' is in effect a history and a manifesto. It is written out of the fear that 'if the Germans win the war, what will the world know about us?' The fear is not that they will determine what history records but, more significantly, 'we shall be forgotten, drowned out by the voices of the poets, the jurists, the philosophers, the priests. They will produce their own beauty, virtue and truth. They will produce religion' (132). In other words, the oblivion he fears is not merely being written out of history but being subsumed in a culture constructed on the base of suffering which either ignores that suffering or accommodates it to a sense of aesthetics, ethics, values which find no place for those whose lives are forfeit or regarded as of no value.

There are other memories, however, that sustain him. Since he and his fiancée are separated it is only in their memories that they can meet. As he notes, 'even if nothing is left to us but our bodies on the hospital bunk, we shall still have our memories and our feelings' (134). After his earlier remarks, this has the air of a desperate piety, a sentimentality which sits uneasily in the context of his unblinking attitude to a deceptive hope. Indeed, there is a dark current to his work that derives less from his own suffering than from what he witnesses. When he reports a conversation with a member of the *Sonderkommando*, a Jew, who explains that they now start the ovens by putting the heads of young children together and lighting their hair – a joke, as it seems – the narrator remarks, 'this is a monstrous lie, a grotesque lie, like the whole camp, like the whole world' (142). The boundary which he had once assumed circumscribed this place now dissolves until the camp becomes metonymic.

In 'Silence', he tells the story of the beating to death of a man after the camp has been liberated by the Americans. Appealed to by an American officer to hand over members of the SS or collaborators, they applaud. As soon as he leaves, however, they trample the man into the ground. There is no normality to which they can return, having learned truths not to be so easily unlearned.

In 'The January Offensive', a story set in West Germany in the first year after the end of the war, he reports a conversation with a Polish poet in which a group of men explain the lessons they have learned in the camps. 'We said that there is no crime that a man will not commit in order to save himself ... concentration-camp existence ... had taught us that the whole world is really like the concentration camp ... The world is ruled by neither justice nor morality; crime is not punished nor virtue rewarded, one is forgotten as quickly as the other' (168).

It is hard not to read his final stories in the knowledge of the death towards which he was surely already accelerating. He recalls that those about to die had begged those watching them to remember what they saw and 'to tell the truth about mankind to those who do not know it' (175), but later as he sat at his desk wondering which of them to recall, which to pull back into a living world from the realm of the dead, he was troubled, as he confessed, 'by one persistent thought – that I have never been able to look also at myself' (176), except, of course, that he had. For through all his stories we learn, sometimes obliquely and sometimes directly, of a man who was not only aware of guilt and complicity but of the sheer contingency of existence. There is an apocalyptic tone to his work, perhaps most clear in 'The World of Stone', in which the postwar world around him seems liable to 'suddenly float into the air and then drop, all in a tangle' human bodies sucked into a huge whirlpool, 'twisted lips open in terror ... down the gutter ... like water into a sewer' (178–9).

And so, he takes another sheet of blank paper and struggles to discover some connection with those around him, some tender feeling even for his wife, the woman to whom he had written in Auschwitz and who will bear him a child. With 'a tremendous intellectual effort' he attempts 'to grasp the true significance of the events, things and people I have seen. For I intend', he explains, 'to write a great, immortal epic, worthy of this unchanging, difficult world chiselled

out of stone' (180). There would be no such epic, unless it be the
stories in which, so soon after his escape from hell, he tried to express
this stone world. Instead, this man who escaped the gas chamber
chose gas to commit suicide. What did that gesture mean? Were the
memories he pulled back from the abyss finally too much to bear? Is it
a sentimentality to suggest that he thereby joined those he had
watched, himself seemingly immune? Was he hardening his heart to
stone because God had done no less?

In some senses Tadeusz Borowski presents the most troubling
of witnesses. During his time at Auschwitz he did not suffer as others
did. His relationship with the Jews was profoundly ambiguous. Yet he
pursued the implications of what he saw to the point at which (his
apparent flirtation with the Party aside) he stared into a darkness
which finally seemed all-enveloping. Even as he appears a link
between Kafka and Beckett, he distrusted the very form in which he
worked, paralysed, finally, by the need to recall and the ultimate
futility in doing so, the need to bear witness but the absurdity thus
revealed. His last, surely ironic gesture, whether expressing solidarity
or despair, meant that he was underlining the central truth he chose
to take from his experiences, namely that the camps were not,
ultimately, aberrant, but that they had revealed man to himself while
art, so easily enrolled, so eager to reshape experience into exemplary
gesture, deceived in its implication of transcendence, its offer to
supply the very coherence lacking from life.

Arthur Miller, that most liberal of writers, nonetheless,
confronted with the crimes outlined at the Frankfurt trials of the
Auschwitz guards, asked, 'If man can murder his fellows, not in
passion but calmly ... can any civilization be called safe from the
ravages of what lies waiting in the heart of man?'⁴ For Borowski,
nothing, finally, could 'keep the world from swelling and bursting like
an over-ripe pomegranate, leaving behind but a handful of grey, dry
ashes' (179). Nor, surely, was there any need to ask of what those
ashes were composed. On the final page of 'The World of Stone' he
describes himself sitting at his desk, watching the lights of a house
being switched off one by one and feeling a terrible disenchantment
mounting within him. But since the world had not blown away on

355

that day, he pulled his long-abandoned papers from the drawer, desperate to find some meaning, some significance, some purpose in his memories, in his fragmentary records of experiences only a few years behind him. Evidently, on 1 July 1951, he felt either that that meaning would always evade him or that it was too painful to bear.

In 1995, the Swedish poet and author Barbro Karlén, in a television broadcast from Amsterdam, claimed to be the re-incarnation of Anne Frank. It was a claim she repeated in her autobiographical book *And the Wolves Howled*. Karlén was born in Sweden in 1954, to non-Jewish parents. She published her first book of poetry at the age of twelve. It became a best-seller. More books followed, nine by the age of seventeen, but later, after a personal crisis, she changed career, joining the mounted police.

Though *And the Wolves Howled* was described as a novel, she claimed that it had been taken directly from her life. Unsurprisingly, it prompted angry rejections, not least by a man called Binjamin Wilkomirski who had himself emerged as a key figure in Holocaust literature and who was seen as in a unique position to make a judgement about an account which supposedly reached back into childhood, albeit one which, in the case of Barbro Karlén, was not her own. He regarded her as 'simply disturbed', and dismissed her claim and the book as a fraud.

In February, 1998, Anne Karpf hailed a book by a Holocaust survivor. Herself a second-generation survivor, she praised it as one of the great books to have emerged from the camps. She was not alone in doing so. Daniel Goldhagen, whose book *Hitler's Willing Executioners* had sought to broaden the condemnation of Germany's wartime crimes, saw it as a masterpiece. He, in common with many others, found it deeply moving. Arnost Lustig, a survivor, writing in the *Washington Times*, thought it would become one of the five or ten lasting books about the Holocaust. Jonathan Koozol, in *The*

Nation, thought it so morally significant that praise could only demean its purity. In one go, its author was seen as standing comparison with Primo Levi, Elie Wiesel and Anne Frank. A child at the time he had suffered in Majdanek and, in common with Fénelon, Levi and Wiesel, in Birkenau, the author had now reached back to assemble the broken memories of another time and place in an effort not only to explain the traumatising impact of his experiences but to understand himself, to restore a sense of a true identity. Like the protagonist of Sebald's *Austerlitz*, in the immediate aftermath of war his past had been erased, placed, as he and Austerlitz had been, with a family which concealed from him both his true name and his Jewish past. In other words, he was reclaiming something more than a sense of himself. He was rediscovering his faith and, though recapitulating wounding events, restoring a damaged psyche. Only slowly had the truth of those lost days come back to him, and then only in tantalising fragments from which he had to construct a narrative. That, indeed, was the explanation for the book's title, *Fragments*.

After the war the languages he learned were, he observed, never his. They were, he confessed, 'only imitations of other people's speech'.[1] This statement, which appears on the very first page of his book, was, it turned out, an intimation of a truth that would take some time to emerge.

The book, written by a man who believed his name to be Binjamin Wilkomirski, had first appeared in Switzerland, in 1995. The following year it was awarded the National Jewish Book Award for autobiography while in 1997 the *Jewish Quarterly* rewarded it with a prize for non-fiction. Other honours followed. Fifty years after the war, a truth was being told, not unique, to be sure, but one which readers found deeply affecting, not least because it was a story told as if from the point of view of that bewildered child struggling to make sense of the things happening to him, deprived of his family, deprived of any logical or emotional grid against which to plot his apparently random experiences.

It had plainly taken him a lifetime to come to terms with what had happened, even to see a connection between himself and events that seemed to exist in another realm, part dream, part brutal reality. But now connections began to be made. In Israel, a film called *Wanda's List* was shown on television. It featured Wilkomirski searching for his origins. The film was drawn to the attention of a man called Yakov Maroto who had lost his son, Michael Benjamin, in Majdanek. He became convinced that Wilkomirski was that son and contacted him. He faxed a reply: 'For more than 50 years I have lived without parents, and now – could it be that I have found you, my father? Has He made a miracle?'[2] There were, he thought, real connections. A miracle indeed.

In September 1997, on another continent, members of the Wilbur family eagerly awaited Wilkomirski's arrival in their Manhattan home. Like many American survivor names, Blake Eskin explains (himself a member of the same family by marriage), their current one was an invention. Before landing in America they had been called Wilkomirski and they came, like Binjamin, from Riga. They had read *Fragments* and had been moved by it. In their case, however, it was written by someone who was possibly a member of their family, like many others scattered to the winds by the forces of history, though the name was not an uncommon one. That name was not Jewish but was itself a cover to conceal a Jewish identity. They were, as far as they knew, the only Wilkomirskis in Riga where the family had spoken Yiddish. Binjamin's own childhood language, they learned from his book, had been seeded with Yiddish.

Wilkomirski responded to a letter from Eskin's mother, explaining that his own researches had turned up evidence of what seemed to be the family, including an address in Riga that did, indeed, coincide with one that had been occupied by members of the family. The connection seemed to be firming up. The family started sending him details of their history. The letterhead of his initial reply listed the '*BWJ-Archive* on Special Aspects of Contemporary Jewish History in Europe and the Near East', the 'Holocaust Library and Documentation' and the 'Research Site on Polish-Jewish Children of the Shoah'. It seemed clear that writing the book had not merely addressed a private problem but opened up his concern with others like himself. For her part, Eskin's mother began calling him 'cousin'. He may have been looking for some sense of authenticity, but so were they, so long removed from the place of their birth.

Eskin had come to Wilkomirski's book by way of his reading of Anne Frank and Jerzy Kosinski's *The Painted Bird*. Only in *Fragments*, however, was there an account of life in the camp and he was struck by what seemed to him its primal power, the disjointed sense of self, the violence. Wilkomirski joined the family in America at a benefit for the Holocaust Museum.

Who was he? That had been an unending question. When he recalled his early years, with great difficulty, in a series of dislocated images, he seemed to have no secure name and, indeed, no language. His account begins with a startling sentence: 'I have no mother tongue, nor a father tongue either. My language has its roots in the Yiddish of my eldest brother, Mordechai, overlaid with Babel-babble of an assortment of children's barracks in the Nazi death camps in Poland.'[3] Later, he would lose his language entirely, as if it had been seared away in the heat of terror. Indeed, it seems, perhaps, that it was that recollection of silence which set him on his way to writing, in that in later life he read a book about another young boy who had lost his speech in that same Poland, though not in the camps. The book was *The Painted Bird* by Jerzy Kosinski, a book which itself picked up an award and whose reviews praised it for its portrait of Nazi brutalities. It would, one reviewer insisted, stand beside Anne Frank's diary. It was a novel but, as its author confessed to his publisher, and repeated in interviews, it was based on his own experiences, a fact which gave it an additional force.

Kosinski was another man of uncertain identity. He was born in Poland and lived for a time in what appears to have been the same village from which Arthur Miller's family had set out for America in the 1880s, and, indeed, the two men became acquaintances if not exactly friends. The family name was Lewinkopf, transformed into Kosinski when necessity meant the advisability of concealing the family's Jewishness. For a while, like the Frank family, they went into hiding but ultimately decided to hide in plain view, all playing roles, pretending to be Catholics, filling their house with crucifixes, adopting a false name.

The Painted Bird recounts the searing experiences of a boy who becomes detached from his family, wandering the Polish countryside, a victim of superstitious and casually violent peasants. His is a medieval world, commanded by sadists and characterised by sexual predators. He suffers alone, never really accepted, living on sufferance, at physical and mental risk. When he drops a missal in church he is thrown into a sewage pit. Though he is unable to swim he is pitched into a river. When he runs a fever, he is buried to the neck in the earth while crows peck at his face. At first he watches the involuted sexual practices of those among whom he lives, and then himself becomes party to them. Marauders rape all the women in a village and he recalls the assaults in detail. He encounters his parents but does not recognise them for what they are. For some time he is struck dumb, literally unable to articulate what he has seen. It was not until he arrived in the United States, it seems, that Kosinski was able to reclaim a past he had previously filed away in his memory. The book, indeed, was, apparently, in part a product of his new sense of security. He had lived first under the Nazis and then the Soviets. Now, at last, he stood on solid ground and could revisit his past without succumbing to it.

His publishers were uncertain about the book, afraid both of the possibility of libel suits by those pictured, and of prosecution for obscenity. Nonetheless, its sheer force persuaded them and it was enthusiastically received. The paperback quoted from a number of its reviews, including that in the *New York Herald-Tribune*: 'No book has delved so deeply into the "Nazi mentality" in the truest sense and because there is enlightenment to be gained from its flame-dark pages, it deserves as wide a readership as possible.' Elie Wiesel praised it in the *New York Times*.

Perhaps it is not surprising that Binjamin Wilkomirski found inspiration in the book. Here was another young boy who had experienced extremes of deprivation. He had not, to be sure, been confined in a concentration camp but he had been shocked into silence. He had had his identity and religion changed. He had waited many years before he felt able to explore what he had every reason to suppress. Both had witnessed extremes of cruelty, seemingly unmotivated. Both had re-encountered parents and not recognised them. Beyond that, there was the seeming coincidence of the fact that Kosinski had spent some time in Switzerland, where Wilkomirski now lived, and where he had been handed parts of Kosinski's book to read before it was published. As he remarked, Kosinski 'was the first person ever to write about children and their experiences when they were little in Poland. Very matter-of-fact, just as he saw it, whether he understood it or not. It was the most shocking thing I had ever read' (59).

Fragments traces the young Wilkomirski's odyssey (he thought he was born in 1938 or 1939) from what seems to have been Riga in Latvia, where he believed he had been born, though it might, he concedes, have been southern Estonia. Though he reached back to these times through a kind of fog he was, he insisted, blessed with a photographic memory, recalling a saying: 'He who remembers nothing gambles away his future', adding 'If you don't remember where you came from, you will never really be able to know where you're going' (377).

His life, he acknowledges, began with a jumble of images and in order to reconstruct that life he needed 'to give up the ordering logic of grown-ups; it would', he added, 'only distort what happened'. After all, the fact that he was alive was itself 'the living contradiction to logic and order' (378). It was this quality of surrender to an emotional coherence that seems to have explained something of the book's impact.

The opening section recalls a scene during a Riga winter but this quickly defers to a suffocating blackness lit by flashes of memory, beginning with a man seemingly being executed, though the child that was Wilkomirski is unable to perceive it as such. It is, perhaps, his father, though there is no certainty for there is no emotional charge to the account, no sense that this man is intimately connected to him.

Then he recalls being at a station with a woman and travelling with her to Switzerland, jumping ahead in time like Faulkner's Benjy in *The Sound and the Fury* following an associational logic as he feels the retreat of danger, the danger that had characterised the previous images, though nothing is drained of danger since it is adults he associates with his vulnerability. He is on his way to a Swiss orphanage but even while there he is liable to flashbacks. For a moment, indeed, in his fractured narrative, he is back in the more distant past, in a farmhouse with his oldest brother in a Polish forest, though he is unsure how many brothers he had. These are what he calls 'Shards of recollection ... like flakes of feldspar in a great rockscape of childhood memories ... the ones I'm halfway sure about' (395). Into this world intrudes a soldier who seems to rape the farmer's wife, though as a child he is able to do no more than narrate what he imagines himself to see.

Then it is winter and first his brothers and then he are taken away and his journey begins, a journey by train, hence his thoughts of a train journey to Switzerland. Indeed, even as he arrives at what he believes to have been the Majdanek concentration camp, he is back, in his mind, in Switzerland before being drawn back to the camp and his initiation into its strange ways. His mind, it seems, is a patchwork quilt.

The camp is a series of gothic horrors. Two babies are thrown into the barracks, their fingers reduced to bone where they have been eating them. A boy is killed with a punch. Rats dart out of a dead woman's stomach as rats had haunted Kosinski's boy in *The Painted Bird*. In both books dogs are the source of fear. There comes a moment when Wilkomirski is taken to see his mother, as the protagonist of Kosinski's account was suddenly introduced to his parents. Lice pour over his face. When a new boy needs to go to the toilet in the night-time, he advises him to relieve himself where he is. The next day the boy is killed for his actions. Sticks are pushed into penises and then broken off. He climbs over the body of a dead man, his feet sinking in as later he climbs over the dead bodies of the two babies, their skulls smashed open. He had, he explained, never been able to free himself of this mental picture.

Now the memories are interleaved with others, not of the Swiss orphanage but of one in Cracow where he recognised one of those who had shared his fate in the camp. In the German edition she is named as Karola. The name was changed at her request in the English edition to Mila. She had been saved from a selection when an SS man had thrown her and her mother onto a pile of corpses. As a result they became non-people, no longer on the lists and able, therefore, to survive. In Cracow they were 'living among the living, yet we didn't belong with them – we were actually the dead, on stolen leave, accidental survivors who got left behind in life' (440).

In the final days at the camp he had been hidden by some women, burrowing down under clothes, surviving when other children were rooted out and taken away. Someone had suddenly recognised him and called out a name, Binjamin Wilkomirski, though whether it was his name or not was unclear to him at the time. Released from the camp, in a way and for a reason he cannot understand, he finds himself in Cracow, in the orphanage but also begging on the street before what appears to be a pogrom.

Later, supposedly safe in Switzerland, he trusts no one, assuming that in some way this is a continuation of that earlier life. He hoards food, binds his feet with cloth when his shoes are removed to be dried. At school he is shown a picture of William Tell but assumes it is the portrait of an SS officer about to shoot a child. Thereafter, he learns about the Nazis in school and slowly begins to make sense of his memories, though a victim of self-doubt. Why, he asked himself, had he survived? He felt guilty about the boy he had surrendered to death. He had betrayed his mother by calling another by that name. He had left everyone to their fate.

Accordingly, he concealed his true background, ashamed of the madness and filth that had constituted his life. His foster parents in Switzerland instruct him to forget everything as if it had been no more than a dream. If he did speak out he was accused of lying. But, he insisted, 'How can I forget what I'm forced to think about every morning when I wake up, and every evening when I go to bed and try to stay awake as long as possible, for fear of the nightmares?' (493). The irony, however, was that, apparently, it was a dream. He had, indeed, been inventing it, for every word of his account, it turned out, was a lie. He was a fraud. His memories were stolen or invented. There was, indeed, no such person as Binjamin Wilkomirski.

And the book that had inspired him – Jerzy Kosinski's *The Painted Bird*? That, too, it turned out, was also a lie, if we take it to be an account of his own experiences. Far from being separated from his parents, Kosinski had lived with them, and been protected by them, throughout the war. And far from witnessing and being the focus of the startling events he describes, he had instead created a gothic chiller. The semi-pornographic and sadistic actions which he describes in such detail – the torture, sodomy, incest, bestiality – are pure inventions and matched the sado-masochism of the author who made a practice of visiting S and M bars in New York and physically assaulted at least one of his girlfriends. Indeed it transpired that the text was perhaps not entirely his own since 'editors' and 'translators' (he wrote it first in Polish) seemed to have contributed.

Also, for a book that was hailed as offering a particular insight into the Nazis, there was a peculiar absence at its heart. The Nazis play no more than a walk-on part. At the centre of the book lie the Polish peasantry who are presented as living a brute existence, unamenable to moral values, irremediably violent and cruel. If Wilkomirski did, indeed, find inspiration in Kosinski's book, the inspiration seems to have taken the form of a licence to invent, to summon up gothic images that are a product not of a personal experience of the Holocaust but of an imagination seemingly well calculated to provoke the response he wished.

The central figure in *The Painted Bird* seems to exist largely through the blows he receives and the violence he observes. He has nothing so positive as a name or a precise religion, though there are references to church services. He is not, therefore, Jewish, only suspected of being such, that or a gypsy. He quickly abandons all evidences of civilisation, shedding the skin of civility as he grows in experience if not necessarily wisdom.

Jerzy Kosinski was a Jew who at first denied his Jewishness. When Elie Wiesel contacted him, ever sensitive to works set at the time of the Holocaust which are silent about the Jews, he insisted first that he was not Jewish and then that he had thought that a book about a Jew would not have been well received in Poland His identities constantly shifted as if he were afraid to be defined, to be fully known. The false self of *The Painted Bird* was in that sense an expression of his inner uncertainty. The tabula rasa that is the protagonist of his later novel *Being There*, a man onto whom others project their fantasies and needs, seems close to Kosinski himself, whoever that self might be.

Kosinski subsequently published a booklet in which he spoke of the area which exists between language and action and suggested that while a characterisation of *The Painted Bird* as non-fiction might be convenient for purposes of classification it would not be easily justified, a phrase which itself stretches language to transparency. He seemed, in other words, to be identifying a no man's land in which words need not come into alignment with fact. He dealt, he said, in symbols rather than speech. The silence of the character bespoke dissociation from 'something greater'. There was a break, he conceded, from what he called the 'wholeness' of the self. There is something fascinating in Kosinski's defence in that his own language seems to slide effortlessly towards unmeaning even as he makes a case for the insubstantiality of identity and the disengagement of word from referent.

But Wilkomirski, by contrast, had proof that he was telling the truth, not least in the form of Laura Grabowski, a Polish Jew, a child-survivor of Auschwitz-Birkenau who had been experimented on by Josef Mengele and was liberated to the same Cracow orphanage as Wilkomirski. She recognised him and wrote to him in 1997 after reading his book. The two met in Los Angeles in 1998 and performed together for the Child Holocaust Survivors Group of Los Angeles, she being a pianist and singer and he a clarinettist. Their reunion after so long was filmed by the BBC. The problem was that Laura Grabowski was not a Polish Jew, nor was she a child survivor, nor had she been in a concentration camp. She was born not in Poland but Washington State. She was Catholic and not Jewish. Nor, as it happened, was she Laura Grabowski. Her real name was Laurel Wilson. She had subsequently changed it to Lauren Stratford and under that name had published a book called *Satan's Underground: The Extraordinary Story of One Woman's Escape*. Escape from what? Satanic abuse. In this book she was not Polish, but American, and a survivor not of a concentration camp but of sexual abuse. The book invoked infanticide and rape. During her teenage years she had fabricated a number of stories of her own victimisation, practised self-mutilation and threatened suicide.

366

Under the name of Lauren Stratford she lectured and supported sexual abuse survivor groups. In seeking to defend herself against sceptics, she turned, interestingly, to Raul Hilberg's comment on Claude Lanzmann's *Shoah*:

> 'Where's the evidence?' you cry. I quote Raoul Hilberg, the
> great historian who spoke on Claude Lanzmann's epic film,
> *SHOAH: An Oral History of the Holocaust*. In speaking
> of the Nazi Germans and their hideous atrocities, Mr. Hilberg
> says, '... they did not copyright or patent their achievements,
> and they prefer obscurity'. This is also true of those who are the
> perpetrators of cult crimes. They do not copyright or patent
> their achievements, and they prefer obscurity.[4]

Ironically, Raul Hilberg had doubted Wilkomirski's story from the beginning.

Stratford/Grabowski persuaded a woman named Jen Rosenberg – whom she helped to run a website devoted to the Holocaust – to take a pair of pink shoes to Auschwitz in memory of Grabowski's friend Anna (recalled, too, by Wilkomirski), who had died there. Ms Rosenberg did precisely that, depositing them in the crematorium and reciting the Kaddish in memory. Unfortunately, there seems to have been no Anna, though Jen Rosenberg is inclined to believe that whether she existed or not is irrelevant since so many others did die. Falsity is swallowed up in a larger truth.

The transition from victim of ritual abuse to victim of the Nazis seems to have been virtually seamless. In validating someone else, Stratford/Grabowski validated herself. Having been exposed under one name she simply changed her name again, shape shifting from Lauren to Laura and from Stratford to Grabowski-Stratford and then Grabowski (only her social security number remaining constant), and though she did not this time write a book she did write a poem whose opening stanza reads:

> We who are child survivors of the Holocaust
> Have heard the word 'just' one too many times.
> We were just children, too young to remember.

We were just in hiding, not in a camp.

We were just sent to a strange country to keep us safe.

We were just in a ghetto.

We were just in a deportation camp, not in a death camp.

We were just in a death camp, but we survived.[5]

She signed it 'Laura Grabowski, Child Survivor of Auschwitz-Birkenau'. She was reborn, once again under a dark star. She had, she explained, remained silent for over fifty years, afraid to speak. Now she was no longer. She had found the company of other sufferers and through them her identity as a victim was affirmed. As for her confirmation of Wilkomirski's claims, she could not, she explained, offer names, dates or places, or hows, whys, whos and when, only 'memories of the heart' which depended not on evidence but a felt affinity.

As Laura Grabowski, she received funds from an organisation to support Holocaust survivors and from a German woman, the latter supposedly to enable her to visit Wilkomirski, flying first class, she explained, because of her medical condition. Like Wilkomirski, Laurel Wilson was illegitimate and later adopted. Her identity, it seemed, was fluid. She was exposed by a Christian magazine – *Cornerstone Magazine* – which had already exposed her earlier persona.

Doubts about Wilkomirski's account began early. His agent received a letter from Hanno Helbling, of the *Neue Zürcher Zeitung*, expressing concern. He offered no evidence but it was enough to send the agent back to Wilkomirski, who broke down in the face of what he saw as a refusal to listen to survivors. Asked by his publishers to write an Afterword that would address the worries, rather than provide evidence for his assertions, he insisted that his memory could not be wiped clean. He also chose to deny the identity under which he had been living. His birth certificate, which revealed him as Bruno Grosjean, was, he asserted, false. He was taking steps to 'have this identity annulled' (*The Wilkomirski Affair*, 496). 'Legally accredited truth is one thing', he suggests, 'the truth of a life another.' Quite what this last phrase meant was far from clear but it was enough to nerve his publishers to continue with publication and at first the book proved a considerable success.

The attacks began in 1998 with an article in a Swiss newspaper by Daniel Ganzfried, son of a man who had survived Auschwitz, and himself the author of a novel based on his father's experiences. Invited to write about Wilkomirski's book, a work which he found facile and sentimental, he agreed but quickly found dislike deepening to suspicion. He began to undertake simple research and in his article asserted that far from being Binjamin Wilkomirski, the author of *Fragments* was indeed Bruno Dössekker, the illegitimate child of Yvonne Grosjean, born in Biel (Switzerland) in 1941. He had spent time in a children's home and then been placed with a doctor and his wife. He had never been in a concentration camp. In an interview immediately after this article was published, 'Wilkomirski' suggested that 'The reader was always free to regard my book as literature or as a personal document' (131). He could not account for the discrepancy between his memories and available evidence, implying that he had been substituted for Bruno Dössekker who had subsequently emigrated and disappeared.

Raul Hilberg, meanwhile, found various sections of the book improbable to the point of being impossible. He was astounded that the American Holocaust Museum could have invited him to speak. Others rejected these attacks but in 1999 *The New Yorker* published an article called 'The Memory Thief',[6] while, in *Granta*, Elena Lappin exposed 'Wilkomirski's' account as a fabrication.[7] In April 1999, Stefan Maechler, a Swiss historian and an expert on anti-Semitism and Switzerland's wartime treatment of refugees, was commissioned by the Liepman Literary Agency, on behalf the publishers, to conduct an examination of Wilkomirski's story. The result was a thorough, and not altogether unsympathetic, analysis which nonetheless exposed the story as a complete fraud. He checked every detail both of the account offered in *Fragments* and of Bruno Grosjean. The supposed Wilkomirski had insisted that he had been given that identity only on arriving from Poland, being substituted for the real Bruno. In fact, they were one and the same. No part of his story stood up to inspection. He had never left Switzerland but had constructed his story from published accounts. Karola/Mila denied all knowledge of him. He was, in short, a fantasist, though Maechler was inclined to think that his own confused upbringing may have been the source of a text in which the central figure presents himself as victim, a person of uncertain identity bearing psychological wounds.

In retrospect, there are, perhaps, clues built into the text, from the confession at the beginning that he was only capable of 'imitations of other people's speech' (*The Wilkomirski Affair*, 377) through to his observation that images came to him 'like an unstoppable copying machine' (402). He confesses that in Switzerland he had 'tried to be a good actor' (61), simulating the good Swiss citizen, though it had not been clear to him at the time. Describing his drawings of the camp, seemingly inaccurate, he insisted that 'optical memories are often stored ... as mirror images' (69). Having begun by insisting on the reliability of his memory he then confesses to the inadequacy of that memory: 'My mind is empty, I've forgotten everything. I don't know who I am' (443). 'I have some shreds of memory still ... but their meaning is much less clear' (452). 'My memory stops here' (463). 'It's all a blur' (466). Nothing, he confesses, connects to anything else. Nothing is 'in its right place' (444). 'I don't know any more' (452). It is as though he wished to cancel out his statements as he makes them. Vagueness became an aesthetic, a perverse guarantee of authenticity to be contrasted with the fussy demands of the historian for whom facts took precedence over memory: 'I knew I could depend more on my memory than on what is said by the so-called historians, who never gave a thought to children in their research' (71).

In a lecture delivered to the World Congress of Psychotherapy in Vienna he explained, speaking of himself in the third person, that 'After more than a year of being therapeutically assisted in concentration exercises, a client who had very vague recollections initially recalls a scene that takes place outside a building in a city he associated with the name Riga and in which a man, possibly his father, is murdered' (81). As a result, he explained, the 'client' no longer suffered from migraines. Yet this is the same man who insisted on the integrity and intensities of his memories even as they were presented as vague images. The psychotherapist had apparently enabled him to bring order to his memories. These were not, he insisted, a product of therapy since he had first written them down as a child (though that account had been lost). What he was looking for, he explained, was understanding, relief from his confusions.

In July 1991 he had written down his memories and sent them to a friend, asking 'Can it have been like that?' (89), though the person to whom he sent the fax had no specialised knowledge that would have enabled him to decide. The fact was, 'Wilkomirski' explained in a letter, 'a child's memory orders events differently; sometimes it builds bridges between events where there are none, in order to hold on better to individual images' (103).

And what of Yakov Maroto, the man who thought he might be the father of the author of *Fragments* and was encouraged in this conviction by Wilkomirski, despite his description of the apparent death of that father in the opening passages of his book? A DNA test proved there was no relationship. And the Wilkomirskis in America who had thought he might be a cousin? They, too, were in for a cruel disappointment.

To Eva Hoffman, 'what Wilkomirski's imposture makes dramatically clear is how smoothly, pseudoempathy can glide into unseemly vicariousness; how imperceptibly "identification with the victim" can turn into exploitation and the violation of the one thing that ought never be thus used: the pain and death of others' (*After Such Knowledge*, 173–4).

And was it irrelevant that Wilkomirski was busy inventing a specious past at the very moment that Switzerland itself was caught in its own historical contradictions, as its fictions about neutrality, uninvolvement, wartime humanity began to come under increasing attention? It had, it now appeared, been altogether more co-operative with Nazi Germany than had been supposed, while its bank vaults contained not only money looted from half of Europe but deposits from Jews, now dead, which the banks refused to release until full documentation was provided by relatives who could no more be expected to flourish such than they could restore their lost relatives to life. Were Wilkomirski's claims embraced as readily as they were because a repressed collective guilt made challenging him something more than a matter of academic accuracy? Certainly the collective memory of the Swiss – which is to say the displacement of guilt into reassuring myth – might seem to have made them vulnerable to one who had seemingly suffered but ultimately found a haven in a country whose security rested on its apparent immunity to history.

But Wilkomirski was not alone in re-inventing himself, in inserting himself into someone else's history. Martin Gray's *For Those I Loved*, set partly in Treblinka and partly in the Warsaw ghetto, was deeply flawed and prompted a journalistic exposé. Monique Defonseca's *Misha: A Memoir of the Holocaust Years* told the story of a Jewish child put in the care of a Christian family who tries to find her parents when they are taken away to the east. She travels through Europe, getting by on her wits and pretending to be mute even living for a while with two wolves. She seeks her parents in Warsaw and later finds her way to a concentration camp and watches a Nazi rape and murder a Jewish woman. She joins up with another pack of wolves before returning to her native Belgium. Somewhat astonishingly, the book was praised by Elie Wiesel though another endorsement was withdrawn when Bette Greene (the American author of *Summer of My German Soldier*) decided that the book was unbelievable.

In 1978, the Spanish author Enric Marco published his autobiography, *Memoir of Hell*. It told of his arrest in Vichy France as a member of the Resistance, an arrest itself evidence of an alliance between Franco and Hitler. It then detailed his subsequent experiences in Mauthausen and Flossenburg concentration camps where he suffered, he explained, at the hands not of sadists but of brutal bureaucrats. His prisoner number was 6,448. After the war, under Franco, it had not been possible to speak out, but he did now offer himself as a witness, speaking in schools, telling his story to journalists and even addressing the Spanish parliament. On behalf of the survivors of the eight thousand Spaniards who had died in the camps, he pressed for compensation.

In May 2005, he was due to attend the sixtieth anniversary of the end of the war, with the prime minister José Luis Rodriguez, at

Mauthausen. However, at this point it was revealed that he had not been prisoner 6,448, had not been in the French resistance and had never been in a concentration camp. He had spent two years in Germany working in an armaments factory but had returned to Spain in 1943 and not been released, as he had claimed, by the Allies in 1945. He had, he suggested, only half-lied since he had been held by the Gestapo at one time. He had merely changed the scenario a little. The rest, however, he conceded, was a lie. He was sent home from the anniversary. Strangely, and in some degree in common with Wilkomirski, there were some camp survivors who, though shocked, nonetheless felt that he had done valuable work. The problem, of course, is that fake victims pollute the stream of true witness.

Nor were such false testimonies limited to those who were, or presented themselves as being, Jews. In 1993, Helen Demidenko published *The Hand That Signed The Paper*, supposedly based on the wartime experiences of her family, most of whom had been killed in the Ukraine by Jewish Communist Party officials, thus justifying Ukrainian involvement with the Nazis. The book won Australia's Miles Franklin Award and the Australian/Vogel Literary Award. It turned out that she had faked her Ukrainian background. Nor was her real name Demidenko. She was not the daughter of a Ukrainian taxi-driver, as she had claimed, but the Anglo-Australian Helen Darville. Parts of the book were also plagiarised. Far from being based, as she claimed, on her own memories, she stole her memories, and much else, from others.

And just for good measure, it was an Australian publisher that in 2003 published Norma Khouri's memoir, *Forbidden Love*, about a love affair between a Muslim and a Catholic in Jordan which results in an honour killing by the woman's father. It was voted one of Australia's one hundred favourite books. The book, she explained, was a gift to the memory of her friend on whom she had based it. It carried an acknowledgement to God for helping her to write it and see that it got into the right hands. God, however, seems to have had his eye off the ball since the book was a fraud. While claiming to have lived in Jordan, Khouri was in fact an American passport holder who had lived in Chicago from the age of three, finally leaving for Australia with a police and FBI record. There she lived under the name of Norma Albaqueen. A Chicago friend claimed that she had written an earlier book, unpublished, which detailed abuse by her father.

Here is less a chain of memory than a chain of lies. These are not false memories but fictions. These people are guilty of memory theft. They have appropriated history, shifting themselves to the centre of a grand narrative of human betrayal by themselves betraying. They lay claim to significance by presenting themselves as victims, beneficiaries of the suffering of others, basking in the sympathy of those for whom the Holocaust is a mystery to be respected for its motiveless ferocities and for whom its victims have earned a special place if not in heaven then in human attention.

In some sense these are simply fraudsters like any others. In an age of identity theft, when criminals appropriate the identity, and hence bank details, credit cards, of their victims, they no longer seem so strange. What is at stake is often money. They have all been financial beneficiaries of their frauds. Nor is it so unusual for people to present themselves as victims, itself a familiar tactic of those who wish to deny responsibility for their own lives or seek compensation for their supposed sufferings. In the twenty-first century, this is a commonplace of an increasingly litigious culture. But something else is in play. Money does not seem to have been primary. They share something with the assassin whose marginal existence is transformed by attaching himself to history. They live vicariously. They live publicly. They lay claim to that twenty-first-century grail – fame. They emerge out of the shadows into the bright light of attention. They shout their modesties from the rooftops, like pocket Coriolanuses showing their wounds as a route to power, though in their case their wounds are non-existent. They crave love who often, it must be admitted, seem to have lacked precisely that. They propose forces outside themselves to explain inadequacies, anxieties, deprivations, real and imagined. And so they synthesise memories, often extracting what seems to them to be the active ingredient of the concentration camp experience. Not for them the extraordinary reticence shown by so many survivors. They steal memories and when those memories are insufficiently dramatic they tend to show a preference for gothic horrors.

374

In May 1991, Jerzy Kosinski drugged himself with alcohol and sleeping pills, climbed into a bath and placed a plastic bag over his head. He did not commit suicide because of the damage done to his reputation over *The Painted Bird*. He had survived that, if not quite intact. Perhaps his suicide did relate to the genuine tensions of those years in which he and his family had had to masquerade, always aware that their fictions might be exposed for what they were. The lessons of vulnerability are not easily set aside. But he had learned other lessons. Survival, for him, depended on a certain legerdemain. He was a charlatan. Memories were not a pure source, a form of witness. He blended them with fictions, with other people's experiences. They were so much raw material. In life, few people claimed really to know him. Like Melville's confidence man he had the ability to present himself in many guises. That he should have been one inspiration for a Swiss citizen who had a similar wish to reinvent himself is not without its ironies. The chain of unmemory – from Kosinski to Wilkomirski to Grabowski – is in a sense the anti-matter to survivor memoirs, not telling a personal truth on behalf of others, but appropriating other people's memories in the name of the self.

As for Wilkomirski and Grabowski, both have retired into silence, in the case of the former still resisting revelations of his falsity as if he has opted to inhabit the world of his own imagining, so much more dramatic than what he sees as the banality of his own experiences. Wilkomirski has been stripped of all but one of his awards, but there are still those who say of his book that, true or not, it conveys an essential truth about children survivors and that therefore its literal falsity matters less than the witness it bears to an ignored group, as if witness were less a matter of personal experience than of a generalised situation. As for Grabowski, she insists that only the individual can decide if he or she is a survivor, quite as if reality were a matter of choice.

Memory is the carrier of the past, modified, to be sure, reshaped by the telling, serving present purposes and past needs. It is, however, a means of keeping a grasp on that past not always contained in documents, not always recoverable by the historian. It is not itself truth but what individuals believe to be the truth. It is suspect just as it is reliable. It is the source of a necessary resistance to time's alliance with forgetfulness. When it is appropriated, falsified, such thefts and deceptions are no misdemeanours. They work to deny the common ground on which we stand and which is the necessary foundation for present actions and future prospects.

Coda

In *The Year of Magical Thinking* (2005) Joan Didion, struggling to come to terms with the sense of overpowering grief she felt at the death of her husband, confesses, 'I need more than words to find the meaning.'[1] Yet words were all she had. As in Hemingway's 'Big Two-Hearted River', in which a man, traumatised in war, seeks to contain and control his terror by focussing on single actions, so she tries to write her way out of confusion and despair by noting down the details of her day, of her husband's death, and the simultaneous illness which leaves her daughter ill and in hospital.

Yet to do so in the present means to revisit the past and to turn to the past is fraught with difficulties not least because her husband's absence is a presence. Thus she is struck with guilt when she idly turns the page of a book he had left open, as if in doing so she is definitively and finally closing the lid of his coffin. To be alive at all is a reproach. To acknowledge that there is an 'after' is to deny the quicksilver energy of a life now forfeit. She cannot bring herself to give away his shoes because at some level she feels he may some day have need of them. They wait for him now as they have always done. A new day may yet erase a mistake in the cosmos.

And what of memory? Where Sebald spoke of a sense of vertigo, for Didion memory is a vortex with the power to mock her with a knowledge of happiness now nullified, a love stilled by a fault in time. Yet without memory who and where is she? She endeavours to close her ears to echoes, to turn aside from places and names which can only remind her of a life ended, of meaning unspooled by contingency. But ultimately the world refuses such denials.

Just over two months before the publication of a book designed to lay the past to rest through its painful recapitulation, her daughter, her only child, the living evidence of a relationship now ended, died. She was alone, afraid all over again to turn back, to look at photographs, to recall, since what could the past offer but a reminder of loss? Yet what was to be done? Was she to turn her back on the past merely because it had the power to unnerve her? There were two people waiting for her there and how could she ever wish to silence them, to live only in the present, stripped, as it was, of consolation if also of irony?

The Holocaust was a singular event, its particularity insisted upon as if to confer on it a meaning when its chief characteristic lay precisely in its denial of such. Yet at its heart is the all too familiar: sudden and arbitrary death, unbearable loss, memory as simultaneously necessary and unsustainable. There, too, were shoes to be kept safe as if one day they might be reinhabited. And the real fear is the same for the individual confronted with personal loss and a culture confronted with systematised slaughter, that a stone thrown in the pool will cease to send out ripples, that the wound will heal, the clock continue to tick, our lives extend towards an unimagined future, a mist slowly forming behind us.

Bishop Berkeley wrote 'esse est percipi', to be is to be perceived. To witness is to substantiate being. There were those committed to denying that certain events ever happened. Harold Pinter, in his 2005 Nobel Prize address, and writing in the context of America's plausibly deniable acts of violence around the world, remarked, 'It never happened. Nothing ever happened. Even while it was happening it wasn't happening. It didn't matter. It was of no interest.'[2] In *The Forgotten*, Elie Wiesel writes of a man whose memory is being destroyed, little by little, as Alzheimer's attacks. It is the more excruciating because his past contains heroism and shame, because it speaks a truth he must hand on, even as he struggles to assemble the broken fragments of his past. The book carries an epigraph from the Talmud: 'Respect the old man who has forgotten what he learned. For broken Tablets have a place in the Ark beside the Tablets of the Law.' A character is baffled by the ache for memory, objecting that, 'It's human nature to forget what hurts you, isn't it? Wasn't forgetfulness a gift of the gods to the ancient world? Without it, life would be intolerable, wouldn't it?' She is told that 'For a Jew, nothing is more important than memory. He is joined to his origins by memory.' 'So you insist on keeping your wounds open?'[3] she asks. It is something more than this, however, that creates the torment for the man whose memory is dying, for as he cries out in extremis, 'God of Auschwitz, know that I must remember Auschwitz. And that I must remind you of it.'[4]

Jane Urquhart begins *A Map of Glass* (2005) with another man who is suffering from Alzheimer's. It is not only memories that are sliding away from him as he stumbles forward through a winter world, able to recall odd words – snow, walking, winter – but not how they relate to himself or the world which now seems so remote and detached from him. Words themselves no longer connect. His grip on the past loosens with his grasp of a language that will connect him to it. So in *The Forgotten*, Wiesel has a character comment on the fact that

> The gaps between my memory and words seem unbridgeable.
> Despite the perils of syntax, paradox and faded images,
> I'd have hoped for coherence, not perfect but enough to convey
> the essence of memory. Unfortunately, I never managed to
> connect all the fragments to a center; too often the words
> surfaced as obstacles ... Sometimes, thinking of the dead
> whose memory I have sworn to preserve, I told myself, to
> write this story you'd already have to be dead; only the dead can
> properly write their story.[5]

The Forgotten ends as the old man finally runs out of language, a comment simultaneously on the centrality of memory, its pains and impossibilities:

> God cannot be so cruel as to erase everything forever. If He
> were, He would not be our father, and nothing would make
> sense. And I who speak to you cannot say more, for

Primo Levi divided his world into the drowned and the saved, aware, surely, that the distinction was never as sharp as he suggested.

He and others survived to tell their stories but the current was always threatening to pull them down. This book is punctuated with the drowned, not merely those lost in mass slaughter but also suicides, though what brought each individual to such a desperate choice is not to be second guessed. Contingency was not a product only of the camps, nor death unique to that imperium. Max Sebald died on a minor road in a marginal county of England, far from his place of birth. I still remember the telephone call that brought the news. My wife answered and suddenly burst into tears. This is a long way from the death of millions but those millions consisted of individuals and loss is personal before it is public. Tears for a people are touched with rhetoric. Memorials entomb the past. Tears for an individual are intransitive. It is true that the Holocaust gains its force precisely from its scale and its calculated cruelties but, as Camus remarked, tyrants conduct monologues above a million solitudes.

The paths of many of those whose stories are told in this book intersected at Auschwitz-Birkenau and then at Buchenwald, quite as if they obeyed a destiny. They did nothing of the kind. They were taken to these places by those who believed themselves the authors of history, some of them surviving to discover otherwise. Their victims were numbers to them, in the most literal of ways. They were never such to those who bore those numbers or those who lost them to the gas and flames. Sometimes those whose stories we have followed met in the camps, or thought they did. Sometimes they were divided from one another by electrified wire, by language or history. For the moment, though, they shared something, not a secret exactly but a truth that was not theirs alone to hold secure. And the day came when they felt obliged to speak, to write, as the day came for those who did not so suffer to acknowledge that they had lived and suffered and that there was an affinity.

Max Sebald was drawn to this experience because he already felt a connection, indirect, to be sure, but indirection has its particular truth to offer and he dealt in indirection. Nor was history ever fixed and immutable to him. The human mind is free to roam. It can imagine and inhabit both the past and the future and see the patterns formed, patterns which may change with the light, as with the grace of our attention. This is not to deny the power of ineluctable facts but to acknowledge the extent to which those facts are themselves part of a more expansive truth. He who felt an irrational guilt nonetheless was driven by that to create and perceive connections, refusing to be constrained by arbitrary definitions, distinctions, boundaries. His aesthetic was his morality.

Those who have undergone electro-convulsive treatment are liable to lose some of their memories. It is a trade-off: peace of mind for fragments of the past. Who would place their sanity on the table to win back memories, especially if they are of near-disabling loss? Sometimes it is necessary. As an Arthur Miller character remarks in *After the Fall*, 'the past is holy', no matter how dark, no matter how menacing to our sense of ourselves. The past, however, as Max Sebald knew, and showed in book after book, contains its own redemption as well as accusations, not least because it is never finished, not least because it bears the impress of mind, memory and imagination.

Elias Canetti, Sebald noted, spoke of writers following their noses over the chasm of time. It was, after all, what he himself chose to do. But time folding back on itself can create strange ironies. In 1943, in German-occupied Swieciany (now part of Lithuania), a Jewish mother gave her newborn son to an illiterate Polish Catholic in a desperate attempt to save his life. Twenty-three years later that boy, Romuald Waszkinel, knowing nothing of his origins, became a Catholic priest. Nonetheless, he was troubled by vague memories. He recalled being taunted, when young, as a Jew. He finally discovered the truth when he was thirty-five. In 1992, a nun who had herself saved Jewish children during the war visited Israel and discovered survivors from Swieciany who knew Waszkinel's family. As a result he met his uncle and was shown a photograph of the mother who had given him up to save his life. The priest, as Andrew Nagorski pointed out in a *Newsweek* article in 1999,[6] then wrote to the Pope indicating that he would like to change his name to incorporate that of his lost family. The Pope wrote back to him in his new name. Today Romuald Waszkinel wears a silver cross enclosed by the star of David.

In 1943, when the Jewish ghetto in Vilnius was destroyed, a thousand Jews were moved to a nearby forced labour camp.

There, Major Karl Plagge worked to protect them from the SS, falsely claiming that they were skilled personnel. When this was no longer possible, he warned them of their imminent fate. He saved possibly three hundred. In his 1947 de-Nazification trial, as Andrew Buncombe has indicated,[7] though survivors testified on his behalf, he insisted on being designated a fellow traveller. In a letter in 1956 he wrote, 'I was not able to recognise the boundaries where the limit of guilt began or ended and in a broader sense, as a German, I myself bear this guilt. From this plague there was no refuge.' Plagge died the following year. In 2005, however, his actions were remembered, not least because his story had come to the attention of Michael Good, a family doctor from Connecticut who visited what was left of the labour camp where his own mother had been imprisoned. In telling her story, retrieving her memories, he forged a link in another chain and changed the ending of the story of Karl Plagge. Good wrote a memoir – *The Search for Major Plagge* – and in 2005 it was announced that Plagge's name would be inscribed on a remembrance wall in the Garden of Righteousness in Israel.

In 1939, Max Sebald's father was among the German troops who invaded Poland. 'We should recall', Sebald insisted, the 'horrendous occurrences and atrocities' that happened 'as soon as the Germans marched into Poland.'[8] Barbara Stimler, invoked in the opening chapter of this book, who now lives in London, recalls her house in Aleksandrow Kuhjawski, near the German border, being bombed that first day, her neighbours killed instantly. Her family spent time in a concentration camp in central Poland. Her father is believed to have died in Auschwitz. She and her mother were transported to the Łódź ghetto. That mother became paralysed and, to conceal her, Barbara placed her in a hole in the ground. She survived that day but was later taken to her death while Barbara herself was taken to Auschwitz where she was selected for life by Josef Mengele. Then, like so many others, she was marched towards Bergen-Belsen, escaping only because she successfully hid herself in a barn.

After the war, she reached Britain where she said nothing about her experiences, even to her husband. Then, in 1995, she began to tell her story, to retrieve those suppressed memories unique to herself but which intersected with those of many others, hers being part of that chain of memories that take us back to those events that haunted Max Sebald as they continue to haunt not only those who were there and who suffered but those who recognise in the Holocaust a seismic event whose aftershocks still disturb our equanimity sixty and more years on.

Sebald met his first Jew in Manchester. Mayer Hersh, whose mother and three younger brothers were killed in a gassing van in Chelmno and who found himself during the war briefly in Stuttgart where half a century later Sebald would speak, also settled in Manchester. For thirty years he said little about his experiences and could find few who wished to know. Thereafter, he began to speak, and once he had started he could not stop. His memories tumbled out, memories of those he had lost and who he now sought to retrieve and thereby preserve. Memory, fragmentary, flawed, compromised, the source of pain, regret, irony, nonetheless proved a necessary resource, not so much a physiological mechanism as a moral necessity.

For Sebald, though, the history thus recalled reached further back than 1945, 1939 or 1933, when Hitler had come to power. The stain sinks deeper in the wood. He was drawn back, he explained, long before he was born, because 'this is where I come from. This is my identity ... this is where my origins lie. My parents were involved in it and my grandparents' lives led up to it. The mistakes go a long way back.'[9]

And how to travel back to those origins, or indeed to the events which haunted all those gathered in this book, except along a chain of memories, some real, some imagined, but, ultimately, as inescapable as night?

Notes

1. The past remembered

1 Aharon Appelfeld, *The Story of a Life*, trans. Aloma Halter (New York, 2004), pp. v, viii.
2 Vladimir Nabokov, *Speak, Memory: An Autobiography Revisted* (London, 2000), p. 17.
3 George Steiner, *George Steiner: A Reader* (Harmondsworth, 1984), p. 209.
4 Lawrence L. Langer, ed., *Art from the Ashes: A Holocaust Anthology* (Oxford, 1995), p. 599.
5 Peter Barnes, *Auschwitz*, in Elinor Fuchs, ed., *Plays of the Holocaust: An International Anthology* (New York, 1987), p. 123.
6 Elinor Fuchs, 'Introduction', in *ibid.*, p. xxi.
7 Eva Hoffman, *After Such Knowledge: Memory, History, and the Legacy of the Holocaust* (London, 2004), p. 152.
8 Dominick LaCapra, *History and Memory After Auschwitz* (Ithaca, 1998), p. 129.
9 Michael Frayn, *Constructions* (London, 1974), paragraph 260, n.p.
10 Marco Belpoliti and Robert Gordon, eds., *The Voice of Memory: Interviews 1961–1987 by Primo Levi*, trans. Robert Gordon (Cambridge, 2001), p. 3.
11 Steiner, *George Steiner: A Reader*, p. 207.
12 Lawrence L. Langer, *Holocaust Testimonies: The Ruins of Memory* (New Haven, 1991), p. 62.
13 *Ibid.*, p. 79.
14 W. G. Sebald, *Campo Santo*, ed. Sven Meyer, trans. Anthea Bell (London, 2005), p. 161.
15 George Steiner, *Bluebeard's Castle* (New Haven, 1971), p. 3.
16 Steiner, *George Steiner: A Reader*, p. 219.
17 Langer, *Holocaust Testimonies*, p. 49.

18 Avishai Margalit, *The Ethics of Memory* (Cambridge, Mass., 2002), pp. viii–ix.

19 Laurence Rees, 'The Nazi Testimony', *The Guardian*, 10 January 2005, G2, p. 3.

20 Chris McGreal, 'This is Ours and Ours Alone', *The Guardian*, 15 March 2005, G2, p. 6.

21 Ralph Waldo Emerson, *Selected Writings of Ralph Waldo Emerson*, ed. William H. Gilman (New York, 1965), p. 186.

22 Ann Scott, *Real Events Revisited: Fantasy, Memory, Psychoanalysis* (London, 1996), p. 66.

23 Quoted in Margalit, *The Ethics of Memory*, p. 148.

24 Margot Levy, ed., *Remembering for the Future: The Holocaust in an Age of Genocide* (London, 2001), p. 438.

25 David Hare, 'Don't Count on Us to Vote Labour', *The Daily Telegraph*, 5 March 2005, p. 17.

2. W. G. Sebald: an act of restitution

1 W. G. Sebald, *The Guardian*, 21 December 2001.

2 W. G. Sebald, *After Nature*, trans. Michael Hamburger (London, 2002), p. 68.

3 *Ibid.*, p. 81.

4 Christopher Bigsby, ed., *Writers in Conversation with Christopher Bigsby* (Norwich, 2001), vol. II, p. 141.

5 *Ibid.*, p. 145.

6 W. G. Sebald, *Campo Santo*, ed. Sven Meyer, trans. Anthea Bell (London, 2005), pp. 214–15.

7 Bigsby, ed., *Writers in Conversation*, vol. II, p. 143.

8 Maya Jaggi, 'Recovered Memories', *The Guardian*, 22 September 2001.

9 W. G. Sebald, ed., *A Radical Stage: Theatre in Germany in the 1970s and 1980s* (Oxford, 1988), p. 2.

10 James Wood, 'An Interview with W. G. Sebald', *Brick* 59 (Spring 1998), p. 27.

11 W. G. Sebald, 'The Revival of Myth: A Study of Döblin's Novels', Ph.D. thesis, University of East Anglia, 1973.

12 Toby Green, 'The Questionable Business of Writing: W. G. Sebald talks to Toby Green about memory, modern culture and the truth of writing' www.amazon.co.uk/exec/obidos/tg/feature/-/21586/ref%3Ded_art__121649-txt1

13 Bigsby, ed., *Writers in Conversation*, vol. II, p. 148.

14 Jaggi, 'Recovered Memories'.

15 *Ibid.*

16 Tony Kushner, *The Holocaust and the Liberal Imagination: A Social and Cultural History* (Oxford, 1994), p. 214.

17 Sebald, *Campo Santo*, p. 55.

18 Sebald, 'The Revival of Myth', p. 93.

19 Sebald, *Campo Santo*, p. 87.

20 Quoted in Sidney Rosenfeld, 'Afterword' to Jean Améry, *At the Mind's Limits: Contemplations by a Survivor on Auschwitz and its Realities*, trans. Sidney Rosenfeld and Stella P. Rosenfeld (London, 1999), p. 105.

21 Bigsby, ed., *Writers in Conversation*, vol. II, p. 153.

22 Henrik Hamrén, 'I Feel Ashamed', *The Guardian*, 18 April 2005, G2, p. 11.

23 Andrew Buncombe, 'Israel Honours Officer Who Was "Better than Schindler"', *The Independent*, 8 April 2005, p. 32.

24 Primo Levi, *The Drowned and the Saved*, trans. Raymond Rosenthal (London, 1988), p. 154.

25 Bigsby, ed., *Writers in Conversation*, vol. II, p. 145.

26 Sebald, *After Nature*, p. 81.

27 W. G. Sebald and Jan Peter Tripp, *Unrecounted* (London, 2004), p. 79.

28 Bigsby, ed., *Writers in Conversation*, vol. II, p. 160.

29 Sebald, *The Revival of Myth*, p. 168.

30 Jaggi, 'Recovered Memories'.

31 W. G. Sebald, *Vertigo*, trans. Michael Hulse (London, 1999), p. 6.

32 Bigsby, ed., *Writers in Conversation*, vol. II, p. 144.

33 W. G. Sebald, *The Emigrants*, trans. Michael Hulse (London, 1996), p. 21.

34 Kenneth Baker, 'Q & A: W. G. Sebald Up Against Historical Amnesia', *San Francisco Chronicle*, 7 October 2001.

35 Bigsby, ed., *Writers in Conversation*, vol. II, pp. 160–1.

36 Jaggi, 'Recovered Memories'.

37 *Ibid.*

38 Bigsby, ed., *Writers in Conversation*, vol. II, p. 162.

39 Jaggi, 'Recovered Memories'.

40 Bigsby, ed., *Writers in Conversation*, vol. II, pp. 162–3.

41 W. G. Sebald, *Austerlitz*, trans. Anthea Bell (London, 2001), p. 34.

42 Jaggi, 'Recovered Memories'.

43 Sebald, *Campo Santo*, p. 149.

44 Levi, *The Drowned and the Saved*, p. 85.

45 Elie Wiesel, *All Rivers Run to the Sea* (New York, 1994), p. 74.

46 Elie Wiesel, *And the Sea is Never Full* (New York, 2000), p. 150.

47 Elie Wiesel, *The Night Trilogy* (New York, 1990), pp. 7–8.

48 W. G. Sebald, *On the Natural History of Destruction*, trans. Anthea Bell (London, 2003), p. 61.

49 Jaggi, 'Recovered Memories'.

50 Green, 'The Questionable Business of Writing'.

51 Bigsby, ed., *Writers in Conversation*, vol. II, p. 154.

52 Jaggi, 'Recovered Memories'.

53 Bigsby, ed., *Writers in Conversation*, vol. II, p. 155.

54 Green, 'The Questionable Business of Writing'.

55 Sebald, *On the Natural History of Destruction*, p. 74.

56 Jaggi, 'Recovered Memories'.

57 Green, 'The Questionable Business of Writing'.

58 Bigsby, ed., *Writers in Conversation*, vol. II, p. 156.

59 *The Guardian*, 14 February 2005, p. 15.

60 Améry, *At the Mind's Limits*, p. 96.

61 Sebald, 'The Revival of Myth', pp. 180–1.

62 Eva Hoffman, *After Such Knowledge: A Meditation on the Aftermath of the Holocaust* (London, 2004), p. 73.

63 George Steiner, *George Steiner: A Reader* (Harmondsworth, 1984), p. 216.

64 Levi, *The Drowned and the Saved*, p. 19.

65 Bigsby, ed., *Writers in Conversation*, vol. II, p. 156.

66 Sebald, *Campo Santo*, p. 3.

67 Jean Améry, *On Aging: Revolt and Resignation*, trans. John D. Barlow (Bloomington, 1994), p. 18.

68 Garry McCulloch, *Understanding W. G. Sebald* (Columbia, SC, 2003), p. 141.

69 Rolf Hochhuth, *The Deputy*, trans Richard and Clara Winston (Baltimore, 1964), p. 79.

70 George Szirtes, *Reel* (Tarset, 2005), pp. 18, 20.

3. Rolf Hochhuth: breaking the silence

1 Judy Stone, 'Interview with Rolf Hochhuth', *Ramparts* (Spring 1964), reprinted in Eric Bentley, ed., *The Storm Over the Deputy: Essays and Articles about Hochhuth's Explosive Drama* (New York, 1964), p. 42.

2 Rolf Hochhuth, *Soldiers: An Obituary for Geneva*, trans. Robert David MacDonald (London, 1968), p. 53.

3 George Steiner, *George Steiner: A Reader* (Harmondsworth, 1984), p. 230.

4 Nicholas Stargardt, *Witnesses of War: Children's Lives Under the Nazis* (London, 2005), p. 221.
5 Rolf Hochhuth, *The Deputy* (New York, 1964), p. 291.
6 W. G. Sebald, *Campo Santo*, ed. Sven Meyer, trans. Anthea Bell (London, 2005), p. 115.
7 Bentley, ed., *The Storm Over the Deputy*, p. 43.
8 Primo Levi, *The Mirror Maker: Stories and Essays by Primo Levi*, trans. Raymond Rosenthal (London, 1990), p. 166.
9 Kevin Madigan, 'What the Vatican Knew about the Holocaust and When', *Commentary*, October 2001, p. 44.
10 Primo Levi, *Moments of Reprieve*, trans. Ruth Feldman (London, 1986), pp. 99–100.

4. Peter Weiss: the investigation

1 Robert Cohen, *Understanding Peter Weiss* (Columbia, SC, 1993), p. 76.
2 Oren Baruch Stier, *Committed to Memory: Cultural Mediations on the Holocaust* (Boston, 2003), p. 1.
3 Donald Bloxham, 'The Missing Camps of *Aktion Reinhard*: the Judicial Displacement of a Mass Murder', in Peter Gray and Kendrick Oliver, eds., *The Memory of Catastrophe* (Manchester, 2004), p. 123.
4 Jost Hermond and Mark Silberman, eds., *Rethinking Peter Weiss* (New York, 2000), p. 97.
5 W. G. Sebald, *On the Natural History of Destruction*, trans. Anthea Bell (London, 2003), pp. 175–6.
6 Ian Hilton, *Peter Weiss* (London, 1970), p. 48.
7 Klaus L. Berghahn, 'On Auschwitz', in Hermond and Silberman, eds., *Rethinking Peter Weiss*, p. 95.
8 Peter Weiss, *The Investigation*, English version by Alexander Gross (London, 1966), p. 10.
9 Olaf Berwald, *An Introduction to the Works of Peter Weiss* (Rochester, NY, 2003), p. 22.
10 Hermond and Silberman, eds., *Rethinking Peter Weiss*, p. 95.
11 Cohen, *Understanding Peter Weiss*, p. 88.
12 Berghahn, 'On Auschwitz', p. 103.
13 Sebald, *On the Natural History of Destruction*, p. 187.
14 Peter Weiss, *Trotsky in Exile*, trans. Geoffrey Skelton (London, 1970), p. 88.
15 Peter Weiss, *The Persecution and Assassination of Marat as Performed by the Inmates of the Asylum of Charenton under the*

Direction of the Marquis de Sade, trans. Geoffrey Skelton, verse adaptation Adrian Mitchell (London, 1965), p. 34.

5. Arthur Miller: the rememberer

1 Christopher Bigsby, *Arthur Miller: A Critical Study* (Cambridge, 2005), p. 335.
2 Arthur Miller, *Timebends* (London, 1987), p. 523.
3 Arthur Miller, *After the Fall* (London, 1964), p. 30.
4 Miller, *Timebends*, p. 526.
5 Arthur Miller, *Echoes Down the Corridor: Collected Essays, 1944–2000*, ed. Steven R. Centola (London, 2000), p. 63.
6 Daniel Jonah Goldhagen, *Hitler's Willing Executioners: Ordinary Germans and the Holocaust* (New York, 1997), p. 14.
7 Lawrence L. Langer, *Holocaust Testimonies: The Ruins of Memory* (New Haven, 1991), pp. 155–6.
8 Arthur Miller, *Plays Two* (London, 1986), pp. 269–70.
9 Fania Fénelon, *Playing for Time*, trans. Judith Landry (Syracuse, 1997), p. 193.
10 Ian Thomson, *Primo Levi* (London, 2002), p. 169.
11 Primo Levi, *The Drowned and the Saved*, trans Raymond Rosenthal (London, 1988), p. 126.
12 Arthur Miller, *Playing for Time* (New York, 1981), p. 20.
13 Arthur Miller, *Playing for Time* (play version) (Chicago, 1985), p. 91.
14 Miller, *Plays Two*, p. 2.
15 Richard Newman with Karen Kirtley, *Alma Rosé: Vienna to Auschwitz* (Prompton Plains, NJ, 2000).
16 Peter Novick, *The Holocaust and Collective Memory: The American Experience* (London, 1999), p. 275.
17 Goldhagen, *Hitler's Willing Executioners*, p. 102.
18 Arthur Miller, *Danger: Memory!* (New York, 1986), pp. 59–60.

6. Anne Frank: everybody's heroine

1 Peter Novick, *The Holocaust and Collective Memory: The American Experience* (London, 2000), p. 119.
2 David Barnouw and Gerrold Van Der Stroom, eds., *The Diary of Anne Frank: The Critical Edition* (New York, 1989), p. 72.

3 Nicholas Stargardt, *Witnesses of War: Children's Lives Under the Nazis* (London, 2005), pp. 238–9.

4 Michael Kammen, *In the Past Lane: Historical Perspectives on American Culture* (Oxford, 1997), p. 341.

5 Brooks Atkinson, 'Introduction', in Frances Goodrich and Albert Hackett, *The Diary of Anne Frank* (New York, 1956), p. x.

6 Willy Lindwer, *The Seven Last Months of Anne Frank* (London, 2004), p. 4.

7 Elie Wiesel, *From the Kingdom of Memory* (New York, 1990), p. 103.

8 Cynthia Ozick, 'Who Owns Anne Frank?', *The New Yorker*, 6 October 1997, p. 78.

9 Bruno Bettelheim, *Surviving and Other Essays* (London, 1979), p. 247.

10 Bruno Bettelheim, *Recollections and Reflections* (London, 1990), p. 270.

11 Marco Belpoliti and Robert Gordon, eds., *The Voice of Memory: Interviews 1961–1987, by Primo Levi*, trans. Robert Gordon (Cambridge, 2001), p. 235.

12 Philip Roth, *The Ghost Writer* (London, 1979), p. 125.

13 Robert Skloot, ed., *The Theatre of the Holocaust*, vol. II (Madison, 1999), pp. 155–6.

14 *Ibid.*, p. 247.

15 Ellen Feldman, *The Boy Who Loved Anne Frank* (London, 2005), p. 47.

16 Jon Henley, 'Don't Pity Me', *The Guardian*, 18 April 2005, G2, p. 3.

17 Quoted in Belpoliti and Gordon, eds., *The Voice of Memory*, p. 278.

7. Jean Améry: home and language

1 W. G. Sebald, *On the Natural History of Destruction*, trans. Anthea Bell (London, 2003), p. 149.

2 Christopher Bigsby, ed., *Writers in Conversation with Christopher Bigsby* (Norwich, 2001), vol. II, p. 176.

3 Jean Améry, *At the Mind's Limits: Contemplation by a Survivor on Auschwitz and its Realities*, trans. Sidney Rosenfeld and Stella P. Rosenfeld (London, 1999), p. 84.

4 Jean-Paul Sartre, *Anti-Semite and Jew*, trans. George J. Becker (New York, 1965), p. 72.

5 Primo Levi, *The Drowned and the Saved*, trans. Raymond Rosenthal (London, 1988), p. 109.

6 Eva Hoffman, *After Such Knowledge: A Meditation on the Aftermath of the Holocaust* (London, 2004), p. 77.

7 Ian Thomson, *Primo Levi* (London, 2002), p. 396.

8 *Ibid.*, p. 352.

9 Levi, *The Drowned and the Saved*, p. 114.

10 Thomson, *Primo Levi*, p. 335.

11 Levi, *The Drowned and the Saved*, p. 110.

12 Simon Wiesenthal, *The Sunflower: On the Possibilities and Limits of Forgiveness* (New York, 1998), p. 108.

13 Levi, *The Drowned and the Saved*, p. 103.

14 Jean Améry, *On Suicide*, trans. John D. Barlow (Bloomington, 1999), p. 88.

15 Jean Améry, *On Aging and Resignation*, trans. John D. Barlow (Bloomington, 1994), p. 14.

16 Tzvetan Todorov, *Facing the Extreme* (New York, 1996), p. 115.

17 Thane Rosenbaum, *The Golems of Gotham* (New York, 2002), p. 181.

8. Primo Levi: from the darkness to the light

1 Primo Levi, *The Periodic Table* (New York, 1984), p. 61.

2 Primo Levi, *Moments of Reprieve*, trans. Ruth Feldman (London, 1986), pp. 10–11.

3 Primo Levi, *The Drowned and the Saved* (London, 1988), p. 1.

4 Ian Thomson, *Primo Levi* (London, 2002), p. 430.

5 *Ibid.*, p. 160.

6 Primo Levi, *If This is a Man and The Truce*, trans. Stuart Woolf (London, 1979), p. 15.

7 Marco Belpoliti and Robert Gordon, eds., *The Voice of Memory: Interviews 1961–1987 by Primo Levi*, trans. Robert Gordon (Cambridge, 2001), p. 224.

8 Levi, *If This is a Man*, p. 19.

9 Primo Levi, *The Mirror Maker: Stories and Essays*, trans. Raymond Rosenthal (London, 1990), p. 86.

10 Thomson, *Primo Levi*, p. 181.

11 Elie Wiesel, *From the Kingdom of Memory* (New York, 1990), p. 83.

12 Levi, *If This is a Man*, p. 32.

13 Levi, *The Truce*, p. 188.

14 Thomson, *Primo Levi*, p. 202.

15 Levi, *The Drowned and the Saved*, p. 112.

16 Thomson, *Primo Levi*, pp. 232–3.

17 Levi, *The Periodic Table*, p. 139.
18 Thomson, *Primo Levi*, pp. 290–1.
19 Levi, *The Mirror Maker*, p. 107.
20 Wiesel, *From the Kingdom of Memory*, p. 170.
21 Levi, *Moments of Reprieve*, p. 172.
22 Antony Sher, *Primo Time* (London, 2005), p. 25.
23 Martin Amis, *Time's Arrow* (London, 1991), p. 176.
24 Peter Novick, *The Holocaust in American Life* (New York, 2000), p. 14.
25 Christopher Bigsby, ed., *Writers in Conversation with Christopher Bigsby* (Norwich, 2000), vol. II, p. 34.

9. Elie Wiesel: to forget is to deny

1 Elie Wiesel, *From the Kingdom of Memory* (New York, 1990), p. 9.
2 Elie Wiesel, *All Rivers Run to the Sea: Memoirs 1928–1969* (London, 1996), p. 17.
3 Elie Wiesel, *The Night Trilogy*, trans. Stella Rodway (New York, 1987), p. 43.
4 Wiesel, *All Rivers Run to the Sea*, p. 83.
5 *Ibid.*, p. 84.
6 *Ibid.*, p. 85.
7 Ted Estes, *Elie Wiesel* (New York, 1980), p. 18.
8 Elie Wiesel, *And the Sea is Never Full: Memoirs 1969–* (New York, 2000), p. 19.
9 Wiesel, *From the Kingdom of Memory*, p. 166.
10 *Ibid.*, p. 16.
11 Elie Wiesel in conversation with Stephen Lewis, in Lewis, *Art Out of Agony: The Holocaust Theme in Literature, Sculpture and Film* (Montreal, 1984), p. 160.

10. Tadeusz Borowski: the world of stone

1 Jan Kott, Introduction to Tadeusz Borowski, *This Way for the Gas, Ladies and Gentlemen*, trans. Barbara Vedder (Harmondsworth, 1976), p. 11.
2 Albert Camus, *Caligula and Cross Purpose*, trans. Stuart Gilbert (London, 1965), p. 155.
3 Samuel Beckett, *Endgame* (London, 1958), p. 45.
4 Arthur Miller, *Echoes Down the Corridor: Collected Essays, 1944–2000*, ed. Steven R. Centola (London, 2000), p. 66.

11. Memory theft

1 Stefan Maechler, *The Wilkomirski Affair: A Study in Biographical Truth*, trans. John E. Woods (London, 2001), p. 377. In this chapter I am heavily indebted to Maechler's forensic work.
2 Blake Eskin, *A Life in Pieces* (London, 2002), p. 39.
3 Maechler, *The Wilkomirski Affair*, p. 378.
4 Bob and Gretchen Passantino and Jon Trott, 'Lauren Stratford: From Satanic Ritual Abuse to Jewish Holocaust Survivor', *Cornerstone* 28, 117, 13 October 1999, pp. 12–16, 18. Also online at www.cornerstonemag.com/features/iss117/lauren.htm
5 *Ibid.*
6 Philip Gourevitch, 'The Memory Thief', *The New Yorker*, 14 June 1999, pp. 48–61.
7 Elena Lappin, 'The Man with Two Heads', *Granta* 66 (Summer 1999), pp. 7–65.

Coda

1 Joan Didion, *The Year of Magical Thinking* (London, 2005), p. 8.
2 Harold Pinter, 'Pinter v the US', *The Guardian*, 8 December 2005, p. 11.
3 Elie Wiesel, *The Forgotten* (New York, 1992), p. 88.
4 *Ibid.*, p. 10
5 *Ibid.*, p. 146.
6 Andrew Nagorski, 'The Jewish Priest', *Newsweek*, 13 September 1999, p. 30.
7 Andrew Buncombe, 'Israel Honours Officer Who Was "Better than Schindler"', *The Independent*, 8 April 2005, p. 32.
8 Christopher Bigsby, ed., *Writers in Conversation with Christopher Bigsby* (Norwich, 2000), vol. II, p. 143.
9 *Ibid.*, p. 145.

Index

absence, of memory 61
academic writing, Sebald on 40
Adorno, Theodor 33
aesthetics, of Sebald 46–7
air war in Germany, silence about
    98–102, 106
Akhmatova, Anna 23
American Jews, attitude towards
    Holocaust 130
Amerongen-Frankfoorder, Rachel van
    235, 239
Améry, Jean 40, 50, 109, 259, 260,
    262, 290
  on anti-Semitism 277
  arrest by Gestapo 266
  at Fort Breendonk 266–8
  and Auschwitz trials 271
  in concentration camps 268–9,
    274–5
  on concentration camps 272, 273–4
  on cosmopolitanism 269
  exile of 263–4, 265
  on forgiveness 279–80
  on German language 265–6
  on Holocaust 270, 275–6
  Jewish identity of 260–2, 270,
    276–7
  and Levi 278, 279, 280, 301, 310
  life after the war 276, 277
  on memory 281–2
  and the past 269
  on remembering 269–70, 272
  in Resistance movement 265
  and Sebald 6, 86–7, 90, 94–5, 96–7,
    98, 258, 269
  on suicide 280–1, 282, 283
  suicide of 277, 278–9, 282–3
  on torture 72, 266–8
  on victimhood 272

works
  At the Mind's Limits 258, 271
  *Encounter of the Intellectuals
    with Auschwitz* (radio talk)
    271
  Lefeu oder der Abbruch (*Lefeu or
    Demolition*) 258
  *On the Necessity and
    Impossibility of Being a Jew*
    (essay) 260–1
  On Suicide 278, 280–1, 283
  writings of 96, 269, 271, 273, 275
Amis, Martin
  Time's Arrow 313–16
Andersch, Alfred 90, 92–3, 94
angel of history, Sebald's 78
Anielewicz, Mordechai, suicide of 282
Anne Frank Foundation 222
  criticised by Ozick 242
anti-Semitism
  Améry on 277
  encountered by Miller 178
  in German church 146–7
  in Soviet Union 187
Appelfeld, Aharon 8
  on German language 266
  on memories
    of Holocaust survivors 18–19
    of trauma 14
  on silence 7
  The Story of a Life 1, 10, 258
appropriation, of Levi 311, 313–14
Arendt, Hannah 158
  Eichmann in Jerusalem 163
art, role in Nazism 85
Atkinson, Brooks 231
Atlan, Liliane
  Mister Fugue or Earth Sick 8–9
  Un Opéra pour Terezin 9

Index

Auschwitz 96, 133–4, 137–8
  Améry on 273–4
  Amis on 315
  Borowski at 342
  Borowski on 343, 350
  and Dante's inferno 165
  Frank family at 236–8
  Levi at 291, 295–6, 298
  Levi on 290–1, 298
  music in 182, 195, 196–200,
      211, 213
  Weiss's visit to 160
  Wiesel at 323–5
  Wiesel on 236–7, 323, 324, 325–6
Auschwitz trials (Frankfurt, 1964)
      159–60, 163
  Améry and 271
  and *The Investigation* (play, Weiss)
      166–7, 171–2
  Miller at 161, 169, 176–7, 181–2,
      187–9, 355
  Nazi war criminals at 169
  Weiss at 153, 156–7, 160, 172
Austerlitz Station (Paris) 77
Autobahnen, built by Nazism 314

Baer, Richard 295
Barnes, Peter
  Auschwitz 6
Barnouw, David 230
Bauer, Fritz 182
Bechhofer, Susie 69
Belgium, Améry in exile in 263–4
Ben Gurion, David 271
Benjamin, Walter 49, 78
Benn, Gottfried 94
Bentley, Eric
  Are You Now or Have You Ever Been
      119
Bergen-Belsen 200
  Anne Frank at 238–9
Berghahn, Klaus L. 153, 162–3
betrayal, of Frank family 227–8
Bettelheim, Bruno 246, 284
  criticism of Frank family and
      portrayal of Anne Frank 245
  criticism of Jewish passivity 271
  Surviving and Other Essays 242–5
Beyle, Henri Marie (Stendhal) 50–3, 56,
      137
Bialik, Chaim Nachman 330
Birkenau 236–7 (*see also*) Auschwitz
Blanchot, Maurice 208
Blau, Magda 208

blood libel, against the Jews 105
Bloomgarden, Kermit 230
Bloxham, Donald 151–2
Böll, Heinrich
  *The Angel Was Silent (Der Engel
      schwieg)* 100
bombing, of German cities 78–9
Borowski, Tadeusz 283
  at Auschwitz 342
  on Auschwitz 343, 350
  communism of 351
  on concentration camps 342–3,
      350–2
  letters to his fiancée 349–50, 353
  as observer of the Holocaust 348–9,
      350, 353, 355
  poems by 341
  short stories by 342, 343, 352–3,
      354–5
  Auschwitz, Our Home 349–50
  A Day at Harmenz 347–8
  January Offensive 354
  The People Who Walked On 348–9
  Silence 353–4
  *This Way for the Gas, Ladies and
      Gentlemen* 343–6
  The World of Stone 354, 355
  suicide of 342, 355, 356
  on survival 346–7
  youth of 341–2
Brandes-Brilleslijper, Janny 234, 236
Brecht, Bertolt, on Holocaust 158
Britain
  attitudes towards Holocaust 35–6
  Sebald's move to 34–7
Broch, Hermann 192
Brook, Peter 146, 156
  on Weiss 173, 174–5
Browne, Sir Thomas
  Urn Burial 67
Buncombe, Andrew 382
Burton, Robert 88, 89
Busch, Wilhelm 117

Calvino, Italo 293
Camus, Albert 124
  The Fall 183
Canetti, Elias 49, 381
capitalism, and genocide 316
Celan, Paul 5, 283
Chadwick, Owen 147
chains
  of memory 7, 23–4, 89
  of unmemory 375
  of witnesses 23

Chatwin, Bruce 42
childhood memories 22
children
    hidden 75
    of Holocaust survivors 89
church
    awareness of ongoing Holocaust
        121–2 *see also* Pius XII
    in Germany, anti-Semitism in 146–7
Cioran, E. M. 98
cities, German, bombing of 78–9
Cohen, Robert 165–6
collective memory
    and past 86
    of Swiss 371–2
    writers and 85
communication, Levi on 308–9
Communism
    of Borowski 351
    of Weiss 165–6
concentration camps
    Améry in 268–9, 274–5
    Améry on 272, 273–4
    Borowski on 342–3, 350–2
    death in 274–5
    imagining of 133–4, 150
    and intellectuals 273–4, 301–2
    Levi on 291, 296–8, 305–6
    Miller on 181, 182, 186
    Sebald on 46
    suicide committed by survivors of 98
    survival in 296–7, 305–6, 325, 346–7
    and time 95–6
    Weiss on 164, 167–9
    writing in 8–9
contested memories 207–8, 213, 215
Corsica, Sebald's visit to 106–7,
        109–10, 110–11
cosmopolitanism, Améry on 269
Crawford, Cheryl 230
Cykowiak, Zafia 214
Czajkowska *see* Tchaikowska
Czerniakow, Adam, suicide of 282

Dante (Alighieri)
    Divine Comedy 162, 165
    influence on Levi 300
    influence on Weiss 174
Dardenne, Sabine 256
Darville, Helen *see* Demidenko, Helen
De Quinecy, Thomas 314
death
    of Anne Frank 238–9
    in concentration camps 274–5
    fascination with 149

of inhabitants of 'Secret Annexe'
        239–40
    of Sebald 113–14, 380
    in Sebald's works 109, 149
    Weiss's fascination with 149
    of Wiesel's father 327–8
Defonseca, Monique
    *Misha: A Memoir of the Holocaust
        Year* 372
Dembo, Charlotte 13–14
Demidenko, Helen
    The Hand that Signed the Paper 373
denial
    of facts 11–12
    of Holocaust 86
    of memory 17
    of past 251–6
diaries
    of Dardenne 256
    of Filipovic 250
    of Günzel 226
    of Nin 228
Diary of Anne Frank see Frank, Anne,
    diary of
Didion, Joan
    The Year of Magical Thinking 377–8
Dimbleby, Richard 35–6
disbelief, and Holocaust experience 83
distortions
    of memory 10–11
    of reality 305
Döblin, Alfred 88
    Sebald on 32, 39–40
    Wallenstein 32
documentary prose style, of Sebald 42,
    82–3
documentary theatre 31–2, 83, 117, 119
    The Deputy (play, Hochhuth) as 127,
        142–3
    The Investigation (play, Weiss) as
        161, 167
    and representation of Auschwitz 133
dogs, as symbols 49
Dubermann, Martin
    In White America 119
Dunicz-Niwinska, Helena 214

Eden, idea of 1
Eichmann, Adolf 126, 128, 318
    kidnap and arrest of 159
Emerson, Ralph Waldo 21
emigration, of Holocaust survivors 271
Enzensberger, Hans Magnus 100
Eskin, Blake 359–60
Evers-Emden, Bloeme 235

exclusiveness, Jewish 297
exile
  of Améry 263–4, 265
  and languages 97–8, 264–5
  Sebald on 111, 264–5
Eyck, Jan van 47
eye-witness accounts 198
  distrust of 151–2

facts, denial of 11–12
false memories 212
fame, sought by those committing
  memory theft 374
Feldman, Ellen
  The Boy Who Loved Anne Frank
    251–6
Fénelon, Fania
  Playing for Time 96, 194, 196–200,
    211
  criticism of 207–8, 209, 212,
    214–15
  Miller's adaptations of 196, 198,
    200–5, 205–6, 214, 215
Fichte, Hubert
  Detlev's Imitations 78
fictionalisation
  of Holocaust 314
    Wiesel's objections to 333
  in Levi's works 304
Filipovic, Zlata 250
Flaubert, Gustave 111
forgetting 91
  and Holocaust 196
  Miller on 180
  Wiesel on 327, 378–9
forgiveness
  Améry on 279–80
  Levi on 280
Fort Breendonk, Améry at 266–8
Foucault, Michel
  Madness and Civilization 48
Frank, Anne 7, 200
  appeal of 228
  at Auschwitz 236–8
  at Bergen-Belsen 238–9
  at Westerbork 234–6
  death and final months of 233–4,
    238–9
  diary of 223, 225–7, 231, 232
    as example of Holocaust writing
      223
    German edition of 221–2
    modifications and revisions of 222,
      228, 240–2
    publication of 221, 240

reactions to 219–21, 228–9
  readership of 222
  role in Feldman's novel 251–6
  stage play of 118, 229–2, 233, 240
  identifications with 228–9, 357
  Jewish identity of 223, 233
  Levi on 257
  memories of 234–6
  ownership of 233, 240–2, 246–9, 256
  portrayal of 245
    Bettelheim's criticism of 242–5, 245
    by Kops 249–51
    by Margulies 251
    by Roth 246–9
Frank family
  at Auschwitz 236–8
  at Westerbork 234–6
  betrayal of 227–8
  Bettelheim's criticism of 242–5
  hiding in 'Secret Annexe' 224–5
Frank, Otto 221, 222, 224, 226, 229,
  240
Frankfurt trials *see* Auschwitz trials
Frayn, Michael 10
Freud, Sigmund
  on childhood memories 22
  on mourning and melancholy 89
Freudian analysis
  memories invoked by 155–6
  Miller engaged in 184
Furtwängler, Wilhelm 213

Ganzfried, Daniel 369
Gare d'Austerlitz *see* Austerlitz
  Station
genocide, and capitalism 316
German Academy, Sebald's acceptance
  to 112–13
German language
  Améry on use of 265–6
  Appelfeld on 266
  Mann on use of 6
  Nazism's deforming influence on 4–6
German past
  Hochhuth on 116, 119–20
  Sebald's dealings with 38–9, 44–5,
    112–13, 160, 296, 383
German writers
  on persecution of the Jews 102–3
  staying in Germany during Nazism
    93–4
Germans
  shame and guilt about Nazism 43–4,
    44–5, 188, 189, 297, 382
  target audience for Levi 289–90, 296

Index

Germany
  attitude towards Holocaust 160
  bombing of cities in 78–9
  German silence about 98–102,
    106
  church in, anti-Semitism in 146–7
  continuity between Third Reich and
    Federal Republic 162–3, 165
  neo-Nazi party in 86
Gerstein, Kurt 113, 121–3, 152
  character in *The Deputy* (play,
    Hochhuth) 125–6, 128–9, 131–
    2, 137, 138
ghetto
  Levi on 311
  of Warsaw 337
  Wiesel living in 321
Gies, Miep 240, 245
Gilbert, Martin
  The Holocaust 190
Glassie, Henry 151
Goethe, Johann Wolfgang von 25
Goldhagen, Daniel Jonah
  *Hitler's Willing Executioners:
    Ordinary Germans and the
    Holocaust* 189, 216, 357
Goldstein-van Cleef, Ronnie 235, 237–8
Good, Michael
  The Search for Major Plagge 382
Goodrich, Frances 230
Grabowski, Laura 366–8, 375
  *Satan's Underground: The
    Extraordinary Story of One
    Woman's Escape* 366
Gradowski, Zalmen 9
Grass, Günter
  From the Diary of a Snail 102–3,
    125
Gray, Martin
  For Those I Loved 372
Greene, Graham 80
Gröning, Oscar 19
Grünbaum Zimche, Hilde 211
guilt
  of Germans about Nazism 43–4, 188,
    189, 382
  of survivors 160, 191, 271, 289
Gutman, Israel 218

Hackett, Albert 230
Halbwachs, Maurice 86
Hamburger, Michael 154
Handke, Peter 38
  Kaspar 37–8
Hare, David 23–4

Hauptmann, Gerhart 94
Hawthorne, Nathaniel 283
Heck, Alfons 216
Helbling, Hanno 368
Hellman, Lillian 230
Hersh, Mayer 20, 383
Heydrich, Reinhard 128
hidden children 75
hidden connections, in Sebald's works
  84
hidden identity 70
hiding, of Frank family in 'Secret
  Annexe' 224–5
Hilberg, Raul 367, 369
Himmler, Heinrich 200, 215
Hiroshima, survivor
  accounts of 85
history
  angel of 78
  Jews denied to 6
  and past 151
  in Sebald's work 68
Hochhuth, Rolf 31, 113, 161
  criticism of 130
  and German past 116, 119–20
  on representation of Auschwitz
    133–134
  and Sebald 125
  works
    The Deputy (play) 31, 117–18,
      120–1, 123–9, 131–3, 134–8,
      145–6
    as documentary theatre 127,
      reactions to 138–9, 140–2,
      143–5
    Sebald on 129
    weaknesses of 145, 146
    Occupation (novel) 117
    Soldiers (play) 31, 119–20
  youth of 115–16
Hoffman, Eva 8, 271, 371
  *After Such Knowledge: A
    Meditation on the Aftermath
    of the Holocaust* 89
Holocaust
  Améry on 270, 275–6
  Amis on 315
  attitudes towards
    of American Jews 130
    in Britain 35–6
  Borowski as observer of 348–9, 350,
    353, 355
  Brecht on 158
  denial of 86
  experience, and disbelief 83

399

Holocaust *Cont.*
  fictionalisation of 314
  Wiesel's objections to 333
  and forgetting 196
  German attitude towards 160
  Jewish passivity during, Bettelheim
    on 242–5
  Langer on 190–1
  Levi on 290–1, 307
  memories of 190, 208–9, 212, 378
  Miller on 176, 178, 182, 185, 192,
    206–7, 217, 218
  non-Jewish witnesses of 341, 355
  Pope accused of inaction during
    120–1, 123–4, 129, 132–3, 135,
    139, 143, 147
  Sebald's attitude towards 69, 382
  Steiner on 350
  survival of 346–7
  uniqueness of 130, 193–4
  Weiss on 158, 173–4
  and Zionists 130
Holocaust memorials 20–1
Holocaust survivors 190–1
  children of 89
  emigration of 271
  in Israel 271
  and remembering 18–19, 259
  shame and guilt felt by 44, 160, 191,
    271
  Steiner on 348
  suicide of 98, 283–4
  testimonies of 12–15, 16–17, 19–20,
    158–9, 260, 380
    distrust of 84–5, 151–2
    by Levi 286, 288–9
    oral 197
    unreliability of 212
    Weiss's interests in 152–3
  Wiesel as 340
Holocaust (television series), Wiesel's
  criticism of 333
Holocaust writing, *Diary of Anne
  Frank* as example of 223
Höss, Rudolf 293
Howe, Irving 8
Huber, Gusti 233

idea of Eden, metaphor of 1
identities
  hidden 70
  and memory 270
  multiple, of Weiss 166, 173
  of Wilkomirski 360
  see also Jewish identity

I. G. Farbenindustrie 295
images, of the past 15–16
indifference, crime of 120–1
intellectuals, and concentration camps
  273–4, 301–2
*Into the Arms of Strangers: Stories of
  the Kindertransport* (television
  documentary) 69
invented memory 372–4
  by Grabowski 366–8
  by Kosinski 364–6, 375
  by Wilkomirski 362–4, 370–1
Israel, Holocaust survivors in 271
Italy, Miller in 300

Jacobson, Dan 78
Jaspers, Karl
  criticism of *The Deputy* (play,
    Hochhuth) 143–5
  The Question of German Guilt 189
Jewish characters, in Arthur Miller's
  works 178–9
Jewish exclusiveness 297
Jewish identity
  of Améry 260–2, 270, 276–7
  of Anne Frank 223, 233
  of Kosinski 365–6
  of Miller 177, 178, 217, 218
  and remembering 318–19
  of Wiesel 318–19
Jewish religion, kept by Wiesel 323–4,
  326–7, 328–9, 339
Jews
  American, attitude towards
    Holocaust 130
  blood libel against 105
  elimination of, by Nazism 274
  history denied to 6
  non-centrality in accounts of Nazi
    crimes 151–2
  passivity during Holocaust,
    Bettelheim on 242–5, 271
  Sebald's interest in 35, 40, 46, 54,
    64–5
Jong-van Naarden, Lenie de 235, 236,
  237, 239
Julian, St, legend of 111
Jünger, Ernst 94

Kaddish (prayer for the dead) 260
Kafka, Franz
  influence on Levi 306, 307–8
  influence on Sebald 54, 103
  The Trial, Levi on 308
Kanin, Garson 233

Karlén, Barbro
  And the Wolves Howled 357
Karpf, Anne 357
Kazan, Alfred 146
Khouri, Norma
  Forbidden Loves 373–4
Kindertransport 69, 70, 73
Kluge, Alexander 78–9
  New Stories. Nos 1–18 41
Kohl, Helmut 86
Kolbe, Maximilian 125
Koozol, Jonathan 357
Kops, Bernard
  Dreams of Anne Frank 249–51
  The Hamlet of Stepney Green 249
Kosinski, Jerzy 52, 283
  influence on Wilkomirski 361–2, 375
  Jewish identity of 365–6
  The Painted Bird 360–1
    invented memory in 364–6
  suicide of 375
Kott, Jan 341, 342, 343
Kristallnacht 216–17
Kushner, Tony 35

LaCapra, Dominick 9–10
Langer, Lawrence L. 12–14, 16–17, 23
  on Anne Frank's diary 220
  on Holocaust 190–1
  *Holocaust Testimonies: The Ruins
    of Memory* 190, 208–9
languages
  deformation of, Levi on 308
  and exile 97–8, 264–5
  German
    Améry on use of 265–6
    Appelfeld on 266
    Mann on use of 6
    Nazism's deforming influence on
      4–6
  of memory 330–1
  use of 258
    Nabokov's 3–4
    Sebald's 33
  Wiesel on 330, 337–9
Lanzmann, Claude
  distrust of memory 9
  Shoah (film) 335, 367
Lappin, Elena 369
Lasker-Wallfisch, Anita 209, 212, 213,
  214, 215
Lessing, Gotthold Ephraim
  Nathan the Wise 103
Lessing, Josef 195
Lessing, Theodor

  *History as Rationale of the
    Irrational* 140
Levi, Primo 10–11, 44, 95, 98, 102, 141,
  148, 195, 285, 294–5, 329, 379
  and Améry 277–9, 280, 301, 310
  on Anne Frank 257
  appropriation of 311, 313–14
  at Auschwitz 291, 295–6, 298
  on Auschwitz 290–1, 298
  on Bettelheim's criticism of Frank
    family 245–6
  as a chemist 305
  children of 305
  on communication 308–9
  on concentration camps 291, 296–7,
    297–8, 305–6
  Dante's influence on 300
  on deformation of language 308
  depressions of 305, 306, 310
  on distortions of reality 305
  on forgiveness 280
  Germans as target audience for
    289–90, 296
  on the ghetto 311
  on Holocaust 290–1, 307
  on intellectuals 301–2
  and Kafka 306, 307–8
  life after the war 299–300
  on memory 287–8, 293–4, 301–3,
    308, 309
  on necessity to bear witness 286–7,
    291–2, 302
  on Perrone 299
  suicide of 283, 285–6, 310, 313–14,
    316–17
  survivor testimonies of 286, 288–9
  on victims and murderers 306
  Wiesel on 309–10, 313, 323
  works
    anger in 303
    Creation story in 306–7
    The Drowned and the Saved 73,
      199, 278, 286–7, 289, 302, 305,
      307
    fictionalisation in 304
    If This is a Man 10, 278, 286,
      289–90, 291, 292–3, 297, 299;
      amendments to 302; radio
      play of 302;
    stage plays of 304, 311–13
    Moments of Reprieve 299, 304, 309
    The Periodic Table 304, 305
    The Truce 10–11, 304, 305, 316
    The Wrench 305
  as a writer 303

Levi, Primo *Cont.*
  writings of 293, 302–3
Levin, Meyer 229–30
  The Obsession 230
  The Search 229
Lichtenberg, Bernhard 125
Lindwer, Willy 234
Loewenstein, Rudolph 186
London, Jack 301
loss
  of memory 378–9
    and sanity 381
  in Sebald's work 67–8
  transferred 89
Lowell, Robert
  The Old Glory 143, 145
Lustig, Arnost 357
Lutzner, Annie 86

Maaren, W. G. van 227
McCarthyism 130
McCullah, Mark 58, 67
McGreal, Chris 20
Madigan, Kevin 147
Maechler, Stefan 369–70
Maestro, Vanda 300
man
  capacity for murder 139–40
  freedom of choice of 140
  indictment of 139–40
  relationship with past 21–2
  Sebald's hopes for improvement of
    111–12
Mandel, Maria 198, 211
Mann, Klaus 94
Mann, Thomas 6, 116
  The Magic Mountain 273
Marché, Pieralberto 304
Marco, Enric
  Memoir of Hell 372–3
Margalit, Avishai
  The Ethics of Memory 18
Margulies, Donald
  The Model Apartment 251
Maroto, Yakov 359, 371
Mauriac, François 77–8, 331
Mauthausen, Miller's visit to 181
melancholy
  and mourning 89
  Sebald's fascination with 87–9, 111
  of Weiss 155
memorials, Holocaust 20–1
memory
  absence of 61
  Améry on 281–2

Appelfeld on 1, 10, 14, 18–19
chain of 7, 23–4, 89
of childhood 22
collective
  and past 86
  of Swiss 371–2
  and writers 85
contested 207–8, 213, 215
denial of 17
Didion on 377–8
distortions of 10–11
distrust of, by Lanzmann 9
false 212
and Freudian analysis 155–6
functions of 259–60
of Holocaust 190, 208–9, 212, 378
and identity 270
invented 372–4
  by Grabowski 366–8
  by Kosinski 364–6, 375
  by Wilkomirski 362–4, 370–1
language of 330–1
Levi on 287–8, 293–4, 301–3, 308,
  309
loss of 378–9
  and sanity 381
Miller on 180, 214, 216
and the past 375–6
and places 72
Sebald on 25, 27, 29, 40–1, 51–2,
  85–6
in Sebald's works 2, 7, 55, 56, 59,
  61–2, 111
theft of 374, 376
of trauma 10, 14, 50, 288
Vosnesensky on 1
weight of 310
Wiesel on 319, 320, 324, 329, 336,
  337, 339–40
Mengele, Josef 126, 128, 159, 200
Miller, Arthur 108, 130, 156, 158,
  182–3
  anti-Semitism encountered by 178
  at Auschwitz trials 161, 169, 176–7,
    181–2, 187–9, 355
  on concentration camps 181, 182,
    186
  criticism of 207–8, 213, 214, 215
  family of 177, 180
  on forgetting 180
  Freudian analysis undergone by 184
  on guilt of survivors 191
  on Holocaust 176, 178, 182, 185, 192,
    206–7, 217, 218
  in Italy 300

Jewish identity of 177, 178,
  217, 218
and Marilyn Monroe 183, 186
marriage to Morath 179
on memory 180, 214, 216
and the past 176, 179–80, 192
PEN presidency 187
on Vietnam war 193
visit to Mauthausen 181
works
  After the Fall (play) 130, 179,
    182–6, 381
  All My Sons (play) 178, 179
  Broken Glass (play) 216, 217
  Clara (play) 217–18
  The Crucible (play) 130, 176, 180
  Death of a Salesman (play) 176,
    178, 179, 182, 184
  The Doctor Fights (radio series)
    177
  The Golden Years (play) 178
  Incident at Vichy (play) 130, 142,
    179, 186–7, 189–90, 191–2,
    193–5
  Jewish characters in 178–9
  The Man Who Had all the Luck
    (play) 217
  A Memory of Two Mondays (play)
    179
  Playing for Time (screen play) 196,
    198, 200–5, 214, 215
  Playing for Time (stage play) 205–6
  The Price (play) 180, 182
  Situation Normal (wartime diary)
    177–8
  The Story of GI Joe (film script)
    177
  They Too Arise (*No Villain*, play)
    178
  Timebends (autobiography) 179,
    196
  A View from the Bridge (play) 179
Mitterrand, François 340
Mommsen, Theodor 140
Monroe, Marilyn, Miller's relationship
  with 183, 186
morality, in concentration camps 325
Morath, Ingeborg 108, 179, 181, 185
Morgen, Konrad 152
Moulin, Jean 268
mourning, and melancholy 89
multiple identities, Weiss's 166, 173
murder, man's capacity for 139–40
murderers, and victims, Levi on 306
Murrow, Ed 36

music, in Auschwitz 182, 195,
  196–200, 211, 213

Nabokov, Vladimir 3–4, 33
  Sebald on 103
  *Speak, Memory: An Autobiography
    Revisited* 2
Nagorski, Andrew 381
Nazis, testimonies of 19, 27–8
Nazism
  Autobahnen built by 314
  deforming influence on German
    language 4–6
  and elimination of the Jews 274
  role of art in 85
  shame and guilt felt by Germans
    about 42–5, 188, 189, 297, 382
  writers during 93–4
neo-Nazi party, in Germany 86
Newman, Richard 208, 209, 210, 213,
  214–15
Niemöller, Martin 122
Nietzsche, Friedrich Wilhelm 16, 38,
  91, 111, 156
Nin, Anaïs 228
normality, of Nazi war criminals 169
Norwich
  air raids on Germany from 106
  blood libel against the Jews started at
    105
  Sebald's stay in 103–4, 106
Nossack, Hans Erich 40, 41
Novelli, Gastone 72
Novick, Julius 86, 86
Novick, Peter 220, 230
Nuremberg laws, Améry's reaction to
  260–2
Nuremberg trials 159
Nussbaum, Laureen 226

O'Neill, Eugene Gladstone
  Strange Interlude 119
orchestra in Auschwitz 182, 195,
  196–200, 213
ownership, of Anne Frank 233, 240–2,
  246–9, 256
Ozick, Cynthia 228–9,
  230, 233
  'Who Owns Anne Frank?' 240–2

Paolini, Pietro 107
past
  Améry's relationship with 269
  and collective memory 86

past *Cont.*
   confronting of 89
   denial of 251–6
German
   Hochhuth on 116, 119–20
   Sebald's dealings with 38–9, 44–5,
     102–3, 112–13, 160, 296, 383
   and history 151
   images of 15–16
   and memory 375–6
   relationships with
     man's 21–2
     Miller's 176, 179–80, 192
     Sebald's 30, 37–8, 42–3, 73–4, 86–7,
       89–90, 91, 107, 110, 380–1
   and theatre 119–20
Pels, Peter van, fictionalised by
   Feldman 251–6
PEN, Miller's presidency of 187
Père-Lachaise cemetery (Paris) 109
Perrone, Lorenzo 299
Pick-Goslar, Hannah Elisabeth 238, 242
pictures
   of German war atrocities 16
   of ruined German cities 79
   in Sebald's works 81–2, 87
Pinter, Harold 378
Piscator, Erwin 138, 139–40, 142
Pius XII (Pope), accused of inaction
   during Holocaust 120–1, 123–4,
     129, 132–3, 135, 139, 143, 147
places, and memory 72
Plagge, Karl 44, 381–2
Pool, Rosie 249
Pope, *see* Pius XII (Pope)
Princip, Gavrilo 65–6
prose fiction style, of Sebald 42, 82–3
Prynne, Hester 283
pseudo-aesthetic effects, Sebald's
   criticism of 79

Rawicz, Piotr 283
reality, distortions of 305
Redgrave, Vanessa 196
Rembrandt (Harmensz. van Rijn)
   The Anatomy Lesson of Doctor Tulp
     67
remembering
   Améry on 269–70, 272
   and Holocaust survivors 18–19, 259
   importance of 16
   and Jewish identity 318–19
   necessity of 259, 302
   Sebald on 108
   Steiner on 259–60

Wiesel on 318–19, 320, 329–30
Ringelblum, Emmanuel 337
Rosé, Alma 197, 208, 209–14, 215
Rosenbaum, Thane
   The Golems of Gotham 283–4, 313,
     340
Rosenberg, Jen 367
Rosenberg, Walter 122
Roth, Philip
   The Ghost Writer 246–9
Routier, Marcelle 196
Rumkowski, Chaim 311, 320

Sachs, Nelly 338
   *A Mystery Play of the Sufferings of
     Israel* 8
Samuel, Jean 302
sanity, and loss of memory 381
Sartre, Jean Paul 261
   Anti-Semitism and Jew 261
Scheps, Hélène 211, 213
Schramm, Hilde 44
Schröder, Gerhard 86
Schwarzenberg, Josef von 187
Sebald, W. G. (Max)
   on academic writing 40
   aesthetics of 46–7
   and Améry 6, 86–7, 90, 94–7, 98, 258,
     269
   on concentration camps 46
   cooperation with Tripp 47–9
   criticism of pseudo-aesthetic effects
     79
   death of 113–14, 380
   distrust of testimonies of Holocaust
     survivors 84–5
   on Döblin 32, 39–40
   on exile 111, 264–5
   and the German past 37, 44–5, 102–3,
     112–13, 160, 296, 383
   and Hochhuth 125
   and the Holocaust 69, 382
   on improvement of mankind 111–12
   influences on
     of Kafka 54, 103
     of Nazi war crime trials 33–4
   and Jewish experience 35, 40, 46, 54,
     64–5
   languages used by 33
   meeting with Arthur Miller and Inge
     Morath 108
   on melancholy 87–9, 111
   on memories 25, 27, 29, 40–1, 51–2,
     85–6
   and places 72

move to Britain 34–7
on Nabokov 103
in Norwich 103–4, 106
relationship with the past 30, 37–8,
  42–3, 73–4, 86–7, 89, 91, 107,
  110, 380–1
on remembering 108
on role of images 15–16
sense of vertigo 103
visit to Corsica 106–7, 109–11
on Weiss 154–8, 172–3
works 1–2, 4, 7, 87
  After Nature 25, 45–6
  *Alien Homeland (Unheimliche
    Heimat)* 37
  Austerlitz 42–3, 49, 65, 69–78, 95
  death in 109, 149
  The Emigrants 25, 35, 54–64, 82,
    265
  hidden connections in 84
  history in 68
  loss in 67–8
  memory in 2, 7, 55–6, 59, 61–2,
    111
  *On the Natural History of
    Destruction* 78, 90–5, 98, 99
  photographs in 81–2, 87
  The Rings of Saturn 41, 65–8
  Vertigo 4, 27, 265
  writing style of 42, 79–80, 82–3,
    104–5
youth of 25–7, 29–33, 43, 60, 83–4
Zurich lectures 98–102
'Secret Annexe'
  deaths of inhabitants of 239–40
  Frank family hiding in 224–5
Segev, Tom 20
selfishness, and survival in
  concentration camps 325
Shalev, Avner 21
shame
  felt by Germans about Nazism 42–5,
    297
  felt by Holocaust survivors 44, 271
Sher, Antony 311–13
  Primo Time 312
shoes, symbolism of 48–9, 53, 181,
  377, 378
Silberbauer, Karl Josef 227
silence
  about air war in Germany 98–102, 106
  Appelfeld on 7
  right to 85
  suicide as act of 6
Simon, Claude 72

Smith, Stephen 23
Sobol, Joshua 334
Sokurov, Alexander
  Russian Ark 105
Sonderkommandos 306
Soviet Union, anti-Semitism in 187
Steiner, George 4–6, 11, 16,
  121, 314
  on Holocaust 350
  on images of the past 15–16
  on remembering 259–60
  on survivors of the Holocaust
    258–9
  on writers staying in Germany
    during Nazism 93–4
Stendhal (Beyle, Henri Marie) 50–3, 56,
  137
Stier, Oren Baruch
  Committed to Memory 151
Stifter, Adalbert 111
Stimler, Barbara 19–20, 382–3
Stratford, Lauren *see* Grabowski,
  Laura
Stresser, Otto 213
Styron, William
  Sophie's Choice 314
subversiveness, of *The Deputy* (play,
  Hochhuth) 142
suicide
  as act of radical silence 7
  of Améry 277–9, 282–3
  Améry on 280–1, 282, 283
  of Borowski 342, 355, 356
  of Holocaust survivors 98, 283–4
  of Kosinski 375
  of Levi 283, 285–6, 310, 313–14,
    316–17
  Wiesel on 309–10, 313
  Todorov on 282
survival in concentration camps
  Borowski on 346–7
  Levi on 296–7, 305–6
  and selfishness 325
survivors
  guilt of 160, 191, 271, 289
  of Hiroshima, accounts of 85
  of the Holocaust 190–1
    children of 89
    emigration of 271
    in Israel 271
    and remembering 18–19, 259
    shame and guilt felt by 44, 160,
      191, 271
    Steiner on 258–9
    suicide of 98, 283–4

survivors *Cont.*
  testimonies of 12–15, 16–17,
    19–20, 158–9, 195, 260;
    distrust of 84–5, 150; Levi's
    195, 286; oral 287; Weiss's
    interests in 152–3
Switzerland, during Second World War
  371–2

Tchaikowska (Czajkowska), Sofia 211
terror, dislocating time 95–6
testimonies
  of Hiroshima survivors 85
  of Holocaust survivors 12–17, 19–20,
    158–9, 260, 380
  distrust of 84–5, 151–2
  Levi's 286, 288–9
  oral 197
  unreliability of 212
  Weiss's interests in 152–3
  of Nazis 19, 27–8
theatre, and the past 119–20
theatre plays, in verse 127, 145, 167
theft, of memory 374, 376
Theresienstadt 76
Thomson, Ian 291, 300, 302, 304
time
  dislocated by terror 95–6
  experienced in concentration camps
    95–6
  reversal of 314–16
Todorov, Tzvetan 191
  Facing the Extreme 282, 325
Topf (company) 288
torture 72, 96
  Améry on 72, 266–8
trains, symbolism of 73
transferred loss 89
trauma, memories of 10, 14, 50, 288
trials of Nazi war criminals
  writers influenced by 11,
    33–4, 117 *see also* Auschwitz
    trials
Tripp, Jan Peter 47–9, 103
  La Déclaration de Guerre 48

uniqueness, of Holocaust 130,
  193–4
United States
  anti-Semitism in 178
  Jews in, attitude towards Holocaust
    130
unmemory, chain of 375
Urquhart, Jane
  A Map of Glass 379

Vatican *see* Pius XII (Pope)
verse, theatre plays in 127, 145, 167
vertigo, Sebald's sense of 103
Vichy (France) 186–7
victimhood
  Améry on 272
  claims to 374
victims
  decency of 319–20
  identification with 371
  and murderers 306
Vietnam war
  Miller on 193
  Weiss on 174
Vosnesensky, Andrei 1

Waldheim, Kurt 66
Walser, Martin 153
Wanda's List (film) 359
Warsaw, ghetto of 337
Waszkinel, Romuald 381
Weisberger, Lucie 149
Weiss, Peter 11, 82, 90, 97, 153, 155
  at Auschwitz trials 153, 156–7, 160,
    172
  Brook on 173, 174–5
  communism of 165–6
  on concentration camps 164, 167–9
  Dante's influence on 174
  fascination with the dead 149
  on Holocaust 158, 173–4
  melancholy of 155
  multiple identities of 166, 173
  Sebald on 154–8, 172–3
  and testimonies of Holocaust
    survivors 152–3
  visit to Auschwitz 160
  works 154
    The Aesthetics of Resistance
      (novel) 157
    Alexanderschlacht (*Battle of
      Alexander*, painting) 155
    Anatomie (painting) 155
    Discourse on Vietnam 174
    Fluchtpunkt (*Vanishing Point*,
      novel) 157, 158
    Das grosse Welttheater (painting)
      155
    Der Hausierer (*The Pedlar*,
      painting) 154, 156
    The Investigation (play) 149–51,
      161–5, 169–71, 174–5; and
      Auschwitz trials 166–7,
      171–2; criticism of 165; and
      emotion 167–9

Kindesmord (painting) 155
Der Krieg (painting) 155
Leave-Taking (novel) 158
Marat/Sade (play) 156, 174
Der Reiche und der Arme
 (painting) 155
Trotsky in Exile 173, 174
Weizsäcker, Baron Ernst von 125
Westerbork, Anne Frank at 234–6
Wiechert, Ernst 94
Wiesel, Elie 8, 75, 284, 296, 361
 at Auschwitz 323–5
 on Auschwitz 236–7, 323, 324,
  325–6
 death of his father 327–8
 deportation of 322–3
 dispute with Wiesenthal 335–6
 on forgetting 327, 378–9
 ghetto life 321
 and Holocaust fictionalisation 333
 as Holocaust survivor 340
 Jewish identity of 318–19
 Jewish religion kept by 323–4, 326–7,
  328–9, 339
 on language 330, 337–9
 on Levi 309–10, 313, 323
 liberation and life after the war 328,
  329, 331
 living under occupation
  German 321–2
  Hungarian 321
 on memory 319, 320, 324, 329, 336,
  337, 339–40
 as moral arbitrator 340
 on remembering 318–20, 329–30
 on victims, decency of 319–20
 works
  All Rivers Run to the Sea 71, 325
  And the Sea is Never Full 307
  *And the World has Remained
   Silent* 331
  The Forgotten 378–9
  From the Kingdom of Memory
   333, 337–8
  memoirs 322, 324, 326, 327
  Night 77–8, 323, 326, 328,
   331, 332

 writings of 328, 331–2
 Yiddish used by 330–1
 youth of 320–1
Wiesenthal, Simon 27–9, 227, 279
 dispute with Wiesel 335–6
Wilkomirski, Binjamin 52, 357, 375
 doubts about accounts of 368–70
 Fragments 357–8, 362–4
 identity of 360
 Kosinski's influence on 361–2, 375
 lost family found again
  358–60, 371
 memories invented by 362–4,
  370–1
Wilson, Cara 228–9
 Love, Otto 229
Winton, Nicholas 70
Wirth, Christian 152
witnesses
 of Anne Frank's final months
  233–6
 chain of 23
 eye 151–2, 198
 of Holocaust, non-Jewish 341, 355
 Levi on necessity of 286–7, 291–2,
  302
Wittgenstein, Ludwig Josef Johann 58
Wouk, Herman
 The Winds of War 334
writers
 and collective memory 85
 German, on persecution of the Jews
  102–3
 in Germany during Nazism 93–4
 and trials of war criminals 11, 33–4,
  117
writing style, of Sebald 42, 79–80,
  82–3, 104–5

Yad Vashem Museum (Jerusalem)
 20–1
Yiddish, Wiesel's use of 330–1

Zimetbaum, Mala 199
Zionists, and Holocaust 130
Zuckerman, Solly 99
Zurich lectures (Sebald) 98–102